BOOTH #851 HAS THE
FREE APP
FOR THE NY2016 WORLD STAMP SHOW

With over 200 dealers, few attendees will have the time to find those that have what they want and still be able to enjoy the show events and exhibits. Let StampFinder be your personal guide at the show to those dealers who will have what you want. With StampFinder you can tell them what you'll be looking for now so they know what to bring.

Also, fill our your wish list at www.StampFinder.com and you can retrieve it anytime before or during the show on your phone or tablet to see an up to date listing of those dealers who have what you are looking for as well as your itemized list.

The app will also have a daily events calendar and guide to the exhibits.

VISIT OUR BOOTH #851 AT NY2016

Make the best use of your time at the show.
Go to **WWW.StampFinder.com/NY2016** today and let's get started.

Gary Posner, Inc.
They're all here!

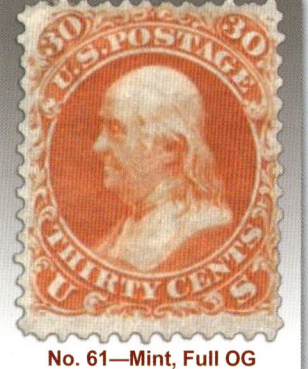

No. 61—Mint, Full OG (100% Sound)

No. 314A Used—Sound

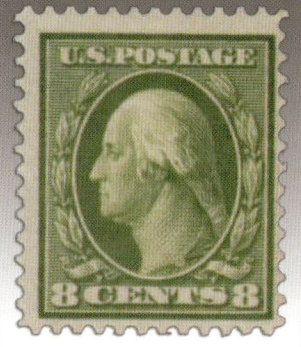

No. 363 Never Hinged

No. 621 Mint Centerline Plate No. Block of 8—Sound

No. 197 Unused (Without Gum As Issued—100% Sound)

Booths 1043 and 1142

No. R2b Used—Sound

BOOTHS 1013 & 1142

Sell HIGHEST Here!
Our success is very much due to our **FAIRNESS** when buying stamps. ALWAYS get our **HIGHEST DOLLAR** offer when selling whether a collection or even a single stamp! We would rather buy 10 collections at a fair price to the seller than try to make a "Big Score" on 1 or 2.

Stop By Our Booths!

See and examine at the show one of the most incredible inventories in the world of the finest United States stamps—from classsic to modern, from the great rarities to the outstanding stamps you need to fill the key places in your album.

"There are many very good reasons why the greatest of United States stamps have consistently passed through our hands. We carefully serve the very personal interests of every individual client. You can feel free to come to us because you can **ALWAYS** trust us to be confidential, expert, fair, and prompt."

We Also BUY GOLD!

"Building Collections by Building Relationships"

GARY POSNER, INC.

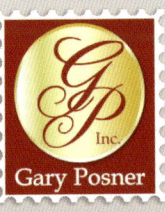

Over 30 years in business • Phone: 800-323-4279 • Fax: 516-599-2145
265 Sunrise Highway • Suite 1-308 • Rockville Centre, NY 11570
Local Ph: 516-599-5969 • Cell 917-538-8133
Email: garyposnerinc@aol.com

www.GaryPosnerInc.com

What Makes a "Great" Cover?
Rarity, Visual Appeal & Philatelic Importance

Visit Booth 1230-1232 to see other "great" covers!

Earliest known combination cover from the United States to Shanghai, China.
Purchased by us recently on behalf of our client for $740,000.00.
Ex: Attwood, Mizuhara

A striking hand-illustrated cover from the famous Patee correspondence,
purchased by us on behalf of our client.
Ex: Matthies

COLUMBIAN STAMP COMPANY

SCARSDALE, NEW YORK   PHONE 914-649-8919   WWW.COLUMBIANSTAMP.COM
EMAIL: sonnyhagendorf@gmail.com

What Makes a "Great" Stamp?
Rarity & Quality

Visit Booth 1230-1232 to see these and other "great" stamps!

Scott No. 166
SUPERB 98!

Scott No. 59
One of the finest known!

Scott No. 360
Choice Blue Paper!

Scott No. C3a
One of the finest known!

Scott 243a
SUPERB 98!

COLUMBIAN STAMP COMPANY

SCARSDALE, NEW YORK   PHONE 914-649-8919   WWW.COLUMBIANSTAMP.COM

EMAIL: sonnyhagendorf@gmail.com

Contents

EDITOR
Matthew Healey

BOOK DESIGN
Niko Courtelis

LAYOUT AND PRODUCTION
Maureen Forys

PRINT CONSULTANT
Paul Golden

PROOFREADING
AND COPY EDITING
Ron Breznay
Benjamin Y. Lee
Marcus Vaska

PRODUCTION ASSISTANT
Peter Le

ABOUT THE COVER
The "I (stamp) NY" design playfully satirizes the iconic "I♥NY" logo, created by Milton Glaser in 1977 for New York's Empire State Development Corp.

8 **Welcome to World Stamp Show–NY 2016**
16 Organizing committee
22 Supporters and donors
28 Volunteers
32 Commissioners and jurors
46 Awards and prizes

50 **Yesterday**
52 Letters carried on Gotham's city streets
68 Nassau Street: the stamp collector's street of dreams
80 Stamp and security engraving and printing in New York
91 New York on stamps: a thematic history

116 **Today**
118 The Smithsonian's National Postal Museum
127 The court of honor and invited exhibits
158 Six days of auctions
166 USPS new issues
176 What is the FIP?
178 The American Philatelic Society and the APRL
187 The Philatelic Foundation
190 The Collectors Club of New York
194 Jenny and the birth of air mail

202 **Tomorrow**
204 The future of philately

225 **The listings**
226 Competitive exhibits by class
296 Index of exhibitors by surname
302 Literature exhibits
312 Society frames
313 Dealers
317 Postal administrations
319 Societies

© 2016 New York Philatelic Exhibition, Inc. except content that remains the copyright of its respective author(s).
Printed in the U.S.A.

It isn't easy, but...

WE CARRY THE WORLD!

SEE OUR *HUGE* STOCK OF UNITED STATES AND FOREIGN

"We carry more stamps at shows than any dealer in the country."

U.S. — *The Works! #1 right up to date, mint, used, plates, BOB, etc.*

FOREIGN — *Millions of stamps, 20¢ to $5,000, A to Z!*

SEE US AT SUPERBOOTH 843
46 feet of counter space, 2 ½ tons of stamps and a courteous staff of eight to serve you.

WHAT MORE COULD YOU WANT?!

~ Jim and Sue Dempsey ~

A&D STAMPS AND COINS
2541 Venado Camino • Walnut Creek, CA 94598
(925) 935-8212 • FAX (925) 935-9277

Welcome, stamp ambassadors

IT IS MY HONOR AND PLEASURE to welcome stamp enthusiasts from around the globe to World Stamp Show–NY 2016. This event has been years in the making, and I salute the tireless efforts of the Organizing Committee, the American Philatelic Society, the American Stamp Dealers Association and my colleagues at the United States Postal Service.

As ambassadors of nations, stamps reflect the traditions, values and history of their home country. The United States hosts a worldwide celebration of these cultural icons only once a decade, and we are making every effort to ensure a spectacular experience for the international collecting community.

As the largest postal organization in the world, the USPS strives to be a leader in all areas of postal product and service innovation. In that vein, we are delighted to introduce some exciting new technology for our philatelic audiences at World Stamp Show–NY 2016.

We will stage several First-Day-of-Issue ceremonies where we will unveil new stamps, including some that commemorate the century-plus tradition of the United States playing host to this week-long pageant of philately.

From the show-opening World of Stamps Day to the closing Topical Collecting Day, I hope that you enjoy eight days of excellence in philatelic exhibiting, an unparalleled dealer presence, scores of postal administrations and stamp societies.

Sincerely,

Megan J. Brennan
Postmaster General and
Chief Executive Officer,
United States Postal Service

Congratulations

THE LONG AWAITED WORLD STAMP SHOW–NY 2016 opens its doors to the world on May 28.

Stamp lovers and philatelists from all over the globe are coming together once again to view the world-class exhibits on display. They will also have the opportunity to do their philatelic shopping at the 200 or so stamp trade booths and five major auctions.

We have granted FIP patronage to 10 world stamp exhibitions from 2011 to 2016, including World Stamp Show–NY 2016.

Having 4,000 frames of competitive exhibits at NY 2016 is certainly a record; it is almost double the number hosted by any other exhibition. All the awards won by the competitive exhibits will be officially registered in our books. As has been the praaice in recent years, the FIP has also donated a Grand Prix award for NY 2016.

The organizing of such a massive stamp show is not an easy task at all. Its fruition is a labor of love, coming from the voluntary efforts of many dedicated lovers of philately. I would like to congratulate the Organizing Committee for this great achievement and I wish NY 2016 every success.

Tay Peng Hian
President
Fédération Internationale de Philatélie

The FIP (known in English as the Federation of International Philately) is the stamp world's leading body, aligned with the Universal Postal Union and numerous other global organizations to unify and promote stamp collecting in nearly 100 countries. Read more about the FIP on page 176.

The best of philately

ON BEHALF OF ALL OF the members of the American Philatelic Society, I welcome you to the stamp show of the decade. Your Society officials, staff and members have been working for several years to organize and promote World Stamp Show–NY 2016.

Ten years ago, the APS contracted with World Stamp Show–NY 2016, an independent not-for-profit organization led by Wade Saadi, to hold this show of all shows.

The American Philatelic Society is the "Federation" in the United States recognized by FIP, the Federation for International Philately, as the representative of all individuals, clubs, associations, etc., within the philatelic hobby in the U.S. It was our responsibility to select a venue, and an organizing committee, for the magnificent show that you are now enjoying.

You are going to find close to 200 dealers of every type of philatelic material imaginable, waiting to show you many items that you might add to your collection. Over 60 philatelic societies and clubs are represented at the show. Their members are present to share with you their interests and hopefully make new members of collectors such as you. Postal administrations from around the world are present to offer you recent stamps and other items from their respective countries. Finally, you cannot miss the 4500 frames of exhibits of all types, including some of the finest and rarest philatelic material in the world. Take the time to stroll around the floor and enjoy everything on display.

The American Philatelic Society is made up of 32,000 members such as you. If you are not a member, visit the APS super booth near the entrance to the show and speak with our staff and volunteers about the services that are available to you.

Enjoy this once in ten years show. Enjoy adding some great material to your collection. Finally, enjoy New York, the greatest city in the world.

Stephen Reinhard
President
American Philatelic Society

WE COLLECT, WE CONNECT

With nearly 32,000 members in more than 110 countries, the American Philatelic Society is the largest, non-profit organization for stamp collectors in the world. Founded in 1886, the APS serves collectors, educators, postal historians, and the general public by providing a wide variety of programs and services.

The American Philatelist
The world's premier stamp magazine.
Editor: Jay Bigalke, ext. 221, jbigalke@stamps.org
Advertising: Helen Bruno, ext. 224, adsales@stamps.org

APEX Expertizing Service
Offers opinions on the genuineness of all stamps.
Director: Mercer Bristow, ext. 205, mercer@stamps.org
Submission: Krystal Harter, ext. 206, krharter@stamps.org

American Philatelic Research Library
Book loans, copy and scan service, reference assistance.
Librarian: Tara Murray, ext. 246
Reference: Scott Tiffney, ext. 241, aprl@stamps.org

APS Stamp Insurance Plan
The best and most comprehensive coverage available.
Toll Free: 1-888-277-6494   E-mail: aps@hughwood.com
Website: www.hughwood.com

Circuit Sales
Our most popular service — $7,500,000 inventory.
Director: Tom Horn, ext. 227, twhorn@stamps.org

Education Programs
Summer Seminar, Internet and Correspondence Courses,
Mentor Service, Youth Programs
Cathy Brachbill, ext. 239, cbrachbill@stamps.org

StampStore.org
Buy/Sell online via our Internet sales site.
Director: Wendy Masorti, ext. 270, stampstore@stamps.org

General Information
Have a question about of our many other services?
Contact: Judy Johnson, ext. 210, apsinfo@stamps.org

STAMPS.ORG
STAMPLIBRARY.ORG

American Philatelic Society
American Philatelic Research Library
100 Match Factory Place, Bellefonte, PA 16823
Phone: 814-933-3803 • Fax: 814-933-6128
E-mail: info@stamps.org

American Philatelic Research Library

AMERICA'S STAMP CLUB

Welcome to New York

IT IS MY DISTINCT HONOR AND PLEASURE to welcome my fellow collectors and guests to World Stamp Show–NY 2016. After a 60-year absence, the U.S. International Exhibition is back in New York City for eight days of philatelic fun.

Stamp collecting may be the "hobby of kings," but all people can embrace it. The extraordinary Court of Honor, Invited Class and society exhibits—not to mention the National Postal Museum—offer every visitor a peek at the crown jewels of philately. The 4,500 exhibit frames showcase all levels, from Championship Class to youth and first-time exhibits.

A walk around the show floor and conference center likewise reveal something for everyone. Dealers and auctioneers cater to every budget, from exquisite rarities to inexpensive covers and albums packed with affordable treasures. The 80-plus postal administrations will take you on a "walk around the world" for the price of a few new issues. Many things are free: the entry-level and youth areas, the opening ceremony, the first-day ceremonies and all the lectures and meetings.

One of the most powerful aspects of any exhibition is its philatelic fellowship—meeting friends and discussing, learning and teaching one another about our wonderful hobby. People from 100 countries are here, and you're sure to find many new friends among them.

I'd like to thank the hundreds of people who came to the fore and tirelessly gave so much of themselves. Our nationwide Organizing Committee, our generous supporters, all the dealers and the U.S. Postal Service—they get the credit for the success of this exhibition. Support and encouragement from all over the United States and around the world has truly made this an International Exhibition.

For more than 175 years, postage stamps have connected people. Welcome to our fabulous celebration of postage stamps.

Warmly,

Wade E. Saadi

Wade E. Saadi
President, World Stamp Show–NY 2016

Thank you

WE ARE THRILLED TO HAVE YOU AS OUR GUEST at World Stamp Show–NY 2016. We have been preparing for your visit for the past ten years!

How many people did it take to produce this once-in-a-decade U.S. International? Most people think it was just a very passionate group of folks known as our Organizing Committee, each of whom played a major role over many years. If you have a chance, please do say "thank you" to them for their extraordinary volunteer efforts.

But we must also remember our amazingly supportive and enthusiastic dealers and postal administrations, including our own USPS. We must also remember the 500 members of more than 75 representing stamp societies, our 500-plus direct service volunteers, our more than 700 exhibitors, more than 200 presenters and dozens of other folks as well. In total, more than 2,000 people have labored long and hard to bring you a successful and exciting stamp show!

How lucky we all are that all of these folks are so committed to strengthening and spreading the news about our great hobby. Our gratitude to all is boundless and genuine… Thank you!

And besides the once-in-a-lifetime opportunity of being able to "shop till you drop" for stamps and view the many gems and rarities on display, we must also remember the Javits Center is located in the middle of the greatest city host city in the world: New York. To start, we are literally just across the street from the entrance to the High Line, a fabulous 1½-mile urban park that ends at the new Whitney Museum of Art.

So please enjoy our big, huge, audacious celebration of stamp collecting, as well as your time in New York City.

All the best,

Steven Rod

Steven J. Rod
Vice-president, World Stamp Show–NY 2016

Join us for these First-Day-of-Issue ceremonies.

★ THE WORLD OF STAMPS DAY ★

World Stamp Show

★ LEARNING NEVER ENDS DAY ★

Repeal of the Stamp Act, 1766

★ ARMED FORCES DAY ★

Honoring Extraordinary Heroism:
The Service Cross Medals

Stamp designs shown may reflect preliminary artwork and are subject to change. Single stamps shown are for illustrative purposes only unless specified for individual sale.

Directors, officers and organizing committee

Directors

President
Wade E. Saadi
New York, NY

Treasurer
Roger Brody
Watchung, NJ

General Counsel
Thomas Mazza
New York, NY

Officers

Vice President
Steven J. Rod
South Orange, NJ

Secretary
Bruce Marsden
Short Hills, NJ

Lighthouse®

World Leaders in Collectors Accessories. Since 1917.

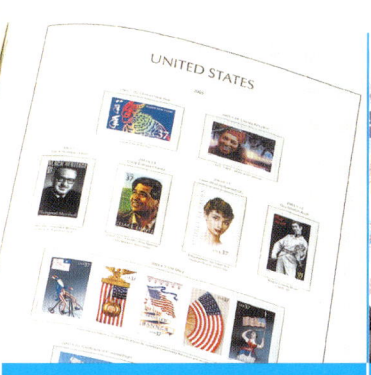

18 styles and interleaves

Many different models with glassine and clear interleaves

| PRE-PRINTED COUNTRY ALBUMS | VARIO STOCKSHEETS AND BINDERS | STOCKBOOKS AND STOCK CARDS |

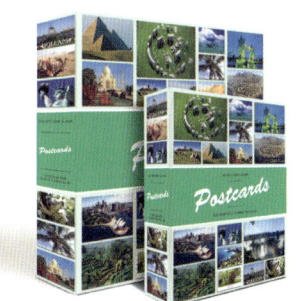
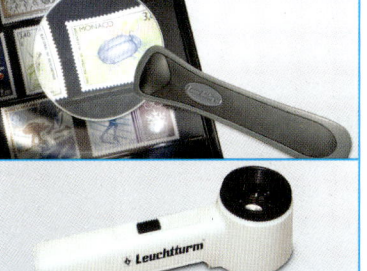
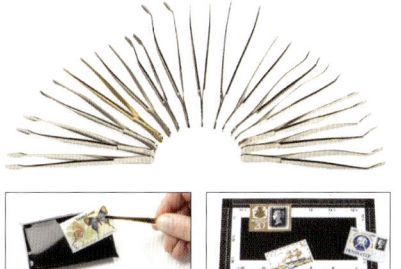

| POSTCARD - AND FDC ALBUMS | MAGNIFIERS AND MICROSCOPES | QUALITY TOOLS AND ACCESSOIRES |

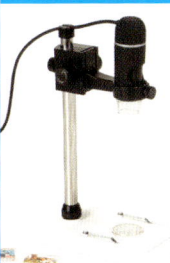

10x-300x, 5 MEGAPIXEL

Visit us at NY2016 World Stamp Show, Booth 837, to view our daily specials.

(888) 269-1513 · www.lighthouse.us

LIGHTHOUSE PUBLICATIONS, INC. · 10 Washington Avenue, Unit B · Fairfield, NJ 07004
Tel. (201) 342-1513 (M-F 9:00-4:30 EST) · Fax (201) 342-7142 · Email: info@lighthouse.us

Committee Chairs

Auctions
Andrew Titley
Dallas, TX

Awards
Gene Fricks
New York, NY

Bourse
Tami Jackson
Leesport, PA

Cachets and Cancels
Henry Scheuer
New York, NY

Commissioner General
Stephen D. Schumann
Hayward, CA

Asst. Commissioner General
Bruce Marsden
Short Hills, NJ

Communications and Exhibition Catalog
Matthew Healey
New York, NY

Design
Niko Courtelis
Portland, OR

Development
Charles Shreve
Dallas, TX

Entertainment and Social
Carol Bommarito
New York, NY

Entry Level and Youth
Michael Bloom
Portland, OR

Functions and Activities
Gail Saadi
New York, NY

Judges and Judging
Stephen Reinhard
Mineola, NY

Chairman of the Jury
Robert P. Odenweller
Bernardsville, NJ

Liberty Club
Alexander Haimann
St. Louis, MO

Committee Chairs (continued)

Marketing and Public Relations
Thomas M. Fortunato
Rochester, NY

Social Media
Janet Klug
Pleasant Plain, OH

Societies and Affiliates
Rodney Juell
Joliet, IL

Volunteers
Mark Butterline
Boston, MA

Committee Members at Large

Ex Officio
Scott English,
American Philatelic Society
Bellefonte, PA

Ex Officio
Megan Orient,
American Philatelic Society
Bellefonte, PA

Ex Officio
Ken Martin,
American Philatelic Society
Bellefonte, PA

Ex Officio
Dana Guyer,
American Stamp Dealers Association
Centre Hall, PA

Executive Assistant
Christine Jimenez
Secaucus, NJ

Entry Level and Youth
Debby Friedman
New York, NY

Database Manager
Eric Jackson
Leesport, PA

Web Site Development
Michael Eastick
Forest Hill, Victoria, Australia

At-Large
Andrew Kupersmit
Metuchen, NJ

Is finding insurance driving you nuts?

Contact Hugh Wood Inc. for all your insurance needs.

Visit our website at www.hughwood.com or call us at 212.509.3777 or email us at info@hughwood.com.

The Gold Standard in REVENUES

Booth 1037

ERIC JACKSON

the hobby's premier dealer of revenue stamps since 1975

Specializing in revenue stamps of the United States and Possessions, Match and Medicine Stamps, Revenue Stamped Paper, Taxpaids, State Revenues, Canada Revenues, AMG Revenues, U.S. and Canada Telegraph Stamps, U.S. Local Post Stamps, Revenue Stamped Paper, and much more. We also maintain an inventory of philatelic literature pertaining to revenue stamps of the world.

Buying & Selling

Eric Jackson
P.O. Box 728 • Leesport PA 19533-0728
Phone: 610-926-6200 • Fax: 610-926-0120
E-mail: eric@revenuer.com
Visit us online at www.ericjackson.com

Donors and supporters

THE ORGANIZERS OF WORLD STAMP SHOW—NY 2016 wish to thank the following people and organizations whose contributions (as of April 1) have been invaluable to making this show a reality.

The Leadership Circle

These show patrons have donated $25,000 or more towards World Stamp Show—NY 2016.

Anonymous
Gordon E. Eubanks, Jr.
Alfredo Frohlich
Joseph Hackmey
Alan and Mitch Holyoake

Vince King
George J. Kramer
Daniel J. Ryterband
Wade Saadi
Charles Shreve

Helen and Harlan Stone
Donald Sundman
Hugh Wood

Donor Sponsors

$50,000 and above:
Collectors Club, NY
www.collectorsclub.org
The Philatelic Foundation
(www.philatelicfoundation.org)
Washington 2006 Exposition

Philatelic Patron

$25,000:
Westpex, Inc.
www.westpex.com

Charitable Foundation Support

$25,000 and above:
TurningPoint Foundation—
    Pavilion Theater

Major Supporters

$10,000 to $15,000:
Carol Bommarito
Roger Brody
James P. Gough
Edward J.J. Grabowski
Larry Hunt
Tami and Eric Jackson
David Zlowe

Liberty Platinum Members

$5,000 to $9,999:
John Barwis
Ian C. Gibson-Smith
Anna Lee
David Gorham

Liberty Gold Members

$2,500:
Murray A. Abramson
James Allen
John Apfelbaum
William P. Barlow, Jr.
Paul Bartolomei
John Barwis
Jonathan Becker
Charles Bentley
Roland Cipolla II
Nancy and Douglas N. Clark
Jim and Sue Dempsey

Anthony M. Dewey
Hugh Feldman
Robert D. Forster
Alexander Haimann
Chris King
Nicholas Kirke
Daniel M. Knowles, M.D.
Thomas W. Lane
Richard C. Malmgren
Robert Wayne Martin
Vernon R. Morris, Jr.

NAPEX
Robert G. Rose
Steven J. Rod
Mark Schwartz
Keith Stupell
Mark Taylor
Steven Walske
Alan Warren
Richard Winter
Alfonso G. Zulueta, Jr.

PALO ALBUMS, INC.
Stamp Albums for Every Country in the World

Palo Albums is your destination for quality stamp albums, stockbooks, stamp supplies and more - the only provider of illustrated and colored pages for every country in the world.

Nowhere else on the planet will you find such a diverse and comprehensive selection.

paloalbums.com | 800-572-5967

The Official Representative of Palo, Lindner & Davo Products.
Visit us at the World Stamp Show NY2016, booth 836.

LINDNER *Das Original*

Liberty Silver Members

$1,500:

Dane S. Claussen
Leonard Hartmann
Robert Johnson
William Johnson
Benjamin Y. Lee
Clifford R. "Rob" Lund
Millard H. Mack
Michael J. and Anna Marie McCabe
Foster Miller
William A. Sandrik
William L. Strauss
Blair Tremere
Hal Vogel
Danforth Walker

Liberty Members

$1,000:

Kees Adema
Anonymous
Akthem Al-Manaseer
Manuel Arango
Ted Bahry
Michael & Faye Bass
Jan Berg
Thomas Bienosek
Lyle Boardman
Allan Boudreau
Robert Boyd
Thomas Broadhead
Mark A. Butterline
Louis Caprario
Richard A. Colberg
Vincent Cosenza
Santiago Cruz
W. Douglas Drumheller
Ann Dunkin
Jack Dykhouse
David Eeles
Dale F. Forster
Thomas Fortunato
Deborah Friedman
Cheryl R. Ganz
Chip Gliedman
Greater Philadelphia Stamp & Collectors Club
Jonas Hallstrom
Matthew Healey & Jacqueline Rubin
Robert R. Hegland
Gary Hendren
John Hotchner
Michael Jacobs
Edgar Jatho
Bill Johnson
Robert Juceam
David A. Kent
Janet R. Klug
Keith Klugman
Yamil H. Kouri
Edward Kroll
Douglas K. Lehmann
Geoffrey Lewis
Michael Ley
Dwayne O. Littauer
Larry Lyons
Kenneth Martin
Thomas Mazza
Edward Mendlowitz
Gordon C. Morison
Ralph Nafziger
Behruz Nassre-Esfahani
Randy Neil
North Carolina Postal History Society
Northeast Federation of Stamp Clubs
James O'Mara
Robert P. Odenweller
Stephen B. Pacetti
Philatelic Club of Will County, Ill.
Marvin Platt
James Pullin
Eric Rasmussen
Stephen Reinhard
Rocky Mountain Philatelic Library
William Schultz
Frederick C. Skvara
K. David Steidley
Clarence Stillions
James Grimwood Taylor
May Day Taylor
Ben Termini
United Postal Stationery Society
Andrew Urushima
Ed W. Wise
Mitchell M. Zais

Supporters

Anonymous
Alan Barasch
Frank Barletta
Alexandru Bartoc
Robert Bialo
Alan Bush
Martha Coleman
Kenneth Coulson
Terry Dempsey
Gladys and John Edward Evan
Vera Felts
Allan Fisk
Eldon S. Fodor
Michael Frank
William Frear
Vinson Friedman
Richard A. Geissler
Paul Glass
Richard Hein
James Hering
Alan Hicks
Carolyn Hollfelder
John Hughey
Norman Jacobs
Kathryn J. Johnson
Rodney Juell
Donna M. Jungreis
Eugene D. Kline
Conrad Klinkner
Todd Leavitt
Kurt and Joann Lenz
Stephen L. Liebman
Brian Liedtke
Bruce Marsden
William A. Matthews
James Mazepa
Maura Muller
Thomas Pallister
Suzanne Pavel
Robert Peck
Barbara J. Poplawsky
Roger P. Quinby
Michael Reed
Adam Rod
Ronald Rohin
Marion Rollings
Henrik Rossell
Robert Sabbagh
Tamaki Saito
Gerald F. Schroedl
Alan Shapiro
Michael F. Simon
Richard E. Small
Richard H. Stanford, Jr.
Jack E. Thompson
Donald Tjossem

Supporters (continued)

Hans van Gils
Joy Venegas
Leslie Vork

Fumiaki Wada
Ryan Walsh

West Essex Philatelic Society
Richard D. Zallen

Corporate Matching Partners

Aetna Foundation
Computer Associates

Society Participation

These groups have made donations securing booth and meeting room space

$2,000 Super Booth Sponsors:

American Topical Association (ATA) *americantopicalassn.org*
Confederate Stamp Alliance (CSA) *www.csalliance.org*
Royal Philatelic Society of London (RPSL) www.rpsl.org.uk
United Postal Stationery Society (UPSS) *www.upss.org*
shared with Postal Order Society (POS) *postalordersociety.blogspot.com*
United States Stamp Society (USSS) *www.usstamps.org*
U.S. Philatelic Classics Society (USPCS) *www.uspcs.org*
U.S. Possessions Philatelic Society (USPPS) *www.uspps.net*

$1,000 Sponsors:

American Association of Philatelic Exhibitors (AAPE) *www.aape.org*
British North American Philatelic Society (BNAPS) *www.bnaps.org*
Collectors Club, NY (CCNY) *www.collectorsclub.org*
International Philippine Philatelic Society (IPPS) *www.theipps.info*
International Society for Japanese Philately (ISJP) *www.isjp.org*
Mexico Elmhurst Philatelic Society International (MEPSI) *www.mepsi.org*
Precancel Stamp Society (PSS) *www.precancels.com*
Scouts on Stamps Society, International (SOSSI) *www.sossi.org*
Society for Hungarian Philately (SHP) *www.hungarianphilately.org*
The Perfins Club (PC) *www.perfins.org*

$500 Sponsors:

American Air Mail Society (AAMS) *www.americanairmailsociety.org*
Canal Zone Study Group (CZSG) *www.canalzonestudygroup.com*
Colombia-Panama Philatelic Study Group (COPAPHIL) *www.copaphil.org*
Ebony Society of Philatelic Events & Reflections (ESPER) *www.esperstamps.org*
Falkland Islands Philatelic Study Group (FIPSG) *www.fipsg.org.uk*
Metropolitan Air Post Society (MAPS) *www.mapsnewyork.org/home.html*
Ottoman and Near Eastern Philatelic Society (ONEPS) *www.oneps.net*
Plate Number Coil Collectors Club (PNC3) *pnc3.org*
Society of Israel Philatelists (SIP) *www.israelstamps.com*

$250 Sponsors:

Carriers and Locals Society (CLS) *www.pennypost.org*
Cuban Philatelic Society of America (CPSA) *www.cubapsa.com*
France & Colonies Philatelic Society (FCPS) *www.fcps.org.uk*
India Study Circle (ISC) *www.indiastudycircle.org*
International Society of Worldwide Stamp Collectors (ISWSC) *www.iswsc.org*
Iran Philatelic Study Circle (IPSC) *www.iranphilately.org*
Military Postal History Society (MPHS) *www.militaryphs.org*
National Duck Stamp Collectors Society (NDSCS) *www.ndscs.org*
Pitcairn Islands Study Group (PISG) *www.pisg.net*
Rossica Society of Russian Philately (ROSSICA) *rossica.org*
St. Helena, Ascension and Tristan da Cunha Philatelic Society (SHATPS) *www.shatps.org*
Sports Philatelists International (SPI) *sportstamps.org*
Universal Ship Cancellation Society (USCS) *www.uscs.org*

Confederate Stamps and Postal History

Visit Me at Booth 1365

Celebrating 50 Years of Expertise in Confederate Philately

- Introduced to Confederates in 1965
- Editor of *The Confederate Philatelist* 1970–1987
- Editor-in-chief of the 2012 *Confederate States of America Catalog and Handbook of Stamps and Postal History*, the APS StampShow 2013 Grand Award winner in literature competition
- Professional since 1973 and called first philatelic auction in 1973
- Collector, exhibitor, writer, researcher, editor, expertizer, and retailer
- Past president of the Confederate Stamp Alliance and winner of countless writing, exhibiting, and service awards
- Former member of the Council of Philatelists of the Smithsonian National Postal Museum
- Member Emeritus of CSA Authentication Service. Member from 1996–2014, former Recording Secretary, and currently an active consultant.

Patricia A. Kaufmann

10194 N. Old State Road • Lincoln, DE 19960

Call: 302-422-2656 • Fax: 302-424-1990

TRISHKAUF@COMCAST.NET

Life Member: CSA, APS, APRL, USPCS
Member: ASDA, CCNY, RPSL

World Stamp Show NY 2016

www.trishkaufmann.com

Schuyler J. Rumsey Philatelic Auctions

An Official Auctioneer for New York 2016

    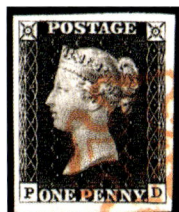

When choosing an auction house, you should also consider the things they don't sell.

Knowledge. Experience. Integrity. Things that cannot be bought, bartered or sold. Yet they're responsible for realizing the highest prices for your stamps. At Rumsey Auctions, we've built our reputation on these qualities as much as on the impressive financial results we achieve for our clients. Please call or email us and let us show you how much we can do for you.

World Stamp Show

| 415 781 5127 | srumsey@rumseyauctions.com | visit us at booth 1031 |

Volunteers

THE ORGANIZING COMMITTEE of World Stamp Show–NY 2016 would like to thank the following individuals who volunteered to assist in making this remarkable event a reality (as of March 15, 2016):

Abad, Razwan
Abram, Sam
Advani, Zeeshan
Agaogullari, Mehmet Edip
Agostosi, Alessandro
Al Attar, Hatim
Allen, James
Anderson, Walter
Atkinson, Al
Awan, Imtiaz
Baker, Richard
Ball, David
Banah, Hesham
Bates, Richard
Belanger, Skip
Bennett, Debra
Bennett, Jeffrey
Benninghoff, Robert
Bergen, Edward
Berkowitz, Joanne
Bernstein, Richard
Best, Deborah
Bloom, Michael
Borofsky, Melvyn
Bouchaqour, Abderrahman
Bowman, Mary Ann
Boyarsky, Jeffrey
Brahin, Jeffrey
Breauer, Bob
Breznay, Ron
Brideau, Bradley
Britt, Mary
Bronner, Michael
Brouady, Christopher
Bubaris, Ginny

Caponi, Rocco
Chen, Wayne
Ching, Fanny
Chitty, Lindsay
Clemmensen, Paul
Click, Irene
Colberg, Richard
Congrove, Jack
Cosenza, Vincent
Costanzo, Paula
Culbert, Daniel
Das, Dilip Kumar
Dempsey, Gerald
Dempsey, John
Dempsey, Terry
Denman, Don
Denys, Jack
Denys, Mary
Devine, Aimee
DiChiara, Joseph
Dimri, Yogesh
Dougherty, James
Dowers, Darryl
Dubois, David
Dunaier, Gary
Ebner, Birgit
Edgcomb, Cheryl
Eisenberg, Joan
Elramly, Mohamed
Forster, Dale
Forster, Jeffrey
Forster, Robert
Foster, Lisa
Frank, Michael
Friedman, Debby

Fuchs, Jeannette
Fuchs, Rainer
Galfotd, Hugh
Gallagher, Heslin
Gamble, Mary
Gamble, Terrence
Gandomani, Amir
Ganz, Cheryl
Geraci, Joseph
Ghosh, Dilip
Gliedman, Chip
Golub, Alvin
Golub, Averell
Gordon, Gabriel
Gottlieb, Stuart
Grabowski, Edward
Gregory, Fred
Gregory, Mary
Haber, Lawrence
Healey, Matthew
Hein, Rick
Held, David
Heller, Don
Hering, Barbara
Hering, James
Hildebrant, Eric
Hofmeyr, Jan
Impenna, John
Islam, Sheikh
Jabson, Jaynee
Jagadeesh, Kariswamy
Jarvis, Bob
Jarvis, Marci
Jeannopulos, Peter
Johnson, Aric

Judge, Richard
Juell, Rodney
Kandil, Moustafa
Kaufman, Ellen
Kaufman, Ken
Kennedy, Dennis
Kent, David
Keto, Karlen
King, Vince
Kirke, Nicholas
Kiskowski, Maria
Kiskowski, William
Kittle, Stephen
Klimley, Ronald
Kroll, Edward
Langhi, Donald
Laveroni, Edward
Lawrence, Frederick
Lee, Benjamin
Liang, Ziqian
Lin, Miranda
Lindemuth, James
Liu, Jia
Lokin, Julius
Luo, Amy
Mady, Tarek
Maguire, Dennis
Maisel, Helena
Maisel, Richard
Manigo, Cheryl
Martin, Robert
Martinez, Gabriel
Matsishena, Olga
McCabe, Annamarie
McCabe, Michael
McClendon, Todd
Metzloff, Peter
Meyer, Geoffrey
Milani, Afshin
Miller, Jacob

Mittal, Ajay
Mohan, Vivin
Moreno Murillo, Juan Manuel
Morginstin, Sid
Morison, Gordon
Morrison, Bill
Muhammad, Zarifa
Nafziger, Ralph
Nogid, Henry
Noh, Barbara
Noll-Morison, Mary Jane
Nugent, Brandon
O'Connor, Timothy
O'Shea, Timothy
Osmolskis, Tadas
Outhier, Charles
Outhier, Yidi
Palladino, Antoinette
Palladino, Nicholas
Patel, Pathik
Patel, Vinaykumar
Pavel, Suzanne
Price, Christina
Provost, David
Reinhard, Jacqueline
Reinhard, Stephen
Rod, Francine
Rodriguez, Omar
Rose, Robert
Ruebush, Trenton
Rufe, Robert
Rusch, Harley
Ryan, Jeff
Sack, John
Sahasrabuddhe, Aniruddha
Sales, Michael
Sandrik, William
Scannell, Caroline
Schaefer, Richard
Schiavoni, Andrew

Schumann, Mary
Schwartz, Rick
Scott, Betsy
Scrivener, Norman
Shapiro, Jeffrey
Sharma, Dinesh
Shestople, Nicholas
Shoults, Gregory
Simrak, Ray
Skoyles, Roger
Sober, Michael
Srinivasan, Vijay Anand
Stafford, Glen
Stafford, Johanna
Stager, Phillip
Stotts, Denise
Stotts, Jay
Sukhram, Dianne
Sussex, John
Taschenberg, Karen
Taschenberg, Richard
Tauber, Stephen
Tawfeek, Ray
Thaker, Bhavin
Thompson, Jack
Thornton, Tiffany
Torre, David
Vaska, Marcus
Verge, Charles J.G.
Walker, Nazlah
Walters, Patrick
Weiss, Lori
Whitman, Joan
Whitman, Robert
Young, Terrence
Zahm, Robert
Ziyan, Mohamed
Zlowe, David
Zwillinger, Steven

Canada Stamp Finder

Specialist in Rare Stamps of Canada and the Provinces

Member of: CSDA, RPSC, BNAPS, APS, CCNY, NSDA, CPS of GB, PTS & IFSDA

The Artemis Collection of Inverted Stamps of Canada
Featuring the Inverted Seaway and other Great Rarities!!!
Mint & Used Singles, Corner Blocks, Covers & More!

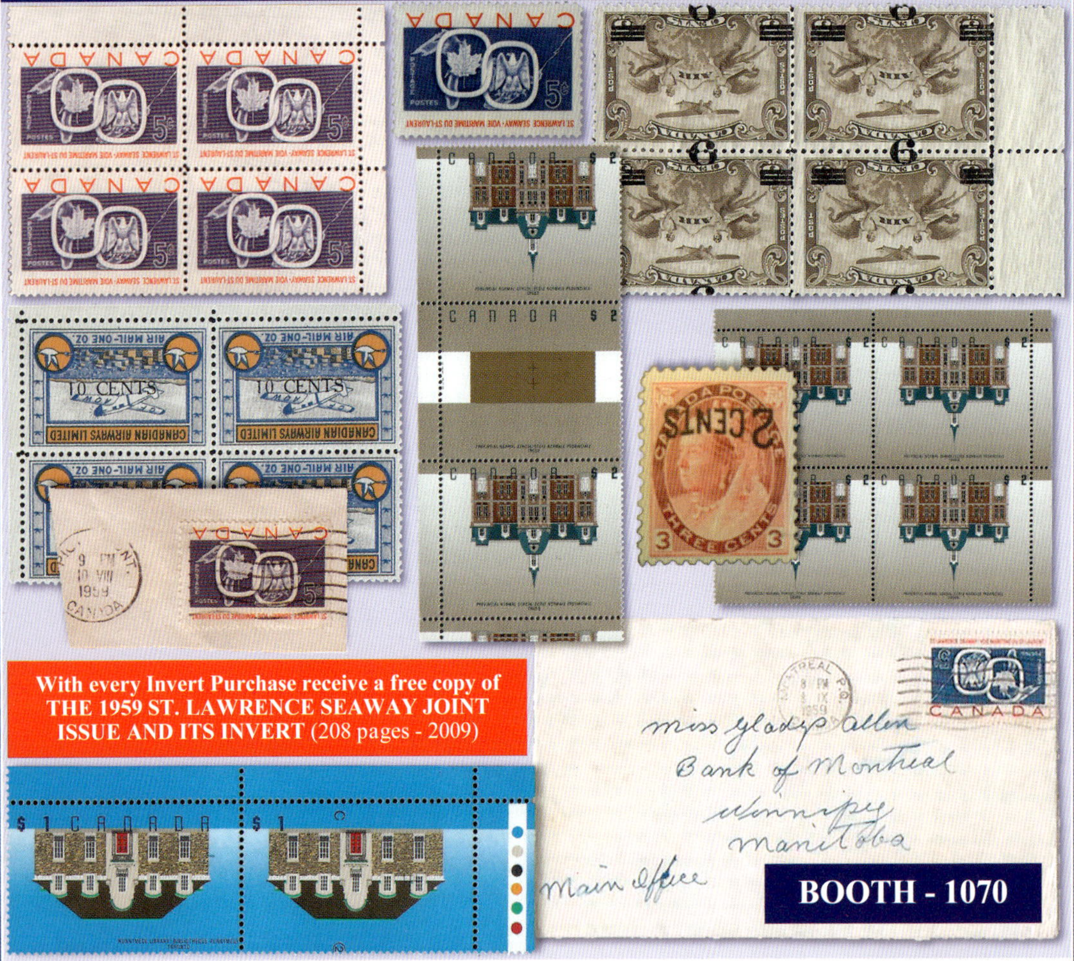

With every Invert Purchase receive a free copy of THE 1959 ST. LAWRENCE SEAWAY JOINT ISSUE AND ITS INVERT (208 pages - 2009)

BOOTH - 1070

Maxime Stephanie Herold
54 Soccavo Crescent, Brampton, ON, L6Y 0W3, Canada
Tel: +1 (514) 238-5751 • Fax: +1 (323) 315-2635
Toll Free in North America: 1 (877) 412-3106
Email: info@canadastampfinder.com • www.canadastampfinder.com

Canada Stamp Finder
Specialist in Rare Stamps of Canada and the Provinces
Member of: CSDA, RPSC, BNAPS, APS, CCNY, NSDA, CPS of GB, PTS & IFSDA

BOOTH - 1070

King George V "Medallion" Issue

Canada Scott #195c-200a   1c to 8c Medallion Issue
Complete set of imperforate pairs with post office fresh color and pristine NH original gum. XF
Catalog Value: $4,200.00   **Net: $1,995.00 USD**

Canada Scott #195DP-200DP   1c to 8c Medallion Issue
An Extremely Rare complete set of large Die Proofs
Catalog Value: Unlisted   **Net: $11,495.00 USD**

Also Available is the UNIQUE Canada Scott #201 DP
13c Citadel in color of issue. EX: Sutherland, Goss & Brigham
Net: $5,995.00 USD (No Photo)

Canada Scott #197cP   3c Medallion Issue "Die II"
Large Die Proof in color of issue with extensive manuscript printer's notation in bottom left corner. A UNIQUE replacement Die Proof, VF, normal mounting abrasion on back of card.   **Net: $2,995.00 USD**

Canada Scott #195c-200a, 199a & 199ai
        1c to 8c Medallion Issue
UNIQUE Never Hinged complete set of imperforate Inscription corner blocks of four including the ONLY imprint blocks of the 5c imperf vertically as well as the only 5c corner block of four imperf vertically and showing the "MAJOR RE-ENTRY" (Pl. 1 UL pos. 10) post office fresh color and XF EXHIBITION SHOWPIECE
Catalog Value: Unlisted   **Net: $31,500.00 USD**

Maxime Stephanie Herold
54 Soccavo Crescent, Brampton, ON, L6Y 0W3, Canada
Tel: +1 (514) 238-5751 • Fax: +1 (323) 315-2635
Toll Free in North America: 1 (877) 412-3106
Email: info@canadastampfinder.com • www.canadastampfinder.com

Commissioners

THE ROLE OF EACH NATIONAL COMMISSIONER is to represent the Federation of International Philately (FIP) in their home country. The commissioners act as personal liaison between each exhibitor from their country and World Stamp Show–NY 2016, ensure that all competitive exhibits have achieved the appropriate qualifications to be displayed at the international level, and physically bring the exhibits to the show. *Please note, the following countries have not appointed a commissioner to World Stamp Show–NY 2016: Georgia, Iceland, Lithuania, Macau, Philippines and Vietnam.*

Commissioner General
Stephen D. Schumann, RDP

Assistant Commissioner General
Bruce Marsden

Federation of International Philately (FIP) Consultant
Bernard Beston

ARGENTINA	AUSTRALIA-1	AUSTRALIA-2	AUSTRALIA	AUSTRIA

Miguel Casielles	Darryl Fuller	Ian McMahon	Ross Wood (Assistant)	Helmut Seebald

BAHRAIN	**BANGLADESH**	**BELARUS**	**BELGIUM**	**BOLIVIA**
Khalid Qassim Behzad	Shafiqul Islam	Konstantin Filobok	Jozef Ghys	Martha Villarroel de Peredo
BRAZIL  Rogerio A. Dedivitis	**BRUNEI DARUSSALAM**  Bakar H. Berudin	**BULGARIA**  Tsvetelina Kostadinova	**CANADA**  Jan J. Danielski	**CANADA**  Robert Pinet (Assistant)
CHILE  Heinz Junge Wenzel	**CHINA**  Frank (Zhifei) Li	**CHINESE TAIPEI**  Mao-Hsin Lin	**COLOMBIA**  Manuel Arango	**COSTA RICA** Luis Fernando Diaz
CROATIA  Ivan Martinas	**CUBA**  José Raúl Lorenzo	**CYPRUS**  Nicos Rangos	**CZECH REPUBLIC**  Vít Vaníček	**DENMARK**  Lars Engelbrecht, RDP

33

Commissioners (continued)

ECUADOR  Jaime Garzón	**EGYPT**  Sherif Samra	**EL SALVADOR**  Guillermo F. Gallegos	**ESTONIA**  Kaido Andres	**FINLAND**  Jarkko Leppänen
FRANCE  Claude Desarmenien	**GERMANY-1**  Walter Bernatek	**GERMANY-2**  Ralph Ebner	**GREECE**  George Thomareis	**GUATEMALA**  Carlos Rivera Grajeda
HONDURAS  Mauricio Mejía	**HONG KONG**  Anna Lee	**HUNGARY**  László Leitold	**INDIA**  Dhananjay S. Desai	**INDONESIA**  Clara Wijarsih
IRAN  Massoud N. Farahbakhsh	**IRAQ**  Mohammad Abd Ali Ibrahim Al-Rubaye	**IRELAND**  Des Quail	**ISRAEL**  Menachem Lador	**ITALY**  Bruno Crevato-Selvaggi

Est 1856
STANLEY GIBBONS
The Home of Stamp Collecting

BY APPOINTMENT TO
HER MAJESTY THE QUEEN
PHILATELISTS
STANLEY GIBBONS LTD
LONDON

Visit us on Stand 1050 & 1051

See the highest quality range of stunning material and meet the Stanley Gibbons team on stand 1050 & 1051 at the show

Great Britain Specialists

Commonwealth Specialists

Publications & Accessories

Specialist award winning catalogues, magazines, albums and stamp accessories.

Visit us on stand 1050

For more information contact our specialists directly
@ Stamps@stanleygibbons.com
or visit our full range at
🖥 stanleygibbons.com

Commissioners (continued)

JAPAN-1 Yoshida Takashi	**JAPAN-2** Kenzaburo Ikeda	**KOREA** Seong-Kwon Kim	**KUWAIT** Khaled Abdul Mughni	**LATVIA** Raimonds Jonitis
LIECHTENSTEIN Jan Huys-Berlingin	**LUXEMBOURG** Guy Jungblut	**MALAYSIA** Tan Chee Hui	**MALTA** John A. Cardona	**MEXICO (COFUMEX)** Jaime Benavides
MEXICO (FIP) Alonso Castillo Osuna	**MONACO** Patrick Maselis	**MONGOLIA** Shagdariin Chadraabal	**MONTENEGRO** Tomo Katurić	**NEPAL** Rishi Kumar Tulsyan
NETHERLANDS A.H.N. Zonjee	**NEW ZEALAND** David Loe	**NORWAY** Ivar J. Sundsbø	**PAKISTAN** Adnan Iqbal Nanjee	**PARAGUAY** Roberto C. Eaton

PERU Carlos A. Brenis	**POLAND** Julian Auleytner	**PORTUGAL** Luis Frazão	**QATAR** Hussain R. Al-Ismail	**ROMANIA** Constantin Milu
RUSSIA Sergey Evtushenko	**SAINT-PIERRE AND MIQUELON** Fabrice Fouchard	**SAUDI ARABIA** Mohammed Kamal Safdar	**SERBIA** Aleksandar Krstić	**SINGAPORE** Henry Ong
SLOVAKIA Vojtech Jankovič	**SLOVENIA** Mihael I. Fock	**SOUTH AFRICA** Peter van der Molen	**SPAIN** Rafael Acuna	**SWEDEN-1** Fredrik Ydell
SWEDEN-2 Cajsa Ojakangas	**SWITZERLAND** Roger Muller	**THAILAND** Sansern Nilrat	**TURKEY** David Franco	**UKRAINE** Dmitro Frenkel

Commissioners (continued)

UNITED ARAB EMIRATES	UNITED KINGDOM-1	UNITED KINGDOM-2	URUGUAY	U.S.A. (EAST)
Ali Abdulrahman Ahmad	Jon Aitchison	Graham Winters	Gabriel Martínez Rouco	Yamil Kouri

U.S.A. (WEST)	VENEZUELA	VIRGIN ISLANDS
Vesma Grinfelds	Pedro Meri	Giorgio Migliavacca

Quality Classic U.S. Stamps & Postal History

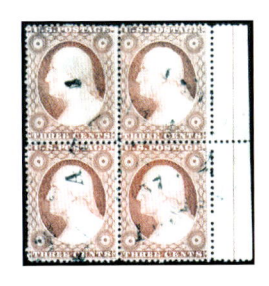

Simply Stated
We Build ...
We Buy ...
We Sell ...

Great Collections

STANLEY M. PILLER & ASSOCIATES

Established 1968
Office: 800 S. Broadway, Suite 201 • Walnut Creek, CA 94596
Mailing Address: P.O. Box 559 • Alamo, CA 94507
Phone: 925-938-8290 • Fax: 925-938-8812
Email: stmpdlr@aol.com • Web: www.smpiller.com

The jury

EACH JUROR HAS BEEN INVITED to judge the competitive exhibits at World Stamp Show–NY 2016 based on their acknowledged expertise in numerous areas and longstanding credentials as international philatelic judges. Many are signatories to the Roll of Distinguished Philatelists (RDP), an honor reserved for the most accomplished members of our hobby in recognition of their lifetime achievements in exhibiting, research, writing and their commitment to philately.

Honorary President
Tay Peng Hian RDP,
Singapore

Honorary Chairman
Robert Odenweller RDP,
USA

Jury Secretary
Stephen Reinhard,
USA

Jury President
Peter McCann RDP,
USA

FIP Consultant
Bernard Beston,
Australia

Jury Vice Presidents

Bernard Jimenez, France

Koichi Sato RDP, Japan

Charles J.G. Verge

Jury members

Fernando Aranaz, Spain

Mark Banchik, USA

Gary Brown, Australia

Chen Yu-An, Chinese Taipei

Prakob Chirakiti, Thailand

Nancy Clark, USA

Santiago Cruz, Colombia

Luis Diaz, Costa Rica

Dila Eaton, Paraguay

Lars Engelbrecht RDP, Denmark *Cross Accreditation*

Darrell Ertzberger, USA

Malcolm Groom, Australia

Jonas Hallstrom RDP, Sweden

Christopher Harman RDP, UK

Suwito Harsono, Indonesia

41

The jury (continued)

Michael Ho, Chinese Taipei

John Hotchner, USA

Alexander Ilyushin RDP, Russia

Muhammed Javaid, UAE

Jørgen Jørgensen RDP, Denmark

Damian Laege, Germany

Lee Bok-Kyu, Korea

Ronald Lesher, USA

Frank (Zhifei) Li, China

Klerman Lopes, Brazil

José Lorenzo, Cuba

Jean-Pierre Magne, France

Jukka Mäkinen, Finland

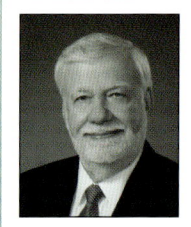

James Mazepa RDP, USA

Thomas Mazza, USA

José Ramon Moreno, Spain

Yigal Nathaniel, Israel

Tono Putranto, Indonesia

Andres Schlichter, Argentina

Barry Scott, New Zealand

Helmut Seebald,
Austria

Ivar J. Sundsbo,
Norway

Tan Chee Hui,
Malaysia

Ross Towle, USA
Assistant Jury Secretary

Brian Trotter RDP,
UK

Danforth Walker RDP,
USA

Patricia Walker,
USA

Robert Wightman,
Switzerland

Apprentices

Neil Cronje, South
Africa

Konstantin Filobok,
Russia

Kathryn Johnson,
USA

Yamil Kouri,
USA

Spas Panchev,
Bulgaria

Igor Pirc,
Slovenia

Expert Group

Chang Chien Pin,
Chinese Taipei

David Petruzelli,
USA

The Global Philatelic Network Rarities Auction

3 June 2016 | Javits Center | New York City, USA

The "ERIVAN" Collection
Selected United States and Confederate States Stamps and Postal History

Pony Express: $2 on westward cover

Waterbury: "Bridgeport Fireman" Fancy Cancel

Nashville, Tennessee: 5c. – one of 2 known tête-bêche blocks of 12, ex Caspary

USA and more "at its best"...

Nashville, Tennessee: 10c. on Adams Express Cover

Baton Rouge: the unique cover with 10c. blue, ex Caspary (1956)

Viewing: Saturday, 28 MAY until Friday, 3 JUNE 2016, BOOTH NO. 729

Official Auctioneer

H.R. Harmer, Corinphila Auktionen, Heinrich Köhler Auktionen and the partners of the Global Philatelic Network are appointed Official Auctioneers at the World Stamp Show in New York.

H.R. Harmer in cooperation with Corinphila, Heinrich Köhler and John Bull

3 June 2016 | Javits Center | New York City, USA

Worldwide Stamps and Postal History

Spanish Philippines: 1854, 5c mint corner block of four with all four different positions

Marion, Virginia: 1861, 10c black on cover to Kingston, TN, most probably the finest example known on cover

Hawaii: 2c Numerals in both shades. The only existing cover with a 4-cent franking and the only entire known with both 2 cent of this issue.

…just a few items from the Worldwide Rarities and "ERIVAN" Collection Auction

Papal State: three-colour-franking incl. 1 scudo on incoming mail cover to the United States

Argentina/Buenos Aires: Liberty Head block of 4 on cover

Also all single lots of the upcoming Corinphila Auction can be viewed at the booth.

H.R. HARMER	CORINPHILA AUKTIONEN AG	HEINRICH KÖHLER AUKTIONSHAUS GMBH & CO. KG	CORINPHILA VEILINGEN B.V.	JOHN BULL STAMP AUCTIONS LTD.
2680 Walnut Ave. Suite AB Tustin, CA 92780 U.S.A. phone ++1 714 389 9178 fax ++1 714 389 9189 info@hrharmer.com www.hrharmer.com	Wiesenstr. 8 8032 Zurich Switzerland phone +41 (0)44 3899191 fax +41 (0)44 3899195 info@corinphila.ch www.corinphila.ch	Wilhelmstr. 48 65183 Wiesbaden Germany phone +49 (0)611 39381 fax +49 (0)611 39384 info@heinrich-koehler.de www.heinrich-koehler.de	Heemraadschapslaan 100 1181 VC Amstelveen/Amsterdam Netherlands phone +31 20 6249740 fax +31 20 6249749 info@corinphila.nl www.corinphila.nl	7/F, Kwong Fat Hong Building 1 Rumsey Street Sheung Wan, Hong Kong phone ++852 2890 5767 fax ++852 2576 5110 info@jbull.com www.jbull.com

Special prizes

Grand Prix d'Honneur
Tiffany & Co. sterling silver tray
gift of Robert P. Odenweller

Grand Prix International
Hand-carved cherrywood vase by Douglas Richard
gift of Fédération Internationale de Philatélie (FIP)

Grand Prix National
Crystal bowl
gift of the American Philatelic Society

Other prizes and awards, listed alphabetically by donor

"Poste près d'Anvers", print
gift of Kees Adema

Solid silver handmade letter carrier
gift of Akthem Al-Manaseer

Native American scrimshaw
gift of American Society for Polar Philately

Orrefor Polaris votive lights
gift of American Society for Polar Philately

Jarrah and Redgum box with sterling silver gum leaves
gift of Australian Federation

Silver Dallah Arabic coffee thermos
gift of Bahrain Federation

Brass hariken
gift of Sheikh Shafiqul Islam, Bangladesh Commissioner

Nakshi flower vase
gift of Ajme Sheikh Nafisa Anjum, Bangladesh Federation

From the Azores to New Zealand, book by Patrick Maselis
gift of Royal Belgian Association of Philatelic Societies (KLBP-FRCPB)

Great Auk stone sculpture
gift of Bernard Beston

Folklore statue
gift of Brazilian Federation of Philately

Sterling bookmark
gift of Eddie Bridges

Spalted yellow-birch wood bowl with brushed silver nameplate
gift of Royal Philatelic Society of Canada

"Year of The Monkey", Malaysian wood-veneer art
gift of Chai Hui Choo

"Serenity Wave Blue" by Becky Ricard Magyar
gift of Nancy and Douglas Clark

Chichen Itzá Pyramid 5 oz/20 pesos silver proof coin
gift of COFUMEX

Sterling serving platter
gift of Collectors Club of Chicago

Alphonse Mucha Award
gift of Society of Czech Philatelists

Post Office Dept. antique eagle sculpture
gift of Diane DeBlois and Robert D. Harris

Exotic wood sculpture "For Philatelic Merit"
gift of Terry Dempsey

Silver falcon sculpture
gift of Emirates Federation

Harvey Mirsky Memorial Award
gift of Gordon Eubanks

Porcelaine de Couleuvre with "Marianne de Briat"
gift of Fédération Française des Associations Philatéliques

To be announced
gift of Luis Frazão

18th Century print of Cartagena, Colombia
gift of Debby Friedman

Fossil wood bookends (Literature prize)
gift of Cheryl Ganz

Leather album
gift of Gibraltar Postal Administration

Waterford cachepot vase
gift of James Peter Gough

Antique stamp box
gift of Arthur Groten

Cliff Schaffer Award
gift of Haiti Philatelic Society

Waterford crystal bell
gift of Elizabeth Hisey

"The Lockhorns", original cartoon art
gift of Bunny Hoest

19th Century wooden box with handle, Zhejiang province
gift of Hong Kong Phila China

Dolphin porcelain figure
gift of Hong Kong Philatelic Society

"PAKISTAN" Overprints on Service Post Cards of British India with Forms Used by Northwestern Railways
gift of Usman Ali Isami

Silver sculpture
gift of Israel Federation

ISJP Robert M. Spaulding Award, Imani plate
gift of International Society for Japanese Philately

Tiffany & Co. "World" box in porcelain
gift of Farley P. Katz

"Homage to Matisse" lithograph by Betsey Carter
gift of Patricia Kaufmann

Native American vase, Tewa tribe
gift of Russell and Janet Klug

"Enchanted Garden", stainless steel bowl with natural brass and Swarovski crystals by Michael Aram
gift of Van Koppersmith

Jewelry box
gift of Korea Federation

Orrefor Polaris bowl
gift of Luca Lavagnino

Lighthouse sculpture
gift of Lighthouse Society

Acoma Pueblo ceramic pot
gift of Bruce and Leslie Marsden

To be announced
gift of Dhirubhai Mehta

Firenation glass flame
gift of Minuteman Press

Montenegro Special Prize
gift of Tomo Katurić, Montenegro Federation

Cash prize (Youth exhibit)
gift of Vernon Morris

"Summer Sun" oil painting by Betsey Carter
gift of Gordon Morrison

Mont Blanc pen
gift of Randy Neil

Wahaika, Maori ceremonial weapon
gift of New Zealand Philatelic Federation

Decorative platter
gift of Lisa O'Kelly

Tiffany & Co. sterling silver and blue glass sugar bowl, c.1909
gift of Philatelic Foundation

Eugene A. Garrett Award
gift of International Philippine Philatelic Society

1860 Register of Vessels with Tax Certificate
gift of Hal Reynolds

Dolphins glass sculpture
gift of Omar Rodriguez

Ercuis silver and gold placard holders
gift of Robert Rufe

Crystal Blanc Grande Planet
gift of Wade and Gail Saadi

Douglas Taylor glass sculpture
gift of St. Petersburg Stamp Club

Fernando Llort glass sculpture
gift of AFISAL—El Salvador Federation

Glass vase
gift of Stephen and Cathy Schumann

Beli Andjeo Special Prize
gift of Union of Serbian Philatelists

Handcrafted chopsticks with ornate wooden case
gift of Association of Singapore Philatelists

Crystal vase
gift of Harlan and Helen Stone

"The Philatelist" ceramic sculpture
gift of Robert Stuchell

Georg Jensen Legacy Prize
gift of Swedish Philatelist Association

"Standing on Top", Cochin ceramic fish
gift of Yu-An Chen, Chinese Taipei Philatelic Federation

Couverture gold or red (Literature prize)
gift of Jean-Jacques Tillard

To be announced
gift of U.S. Philatelic Classics Society

Onofre Frias sculpture
gift of Venezuela Federation

Cheese board with implements
gift of Charles J. G. Verge

Vintage Robert Eckholt art glass, 1993
gift of Patricia S. and W. Danforth Walker

Tiffany Favrile salt celler, 1902
gift of Stephen and Elizabeth Washburne

Clyde Jennings Memorial Award— Arts & Crafts Movement leather case
gift of Richard F. Winter

THE COMMONWEALTH
Your leading International

ifsda

Willard Allman
Willard.S.Allman@gmail.com

Exclusively
British Commonwealth
Postal History

All areas excl GB & BNA. Exotic frankings, usages & cancellations, interesting instructional marks, censored mail. Emphasis on pre-1953.

David Morrison Ltd.

africonect@aol.com *www.forpostalhistory.com*

**British Commonwealth Postal History.
Unusual postal incidents;
shipwreck & train crash mail,
floods & mail robberies!**

CompuStamp

Worldwide postal history with an emphasis on British Commonwealth, French & German Colonies.

Left: Australia Western Australia 1903 Perth OHMS Envelope

Right: Australia New South Wales 1875 Brouchton Creek Mourning Envelope

Contact Gary DuBro by email: Compustamp@aol.com | www.Compustamp.com

SUPERTEAM!
British Commonwealth Dealers

BRITISH AFRICA!
Fine Stamps, Proofs, Varieties & Covers

Try a new source... **www.filat.ch**

Filat AG

Richard Johnson awaits you at **Stand 1360**

Doreen Royan & Associates (Pty) Ltd.

www.doreenroyan.com
royan@icon.co.za

1840-1970 Rarities, Errors & Varieties
from Great Britain & British Commonwealth.

See us on
Superstand 1257, 1261 & 1360

FIVE expert dealers, FIVE world class stocks!
All in one booth for your convenience.

Contact us for special requests and your Commonwealth needs.

YESTERDAY

Detail of the 1845 New York Postmaster's Provisional, printed by the firm of Rawdon, Wright and Hatch. The magenta ink across the face is the initials of Alonzo Castle Monson, assistant postmaster, who validated many of the stamps prior to use. Image courtesy of Robert A. Siegel Auction Galleries.

Letters carried on Gotham's city streets

by Scott R. Trepel

New York City in the mid-1800s

THE 1840s PROVED TO BE THE PIVOTAL DECADE for change in the United States postal system. Rapid developments in transportation, settlement of territory west of the Mississippi, the influx of immigrants to America, and the country's emergence as one of the world's industrial and financial giants all contributed to the increased demand for mail communication.

Much of the change in the postal system was spawned in New York. By 1840 the city had become the nation's largest and most active urban

Scott Trepel has been a stamp auctioneer for the past 36 years. He has authored numerous articles on philately and continues to develop new sources of information and avenues of research. His wife, Katie, is a television journalist and comedy writer/performer.

View of the Old Dutch Church on Nassau Street in downtown Manhattan, which housed the post office from 1845 to 1875 (lithographed by Endicott). Photo courtesy The New York Public Library Digital Collection

1842 map of New York City marked with the locations of post offices and other significant postal entities (see key below)

1. *Rotunda post office at City Hall Park near corner of Chambers and Center Streets (1838-1844)*
2. *Main post office in Old Dutch Church on Nassau Street between Liberty and Cedar (1845-1875)*
3. *Merchant's Exchange branch post office at William Street and Exchange Place (1837-1845)*
4. *Chatham Square branch post office (1845-1846)*
--- *Northern boundary of post office delivery in 1842*

53

Interior view of the post office in the Old Dutch Church in 1845 (lithograph by Endicott).

metropolis, having surpassed Boston and Philadelphia fifty years earlier. Steamboat transportation along the Hudson River, transatlantic steamship service through the port of New York, and a sprawling railroad network with New York as its hub attracted commerce and people thirsty for jobs and prosperity, despite the depression that started in 1837.

In 1840 there were 313,000 residents in New York City, plus another 92,000 men, women and children who had just stepped off ships arriving from Europe. The city's residential boundaries continued to expand north of Canal Street, but the post office remained downtown.

From 1838 to 1844 the post office was situated in the Rotunda building located on the northeast corner of City Hall Park, near the corner of Chambers and Center Streets. In 1845 it was moved to the Old Dutch Reformed Church on Nassau Street between Cedar and Liberty Streets. At these two offices, the city's postmasters, clerks and carriers performed their duties.

Robert H. Morris, postmaster (1845-1849)—his predecessors were Jonathan J. Coddington (1836-1842) and John Lorimer Graham (1842-1845)

U.S. POSTMASTERS GENERAL 1829–1864 (AS CABINET APPOINTMENTS)

William T. Barry	9 Mar 1829–30 Apr 1835
Amos Kendall	1 May 1835–18 May 1840
John M. Niles	19 May 1840–5 Mar 1841
Francis Granger	6 Mar 1841–12 Sep 1841
Charles A. Wickliffe	13 Sep 1841–5 Mar 1845
Cave Johnson	6 Mar 1845–7 Mar 1849
Jacob Collamer	8 Mar 1849–22 Jul 1850
Nathan K. Hall	23 Jul 1850–30 Aug 1852
Samuel D. Hubbard	31 Aug 1852–6 Mar 1853
James Campbell	7 Mar 1853–5 Mar 1857
Aaron V. Brown	6 Mar 1857–13 Mar 1859
Joseph Holt	14 Mar 1859–11 Feb 1861
Horatio King	12 Feb 1861–4 Mar 1861
Montgomery Blair	5 Mar 1861–23 Sep 1864

NEW YORK POSTMASTERS 1828–1864

Samuel L. Gouverneur	19 Nov 1828–4 Jul 1836
Jonathan J. Coddington	5 Jul 1836–13 Mar 1842
John L. Graham	14 Mar 1842–2 May 1845
Robert H. Morris	3 May 1845–13 May 1849
William V. Brady	14 May 1849–31 Mar 1853
Isaac V. Fowler	1 Apr 1853–16 May 1860
John A. Dix	17 May 1860–15 Jan 1861
William B. Taylor	16 Jan 1861–20 Mar 1862
Abram Wakeman	21 Mar 1862–18 Sep 1864

The opportunity to profit by carrying mail for local residents induced entrepreneurs in several cities to launch private posts. New York, with its dense population and need for local delivery, was ripe territory for start-ups. The bitter contest between government and private enterprise reached its zenith in the 1840s and 50s, and nowhere was it fought harder than on the streets of New York.

New York's Post Office Carriers

The tradition of a postman taking letters to and from the post office for a small fee dates back to colonial times. The term penny post refers to the customary charge per letter of one British penny (worth 2¢). A postman could be in business on his own or working for the post office. The official postal employees were known as carriers.

Postmasters wanted all letters to be promptly delivered to the addressees, for two reasons. Most letters were sent collect, so the government did not receive postage until a letter was delivered, and unclaimed mail clogged the system. If a resident gave the post office instructions and an address for carrier delivery, letters would be sent immediately. Letters that were not picked up at the post office within a day or two were automatically delivered by a carrier for the additional fee. Patrons could

1837 letter from Boston with a pointing hand and instructions to New York carrier, "Will The Penny Post deliver this as soon as he possibly can…"

*Complete sheet of 42 of the City Despatch Post 3¢ stamp—
the first adhesive stamp issued in the Western Hemisphere*

Unless otherwise credited, all images of stamps and covers in this chapter © Siegel Auction Galleries, Inc.

also have their letters brought to the post office or delivered to other local addressees by the carrier. Letter drop boxes were used for convenience.

The fee-based carrier system authorized by Congress in 1836 established a maximum 2¢ charge per letter, but the charges varied by city. This system remained in effect until 1863, when free carrier service was mandated by Congress.

As New York's population grew, the number of carriers grew, but the city's postmasters struggled to keep up with demand.

The City Despatch Post of 1842

The City Despatch Post was established in February 1842 by Alexander M. Grieg. It is said that Greig was encouraged to start the enterprise by his friend, an Englishman named Henry Thomas Windsor, who arrived in the U.S. in May 1841. Windsor had been inspired by Great Britain's postal reforms under Sir Rowland Hill.

The predecessor firm to the City Despatch Post was the New York Penny Post, which began delivering letters in January 1840. The proprietors of this post, the first of its kind in New York, sold the good will and assets to Greig in January 1842.

Shown to the right is a letter with the datestamp of the New York Penny Post, whose good will and assets were acquired by Alexander M. Greig (below), founder of the City Despatch Post.

City Despatch Post stamp used February 3, 1842, on the post's printed advertisement from the first week of operation

57

The City Despatch Post operated as a private firm for approximately six months, from February to August 1842. During this time, it introduced significant conveniences and services, such as letter boxes placed throughout the city, three daily deliveries for 3¢ per letter, adhesive stamps, free service for newspaper editors, delivery of large parcels, and registration of valuable letters.

The 3¢ City Despatch Post stamp was the first adhesive stamp issued in the Western Hemisphere. It followed Great Britain's Penny Black and Two-Pence Blue by a mere 21 months and predated the U.S. 1845 Postmasters' Provisionals and 1847 General Issues by three and five years. The stamps were printed in sheets of 42 from an engraved steel plate.

In August 1842 Greig's City Despatch Post was bought by the government and reestablished as an official carrier department. The U.S. City Despatch carried letters between two points within the city, to the post office drop box, and to the post office for out-of-town mails. Carriers employed by the post office continued to deliver letters received from out of town (for a fee), but this function and those carriers were separate from the U.S. City Despatch.

New 3¢ stamps with the inscription "United States City Despatch Post" were printed from a plate of 50 subjects. Issued in August or September 1842, these are the first adhesive stamps issued under federal authority. 3¢ included 2¢ for carrier service and 1¢ for the drop-letter postage.

The U.S. City Despatch Post served New York's residents until November 1846, when it was sold to Abraham Mead, a letter carrier, who re-named it the Post Office City Despatch. Mead and his successors ran the local post from 1846 until 1852.

The government sold the U.S. City Despatch Post in 1846 because the major rate changes in July 1845—specifically the increase in drop-letter postage from 1¢ to 2¢—made the City Despatch much less competitive with local posts that charged only 2¢ per letter.

Greig's "City Despatch Post" 3¢ stamp at left and the new "United States City Despatch Post" version issued by the government after it bought the post and established it as New York's carrier department

U.S. City Despatch Post carrier stamp used on a Valentine envelope

Rare use of five U.S. City Despatch Post stamps to prepay carrier fee and 12½¢ intercity postage to Philadelphia

"Pr. City Despatch Post" on this ca. 1848 cover to West 21st Street indicates delivery by the local post after it was sold by the government

The Independent Mails of 1843-1845

The rise of the *Independent Mails*—private firms that carried intercity mail—resulted from public agitation for cheaper postage. Beginning with Hale & Co. in December 1843, the Independents would carry a letter across a far-reaching network of railroad and steamboat lines. They competed with the federal postal system and flourished in 1844 and 1845, until Congress passed laws to reduce postage rates and strengthen the federal postal monopoly laws.

The Independent Mail companies introduced numerous innovations, including adhesive stamps and quantity discounts to encourage senders to prepay postage. Companies were able to cover greater territory by linking routes, and letters could be delivered directly to recipients by forming cooperative ventures with private local posts, such as Boyd's City Express in New York.

Messengers on trains running between New York, Philadelphia and Boston carried the largest volume of Independent Mail. Hudson River steamboats were also used, and by following the Erie Canal, the Independent Mail routes were extended west from Albany to Buffalo. From there the railroads and Great Lakes steamers brought mail to Cleveland, Chicago, Detroit and other cities in the midwest.

59

Letter addressed to James Gordon Bennett of the New York Herald, carried by Hale & Co. from Baltimore to New York and delivered by Boyd's local post for free

Triple-rated letter carried by American Letter Mail Co. from New York to Boston

Three different companies carried this letter from the midwest to Connecticut, and stamps were applied along the way to prepay postage and credit the next company with its share

Postmaster General Charles A. Wickliffe—the postmaster general who approved the acquisition of the City Despatch Post—fought Independent Mail companies. Once they were defeated in July 1845, Wickliffe faced another competitive threat from the private local posts, which proliferated in cities like New York during the 1840s and 50s.

Competition from Local Posts

Private local posts sprang up in cities around the U.S. during the 1840s, and New York had the largest number. Many were short-lived, one-man operations. Others became major enterprises that prospered for years.

The biggest and longest-lasting was the firm founded in June 1844 by a former auctioneer, John T. Boyd. Starting with more than 200 mail boxes around the city, mainly in drug stores and hotels, Boyd's City Express carried hundreds of letters daily, between city residents and to the post office. During its first year of existence, Boyd's also delivered mail for Independent Mail firms, until intercity mail transportation was banned.

Another major player in the New York local posts scene was Aaron Swarts, a former grocer who had worked in the Chatham Square branch post office in 1845 and 1846. In January 1847, after the branch office was closed, Swarts filled the void by starting his "Chatham Square Branch Post Office," which had no official status, but Swarts capitalized on the name and public's familiarity with the location.

Postal officials watched as local post companies siphoned off letter-carrying business in major cities, particularly New York and Philadelphia. They tried to prohibit private enterprises from competing with the Post Office

New York local post stamps of the 1840s and 50s with quaint names and images

A letter box is shown on this stamp for Clark & Co.'s local post in New York

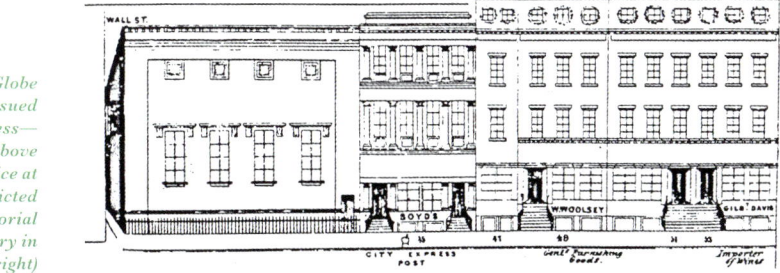

Large green Eagle & Globe stamp—the first type issued by Boyd's City Express—used in July 1844 (above right) and Boyd's office at 45 William Street depicted on Lowenstrom's Pictorial Business Directory in 1850 (right)

by enacting laws that declared all city streets to be *post roads*, over which the federal government had exclusive right to transport mail. This legal maneuvering was unsuccessful.

By the 1860s, however, postal laws and the growth of official carrier service began to have an effect on the local posts. In July 1863 a new system went into effect, in which carriers were paid salaries and the extra fee was abolished. After that, only a few local posts managed to survive by functioning more as messenger services than mail delivery operations.

New York's Carrier Department Fights Back

After the government sold the U.S. City Despatch Post in 1846, New York's carrier department struggled in competition with local posts. Toward the end of 1848, there was some talk of Swarts and his operation becoming an official postal division, but it never materialized.

Around the same time, in January 1849, the carrier fee in large cities was reduced from 2¢ to 1¢ by order of Postmaster General Cave Johnson. In New York, a postal employee named Robert Roberts was placed in charge of the revamped carrier department. These moves were designed to make the carrier service in big cities more competitive with local posts, but in New York the local posts continued to thrive.

In 1851, under Postmaster William V. Brady and Postmaster General Nathan K. Hall, new carrier fees were set in New York. They eliminated the charge for letters taken to the post office, an attempt to undercut the local posts. The 2¢ fee remained the same on letters delivered from the post office, since local posts had no practical way to claim inbound mail. Intra-city letters were charged 1¢, but if dropped at the post office, an extra 1¢ drop-letter postage was required. Over the next nine years, the Post Office continued to try competing with the private local posts, but they faltered in a business built on service, convenience and goodwill.

In 1860, Congress established a uniform 1¢ carrier fee for letters taken to or from the post office. With the fee capped at 1¢, postal officials began a concentrated effort to put the local posts out of business. Boyd's closed in August 1860, but in Philadelphia a lawsuit brought by the government against the biggest private post was being fought in the Courts. The

Embossed "Star Die" envelope with 1¢ for carrier fee and 3¢ for postage, used in 1861 with 7¢ in stamps to pay the 10¢ rate

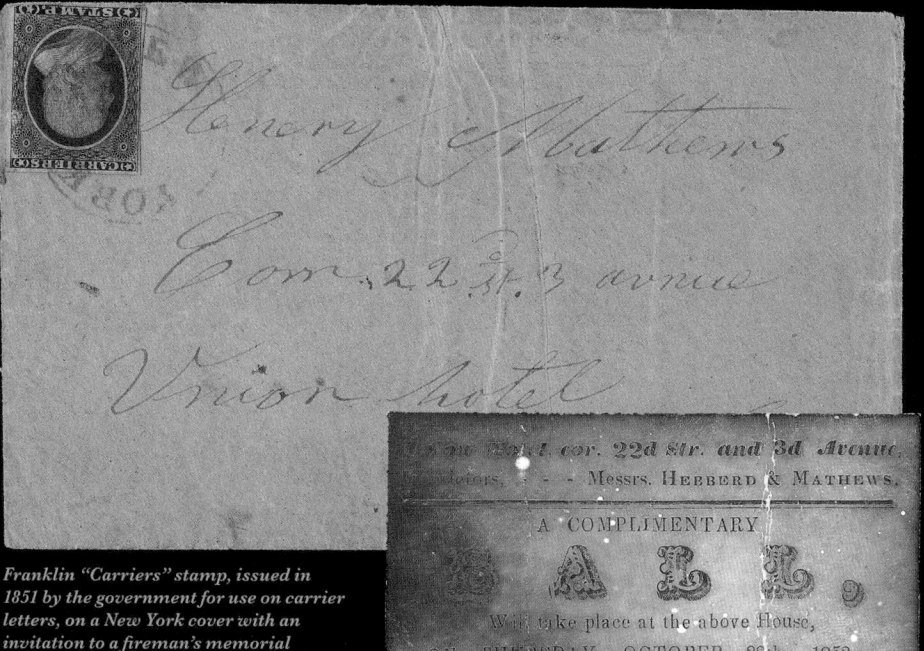

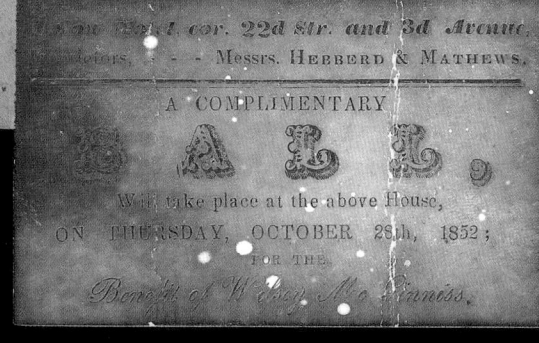

Franklin "Carriers" stamp, issued in 1851 by the government for use on carrier letters, on a New York cover with an invitation to a fireman's memorial

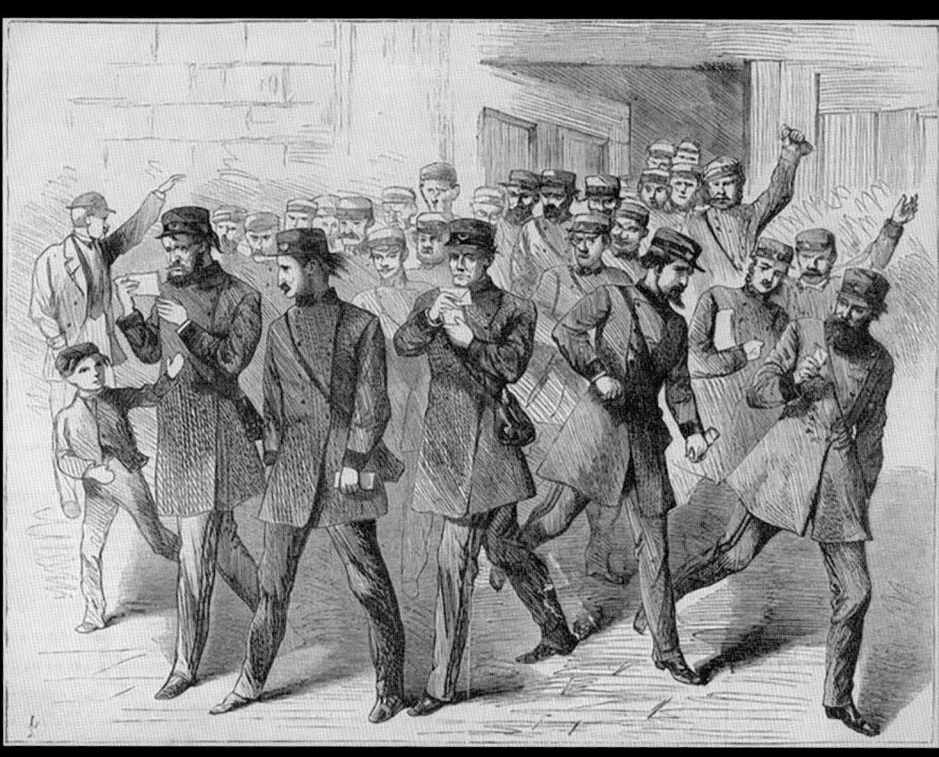

"Morning start of the New York City mail-carriers in their new uniform" Harper's Weekly, December 26, 1868

decision in November 1860 went against the government, and local posts were once again free to do business on city streets, but their decline was inevitable in the face of improved government carrier service. After 1860, the local posts throughout the country faced extinction.

The Private Expresses

The government's fight against local posts and intercity Independent Mail companies did not carry over to all forms of mail. Expresses that carried letters over routes not serviced by the government or that paid government postage in addition to express fees were allowed to operate.

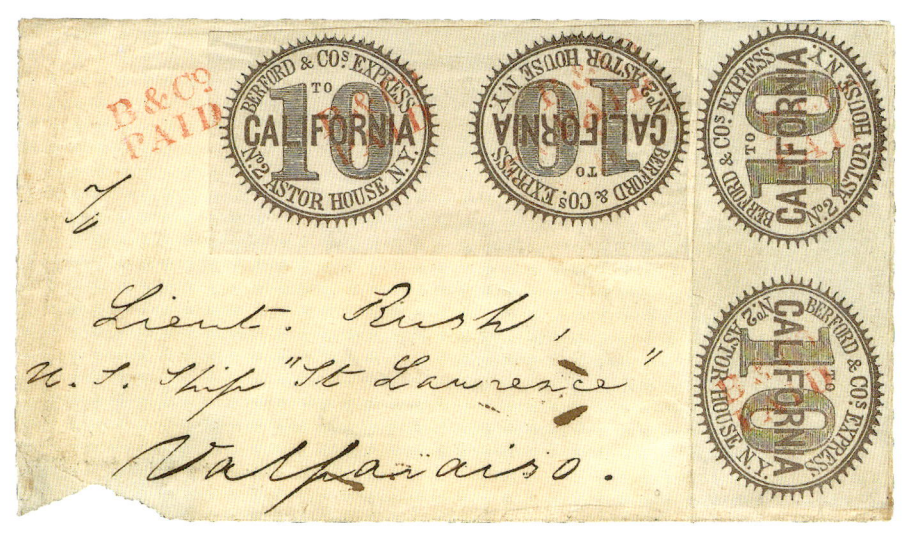

Berford & Co., located at 2 Astor House, carried mail to and from other countries

Carried by the legendary Pony Express from Missouri to California, this printed Wells, Fargo & Co. envelope was first sent by mail from New York in August 1861

64

Private Messenger Services

The successful government campaign to take over city mail delivery in the 1860s forced the local posts out of business. Boyd's carried on by becoming a messenger service, rather than a competing letter carrier, something that George Hussey had been doing in New York since 1854.

The distinction appears subtle, but there was a major difference between an impromptu messenger service and a company that kept drop boxes for public use around the city, picked up and delivered mail on regular routes, and carried letters to the post office for mailing. The federal Post Office had a monopoly on that sort of activity.

Instead, Hussey's Post and Boyd's City Dispatch delivered notices and bills for banking, insurance and other kinds of companies. They stayed clear of running afoul of the Post Office until 1883, when authorities shut down Hussey's Post.

The conflict between government and private enterprise in business has manifested itself in many historical events, but none so passionately and long-lasting as the fight over the right to carry the mail. New York was one of the war's major battlegrounds during the mid-nineteenth century, and for stamp collectors and postal historians it supplied a trove of fascinating items.

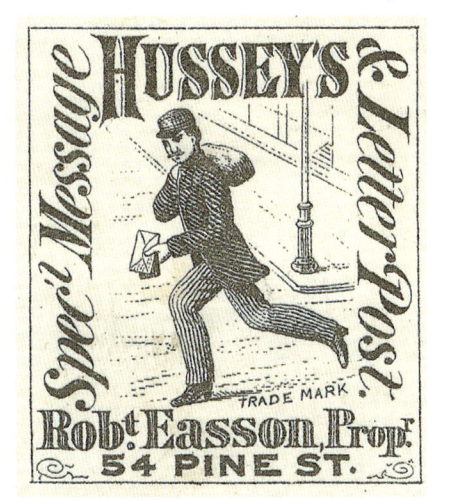

Hussey's Special Message & Letter Post operated from 1854 to 1883

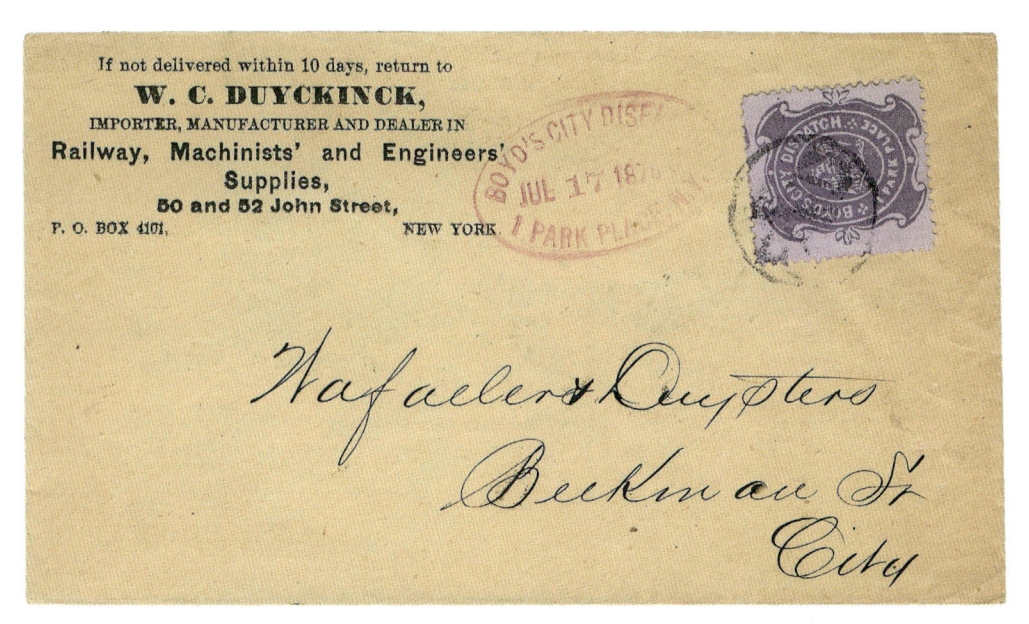

A bill or advertisement was contained in this cover carried by Boyd's City Dispatch

Henry Gitner Philatelists Inc

From Classic to Modern, Henry Gitner Philatelists can fill your collecting needs

Free Price Lists

From A-Z:
Artmaster Artwork and Proofs
Austria
Austrian Black Prints
Belgian Imperfs and Proofs
France
French So. Antarctic
French Polynesia
Germany
German Specimen Overprints
Guyana
Iceland
Israel & Palestine
Kosovo
Liechtenstein
Marshall Is, Micronesia & Palau
Marshall Is Press Sheet Archives
Monaco
Ryukyu Is.
St. Pierre & Miquelon
Switerland
Swiss Officials
United States
US Confederate States
US Ducks
US Graf Zeppelins
US Shanghais
US Savings Stamps
US Washington – Franklins
US Cut Squares
US Farleys Special Printing
US Photo Essay & Autographed PB
US Autographed Covers
US Dignitary Presentation Albums
US Postmaster General Covers
Worldwide Artist Die Proofs
UN including Personalized Sheets
Vatican
Zeppelin and Aerophilately

With over 20 rooms of stamps, our price lists are only a fraction of our stock!

Now You Can Own The 2013 Right Side Up Jenny!

US 4806e XF-90 Singles
~~$15,000.00~~
Now $14,000.00!!
LL Position sold
Others Available, Your choice!
(Only one other sheet has been broken)

We Buy! We Pay TOP PRICE for Your Right Side Up Jenny!!

Visit our online Store at
www.hgitner.com

1000's of better U.S and Worldwide listed from $5. to $$$ rarities!!
Pricelists at left can also be viewed

We Buy US & the World!

As one of America's largest stamp retailers, we need all your stamps! Few others can pay as much for you stamps as Henry Gitner. Especially needed – all mounted collections for U.S., Asia, British Commonwealth, Europe and Worldwide. All stamps and Postal History of China wanted.
Phone today for our top prices on your holdings. Or ship your stamps with confidence for our fast, fair offer. We travel for large holdings.

Henry Gitner is your Headquarters for Specialized Topicals

We have just what you are searching for to enhance your collection or add to your exhibit!

Large Stock of U.S. Errors

US #1381 missing black engraved writing
.........................$500.00

Henry Gitner Philatelists Inc

P O Box 3077, 53 Highland Ave, Middletown NY, 10940
Toll Free 1-800-947-8267 Tel 845-343-5791 Fax: 845-343-0068
Email: www.hgitner@hgitner.com
Visit our new and expanding website at www.hgitner.com
Philately –The Quiet Excitement

Something for Everyone...
From Classic to Modern, Henry Gitner Philatelists can fill your collecting needs!

Booth 1136

Switzerland 3L1 F - VF "Basel Dove" Used sound but tiny nick at bottom - bright color with Sismondo cert cv 13,500.00..........$4000.00

US 350 Washington / Franklin XF - Sup NH— Extraordinary for this scarce coil.....$900.00

US Shanghai Overprint Scott K16 F - VF NH $2.00 on $1.00 .... $675.00

Ireland 392a NH, Color error with value and inscription missing. With certificate. $950.00

Covers & Postal History!

Austria Death Mask + S.S. lightening striking Austria and death taking off Hitler mask. Unissued but like B171 - B178 cv 2100.00 Rare! $1600.000

Vatican 40 VF XF LH Signed cv 450.00 ...$350.00

Liecht 1932 Scott O2 Used VF Mi O2A .....$900.

Hundreds of Europe and Colonies Stock books!
Pick out the sets or singles you need!

Newfoundland C18 XF NH cv 500.00 .. $400.00

US 75 F LH Pristine Full OG barely hinged - appears NH. Rich red brown color cv 5750.00 (PSE). ...$1500.00

U.S., British Colonies and Foreign Country Collections!!
From $100. to thousands!

US C13-C15 XF NH ....$2650.00.........$2400.00
Show Sale on all C13-15!

US FDC's!

US Ryukyu Is 46, 48TC5 XF NH Set of 2 imperf trial color proofs in black with red specimen ovpt. cv 1500.00 .... $1000.00

France 20 (Yv 17Ba) XF OG NH from Wm. Gross collection. Extraordinary Color & Freshness. Signed Calves. Among the finest in existence (cv. €2800.00 as Hinged)......$3750.00

Great U.S. Stock 1847 on!
50+ books of better USA!

Germany.OSS Forgeries Michel 15-17 VF/XF NH set of 3 (rare, centered so nicely) $210.00

Israel 7 - 9 Tabs XF NH One of the finest sets we've seen! .... $4500.00........$4000.00

US 116L4 Local Mint Unused F - VF Sound! 1862 1 cent PIPS Daily Mail **Brooklyn** , NY $750.00

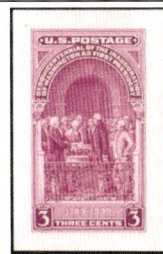

US 854P-2 Washington Inauguration, small die proof $1250.00

At one time, there were so many stamp dealers at 116 Nassau Street that the building was officially named the Stamp Center. 1954 photograph reproduced by permission of the Museum of the City of New York.

Nassau Street— the stamp collector's street of dreams

by Steven J. Rod

Steven J. Rod is an independent non-profit consultant who has spent his life promoting stamp collecting. He is a co-editor of the Encyclopedia of United States Stamps and Stamp Collecting, with a second edition being published at World Stamp Show–NY 2016. He has served as an officer of the American Philatelic Society, is a governor of both the United States Stamp Society and the Collectors Club of New York and served on the Council of Philatelists of the Smithsonian's National Postal Museum. His 20-frame exhibit on the history of Nassau Street was presented at the Collectors Club in 2012. He lives in South Orange, N.J.

NEAR THE SOUTHERN TIP OF MANHATTAN, in the Financial District, lies a narrow thoroughfare, just a few blocks long, called Nassau Street. It starts at Wall Street and runs north as far as Spruce Street, by the on-ramp to the Brooklyn Bridge, just one short block east of Broadway and Park Row. Its northern end faces City Hall.

It was named in the late 17th century in honor of William of Orange-Nassau, the Dutch prince who became King William III of England.

Beginning in the late 20th century and continuing for almost a century, Nassau Street enjoyed a glorious period as the center of stamp collecting in New York City.

The earliest known selling of stamps by one person to another has been traced back to the 1860s and 70s at both City Hall Park and a church located around the corner from Nassau Street.

In those neonatal days of stamp collecting, there was little understanding or regard for the condition of a stamp. Dealers and collectors would display the stamps they wanted to sell by pinning or tacking them to a show board. To this day, classic 19th century stamps can be found with the remnants of pinholes dating to this practice.

Beginnings

The history of our hobby records that a young man from England, J. Walter Scott (1842–1919), was the first "stamp dealer" to sell postage stamps for collectors on Nassau Street in 1861. Scott would eventually publish an annual price list, and his family name would go on to be synonymous with the stamp collecting hobby. Today, we still depend on the annual publication of the Scott *Standard Postage Stamp Catalogue*.

Soon after that, in 1863, William P. Brown (1841–1929) set up a retail shop at no. 65. Known as "Willie Brown," he was the first to formally develop a stock of stamps, or an inventory, for his customers to draw upon.[1]

Starting in the 1890s, more and more dealers began migrate to Nassau Street to establish their businesses. At one time, there were as many as 50 stamp dealers clustered together in the northernmost three-block strip of the street.

Although they catered to thousands of stamp collectors who visited each week from near and far, the dealer-to-dealer buying, selling and swapping

1. For a complete narration of Brown as the first Nassau Street dealer, see The Romance of Stamp Collecting by Ernest A. Kerr. New York: Thomas Y. Crowell, 1947 pp. 91–95.

A hand-tinted World War I-era picture postcard of Nassau Street, looking north from Liberty Street. The block in the foreground would be demolished to make way for the Federal Reserve Building (built 1919–1924). The tower at no. 116 is faintly visible in the distance, tinted pink and inscribed "Morton Hotel" just below the roof.

that took place at a frenetic pace, six days a week, were as important as the retail sales. Dealers could walk next door, upstairs, or to the next block minutes after purchasing some stamps and offer them at a profit to another dealer they knew would want them.

A few of the early dealers on Nassau Street would open a new shop or office only to close it again within a few short months, disappearing in the middle of the night when they could not meet their obligations. Many more, however, were highly successful, and the best of them would occupy their Nassau Street addresses for many years. Such was the case with the Nassau Stamp Company.

Founded in 1894 and purchased in 1899 by John J. Klemann (1870–1945), the Nassau Stamp Company was located at number 70 for more than half a century. Klemann was directly involved in almost every major stamp story occurring from 1899 to the 1950s.

Most memorable was the publicity surrounding the 1918 discovery at a Washington, DC post office, by a young clerk named William T. Robey, of a sheet of 24¢ air mail stamps with inverted centers.

Robey's find and the instant profit he made on the error, known as the "Inverted Jenny" after the Curtiss JN-4 biplane depicted in the stamp's vignette, would lead many members of the public to believe it was possible to garner large riches through stamp collecting, even when buying from the post office.

Robey knew that New York and Nassau Street were the center of the American stamp trade, and he quickly took a train up from Washington to attempt the sale of his wonderful purchase. After several unsuccessful attempts to sell the sheet, he returned to his hotel room—where he found Klemann waiting for him.

The story goes that Klemann offered Robey $2,500 for the full pane of 100. Robey countered that a dealer named Phillip Ward in Philadelphia

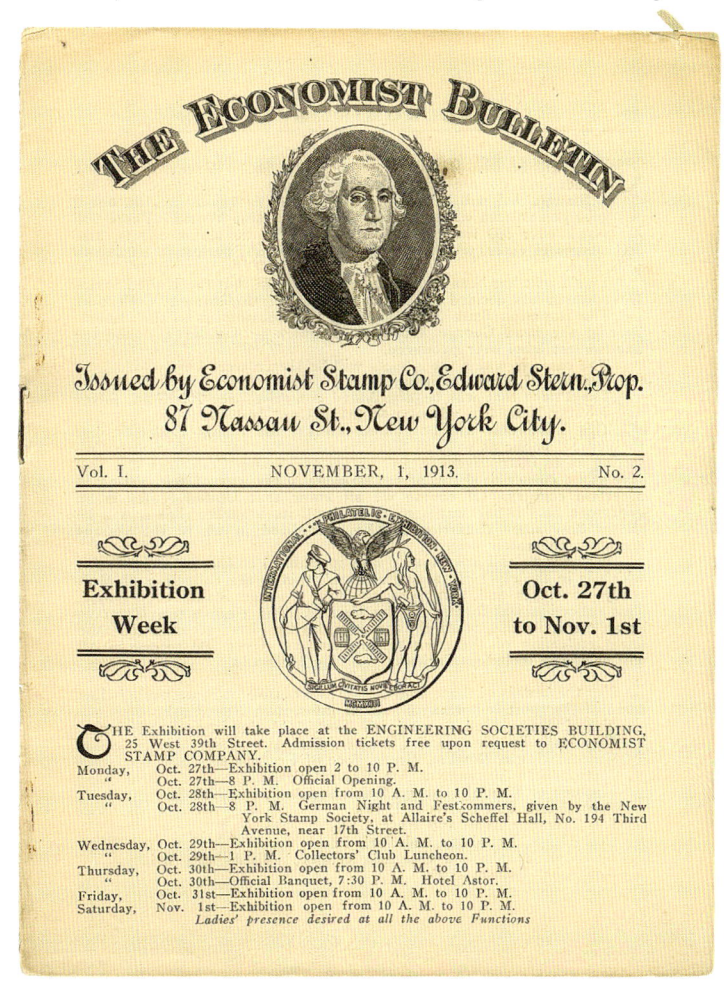

The cover of the second issue of a bulletin published regularly by Edward Stern, the famed proprietor of the Economist Stamp Company, located on Nassau Street for nearly 50 years.

had already offered him $10,000 for the pane, a figure Klemann is said to have called "crazy."

But Robey soon sold the sheet for $15,000, to a savvy Philadelphia dealer named Eugene Klein, who would himself quickly turn a $5,000 profit reselling the sheet to the famous collector, Edward H.R. Green.

This is an interesting anecdote because Klemann was considered one of the most knowledgeable dealers of his time. Why did he offer so little? Presumably he, like many in those heady days, was assuming that a second, third or even a fourth pane of the prized air mail inverts would presently emerge, lowering their rarity and value.[2]

Getting established

The Economist Stamp Company at number 87 was owned by Edward Stern (1880–1953), a serious philatelist and leading Nassau Street dealer for more than 50 years. His magazine, *The Economist Bulletin*, had its debut in 1913 and was published for 247 issues through 1939.

It was one of a number of Nassau Street stamp dealer house organs given or mailed to customers. Many of these publications contained original research and articles that could not be found anywhere else.

A registered cover from Stern addressed to Philip Ward in Philadelphia bears a reference to "Nassau Street" that is in some ways an allegorical statement: while of course there was a large concentration of stamp dealers in New York City, on Nassau Street in particular there was a close-knit network of dealers trying to foster a reputation for honesty and integrity.

This was further advanced by Max Ohlman's role in founding the American Stamp Dealers' Association here in 1914. Ohlman (1881–1957), first at no. 77 and later at no. 116, was a leading Nassau Street dealer, and the man most responsible for the formation of the ASDA. He gained

2. *For the complete and detailed story of the Inverted Jenny, see* Jenny! *by George Amick. Sidney, Ohio: Amos Press, 1986. Chapter 7 details Robey's sale of the sheet.*

Wax seal of the Economist Stamp Company on the reverse of a registered, return-receipt cover to stamp dealer Philip H. Ward in Philadelphia.

A 1913 envelope from the firm of Max Ohlman, bearing an advertisement illustrated with a stamp from the Pacific island of Tonga

great fame within the hobby when he became the preferred auction house at which New York State governor—and later U.S. president—Franklin D. Roosevelt would bid on stamps for his collection.

Ohlman told the story of his long awaited invitation to visit FDR at the White House, and his disappointment when he discovered upon arrival that it was not a personal audience, but that a number of other people were also present. A cover, hand addressed by Ohlman, shows his large, distinctive handwriting.

The Nov. 28, 1942 issue of *Stamps* magazine had an article proclaiming that "just 50 years ago this month the J. M. Bartels Company, then located at Alexandria, Virginia, the owner's native state, issued their first price list. Subsequently the firm moved to Washington and Boston and has since been located in New York for the past 32 years."

J. Murray Bartels (1872–1944) became a stamp dealer at age 20 and settled his stamp business at Nassau Street in 1911. He was considered the preeminent authority on United States stamped envelopes and the stamps of the Philippines, Panama and the Canal Zone, and his publications in those areas were considered the standard reference guides at the time.

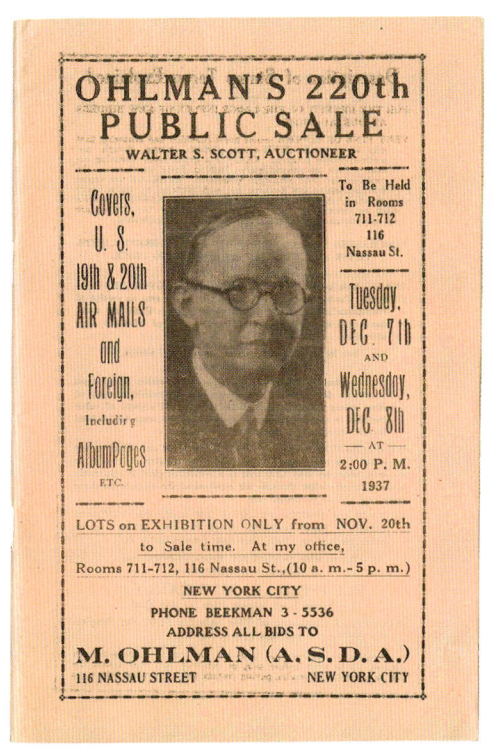

A 1937 ad for one of Max Ohlman's public auctions. The sale would be called by Walter S. Scott, son of pioneer stamp dealer and publisher J. Walter Scott, founder of the Scott catalogs.

A registered cover to Germany from the firm of J. Murray Bartels, one of Nassau Street's leading dealers

Registered 1926 cover from the Economist Stamp Co. to John Kay, a prominent collector in Detroit. It is interesting that even at this late date, stamps of the 1893 Columbian series were considered usable as postage.

His first book, published in 1897, was *J.M. Bartels and Co.'s Catalogue and Reference List of the Stamped Envelopes, Wrappers and Letter Sheets*. It had three subsequent editions through 1911. Bartels also wrote *Envelopes of the United States* with several editions published from 1930 to 1938. Prescott H. "Pep" Thorp succeeded Bartels in this field, publishing subsequent catalogs under the name "Thorp-Bartels".

Stamps magazine noted that Bartels's company was one of the oldest stamp auction firms in existence, having held its first auction sale in 1898, and was preparing its 334th at the time of the article. Bartels's 337th sale, in 1944, would be his last, and he died on Oct. 5 that year.

Bartels's obituary, in the Nov.1944 issue of the American Philatelist, noted that when he passed away at age 73, he "was one of the best known American philatelists and had been active in the stamp business for over 50 years."

Bartels is also famous, or infamous, for having his name on the Troughton v. Bartels case. Bartels had bought an old cover, franked with a rare Baltimore postmaster's provisional, from a woman of a certain age who entered his shop one day to sell a relative's collection. When the news broke that Bartels had promptly resold the Baltimore cover for many multiples of what he offered the woman, her nephew sued Bartels and won. A complete description of this landmark case appeared in the 1986 American Philatelic Congress Book.

Nassau Street dealers were typically friendly with one another, but they were also in stiff competition with one another. Individual dealers generated more than 50 years of annual printed price lists, from which collectors all over the country could place orders by mail.

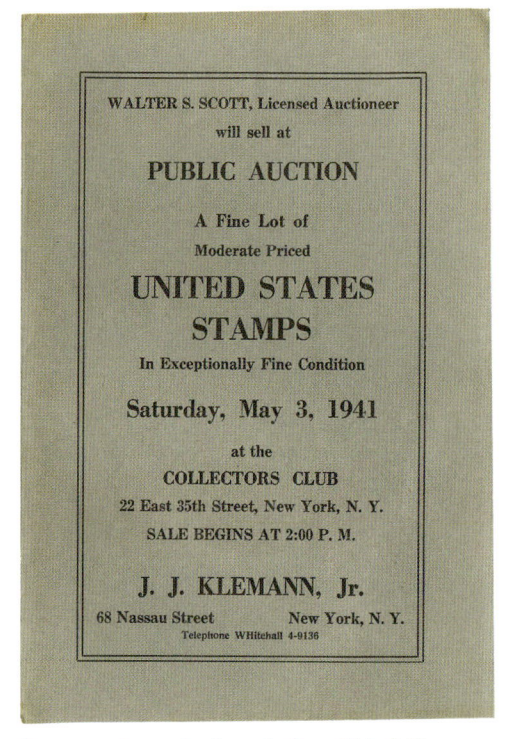

Stamp-auction catalog from the firm of John J. Klemann, one of the legendary dealers of Nassau Street. The 1941 sale, called by auctioneer Walter S. Scott, took place at the Collectors Club, 22 East 35th Street.

A 1929 registered cover from the Burger brothers' firm at 90 Nassau Street

Two of the most colorful dealers of all time were the Burger brothers, Gustav (1867–1952) and Arthur (1868–1949). The Burger firm, at no. 53, was known for its prices, which had the reputation of being the highest on the street. Other dealers would hold informal contests to see who could make money from dealing with the Burgers. It was considered a feat in New York to make a profit on a Burger transaction!

International exhibitions

World Stamp Show–NY 2016 is the 11th international philatelic exhibition to be held in the United States, having been held roughly once a decade since 1913. All of the exhibitions through 1956 were held in New York.

One of the most significant indicators of the power and influence of Nassau Street on the stamp hobby was the prevalence of its dealers on the Organizing Committees of the 1913, 1926, 1936, 1947 and 1956 shows. The Economist's Stern was among the active organizers of our first exhibition in 1913.

It is unlikely that our country's history of great philatelic exhibitions could have been as successful in both the immediate goals of buying, selling and exhibiting stamps and the long-term goals of supporting and growing the hobby for future generations without the collective energy, vision and business acumen of this concentration of experienced dealers.

The tiniest known Nassau Street stamp dealer cover, a self-addressed envelope to the Burger brothers, dating from 1902.

Moving on

Nassau Street was the title of a book written in 1960, reprinted several times and revised in 1988, describing this heyday of New York's stamp business. It was the most famous and notable volume written by Herman 'Pat' Herst Jr., a stamp dealer located at 116 Nassau Street.

The ironic part of Herst's being associated with the name Nassau Street is that he was also one of the first Nassau Street stamp dealers to pack up and leave.

From his spacious office at no. 116, he left the big city in 1946 and established his office in his new

75

home in Shrub Oak, NY, about an hour north of Manhattan. In his book, he recounted with glee how the local townspeople marveled that he could remain in business despite being located across the street from the local post office.

There was only one high rise on Nassau Street during the period when stamps dominated. All the rest of the dealers were in ground-floor store fronts or 2nd and 3rd floor walk-ups.

Shown towering over the street on the right is the 12-story office building at no. 116. At the zenith of "the Street of Stamps", no. 116 was known as the Levi P. Morton Building, named in honor of Benjamin Harrison's vice president, who later went on to be governor of New York State.

More than 70 stamp dealers were housed at no. 116 at one time or another, with about 30 to 40 at any given time.

These included dealers whom experienced philatelists long associated with different addresses altogether, such as the legendary auctioneer John A. Fox, who for most of his career was located in Floral Park, NY.

Another was Robert A. Siegel, a very popular auctioneer who also occupied an early office in the tower at no. 116 before moving on to his Fifth Avenue and East 57th addresses as his business prospered. Although Bob Siegel died in 1993, the firm bearing his name remains one of the most important stamp auction firms in the world, playing an important role at World Stamp Show–NY 2016.

Pat Herst occupied space at no. 116 from 1936, when he took his first office as a professional stamp dealer after leaving a full time position on Wall Street, which he had kept long to raise enough money to go into stamp dealing full time.

The term "Nassau Street" was as much an idea as it was a street in New York, and there were a myriad of stamp dealers whose offices were

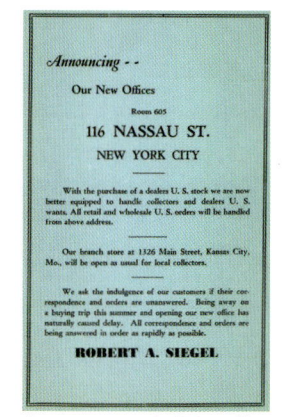

Announcement in Robert Siegel's 25th auction catalog of his impending move from Kansas City to New York (1934).

A patriotic World War II-era cover from Pat Herst's office at no. 116 to George Linn, the founder of Linn's Stamp News.

[3. See K. David Steidley's article on the life story and contributions of "Toasty" in the Collectors Club Philatelist, Vol. 92. No. 1, Jan.-Feb. 2013]

not located exactly on Nassau Street, but somewhere nearby in lower Manhattan.

Herman "Toasty" Toaspern (1893–1936) was one of these. He had been Bartels's bookkeeper and had a deep interest in stamps and postal history. There are a number of covers today that are sought after because they have the "Toasty" hand-stamp, showing they passed through his hands.[3]

The end of an era

Another long time Nassau Street dealer was the Subway Stamp Shop, named for its origins in the subway underpass at Fulton and Nassau Streets, and spent most of its history at no. 111. It was owned by Virginia and Hugh "Mel" Goldberg, who often referred in their customer letters to the glorious Twin Towers of the World Trade Center, just around the corner.

Subway was the last dealer to remain on Nassau Street, occupying a crowded second-floor shop filled with packets and stamp-collecting supplies. The Goldbergs held out until Aug. 1994, just about 100 years after the first wave of stamp dealers started to arrive. They relocated their firm to Altoona, Pa. where it remains today, doing most of its business by mail-order and online.

In its heydey, Nassau Street was the thrilling center of the hobby, boasting wall-to-wall stamp dealers and stamp collectors—sort of what we have on the Internet today.[4]

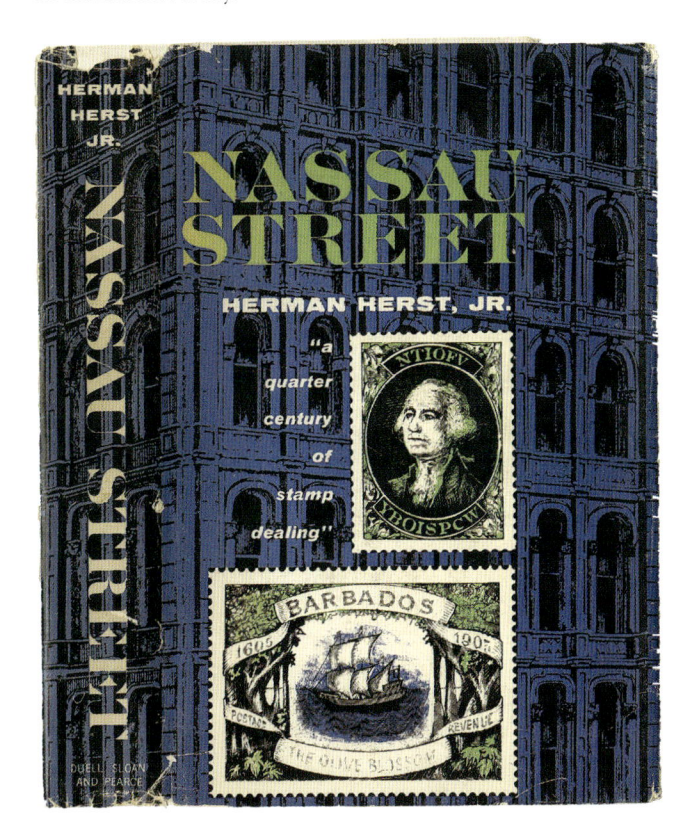

[4. There is a wonderful, full-color walking tour of Nassau Street at http://forgotten-ny.com/2012/11/nassau-street-manhattan/]

The dust jacket of an early printing of Herman "Pat" Herst Jr.'s memoir, Nassau Street.

American Stamp Dealers Association, Inc.

Buy or Sell with Confidence
from Any of Our Members

Integrity • Honesty

Expertise • Dedication

Reliability • Hobby Builder

Look for this logo wherever stamps are sold!

Established 1914

Looking for a dealer in your area?
Visit our website and
select "Find a Dealer"

For more information, call Toll Free: 1-800-369-8207
E-mail: asda@americanstampdealer.com

www.americanstampdealer.com

Eastern Auctions Ltd.

P.O. Box 250 - Bathurst - New Brunswick - E2A 3Z2 - Canada
Tel: 1(506) 548-8986 - Fax: 1(506) 546-6627
Toll Free Tel: 1(800) 667-8267 - Fax: 1(888) 867-8267
email: easternauctions@nb.aibn.com - website: www.easternauctions.com

Canada's Most Trusted Auction House
Unparalleled Results and Unmatched Expertise

Consignments Welcome

Visit Us!

Booth #1342

Buying & Selling

Your Reliable Source for British North America Philately

P.O. Box 450 - Bathurst - New Brunswick - E2A 3Z4 - Canada
Tel: 1(506) 546-6363 - Fax: 1(506) 546-6627
Toll Free Tel: 1(800) 667-8267 - Fax: 1(888) 867-8267
email: glstamps@nb.aibn.com - website: www.garylyon.com

Gary J. Lyon (Philatelist) Ltd.

Stamp and security engraving and printing in New York City

by Bruce L. Johnson

BEGINNING IN THE 17TH CENTURY, New York City played an increasingly central role in engraving and printing stamps, bank notes, and stock certificates for much of the world. Although it was not an exclusive role, New York's position as a center of commerce and finance resulted in a concentration of trades supporting those activities.

Many a collector has noticed the tiny inscriptions at the foot of some of the world's finest stamps, reading "American Bank Note Company, NY" or similar wording. This article tells the story of some of the leading firms and how they came to produce the world's stamps—even as American stamps, paradoxically, came to be produced exclusively by the government Bureau of Engraving and Printing in Washington, D.C.

William Bradford: New York's first printer

William Bradford's early contributions had set the direction for what New York would become as the city matured. After working as a printer in Pennsylvania for ten years, Bradford moved to New York City in 1693. His print shop was at what is now 81 Pearl Street.

Governor Fletcher appointed him public printer, New York's first; he held that position until 1742. Although a couple of undated pieces may have appeared earlier, with no place of printing noted, Bradford published a Proclamation of Governor Fletcher of New York in 1693, the first item ever printed with New York named as the place of publication.[1]

Bradford was quite prolific, and from 1693 through 1743 he printed more than 400 pieces, including, in 1727, the first history of New York.[2]

In addition to printing currency (see below), William Bradford was responsible for several other "firsts" while working in New York City:
- In 1710, the first American edition of *The Book of Common Prayer*;
- In 1714, Governor Robert Hunter's *Androboros*, the first known play written and published in the North American British Colonies;
- From 1725 to 1755, the *Gazette*, the first newspaper in New York City;
- In 1731, the first map of New York City; it primarily depicted what is now downtown Manhattan, with the street layout accompanied by a key assigning letters and numbers to important buildings and churches.

Bruce Johnson has a Ph.D. in Library & Information Studies from the University of California at Berkeley. He has directed historical libraries in California and Indiana for over 30 years, and has published widely on historical bibliography, printing and publishing. He served as secretary of the Graphics Philately Association, and edited its quarterly publication, Philateli-Graphics, for many years. He lives in Laguna Woods, Cal.

1. The full imprint reads: By His Excellency Benjamin Fletcher, Captain General and Governor in Chief of Their Majesties Province of New-York . . . A Proclamation. Whereas I am given to understand that sundry souldiers and marriners have deserted Their Majesties service . . . Given under my hand and seal at Fort William Henry, the thirteenth day of November, 1693. . . . [New York]: Printed and sold by William Bradford, printer to Their Majesties, King William and Queen Mary at the Sign of the Bible in the city of New-York, 1693.

2. Cadwallader Colden. The History of the Five Indian Nations Depending on the Province of New-York in America. New York: William Bradford, 1727.

United States 15¢ and 24¢ issues of 1861-66, with experimental security grills (type F), in blocks of eight showing the marginal imprints of the National Bank Note Company of New York. From the collection of William H. Gross, images courtesy Robert A. Siegel Auction Galleries

Bank note printing in New York

New York was the third of the original 13 colonies to print paper currency. William Bradford printed the first New York "emission," dated 31 May 1709, and acceptable for taxes and other public payments to the treasury. The bills were printed four notes to a sheet with a wood-cut design, in four denominations: five shillings (in two variants), 10s (also in two variants), 20s, 40s, and £5.

Although the first U.S. coins were struck in 1793, it wasn't until the mid-19th century that the federal government printed the first currency. Until then, and with minimum regulation, more than 1,600 local state-chartered, private banks, including those in New York, issued paper money. State bank notes, however, with more than 30,000 varieties of color and design, were easily counterfeited.

During the Civil War, Congress authorized the U.S. Treasury to issue paper money for the first time in the form of non-interest bearing treasury notes called "demand notes." Instead of minting coins, which was a more expensive and logistically difficult proposition, private companies received contracts to print the notes, which were redeemable in gold or silver coin "upon demand."

After the Legal Tender Act of 1862, and under contract with the government, so-called "greenbacks" were engraved and printed in New York by both the American Bank Note Company and the National Bank Note Company. Money historian Gene Hessler notes that "the best of the early 19th-century engravers found security in bank note engraving."[3] Their identities, however, are not known to posterity.

Although the currency was produced in New York, the Department of the Treasury was involved with preparing the currency for distribution from a Washington, D.C. office variously known as the "Printing Bureau," the "Small Note Bureau," the "Currency Department," and the "Small Note Room." After an assemblage of clerks signed the notes by hand, a staff of clerks physically cut the sheets (four notes to a sheet), also by hand, before bundling them for distribution. Such manual labor-intensive methods would be brought to bear in the production of early postage stamps as well.

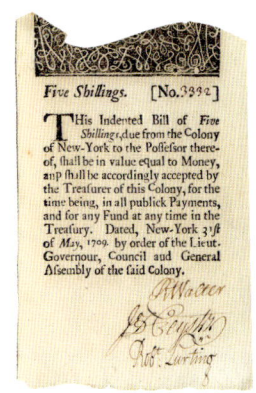

Bradford's Five Shilling Note

3. Ibid

An unissued example of the first United States Treasury note, used to raise funds during the War of 1812. It was an interest-bearing loan instrument, rather than currency.

In the United States, the second half of the 19th century is often termed engraving's "golden age". Engravers' ability to render "life-like portraits and breathtaking vignettes in steel for postage stamps and…bank notes and bonds…was their true forte."[4]

4. Ibid

Postage stamp printing in New York

The first adhesive postage stamp in the Western hemisphere, a greyish three-cent stamp featuring the head of George Washington, was issued for by Greig's City Despatch Post, a private courier firm, in New York in 1842—five years before the U.S. government issued its first postage stamps.

The City Despatch Post stamps were engraved on steel by Rawdon, Wright & Hatch and printed in New York in sheets of 42. When Greig's agency was taken over by the federal government after six months, it continued using the same stamp, simply changing its lettering to "United States City Despatch Post."

Congress approved new postal rates in 1845, but did not provide for a national postage stamp issue until 1847. In the interim, postmasters in 11 different cities and towns, including Robert H. Morris in New York, produced their own "provisional" stamps.

Unused block of sixteen of the first United States postage stamp, printed in New York City in 1847 by Rawdon, Wright, Hatch & Edson. From the collection of William H. Gross, image courtesy Robert A. Siegel Auction Galleries.

For a century, the American Bank Note Company of New York was a prolific producer of stamps and paper money for the whole world. Shown here are an 1897 Newfoundland stamp, a 1914 banknote for China, a 1940 stamp for El Salvador and a 1947 color trial printing of a banknote for Cuba.

The firm by then known as Rawdon, Wright, Hatch & Edson delivered 3,590 sheets of 40 stamps, with a portrait of Washington and a denomination of 5¢, to the New York post office in July 1845. The stamp paid for delivery of a letter up to a distance of 300 miles. Morris eventually distributed his New York provisional stamps to post offices outside the city, to be used on letters bound for a New York address, or on letters that would pass through New York to their final destinations.

Rawdon, Wright, Hatch & Edson subsequently won the United States government contract to print postage stamps, producing the issues of 1847–1851. The design of the two stamps introduced in 1847 was similar to the New York postmaster's provisional. For a century and a half these remained the only U.S. stamps to bear a printer's imprint: the tiny letters R.W.H.E. at the foot of the design.

It made sense that governments would turn to a bank note printer to make postage stamps: as paper that bore value (the promise to deliver a letter at any time in the future), stamps needed to be just as secure from counterfeiting as money.

Of the five private firms that printed stamps for the United States during the classic period, from 1847 to 1893, Rawdon, Wright, Hatch & Edson produced the fewest; historians agree, however, that its artistry set the standard for succeeding U.S. printing and engraving firms, including the American Bank Note Company, of which it was a part.

Until July 1894, when the federal government's Bureau of Engraving and Printing assumed the task, private firms designed and produced all federal postage stamps and experimented with every aspect of the stamp-making process, seeking out innovations in security and convenience.

The National Bank Note Company was the contractor for printing United States postage stamps from 1861 to 1873. During that period, it introduced such innovations as perforating and gumming by machine to replace the manual tasks of gumming and cutting apart by hand. The National Bank Note Company also experimented with applying grills, or waffle-like impressions, to prevent the fraudulent removal of cancellations from stamps, while other firms produced essays for a dizzying variety of printing techniques and papermaking devices in an effort to improve the humble postage stamps.

American Banknote Company

The American Banknote Company was perhaps the most significant of the several engraving and printing companies based in New York, and would become the world's foremost producer of stamps, bank notes and other securities.

The company had a long and tortuous history of mergers and take-overs, dating back to 1795, when Robert Scot, the chief engraver of the United States Mint, formed a bank-note engraving business that would become Murray, Draper, Fairman & Co. in 1810. It printed the first United States treasury notes in 1812.

Ralph Rawdon established an engraving and printing firm in 1816 at Albany, New York. His younger brother, Freeman Rawdon, created his own independent firm sometime after 1825. Each of them established companies with other engravers, but the firm that finally emerged in 1832 was Rawdon, Wright, Hatch, & Company. Tracy R. Edson became the firm's administrator in 1847, and Rawdon, Wright, Hatch & Edson won the United States government contract to print the first federally issued postage stamps in New York City in 1847.

The transformations in managing partners and offices that began in 1832, when Edson joined the company, culminated in a final merger in 1858. Seven engraving firms, including Rawdon, Wright, Hatch & Edson (the only company whose principal seat of business had been New York) merged to form the American Bank Note Company.

American Bank Note Company had its headquarters at 55 Wall Street, in the Merchants Exchange Building. In 1867, it moved to 142 Broadway, corner of Liberty Street; to 78–86 Trinity Place in 1882; and to 70 Broad Street in 1908.

International expansion

During the American Civil War, the work done by American Bank Note Company did not go unnoticed in other countries. As early as 1862, the national banks of both Greece and Colombia had placed orders for currency. Within three years, Peru had placed an order for government bonds, and from Argentina came an order for postage stamps.

Other orders followed: from the Lima, Peru branch of an English bank, and from the National Bank of Italy, in Florence, to cite but two. Albert Goodall, a company employee who eventually became American Bank Note Company's president, traveled extensively soliciting foreign business, especially after business in the United States came to a standstill during a post-Civil War letdown in currency needs. It seemed as though the words "American Bank Note Company" engraved on the currency of a foreign country created a confidence in the currency itself.

Another New York engraving company, the National Bank Note Company, had been established in 1859 through the merger of several other firms. Within twenty years, in 1879, National Bank Note Company and the Continental Bank Note Company, both of which had taken turns printing U.S. stamps from 1873 to 1894, merged with American, under the latter firm's name.

The business thrived, and during the 19th and early 20th centuries, the new American Bank Note Company did business world-wide, receiving orders to design, engrave and print postage stamps, bank notes and securities from 115 countries, from Afghanistan to Yugoslavia.

Other engraving companies occasionally protested the apparent strangle-hold the American Bank Note Company appeared to have on the engraving and printing of securities. One complaint was that American "was so strong in artistic and scientific skill, reputation, equipment and resources that it was hard to compete with."[5]

Paper was one such resource. Crane & Company, a paper manufacturer in Dalton, Massachusetts, had been supplying paper for bank notes since 1842 and American Bank Note Company was a major customer. In 1844, Zenas M. Crane began putting parallel silk threads into the currency paper his company was making,

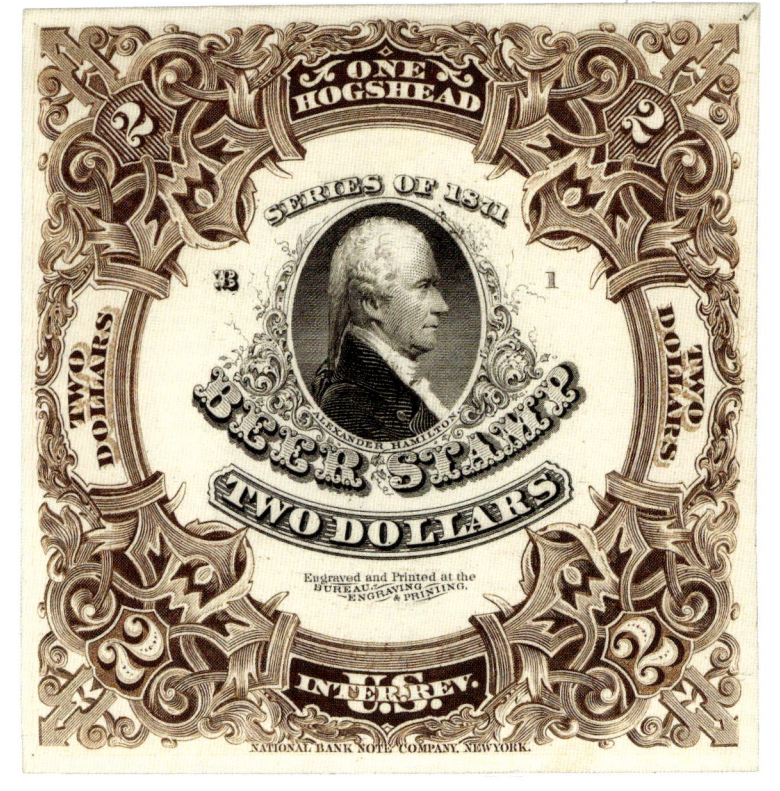

5. *Griffiths, page 51*

1871 revenue stamp to pay the $2 tax on one hogshead (64 gallons or 245.5 liters) of beer, engraved by the National Bank Note Co. of New York and printed by the Bureau of Engraving and Printing in Washington, D.C.

American Bank Note Company stock certificate

6. *See especially Gene Hessler, The Engraver's Line: An Encyclopedia of Paper Money & Postage Stamp Art (Port Clinton, OH: BNR Press, 1993), x, 437; and Gene Hessler, The International Engraver's Line (Cincinnati: Gene Hessler, 2005), x, 531.*

7. *Gene Hessler, The Engraver's Line, page 142–43. 5. Ibid., page 33.*

an innovative attempt to discourage counterfeiting.

When Crane was later prohibited from supplying its silk thread paper for currency to anyone but the BEP, American Bank Note Company developed "planchettes" that it sent to Crane for use in the currency paper it was making. Planchettes are small paper discs, which are embedded in the paper during manufacturing to make counterfeiting very difficult.

Stock certificates and bonds were a major component of the work done by American Bank Note Company. The industrial expansion of the United States in the late 19th century was often based upon public financing, and American played a large role in engraving and printing the requisite stock certificates and bonds during that period.

As with currency, a significant concern of companies issuing securities remained the danger of counterfeiting. In 1874, the New York Stock Exchange went so far as to recommend that securities not be printed or lithographed, but rather engraved for the protection of both the company and the public; American Bank Note Company was ready, willing, and able to fill that need.

Some of the world's most beautiful bank notes were designed by major American artists working for American Bank Note Company. Will Low, Edwin H. Blashfield and Walter Shirlaw, for example, designed, respectively, the $1, $2, and $5 silver certificates of 1896. The same was true for various securities: the same designers and engravers who worked on postage stamps also worked on security documents.

The number of designers and engravers working for the American Bank Note Company during the century and a half in which it dominated worldwide production of stamps and securities is estimated to have been in the many hundreds.

Several sources provide detailed information, including illustrations of their work,[6] but one engraver in particular serves as an example.

William A. Grant headed the engraving division at American Bank Note Company in 1908, when the Imperial Chinese Government asked him to help organize a Chinese Bureau of Engraving & Printing. This he did, as well as designing Chinese bank notes, including one featuring a portrait of Prince Chün.[7]

In 1911, American Bank Note Company merged with United Bank Note Corporation, but continued to operate in New York as American Bank Note Company. It subsequently became a subsidiary of United States Banknote Corporation, a holding company, which changed its name to American Banknote Corporation.

The American Bank Note Company printed the Overrun Nations stamps of 1943–1944, using a two-step, multi-color process to render each nation's flag in its correct colors.

87

Part of the 1943–44 set honoring countries overrun by the Axis powers in World War II. During the long period when the Bureau of Engraving and Printing produced all U.S. stamps, an exception was made for this series because the American Bank Note Co. was capable of printing the flags in full color.

The recent history of today's Banknote Corporation of America begins with Richard Sennett, employed by the Bureau of Engraving & Printing (BEP) in Washington, D.C. until 1979, when he left to join American Banknote. While at American, Sennett received the first contract for printing United States postage stamps outside the BEP since 1894, thus inaugurating the late-20th century privatization of postage stamp printing in the United States.

In 1987, he founded Sennett Enterprises, and in 2004, acquired Banknote Corporation of America. Sennett Security Products continues to print stamp products for the United States Postal Service.

20th-Century Engraving & Printing in New York

Between 1900 and mid-century, about 20 percent of all printers and publishers in the country were working in New York. The Encyclopedia of New York City neatly summarizes the situation in 1940: "The federal census of manufacturers found that New York City has more than 18,400 compositors and typesetters, 7,700 other printing workers, 700 electrotypers and stereotypers, 3,600 photoengravers and lithographers, and 3,400 press workers and plate printers."[8]

8. Kenneth T. Jackson, Editor. The Encyclopedia of New York City. 2nd Edition. New Haven & London: Yale University Press; New York: The New-York Historical Society [2010], page 1038.

Besides Banknote Corporation of America, now with offices in North Carolina, and Sennett Security Products, Ashton-Potter (USA) Ltd. has been printing U.S. postage stamps since about 1990. Ashton-Potter is one of Canada's largest commercial printers, which also prints postage stamps for Canada Post; Ashton-Potter (USA) Ltd. is headquartered in Buffalo, New York.

Further reading

Berry, W. Turner and H. Edmund Poole, *Annals of Printing: A Chronological Encyclopaedia from the Earliest Times to 1950*. London: Blandford Press, 1966.

Clair, Colin, *A Chronology of Printing*. New York & Washington: Frederick A. Praeger [1969].

Griffiths, William H., *The Story of [the] American Bank Note Company* [New York: American Bank Note Company, 1959].

Hackleman, Charles W., *Commercial Engraving and Printing*. Indianapolis: Commercial Engraving Publishing Company, 1924.

Hessler, Gene., *The Engraver's Line: An Encyclopedia of Paper Money & Postage Stamp Art* [Port Clinton, OH: BNR Press, 1993].

Toppan, Robert Noxon, *A Hundred Years of Bank Note Engraving in the United States, 1795–1895*. New York: [American Bank Note Company], 1896.

The World's Leading Auctioneers for China & Hong Kong

PRC unissued Mao's Inscription to Japanese Worker Friends
Realized US$1,150,000

Small One Dollar
Realized US$890,000
The Rarest Regularly Issued Classic Chinese Stamp

Sinkiang Transposed Characters Error: middle stamp in strip of three
Realized US$385,000
One of the Four Treasures of the Republic

**Experience   Worldwide Distribution   Preeminent Expertise   Superior Realizations
Outstanding Material   Auctions in Hong Kong, the Center of Chinese Philately**

Whether you're a buyer or seller, you should be dealing with
the world's largest full-line auctioneers of China & Hong Kong.
See us at Booth 833.

interasia auctions

interasia auctions limited
Suite A, 13/F, Shun Ho Tower, 24-30 Ice House Street, Central, Hong Kong
tel: +852 2868 6046   fax: +852 2868 6146   email: info@interasia-auctions.com
www.interasia-auctions.com

For One of the World's Most Complete U.S. Inventories

See us at Booth 937

or visit our website: www.millerstamps.com

From the Classics to the Back-of-the-Book, including Errors Confederates, Ducks, and U.S. Possessions.

DARN! *I should have bought my stamps from*

MILLER'S STAMP CO.

— *A name you can trust since 1969* —

12 Douglas Lane, Suite 11 • Waterford, CT 06385
Phone: 860-908-6200
E-mail: stamps@millerstamps.com

World Stamp Show NY 2016

New York City: a thematic history

Excerpted and updated from The Philatelic Foundation's New York City on Stamps *by Mary Ann Owens and George T. Guzzio, originally published in 1992 as part of its educational program. Reproduced with kind permission.*

THE THEMATIC HISTORY OF NEW YORK CITY is reflected in the philately of both the United States and the rest of the world. Together, they commemorate many interesting aspects of the history and the people who have made New York the great city it is today.

The following subjects and illustrations are only a representative sampling of the history and philately of New York. Anyone looking to begin a New York-themed collection is strongly encouraged to do their own research and develop a narrative and perspective of their own.

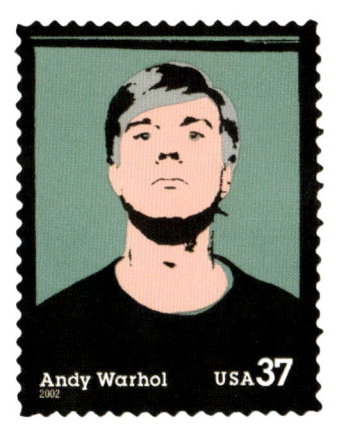

91

Discovery, exploration and settlement

INSPIRED BY THE ADVENTURES AND TALES of Marco Polo and the voyages of Christopher Columbus, explorers from several countries crossed the Atlantic and claimed the land they saw for the rulers who financed them. Since these were frequently the same lands, the claims often led to later conflicts.

1524: Giovanni da Verrazano, an Italian in the service of Francis I, king of France, sailed the American coastline from Georgia to Maine, claiming possession of the area he called New France. It is believed he sailed into New York Harbor.

1609: Henry Hudson, an Englishman in service to the Dutch East India Company, sailed his ship *Half Moon* into New York Bay and up the North (later Hudson) River to present-day Albany. He claimed this area for the Netherlands.

1647: Peter Stuyvesant became governor of New Netherlands, a position he held until Dutch rule ended. A year after arriving, he organized the first volunteer firemen in America. Stuyvesant's ideas were not popular, however. His concept of local government met protests, resulting in the Netherlands making **New Amsterdam** a "burgh", the first organized municipality in the Americas.

1657: Stuyvesant's order to fine anybody allowing a Quaker to stay in his house overnight was loudly protested by the English in Flushing. The governor's answer has become known as **the Flushing Remonstrance**, the first example of ordinary people speaking out for religious freedom and winning.

1664: England, at war with the Dutch, decided to take over the rich fur trade in New Netherlands and sent warships to New Amsterdam Harbor. Stuyvesant gave up without a shot and New Amsterdam became **New York**.

1776: On September 19, New York was occupied by Lord William Howe after the English defeated the Continental Army at the **Battle of Long Island**. Following a further defeat at **White Plains** on Oct. 28, General George Washington gave up New York and fell back to New Jersey. He regained New York City again in 1783.

1787: New York appointed three delegates, including **Alexander Hamilton**, to represent it at the Constitutional Convention in Philadelphia. To help overcome New York's reluctance to sign the Constitution, Hamilton joined John Jay and James Madison to publish *The Federalist*, a series of essays they wrote to win support for ratification. Hamilton was the only delegate to sign for New York, since the others were not in favor of a strong central government.

Henry Hudson c 1560-1611
7½p
POSTAGE
U.S.A.
3¢
300TH ANNIVERSARY OF NEW YORK CITY
Religious Freedom
IN AMERICA
1657
THE FLUSHING REMONSTRANCE
1957
3¢ UNITED STATES POSTAGE
1776
1926
UNITED STATES POSTAGE
CENTS 2 CENTS
UNITED STATES POSTAGE
1776
1951
WASHINGTON SAVES HIS ARMY AT BROOKLYN
3¢
NEW YORK 1673
SAN MARINO
L.200
COURVOISIER S.A.
NEW YORK 1973
SAN MARINO
L.300
UNITED STATES POSTAGE
3¢
1757
1957
ALEXANDER HAMILTON
FEDERAL HALL, N.Y.C.
BICENTENNIAL

Statehood

NEW YORK was the 11th of the 13 original colonies that voted for statehood under the U.S. constitution.

1788: On July 26, New York **ratified the Constitution** by a vote of 30 to 27. Hamilton had led the delegates for ratification with the others agreeing because certain provisions were added in the Bill of Rights. New Hampshire's vote on June 21 had put the Constitution into effect, and New York knew it could not live outside the Union of States.

The **U.S. constitution** would prove such an powerful example of democracy that dozens of countries honored its sesquicentennial with commemorative stamp issues, many depicting New York's Statue of Liberty.

1789: The first national capital was New York. At **Federal Hall**, George Washington was inaugurated the first president. When the city ceased to be the capital in August 1790, Abigail Adams, wife of the vice president, commented on the move from New York, "When all is done, it will not be Broadway."

The **U.S. constitution** would prove such an powerful example of democracy that dozens of countries honored its sesquicentennial with commemorative stamp issues, many depicting New York's Statue of Liberty.

1847: Under the Act of March 3, 1847, the contract to print the **first U.S. stamps** was awarded to Rawdon, Wright, Hatch & Edson in New York. Using standard portraits in stock, it produced stamps ready for sale on July 1 in New York. In 1858 the firm was one of seven that formed the American Bank Note Company.

1862: John Ericsson, a Swedish-born inventor living in New York, designed the turreted, iron-clad ship **Monitor** launched at Greenpoint, Brooklyn on January 30, 1862. Her March 9th Civil War battle with the Virginia led to modern battleships.

1898: On Jan. 1, the separate boroughs and villages surrounding Manhattan Island united to become **New York City**. The city's five boroughs are Manhattan, the Bronx, Staten Island, Queens and Brooklyn. Each has its own government as well as representation on the city council.

MONITOR✻VIRGINIA
USA32
1995

U.S.POSTAGE
1803
1889
JOHN ERICSSON MEMORIAL
5 CENTS 5

UNDER AUTHORITY OF
ROBERT E. HANNEGAN, POSTMASTER GENERAL
PRINTED BY THE
TREASURY DEPARTMENT
BUREAU OF ENGRAVING AND PRINTING
IN COMPLIMENT
TO THE CENTENARY INTERNATIONAL
PHILATELIC EXHIBITION
U.S. POST OFFICE 5 FIVE CENTS 5
U.S. POST OFFICE X TEN CENTS X
100TH ANNIVERSARY
UNITED STATES POSTAGE STAMPS
NEW YORK, N.Y., MAY 17-25, 1947

REPUBLICA ESPAÑOLA
1 PESETA
CORREOS
AEREO
+ 5 Pts
1 PESETA
CONMEMORATIVOS CORDIALIDAD DE LA REPUBLICA ESPAÑOLA
A LOS AMIGOS DE LOS ESTADOS UNIDOS DE AMERICA
1787-1937

UNITED STATES POSTAGE
1898 THE CITY OF NEW YORK 1948
GOLDEN ANNIVERSARY
5¢ U.S.AIR MAIL 5¢

U.S.POSTAGE
SESQUICENTENNIAL OF THE INAUGURATION OF WASHINGTON AS FIRST PRESIDENT
1789-1939
3 THREE CENTS 3

July 26, 1788
New York
USA
25

UNITED STATES POSTAGE
LINDBERGH AIR MAIL
NEW YORK
PARIS
10
CENTS
10

U.S.
POSTAGE
5c
ERIE CANAL
1817 1967

HUDSON-FULTON CELEBRATION
1609
1909
U.S. POSTAGE
2
2
TWO CENTS

UNITED STATES
OF AMERICA
2
2
FAST EXPRESS
POSTAGE TWO CENTS

Omnibus 1880s
1 USA
BROADWAY & 23 ST.
WALL ST. FERRY
MADISON AV.
3

FIRST
STEAMSHIP
TO CROSS
THE
ATLANTIC
3¢
1819
1944
UNITED STATES POSTAGE

ROBERT
FULTON
1765-1965
U.S. POSTAGE
5c

Transportation

BECAUSE PEOPLE HAVE ALWAYS BEEN keenly interested in the best ways to get themselves and their products from one place to another in the ever-expanding United States, innovations, inventions and improvements have been introduced for various means of transportation to fulfill this necessity.

1807: Two hundred years after Henry Hudson sailed up the Hudson River, **Robert Fulton's Clermont**, the first steamship, made the same journey.

1817: To get produce to big city markets faster, New York governor De Witt Clinton convinced the state legislature to build the 365-mile **Erie Canal**. New York City became a leader in eastern shipping.

1819: The steamship **Savannah**, built in New York, sailed to Savannah, Georgia before leaving on May 22 for her maiden voyage to Liverpool, England, the first steamship to cross the Atlantic.

1832: The **first street cars** in the United States, drawn by horses, operated in New York City. By the 1880s, the horse-drawn **omnibus** was a familiar sight in New York.

1901: The **Empire State Express** was on New York Central Railroad's run between New York and Buffalo. It set speed records on the Mohawk Valley section of the line.

1918: On May 15, the first regularly scheduled **U.S. air mail service** began between New York, Philadelphia and Washington, charging 24¢ per half ounce. The linchpin of this new service was the trusty Curtiss JN-4 biplane, built near Buffalo, NY.

1927: Roosevelt Field, Long Island, was the site from which **Charles A. Lindbergh** took off on May 20 for his historic trans-Atlantic solo flight to Paris. After he completed his flight and returned to New York, Lindbergh was treated to a hero's welcome and a parade through Manhattan

The British Empire Specialists

BOOTH # 857

We are important Buyers of British Empire, German Colonies, Worldwide and US Rarities and Specialized Collections.

Pre-1936 Aden to Zululand & German Colonies
Stamps, Varieties and Postal History

Are you trying to fill those pre-1936 gaps in your collection? We can help you build your collection with our extensive mint and used British Empire stock.

Our Public Auctions offer an important and comprehensive selection of Great Britain and British Empire

Colonial Stamp Company

5757 Wilshire Blvd., Penthouse 8, Los Angeles, CA 90036 USA
Tel: +1 (323) 933-9435 Fax: +1 (323) 939-9930
Tel: 1 (877) 272-6693 Fax: 1 (877) 272-6694
E-Mail: *info@colonialstampcompany.com*
URL: *www.colonialstampcompany.com*

Members of: ASDA, PTS, IFSDA, APS, CSDA, International Society of Appraisers

PARADISE VALLEY
Stamp Company, Inc.

France and French Colonies

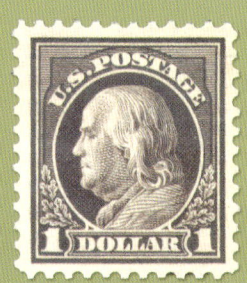

United States

British Commonwealth

Worldwide

A Company by Collectors for Collectors.

- Weekly Internet Sales at **www.stamp-one.com**
- Fair Prices & Fast Service
- Accurate Descriptions
- Friendly and Approachable Staff

Paradise Valley
Stamp Company, Inc.
PO Box 2884
Concord, NH 03302
Phone (603) 223-6650
Fax (603) 223-9651
pvsc@stamp-one.com

APS NSDA ifsda ASDA

Meet us at booth 1071 at the World Stamp Show in New York

NY 2016

Landmarks

NEW YORK HAS ALWAYS BEEN a mecca for tourists with a wide variety of interests. Historic, cultural and entertainment attractions abound.

High on the list of sights would be the **Statue of Liberty**, designed by **F. Auguste Bartholdi** of France as a gift to the United States. Built from the early 1870s to 1884, it was officially presented in Paris to the American ambassador on July 4th. Earlier, the torch and right arm were displayed at the Philadelphia Centennial Exposition in 1876. The head with its seven-spike tiara (one for each continent) was on view at the 1878 Paris Exposition. The statue was dedicated in 1886.

Joseph Pulitzer, publisher of the New York World, promoted the fund for financing the statue's base. Most of the money came from school children.

The first major, and most famous, bridge connecting New York's island boroughs was the **Brooklyn Bridge**. John Roebling, the designer, died in 1869 following a freak ferry boat slip accident the year construction started. His son Washington built the bridge, which was dedicated May 24, 1883. Both President Chester Arthur and Governor Grover Cleveland walked across the bridge and participated in the dedication ceremonies. At the time, the Brooklyn Bridge was the longest suspension bridge, with a span of 1,595 feet and a roadbed 133 feet above the East River.

Other bridges that have been remembered philatelically are the George Washington Bridge over the Hudson River, the 59th Street Bridge (also called the Queensboro Bridge or the Edward I. Koch Bridge) over the Hudson River, and the **Verrazano-Narrows Bridge** connecting Staten Island with Brooklyn at the entrance to New York Harbor.

Central Park's 840 acres (about the size of Monaco) are New York's "Jewel of Manhattan." The park was designed by Federick Law Olmsted and Calvert Vaux, the winners of an 1857 competition. They also designed Prospect Park in Brooklyn.

In the northwestern section of Central Park is Summit Rock, crowned by Sally Farnum's equestrian **statue of Simon Bolivar**, Venezuelan liberator, dedicated in 1951.

At the southwest corner of Central Park, on Columbus Circle (where the Time Warner Center is now), the **New York Coliseum** held many events, including the 1956 International Philatelic Exhibition.

However, the most famous Manhattan landmark is still the **Empire State Building**. From the harbor or up close, it is equally impressive to behold.

50c
+25
POSTES
POSTES
RF
AIDE AUX RÉFUGIÉS

U.S. POSTAGE
3¢
SAGAMORE HILL, OYSTER BAY, N.Y.
HOME OF THEODORE ROOSEVELT

USA
22
F.A. Bartholdi, Statue of Liberty Sculptor

FREDERICK LAW OLMSTED
USA
33
LANDSCAPE ARCHITECT

3¢
U.S. POSTAGE
FIFTH INTERNATIONAL PHILATELIC EXHIBITION
NEW YORK COLISEUM 1956

"OUR REPUBLIC AND ITS PRESS WILL RISE OR FALL TOGETHER"
1847 1947
JOSEPH PULITZER
3¢
UNITED STATES POSTAGE

5¢ U. S. POSTAGE
MANHATTAN
JERSEY CITY
BROOKLYN
STATEN I
VERRAZANO-NARROWS BRIDGE

E.E.U.U. DE VENEZUELA
30
CORREO AEREO
SIMON BOLIVAR
TRASLADO DE LA ESTATUA DEL LIBERTADOR EN NUEVA YORK 19 DE ABRIL DE 1951
CENTIMOS

Chrysler Building
NEW YORK, NY
USA
37
1930
HEROES
USA
FIRST-CLASS +
2001
NEW YORK WORLD'S FAIR 1964
1965
5c
U.S. POSTAGE
Stanford White 1853-1906 NYU Library New York
Architecture USA 18c
32
USA
Empire State Building
UNITED NATIONS · NATIONS UNIES · ОБЪЕДИНЕННЫЕ НАЦИИ
NACIONES UNIDAS
1½c
Yankee Stadium, New York City
USA34
2001
32
USA
News of victory hits home, Aug. 14-15, 1945
METROPOLITAN OPERA
1883
1983
USA
20c

Similarly impressive—and considered by many the more beautiful of the two—is the art-deco **Chrysler Building** on 42nd Street. Its owner, Walter P. Chrysler, was also a noted stamp collector.

Nearby, **Grand Central Terminal** is one of the most celebrated railway stations in the country, with some 21 million visitors a year passing through. A major renovation in the 1990s restored the celestial ceiling of the main concourse, after decades of discoloration by tobacco smoke.

The **Metropolitan Opera** celebrated its 100th birthday in 1983 and 25 years in its Lincoln Center home in 1991. The stamp shows the proscenium from the Met's old home and the front door arches of its new home.

New York has hosted a **World's Fair** twice in Flushing Meadow Park in Queens. The first ran from 1939 to 1940. The second also ran two years, 1964–65, using some of the buildings from the first.

The former **New York University library**, designed by Stanford White (who also designed the façade of the Collectors Club building at 22 East 35th Street), is now part of the Bronx Community College campus.

In 1946, the **United Nations** accepted an 18-acre tract next to the East River for its permanent headquarters. A square near U.N. headquarters is named for Sweden's Dag Hammarskjold, who served as Secretary-General from 1953 until he died in an African airplane crash in 1961.

Times Square, where a lighted ball drops every New Year's Eve and crowds thronged to celebrate the end of World War II in 1945, today draws millions of international tourists to its theaters, shops and restaurants.

Several of New York's sports stadiums have been famous landmarks during their time, including the Polo Grounds (Manhattan), the original **Yankee Stadium** (the Bronx) and Ebbets Field (Brooklyn). Sadly, all three have been demolished.

Many visitors stop at the 9/11 Memorial in lower Manhattan, site of the Twin Towers of the World Trade Center, to pay their respects to the victims and **heroic rescuers** of the 2001 attack.

In the 21st century, the conversion of a disused elevated freight railway line into the **High Line park** has attracted visitors from around the world and led to the revitalization of Manhattan's west side.

For Outstanding United States stamps…
See Volovski Rarities at booth #937

Scott #1 Rare mint stamp!
VF-OG-LH
w/2000 PFC $4,000.00

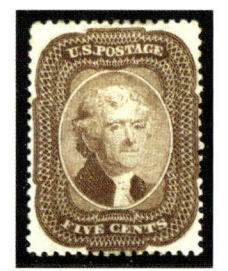

Scott #29 - Tremendous color!
XF-OG-LH
w/1989 PFC $5,000.00

Scott #47 - Only 454 sold!
XF-unused, no gum as issued.
w/2016 PSE $5,500.00

Scott #101 - Rare grill.
VF-OG-LH stunning!
w/2015 PSE $7,950.00

Scott #120a - Ungrilled 24c
VF-OG-LH
Few are known to exist.
w/1998 PFC $12,500.00

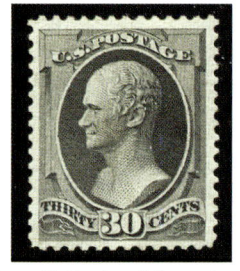

Scott #165 - Condition rarity.
XF-OG-LH
w/2000 PFC $6,000.00

Scott #166 - 90c Perry
XF-Large Part OG
w/1982 PFC $1,900.00

Scott #229 - Jumbo!
VF/XF-OG-NH
w/2016 PSE cert. VF-XF-85J
$3,250.00

Scott #LO2 - Matchless GEM!
Superb-OG-NH
w/2016 PSE cert. graded GEM-100J.
$3,000.00

Scott #524 F/VF-OG-NH plate block $3,995.00
We have an enormous selection of better
plates - please check out our stock!

CSA #10 Frame Line
VF/XF-unused, no gum
A major rarity!
w/2016 PSE $7,000.00

Our selection of TOP QUALITY stamps and plate blocks is second to none! Please stop by and introduce yourself.

Larry Volovski   -   Volovski Rarities   -   Booth #937
Post Office Box 208, Thomaston, CT 06787
(860) 480-0186   VolovskiRarities@sbcglobal.net

WANTED TO BUY - Your U.S. stamps, covers and plate blocks.   **FREE APPRAISALS** - No obligation.

UN STAMPS

World Stamp Show NY 2016

UNPA first day ceremonies:
Saturday, 28 May 2016 (UN Peacekeepers) and
Monday, 30 May 2016 (WSS/UNPA New York office 65th Anniversary special event sheet)

WORLD STAMP SHOW
NEW YORK CITY 2016
BOOTH # CC329

UN Postal Administration
P.O. Box 5900, Grand Central Station,
New York, NY 10163-5900, USA
Tel : 1-800-234-8672, Fax 1-917-367-1400

Email: unpanyinquiries@un.org
Website: https://unstamps.org

People

NEW YORK HAS BEEN HOME at some time to many people who have made a name for themselves in a variety of human endeavors, from government to business to the arts to sports. Some have also appeared on stamps.

Of the four U.S. presidents born in New York State, only one was born in New York City. Theodore Roosevelt (1858–1919) was born in Manhattan at 28 East 20th Street and spent his boyhood days there. His birthplace is now a museum. Roosevelt was New York's police commissioner in the mid 1890s and governor from 1988 to 1901. In 1900 he was elected vice president and succeeded to the presidency as the nation's youngest leader when McKinley died in September 1901. He was elected president in 1904. He died at his home, **Sagamore Hill**, Oyster Bay, Long Island, which is also maintained as a museum.

Franklin Delano Roosevelt (1882–1945) was born up the Hudson River in Hyde Park (also open to the public), within commuting distance of New York City. He attended Columbia Law School and practiced law in New York from 1920 to 1928. He was New York governor from 1929 to 1933, then president from 1933 until his death.

New York was also home to three men who served as chief justice of the United States Supreme Court. The first was **John Jay** (1745–1829) and the second was Charles Evans Hughes (1862–1948).

The third was **Harlan Fiske Stone** (1872–1946), who led the court from 1941 to his death. He received his law degree at Columbia in 1898, taught law there beginning in 1902, and became dean of the law school in 1910. He sat as an associate justice from 1925 to 1941.

Fiorello H. LaGuardia (1882–1947) has been the only New York mayor (1933–45) remembered on a stamp. An interpreter at Ellis Island, he graduated from New York University Law School (1910) and was elected a U.S. Congressman. Born in New York, he also died there. Schools, streets and an airport bear his name.

Giuseppe Garibaldi (1807–82) was one of many world political and military figures with a personal connection to New York. He arrived in 1850 as an exile from Italy and became an American citizen. He lived on Staten Island that winter, employed as a candlemaker. His former home is maintained as a historical site. In 1854, he returned to Italy and led it to unification. Many business figures have had prominent ties to New York, leaving their mark on the city in one way or another.

32 USA
Frederick Douglass
1995
Lou Gehrig
USA 25
Duke Ellington
22 USA
UNITED STATES POSTAGE
3¢
HARLAN F. STONE
GIUSEPPE GARIBALDI 1807-1882
200
ITALIA
I.P.Z.S. ROMA 1982
Adolph S. Ochs
PUBLISHER
13c USA
USA 29
FANNY BRICE
Babe Ruth
USA 20c
JOHN JAY
15¢
U.S. POSTAGE
U.S
LaGuardia/14¢

Marianne Moore
25 USA
American Poet 1887-1972
Jackie Robinson
Black Heritage USA 20c
POSTE ITALIANE
ARTURO TOSCANINI
1867-1957
L.40
1967
Herman Melville
USA 20c
UNITED STATES POSTAGE
SAMUEL GOMPERS
3¢
CHAMPION OF LIBERTY
IGNACY JAN PADEREWSKI
POLISH STATESMAN ARTIST
8¢
UNITED STATES POSTAGE
GEORGE M. COHAN
Yankee Doodle Dandy
Performing Arts USA 15c
DEUTSCHE BUNDESPOST
70
Carl Schurz
Für die Freiheit in Deutschland und Amerika
1776-1976
UNITED STATES POSTAGE
HORACE GREELEY
4¢
UNITED STATES POSTAGE
4¢
ANDREW CARNEGIE
THEODORE E. STEINWAY
FÜRSTENTUM LIECHTENSTEIN
1883 1.30 1957
UNITED STATES POSTAGE
5 CENTS CENTS 5
WALT WHITMAN

Andrew Carnegie (1835–1919) was a successful industrialist and philanthropist. In 1901, he offered New York City 65 branch library buildings on city-owned sites. His offer was accepted, and most of the "Carnegie libraries" are still open today as part of the New York Public Library system.

Samuel Gompers (1850–1924) was a cigarmaker in New York, as his father had been in London before the family emigrated. He reorganized the Cigarmakers' Union, founded what became known as the American Federation of Labor (AFL) in 1881 and held its presidency in 1886–94 and from 1896 to his death.

Theodore Steinway (1883-1957) of the Steinway Piano Company was also a highly respected philatelist and a leading figure of the Collectors Club of New York. His family came from Germany in the 1850s and founded the piano company in 1853.

Musicians and composers make up one group of prominent New Yorkers. Their performances and compositions have been major attractions for many visitors to the city each year.

George M. Cohan (1878–1942) was famous for his patriotic songs like "Over There" and "You're a Grand Old Flag". He wrote for the Broadway stage for more than 20 years. He died in New York. A statue of him stands prominently in Times Square.

Duke Ellington (1895–1974) also lived and died in New York. His five years at the Cotton Club in Harlem brought world-wide fame. He was the jazz master of his time —composing, arranging, playing.

Arturo Toscanini (1867–1957), Italian conductor, led the Metropolitan Opera from 1908 to 1915, the New York Philharmonic Orchestra from 1929 to 1937, and the NBC Symphony Orchestra (formed especially for him) from 1937 to 1954. He died in retirement in New York.

Actors and other performers have always gravitated to New York's stages.

Fanny Brice (1891–1951) was born in New York, began entertaining at 13 as a singer and comedienne, performed in Ziegfeld's "Follies" in New York at 19. Her life was the subject of the popular Broadway play "Funny Girl".

Ignacy Jan Paderewski (1860–1941) was a well-known Polish pianist and composer who made his New York debut in 1891 at newly opened Carnegie Hall, during a trip sponsored by the Steinway Piano Company. He took time off from music to be Poland's first prime minister and foreign minister in 1919, returning to the concert tour in 1923.

Many artists, writers, journalists and editors spent at least part of their lives in the city.

Frederick Douglass (1817–95) wrote of his arrival in New York, after escaping slavery in Maryland, that "a new world had opened upon me." He was a great orator and a leader of the abolitionist movement, as well as a writer and newspaper publisher.

Horace Greeley (1811–72), founder of the *New York Tribune* in 1841, was its editor for 30 years. Earlier he had published the *New Yorker* magazine. He served one term in Congress from 1848–49. Greeley encouraged young people to go and settle the American West.

Herman Melville (1819–91) was born and died in New York. He had a long career as a seaman, which was reflected in *Moby Dick* and his other novels. He served as U.S. Customs inspector on New York docks from 1866 to 1885.

Marianne Moore (1887–1972) wrote poems and prose essays, taught and was acting editor of *The Dial* magazine in 1925–29. She moved to Greenwich Village during World War I and to Brooklyn in 1929.

Adolph S. Ochs (1858–1935) took over the financially strapped *New York Times* in 1896 and managed it until his death. Today a leader in digital media, the paper still uses the slogan "All the News That's Fit to Print."

Carl Schurz (1829–1906) was a German revolutionary who came to the United States in 1852. After serving as U.S. Secretary of the Interior from 1877–81, he moved to New York to become editor of the *Evening Post* newspaper and *The Nation* magazine from 1881–84. A park on Manhattan's Upper East Side is named for him.

Andy Warhol (1928–87) was a leading figure of the New York art scene in the 1960s. He excelled in fusing commercial and fine art, high-brow and low-brow cultures. Warhol's paintings have fetched some of the highest prices ever paid for art. He also worked in film and managed the Velvet Underground rock group.

Walt Whitman (1819–92) grew up in Brooklyn Heights, taught school and wrote articles. From 1846–48 he edited the *Brooklyn Eagle* newspaper. His collection of poems, *Leaves of Grass*, gained him lasting fame.

New York athletes have been renowned in many sports, including baseball, football, basketball, hockey, soccer, track and tennis.

Lou Gehrig (1903–41) dropped out of Columbia University after two years for the financial rewards of playing baseball for the New York Yankees. His record for consecutive major-league games played—2,130—stood for 56 years. The disease he died of, amyotrophic lateral sclerosis, is commonly called Lou Gehrig's disease. He was inducted into the baseball Hall of Fame in 1939.

Jackie Robinson (1919–1972) was the first black major league baseball player when he joined the Brooklyn Dodgers in 1947. He was voted Rookie of the Year in 1947 and the National League's most valuable player in 1949. He retired after the 1956 season and was elected to the Hall of Fame in 1962. In 1997, the Interboro Parkway connecting Brooklyn and Queens was renamed in his honor.

George Herman "Babe" Ruth (1895–1948) was playing baseball for the New York Yankees (1920–34) when he hit his record 60 home runs in a season (1927). He was elected to the Hall of Fame in 1936 and was a coach for the Brooklyn Dodgers in 1938.

Artikelnummer
351364
Aanvang verkoop
14 september 2015

postnl

USA

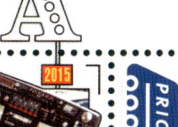

Hotdog USA, Jan Cremer, 1967

Kid Freeze, Circa 1984 (foto: Jamel Shabazz)

Jan-Kees, Verwijzing naar de Nederlandse oorsprong van de naam "Yankees"

Haarlem en Breukelen, Verwijzing naar de stadsnamen Haarlem en Brooklyn

Stadhuis/bibliotheek Den Haag, Richard Meier, 1984 (foto: Kim van Dommele)

High Line, Piet Oudolf, 2006

H.P. Berlage (1), die in 1913 zijn 'Amerikaansche reisherinneringen' publiceert, is niet de enige Nederlandse architect die onder de indruk is van de architectonische ontwikkelingen aan de andere kant van de Atlantische Oceaan, en in het bijzonder van één persoon, Frank Lloyd Wright (1867-1959), die met "een geest vrij van traditie" van invloed is op zowel De Stijl als de Amsterdamse School. De architect Hendrik Wijdeveld (2) is zelfs zo

Wendingen, Volume VII, Nr. 1-7. 1925.

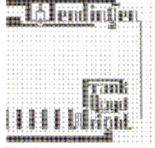

"This is a fine piece of work!"

Ontwerp: Strange Attractors Design: Catelijne van Middelkoop, Ryan Pescatore Frisk

VIA WENDINGEN, OVER EEN WITTE REGENBOOG, TOT AAN DE HIGH LINE.

ARCHITECTUUR.

onder de de indruk van Wright dat hij meerdere nummers van het kunsttijdschrift Wendingen wijdt aan diens werk. De bewondering is wederzijds; "Wijdeveld begrijpt mijn architectuur. Ik geloof dat Nederland het ver zal schoppen op het gebied van architectuur." In 1986 vindt in Den Haag de tot dan toe meest spraakmakende prijsvraag in de Nederlandse architectuurgeschiedenis plaats; het ontwerp van een nieuw stadhuis.

High Line *Piet Oudolf (2006)*
Stadhuis *Richard Meier (1986)*

De vakjury selecteert het ontwerp van Rem Koolhaas (1944), die tot dan toe vooral bekend is door zijn boek Delirious New York. De bewoners en het stadsbestuur verkiezen echter het imposante, open en witte ontwerp van de tien jaar oudere Amerikaanse architect Richard Meier (1934). "Wit is de mooiste kleur die er is, je kunt er alle kleuren van de regenboog in zien", aldus Meier.

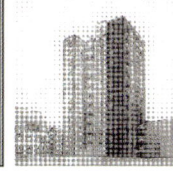

GRENZELOOS NEDERLAND
VERENIGDE STATEN
VAN AMERIKA

Ook tuinarchitect Piet Oudolf (1944) bewijst dat het goed is om bepaalde opvattingen te herwaarderen; "Een tuin moet vier seizoenen de moeite waard zijn... Naast de bloemen spelen ook de zaden, dode bladeren en plantenresten een actieve rol in de schoonheidsbeleving. Bruin is ook een kleur." Dit vernieuwende perspectief komt onder meer tot zijn recht op de 2,3 km lange High Line in New York waarvoor Oudolf in 2006 de beplanting ontwerpt.

De Wolkenkrabber. J.F. Staal. 1932. Onderdeel van Plan-Zuid. (H.P. Berlage)

(1) 1856-1934
(2) 1885-1987

8 714341 085320

WHAT ARE YOU LOOKING FOR?

Is this the place to find it?
Stop by and see!

HERE'S THE PLACE! — Booth 1236
It's our booth number here at
WORLD STAMP EXPO—NY 2016.
We've filled our stock with a vast array of outstanding material at such great prices that you'll pull up to a screeching halt and stop by right here! –Mark Eastzer

"From FULL SHEETS of more than 125 years of U.S. stamps—to amazing inventories of wonderful U.S. and Worldwide stamps (and covers, too), you'll find our booth to be THE PLACE for ATTRACTIVE PRICES and lots of DISCOVERIES. BUT WAIT! Check this: We are one of the TOP BUYERS in America of Stamps, Covers & Entire Collections. We won't hem and haw—we'll give you a GOOD PRICE! Drop by our booth and have some FUN!"

Mark Eastzer
President

MARKEST Stamp Co.

Box 176 • Lynbrook, NY 11563
Phone: 1-800-470-7708
Fax: (516) 599-1180
Email: markest@optonline.net

www.markest.com

Thank you.

Randy L. Neil arrived in New York City 60 years ago this month to attend FIPEX, the Fifth International Philatelic Exhibition, as a junior exhibitor and fledgling grade school writer. His very first article appeared that same month in the May 26, 1956 issue of *Weekly Philatelic Gossip*.

Your gracious support—not to mention the wonderful help, encouragement, suggestions and criticisms received from so many of you—is responsible for the continual publication of the four magazines shown on this page. Place the latter alongside the greatest "stable" of writers ever assembled to produce a philatelic medium and it is an association that has fulfilled a lifetime dream. Periodicals are very much the lifeblood of philately and the building of our pastime's underpinnings for the future. That you care enough to read our output is a rare and cherished privilege. Thank you.

Editor/Designer

THE EXCELSIOR COLLECTION

Booth 1237

Since 1989, it has been our mission to supply top quality stamps and covers at fair prices to stamp and postal history collectors throughout the world. We are dedicated to serving the philatelic world with honesty, fairness and integrity.

Specializing in —
Worldwide • British Commonwealth
U.S. Postal History • Worldwide Postal History
Worldwide Collections

Send for our top quality approvals.
We pay postage both ways.

We are serious buyers of stamp collections and covers. When it is time to sell, let us know.

The Excelsior Collection
P.O. Box 487 • Scotch Plains, NJ 07076
Phone: 1-908-875-3042
E-mail: bob@theexcelsiorcollection.com
Website: www.theexcelsiorcollection.com
Our eBay Seller ID: excelsiorcol2hh2

Murray Payne Ltd British Commonwealth & KGVI Specialists

Visit the Murray Payne team on Stand 1051

to view our full range of British Commonwealth stamps

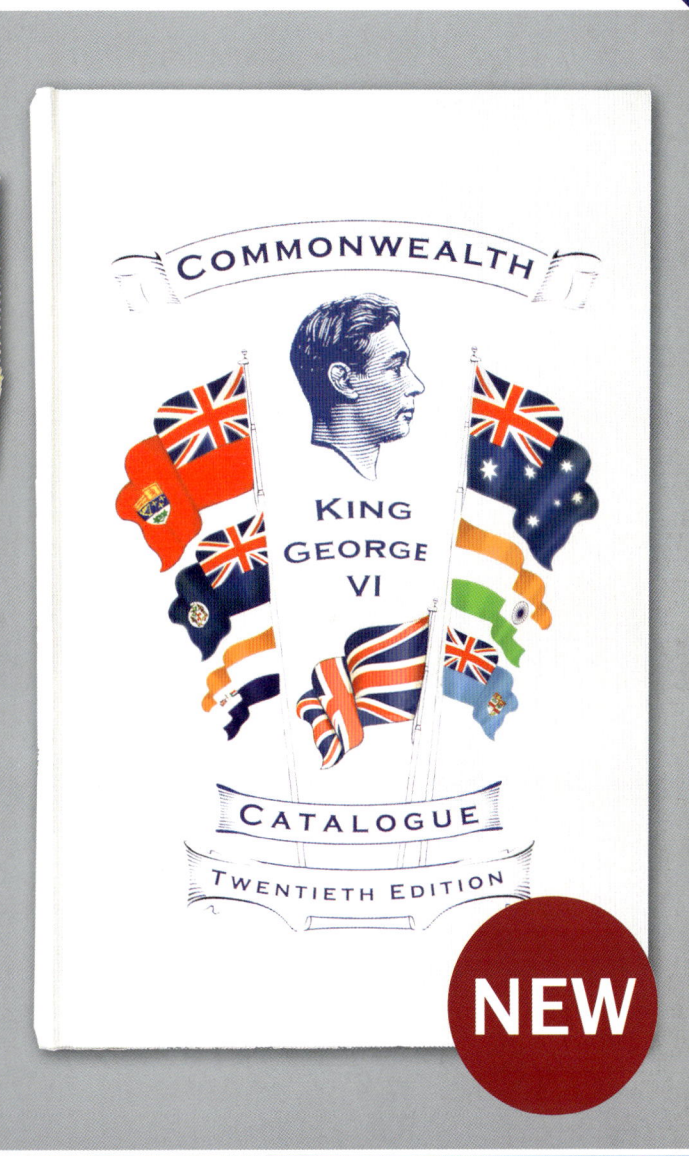

Visit us on Stand 1051

COMMONWEALTH

KING GEORGE VI

CATALOGUE

TWENTIETH EDITION

NEW

Murray Payne Ltd, PO Box 1135, Axbridge, Somerset BS26 2EW, United Kingdom

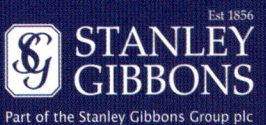

@ info@murraypayne.com

www.murraypayne.com

Tel: +44 (0) 1934 732511

STANLEY GIBBONS — Est 1856
Part of the Stanley Gibbons Group plc

TODAY

Overhead bower of larger-than-life stamp designs in the William H. Gross Stamp Gallery at the Smithsonian's National Postal Museum. Visitors are literally enveloped by stamps as they move about, discovering the magical world of philately. Image courtesy of the museum.

Damus Petimus

Que Vicissim

GUIANA.

Smithsonian National Postal Museum

Opposite: The world's rarest and most expensive postage stamp and the world's most valuable object by weight: the British Guiana 1-cent black on magenta of 1856, auctioned in New York in 2014 for $9.48 million. From the collection of Stuart Weitzman, courtesy Smithsonian National Postal Museum. This and other items indicated with a star (*) are displayed at World Stamp Show–NY 2016.

Above: the reverse of the stamp, showing various owners' marks and signatures.

Top right: The "Windows into America" installation (2013) on the museum façade, at night.

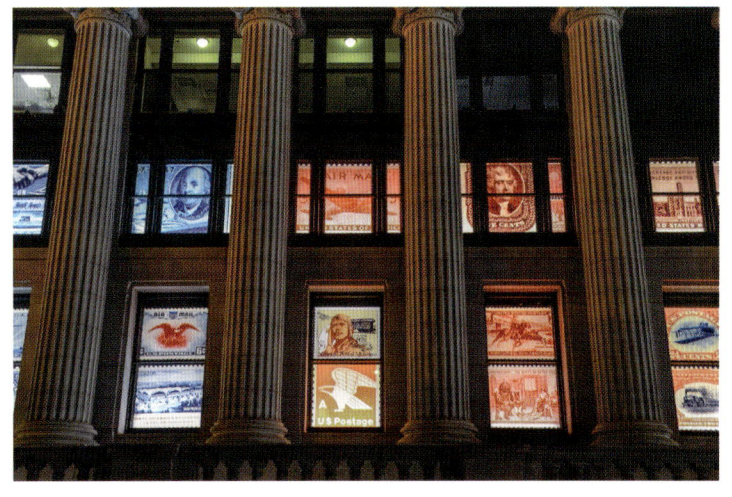

THE SMITHSONIAN'S NATIONAL POSTAL MUSEUM is dedicated to the preservation, study and presentation of postal history and philately. It has the largest and most comprehensive collection of stamps and philatelic material in the world – nearly 6 million items – including postal stationery, vehicles used to transport the mail, mailboxes, meters, cards and letters and postal materials that predate the use of stamps.

This rich history is available free of charge to scholars, philatelists, collectors and visitors from around the world. The museum occupies over 100,000 square feet of the historic City Post Office Building, built in 1914 next door to Union Station, with a third of that space devoted to exhibition galleries. The United States Postal Service, which co-founded the museum, continues to support it financially.

The William H. Gross Stamp Gallery – the largest stamp gallery in the world, completed in 2014 at a cost of $8 million – is named for the financier and philanthropist who has played a leading role in its funding.

Among the most important holdings is a complete collection of all U.S. postage stamps dating back to 1847, as well as other important artifacts going back to Colonial times and of course prestigious philatelic items from around the world.

A U.S. Postal Service stamp store, museum store and a 6,000-square-foot research library complement the exhibition halls.

Exhibitions

The museum atrium has a 90-foot-high ceiling with three vintage airmail planes suspended overhead, a reconstructed railway mail car, an 1851 stagecoach, a 1931 Ford Model A postal truck and a contemporary Long Life Vehicle postal truck. Among its permanent exhibitions are: "Binding the Nation," "Systems at Work," "Moving the Mail," "Mail Call," "Customers and Communities," "Pony Express: Romance vs. Reality."

Visitors can walk along a Colonial post road, ride with the mail in a stagecoach, browse through a small town post office from the 1920s, receive free stamps to start a collection and more. Museum presentations bring to life the story of "Owney," the mascot dog of the Railway Mail Service, and tell the history of U.S. mail trains.

The museum's website, postalmuseum.si.edu, offers virtual exhibits, articles and information about collection objects, academic research and access to social media platforms, while many of the items in the collection can also be seen at arago.si.edu.

Research

With more than 40,000 volumes and manuscript holdings, the National Postal Museum's Library Research Center—a branch of Smithsonian Libraries—is among the world's largest philatelic and postal history research facilities. The library is open to the public by appointment only.

Above: The "Moving the Mail" exhibit in the museum's atrium, with a variety of historic transportation methods including a stagecoach, vintage and modern mail trucks and a Standard biplane.

Amelia Earhart's flight suit from the 1920s.

Clockwise from top: a letter-card mailed aboard the RMS Titanic on April 10, 1912, just before it departed on its fateful voyage; a 5¢ Hawaiian "Missionary" stamp of 1851; a letter autographed by Amelia Earhart and carried on her solo, non-stop trans-Atlantic flight, the first by a woman; the original artwork models for the first two U.S. postage stamps, issued in 1847.

Public Programs

The museum offers a variety of free educational and outreach programs throughout the year for visitors of all ages. Programs encourage and enable visitors to create their own greeting cards, discover the art of letter writing, explore the hobby of stamp collecting, participate in heritage hunts and more.

"Postmark," the museum's official e-newsletter, is published monthly. Exhibition catalogs, educational materials, museum brochures and a three-month calendar of events are published throughout the year.

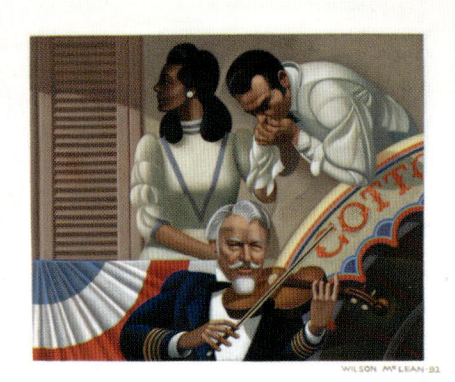

Above: Original artwork by Wilson McLean for the 1993 29¢ "Showboat" stamp, part of the Legends of American Music series. The painting is part of the exhibit "New York City: A Portrait through Stamp Art", featuring works from the USPS Postmaster General's collection. (*)

About the Museum

The National Philatelic Collection was established at the Smithsonian in 1886 with the donation of a sheet of 10-cent Confederate postage stamps. Gifts from individuals and foreign government agencies and occasional purchases have increased the collection.

From 1908 until 1963, the collection was housed in the Smithsonian's Arts and Industries Building on the National Mall. In 1964, the collection was relocated to the National Museum of History and Technology (now the Smithsonian's National Museum of American History), and its scope expanded to include postal history and stamp production. It opened as the National Postal Museum in its present location in July 1993.

Facing page, top: a collection of mailboxes from around the world, in "Stamps around the Globe" exhibit at the William H. Gross Stamp Gallery.

Facing page, bottom: "Connect with U.S. Stamps" (foreground) in the Gross gallery.

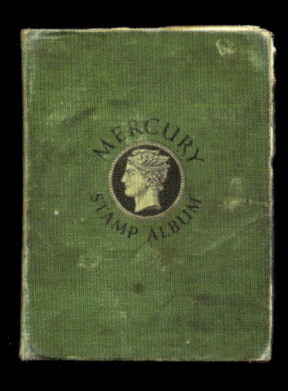

Clockwise from top: a proof of the one-penny tax stamp authorized by the Stamp Act of 1765, whose enactment and repeal laid the groundwork for the American Revolution; a cover, partly damaged by fire, with a unique strip of three of the 13¢ Hawaiian Missionary stamp of 1851; a lunar mail cover carried on the Apollo 15 mission in 1971 (on loan from the Postmaster General's collection); the cover of John Lennon's boyhood stamp album. (*)

FREE

To
The Honble John Hancock Esqr
In
Philadelphia

York, July 4

Letter sent on July 4, 1776 to John Hancock, the most prominent of the signatories of the Declaration of Independence. (*) Gift of George Kramer.

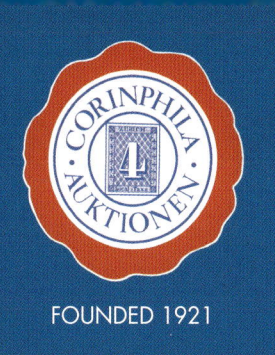

205 - 208 CORINPHILA AUCTION
15 - 18 JUNE 2016

CORINPHILA AUKTIONEN
FOUNDED 1921

SOME FINE ITEMS FROM OUR UPCOMING AUCTION IN ZURICH

CORINPHILA AUKTIONEN AG
WIESENSTR 8
8032 ZURICH · SWITZERLAND

PHONE +41-(0)44-3899191
FAX +41-(0)44-3899195
info@corinphila.ch
www.corinphila.ch

CORINPHILA VEILINGEN BV
HEEMRAADSCHAPSLAAN 100
1181 VC AMSTELVEEN
AMSTERDAM · NETHERLANDS

PHONE +31-20-6249740
FAX +31-20-6249749
www.corinphila.nl · info@corinphila.nl

VIEWING AT BOOTH 729

WORLD STAMP SHOW NEW YORK 28 MAY - 4 JUNE 2016

All single lots of the 205 - 208 Corinphila Auction will be presented for viewing at the World Stamp Show NY2016. Please visit booth 729.

www.corinphila.ch

- Lot descriptions and photos available as PDF
- Online Live Bidding: Registration online
- Online Auction Catalogue with „search functions"

For us, *history is a collectible*

BOLAFFI
Antique collectibles since 1890
TORINO MILANO VERONA ROMA

World Stamp Show | New York, May 28 – June 4, 2016
Jacob Javits Center | Booth K 957

Court of Honor

Below: The earliest known example of the world's first postage stamp, the famous Penny Black, on a document dated April 10, 1840—nearly one month prior to its first day of use. From the personal archive of Robert Wallace (1773–1855), member of Parliament and leader of the British postal reform movement of the 1830s. Also attached to the document is an early proof of the letter sheets designed by William Mulready. From the exhibit of Alan Holyoake

EVERY MAJOR, INTERNATIONAL PHILATELIC EXHIBITION faces the question of what to do with stamps, postal history and other items that might be of great public interest but do not fall within the rules for competitive showing.

This question is solved with the Court of Honor and the Invited Class, where top rarities and crowd pleasers can be shown: famous or significant items from leading collections; one-of-a-kind exhibits that have "maxed out" at Champion-class level; rare philatelic material owned by royalty, celebrities or museums; and ephemera and objects that are of great interest to the collecting world, even though they might not be strictly "philatelic."

Visitors to World Stamp Show–NY 2016 are being treated to what is likely the finest assemblage of such rarities ever shown in one place. Our heartfelt thanks to all those who have graciously agreed to share their treasures here.

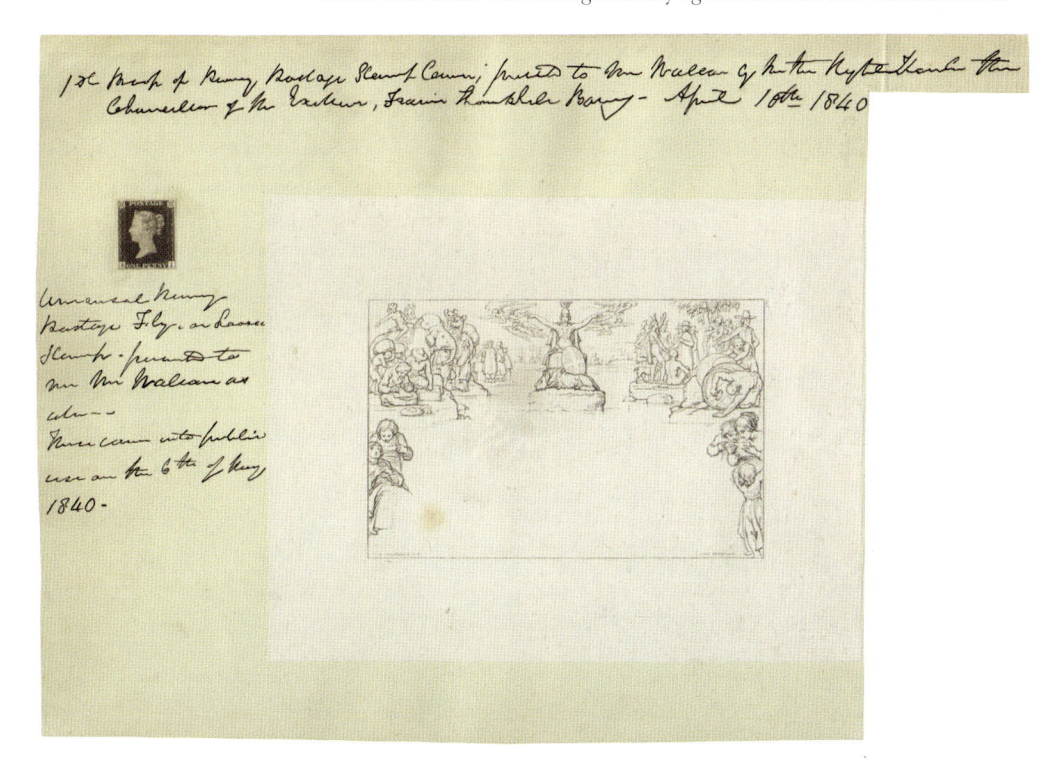

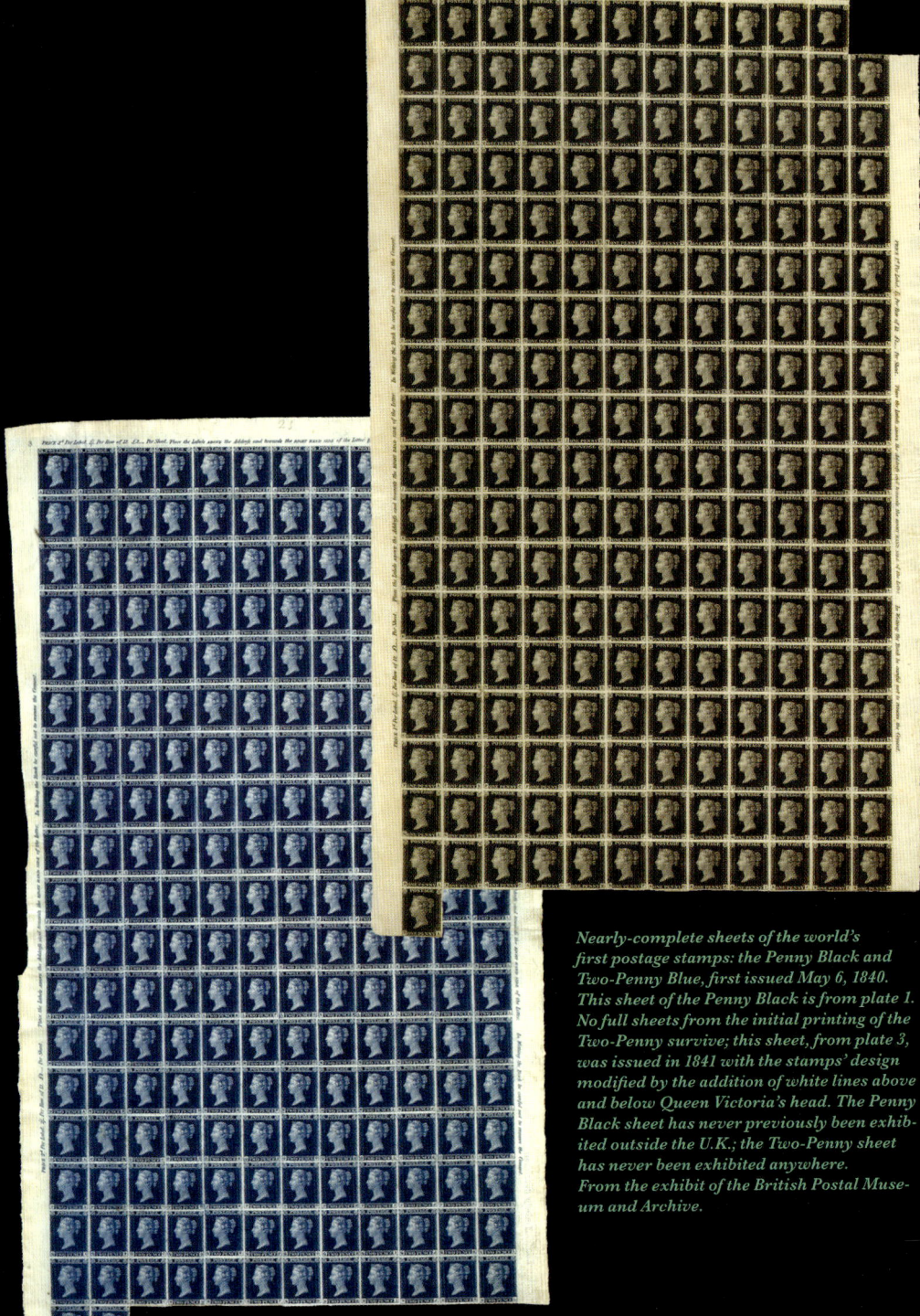

*Nearly-complete sheets of the world's first postage stamps: the Penny Black and Two-Penny Blue, first issued May 6, 1840. This sheet of the Penny Black is from plate 1. No full sheets from the initial printing of the Two-Penny survive; this sheet, from plate 3, was issued in 1841 with the stamps' design modified by the addition of white lines above and below Queen Victoria's head. The Penny Black sheet has never previously been exhibited outside the U.K.; the Two-Penny sheet has never been exhibited anywhere.
From the exhibit of the British Postal Museum and Archive.*

Listed alphabetically by exhibitor

Frame 197 — **Stamps of the 1869 Pictorial Issue**
Anonymous Collector
The 1869 Pictorial Issue includes the first bicolored United States postage stamps, and the first to show themes other than portraits. This issue also produced the first inverted-center errors.

178–182 — **The Roll of Distinguished Philatelists**
Jon Aitchison
The historic Roll of Distinguished Philatelists was inaugurated in 1920. All five sections of it are exhibited here, with an explanation about its history and relevance.

183–184 — **"No Taxation Without Representation": The Stamps that Caused the American Revolution**
Joseph Antizzo
Documents bearing stamps required under Britain's Stamp Act of 1765, for use in the American Colonies.

132–133 — **The Stamps that Changed the World**
British Postal Museum and Archive
Unique registration sheets (also known as imprimatur sheets) of the world's first adhesive postage stamps, the Penny Black (plate 1, before hardening) and the Twopenny Blue (plate 3). The latter sheet is exhibited here for the first time ever.

194 — **The Great Americans Issue: Production Varieties**
Roger Brody
Errors, freaks and oddities, including major plate, perforation and color-omission errors, of the Great Americans series of U.S. definitive stamps (1980–99). Many pieces are unusual, some unique and several are the source for catalog listings.

131 — **The Ball Invitation Envelope**
Vikramm Chand
Lady Gomm, wife of the governor of Mauritius, used the colony's new "Post Office" stamps in 1847 to mail out invitations to a ball. Only three of these covers survive, with this being the only one in private hands.

196 — **Highlights of Indian Territory Postal History**
Joe Crosby
Covers of historic and philatelic importance from Indian Territory, from the earliest known until the day it became a part of the state of Oklahoma (1824–1907).

198 — **Spanish Colonial "Papel Sellado": the First Issue 1640–41 and Its Usages**
Ralph Ebner
Printed in Spain and shipped in two fleets—one via Panama to Lima for Peru and another to Veracruz for Mexico and from there to the Philippines—these classic papers tell the story of the first taxation in the Americas.

122 — **Colombia: Plating Study of the 1861 Peso Stamp, Changing Philatelic History**
Alfredo Frohlich
A new plating of Colombia's 1861 Peso stamp: A new discovery changing the philatelic history of the most elusive classic stamp of Colombia.

Frames 118–121

World Rarities
Club de Monte Carlo

Co-founded by the late Prince Rainier III as an elite, international gathering of the owners of top philatelic rarities, the Club de Monte Carlo includes several institutions and about 100 leading philatelists. It is now headed by Patrick Maselis, appointed by HSH the Prince Albert II in 2009. This exhibit gathers in one place extraordinary items from nearly 50 of its members:

Channel Islands: Cover from the Island of Herm to South Africa
Jon Aitchison

Only known cover from the island of Herm with a registration label.

Serbia: Bisected 4 Para with Portrait of Michael III Obrenovitch
Predrag Antić

Letter from Saxony to Valjevo that passed through the Austrian post office to the Serbian post office in Belgrade. This is the only bisect of this issue known used in Belgrade.

Cuba: 1914 Air Mail Crash during Attempt to Link Cienfuegos with Havana
Fernando Aranaz

Pilot Jaime Gonzalez crashed at take off, but survived. Very few covers were created for the occasion.

Denmark: First Month of Use of the 2 Rigsbankskilling Stamp
Claes Arnrup

Only two letters have come down to us from the first month of use. This one of May 12, 1851, is the earliest date known.

Assini: French Post Office on the Gold Coast of Africa
Paolo Bianchi

Fewer than 10 letters are known from the Assini post office. In 1863, 1 franc was the double rate for letters passing through the English Channel.

Great Britain: The World's First Three Stamps on One Cover
Alberto Bolaffi

Cover of July 7, 1841 to Thirlestane Castle in the Scottish Borders. Franked with a Twopenny Blue of 1840, the letter was redirected to Dunse in Berwickshire with a Penny Black of 1840 and a Penny Red of 1841.

Victoria: Cover from Melbourne to the Confederate States of America
Carol Bommarito

Cover addressed to Richmond, Virginia dated March 25, 1861. The letter reached New York but was returned to sender because postal services to the Confederate capital had been suspended.

Clockwise from top: 1¼-piaster Turkish Empire with inverted center, overprinted "Iraq in British Occupation/4 An." (exhibited by Akthem al-Manaseer); 1858 cover from Monaco to the U.S. with 40- and 80-centesimi Sardinian stamps (HSH the Prince Albert II); 1863 letter from Belgium to Norway, with private trial perforations on all stamps (Patrick Maselis); largest recorded multiple of U.S. 1851 3¢ stamp, from early printing in brown-orange shade (Wade Saadi).

Top to bottom: corner-margin example of Britain's unissued King Edward VII 2-penny Tyrian Plum (Ian Gibson-Smith); 1845 cover with irregular block of six of 5¢ New York postmaster's provisional (Mark Schwartz); 1861 letter from Australia to Virginia, stopped and sent back at New York because of the Civil War (Carol Bommarito); block of six of high-value Iraq 25-rupee official stamp of 1931 (Alfred Khalastchy)

Club de Monte Carlo, continued

Kingdom of Naples: Savoy Cross Mixed Franking on a Newspaper
Giacomo Bottacchi

Exceptional mixed franking on a newspaper corresponding to the rate for three newspapers.

Mozambique: Letter Forwarded in 1858 by David Livingstone
Maurice Boule

Originating in Marseilles, this is probably the oldest franked letter from this region. At the time, the great explorer was serving as Her Majesty's Consul for the East Coast of Africa. One of the jewels of consular mail.

France: War Department Camp de Cavalaire Letter, March, 1871
Stephane Boule

Only two letters are recorded with postage stamps cancelled with this camp mark. One of the major military-mail rarities of the Franco-Prussian war.

Canada: London-to-London Flight Cover, 1927
Paul Buchsbayew

Unique survivor of an ill-fated North Atlantic air crossing from London, Ontario to London, England. After an aborted first attempt, one envelope was not put back on the plane when the crew left again. The plane, crew and remaining mail were all lost in the ocean.

Sardinia: Fourth Issue Used in the County of Nice
Giorgio Colla

Letter to London bearing six 80-centesimi stamps of the fourth issue with the effigy of Victor Emmanuel II. An exceptional franking of the eight-fold rate.

Colombia: United States of New Granada Strip of Four
Santiago Cruz

Showing sheet margins on three sides, this newly discovered multiple illustrates the composition of the printed sheets.

Philippines: Reconstruction of the Plates of the First Issue
Antonio Cuesta

Especially notable in this plating of the 10-cuartos first issue is the exceptional block of 20 with sheet margins on three sides, making it an unmatched ensemble.

Hawaii: Famous "Missionary" Issue on Cover
Gordon Eubanks

This 1852 letter from Lahaina on Maui, franked with a 5¢ stamp, was forwarded to Honolulu by G.D. Gilman with their cachet, the only example so far recorded.

Monaco: Princess Charlotte Wedding Surcharge on 5 Francs Orphan
Véronique Fissore

Only 21 gutter pairs were printed. This one is probably the most beautiful of the five or six examples that survive.

Schleswig-Holstein: Stamp of Holstein Used Bisected from Altona to Hamburg
Joachim Friedsch

This stamp with widely spaced lines is a rarity on cover, and bisected it is unique.

Club de Monte Carlo, continued

Panama: First Pre-Philatelic Postmark
Alfredo Frohlich
This letter to Guayaquil, today in Ecuador, dates from 1777. The manuscript Panama postmark is abbreviated. First letter with a postmark known from this state.

Italy: Modena-Sardinia Mixed Franking
Tito Giamporcaro
Fewer than a dozen are known besides this one, addressed to a soldier of the Modena brigade in Rimini on March 28, 1860. This is the last date of use of a provisional-government stamp.

Great Britain: The Unissued 2 Penny "Tyrian Plum"
Ian Gibson-Smith
After the death of King Edward VII, the entire run of the new monochrome 2-penny stamp was destroyed. Just a dozen copies survived and this one, a corner sheet-margin example, is the most beautiful of them.

Monaco: Sardinian Fourth Issue, Used in the Principality
HSH the Prince Albert II
Envelope sent from Menton to the United States franked with an 80-centesimi stamp of the fourth issue. This value used in the Principality is only recorded on four covers.

Spain: 2 Reales of 1851 on Cover
Carlos Gutiérrez Garzón
This composition of the franking with a 6-reales stamp on a legal document from Burgos to Laredo is unique.

Morocco: Spanish Post Office at Meknes
Maurice Hadida
Unique registered letter sent from Meknes to Zaragoza, Spain in 1877. For the registration, the stamps are cancelled in the center with a postmark stating "Certificado" and the name of the city.

The Anglo-Zulu war of 1879
Alex Haimann
Envelope mailed in Feb. 1879 to a British officer in Beckenham, south of London, via a Cape Town forwarding agent, illustrated with a beautiful pen drawing depicting a Zulu warrior with the caption "GET-OUT-OF-WAY-Y-O"

United States: 1861 New Orleans Postmaster Proof
Leonard Hartmann
This proof is a valuable witness of the printing process during the Civil War because it is the only one that was preserved from anywhere in the C.S.A.

Great Britain: Earliest Dated Penny Black, with Proof of Mulready Envelope
Alan Holyoake
The document was presented to Robert Wallace, a champion of postal reform, on April 10, 1840 by Francis Baring, Chancellor of the Exchequer. It is the earliest dated Penny Black.

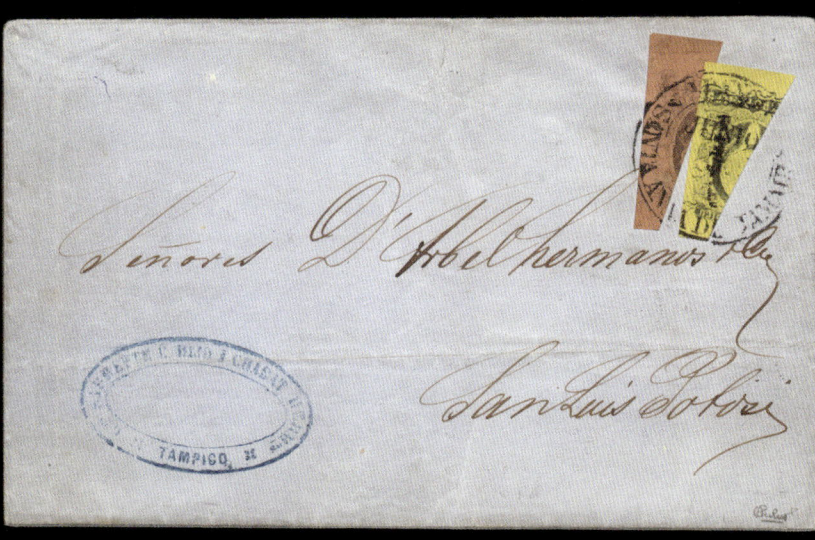

From top: Unique die proof of New Orleans postmaster's provisional 5¢ stamp (Leonard Hartmann); 1868 1¢ Franklin with Z-grill (William H. Gross); Mexico cover franked with two bisected stamps— half of 8-reales and half of 4-reales (Omar Rodriguez); unique 1927 cover from ill-fated flight attempt from London, Ont. to London, England (Paul Buchsbayew)

Club de Monte Carlo, continued

Belgium: Three-Color franking of the three values of the Medallions perforate issue to the British Guiana
Jan Huys-Berlingin

Letter of 1 Nov. 1864 from Ghent via London and Southampton to British Guiana. The only known letter with all issues of the reign of Leopold I to this unusual destination.

Holy Land: 1906 Registered Letter with Declared Value
Itamar Karpovsky

This letter was transported by closed pouch from Safed in Galilee to the Austrian Post Office in Beirut and then onward to Bucharest. One of the highest frankings (74¾ piasters) sent via the Austrian postal system in the Levant.

Iraq : Faisal ibn Hussein 25 rupees in a block of 6
Alfred Khalastchy

With a face value of 25 rupees, huge at the time, few collectors could acquire and therefore multiples are uncommon. This block is currently the largest known.

Schleswig-Holstein: Three-Color Franking to New Zealand
Christopher King

Letter with a three-color franking of Denmark's first stamps, sent in 1862 from Wyk auf Föhr to New Zealand.

Spain: Superfluous 19 Cuartos Franking
Angel Laiz

Registered letter from Las Palmas, in the Canary Islands, to Lyon. The regular rate was 24 cuartos for a registered letter. A unique superfluous franking.

Mariana Islands: The 6 Centimos Value
Rafael Maccaron

The first stamps of this former Spanish colony were those of the Philippines with a hand-stamped overprint. One of the six values, the 6 centimos, was issued in a quantity of just 50 stamps. Presented here in a unique block of four.

Iraq: Turkish Inverted Center Overprinted "Iraq in British Occupation"
Akthem Al-Manaseer

The 1¾-piastre of the Ottoman Posts exists with inverted center. At least one sheet received a 4-anna surcharge by British forces occupying Baghdad in 1918. Only four used examples are recorded.

United States: Letter Signed by Peter Stuyvesant
Patrick Maselis

Stuyvesant was Director General of the New Netherlands from 1647 to 1664. This document was signed in the village called New Amsterdam, nowadays better known as New York. One of seven letters by this illustrious personality recorded in private hands, it is a treasure of the New World.

Naples: The Savoy Cross in a Block of Eight
Bernardo Naddei

This cancelled block of eight is unique and in an exceptional state of preservation.

BARDO STAMPS

YOUR Headquarters for Classic and Modern U.S. Stamps On-the-Road and Online

We are your go-to dealer whether you're looking for regular Scott numbers or if you're a collector of specialized modern United States including Perforation Varieties, Tagging Varieties, Tagging Omitted, Bureau Precancels, Imperforated Errors and EFOs.

We are on the road more than 35 weeks a year bringing our outstanding stock to collectors at local and national shows. Visit our website — **bardostamps.com** — to see our show calendar. We look forward to seeing you down the road at an upcoming show.

Send us your want lists.

Bardo Stamps Online Catalog

Our catalog features more than 4,600 items. For ease of navigation, it is divided into three sections: General • Back-of-the-Book • Modern Varieties Search the site by using a Scott Number, description, topic or any other pertinent information.

Visit us online at bardostamps.com

BARDO STAMPS

P.O. Box 7437
Buffalo Grove, IL 60089-7437

E-Mail: jfb7437@aol.com
Phone: 847-634-2676
Cell: 847-922-5574

Club de Monte Carlo, continued

Japan: Three-Color Franking of The 'Cherry Blossom' issue
Yigal Nathaniel

An exceptional franking of 27 sen, which represents 13 times the single rate (2 sen) and 1 sen additional delivery fee on this weighty envelope from Shizuoka to Okabe, 5 Nov. 1874.

Italy: First Italian Postage Due stamp
Federico Pincione

Issued January 1, 1863, this block of 24 with full original gum, in an extremely fresh shade of ochre, is one of the treasures of the Italian kingdom.

Belgium: The 40 Cent "Medallions" Issue of October 1849
Jean-Claude Porignon

This block of four of the 40 cent, mint with complete sheet margins in this vermilion shade, appears to be unique.

Czechoslovakia: The 10 Korona Parliament Overprinted "Pošta Ceskoslovenska 1919"
Ludvík Pytlíček

Not more than 164 copies of the 10-korona stamp were overprinted and the block of four is one of the jewels of these provisional issues.

Mexico: Two Bisects on the Same Envelope
Omar Rodriguez

Halves of an 8-reales stamp and a 4-reales stamp were used to make up the 6-reales rate for this letter from Tampico to San Luis Potosi. A very rare combination.

France: The "Paris/Exposition" Date Stamp from 1872 Home Economics Exposition
Michel Rozenblat

Only two or three examples of this "Paris/Exposition" date stamp and lozenge-shaped "P.EX" postmark have survived.

United States: The 1851 3¢ in Block of Eight from the Early Printing
Wade Saadi

This block in used condition of the brown-orange shade, issued in September 1851, is the largest multiple recorded.

United States: 5¢ New York Postmaster's Provisional Block of Six on Cover
Mark Schwartz

The 30¢ rate for this letter to Buffalo was for a letter weighing between one and one-and-a-half ounces. This is the second-largest block known on cover.

Brazil: The 30 Reis, Type II on Thick Paper on Cover
Olivier Stocker

Cover sent from Rio de Janeiro to Barbera in 1845 with a pair of the 30-reis, type II stamp on thick paper. Only two or three other examples reported. Unique in a pair and on cover.

In an Industry Where Tradition Matters…

Keith A. Harmer

The Harmers look forward to seeing you at **Booth #671.** For your viewing and buying pleasure we offer:

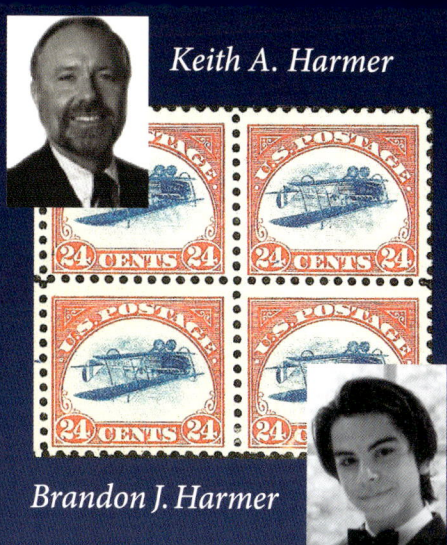

Brandon J. Harmer

Private Treaty

Classic US, Great Britain & Commonwealth, and Foreign Stamps and Postal History

Bernard D. Harmer Stamp Boxes, Letter Scales, Framed Art and Valentines

Viewing of our Upcoming Summer Auction.

Consultations with our Auction Department to discuss:

The sale of your collection or rarities.

Questions you may have regarding the market.

Harmers International Inc.

NOT Affiliated with H.R. Harmer, Inc.

Also Offices In London.
(P) 01144 207 989 3700

1325 Echo Hill Path, Yorktown Heights, NY 10598
Phone: 212.532.3700   Email: info@HarmersInternational.com
www.HarmersInternational.com

Club de Monte Carlo, continued

Mexico: Heavy Envelope Front Franked with 38 Reales
Enrique Trigueros
This three-color franking with the very scarce 8-reales stamp of the first issue of 1856, sent from the island of Carmen in Campeche, is considered one of the most outstanding pieces of this issue.

Cape of Good Hope: Cover from Cape Town to Constantinople, 1862
Brian Trotter
A 2-shilling-and-4-pence franking to an unusual destination. Only two such covers recorded from this period.

Belgium: All Three 1851 Values on Letter from Ostend to Hong Kong
Erwin Van Tendeloo
An exceptional journey for this rare three-color franking to a faraway destination in 1857.

Switzerland: October 1, 1849 Letter
Jean Voruz
An exceptional combination of a "Large Eagle" and an old newspaper hand-stamp. There are only two covers known dated on the first day of establishment of Swiss federal mail service.

British Guiana: The Unique One Cent Black on Magenta of 1856
Stuart Weitzman
The most legendary, the most valuable, the most famous and most honored stamp in the world of philately.

Switzerland: Earliest Known Use of the 2½ Rappen for Local Service
Takashi Yoshida
Use of stamps was not mandatory until September 30, 1850. Only four stamped covers are recorded prior to that date and this one dated June 28, 1850 is the earliest known.

Romagna: Exceptional Use of 8 Baiocchi Bisect on Cover
Alessandro Zanini
This letter from Pontelagoscuro, near Ferrara, to Venice in February, 1860 required a 4-baiocchi franking, paid for with a bisected 8-baiocchi stamp.

Frames 114–116	**Iconic Rarities of United States Philately** *William H. Gross* An extraordinary display of many of the most iconic rarities in United States philately, from Postmasters' Provisionals through the 20th Century.
123–130	**Ceres: France's First Issues** *Joseph Hackmey* The first issues of France (1849–50) with unused and used examples, as well as covers showing rates, destinations and rare tête-bêche examples.
170–177	**The Colon Stamps of Chile** *Joseph Hackmey* The first issues of Chile (1853–65) with unused and used examples, as well as covers showing rates and destinations.

Top to bottom, from the William H. Gross exhibit of iconic United States rarities: The unique plate-number and imprint block of ten of the 1875 reissue of the 1869 90¢ Pictorial issue; the unique Pony Express cover from San Francisco to Prince Edward Island, bearing a $2 red Pony Express stamp; the largest known mint multiple of the 1847 10¢ Washington stamp.

Top to bottom: block of eight of 1857 1¢ Franklin stamp displaying "relief bruises" (David Zlowe); 1846 cover bearing Millbury, Mass. 5¢ postmaster's provisional (William H. Gross); 1872 cover from New York to Brazil, with unique on-cover example of un-grilled 90¢ stamp of 1870 (Nicholas Kirke); 1908 2¢ Washington type I vertical coil pair (William H. Gross).

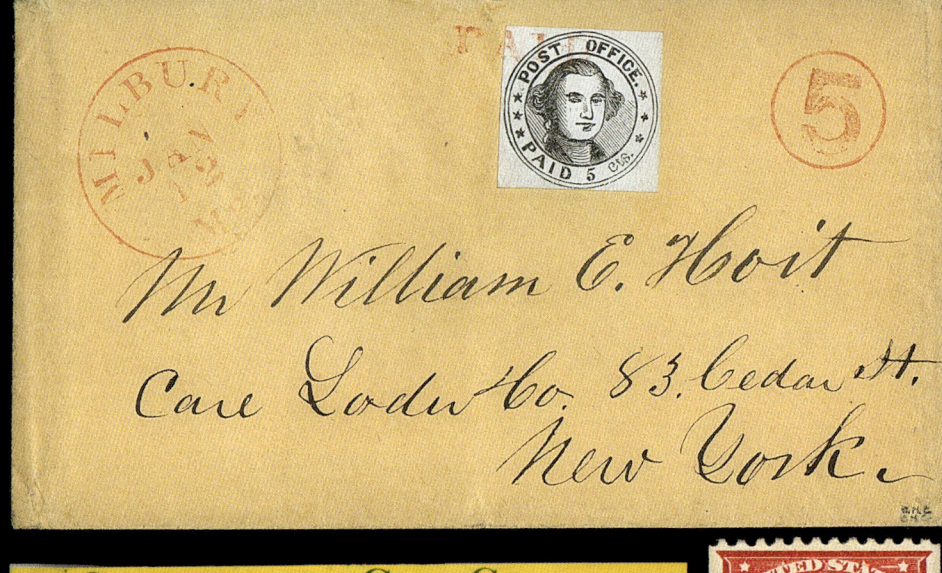

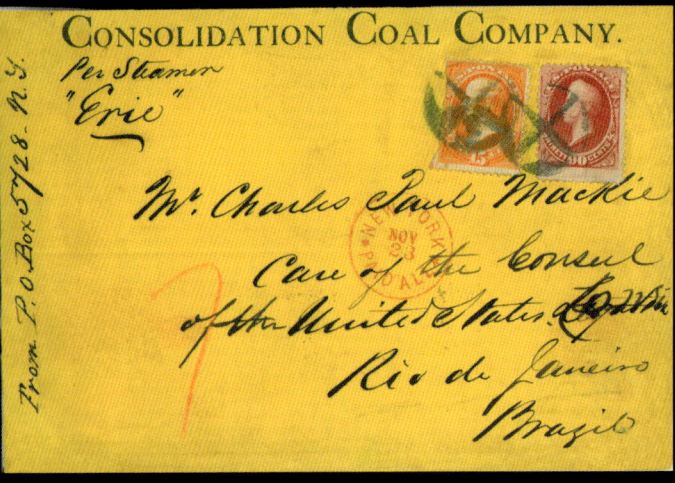

Frames 101–105	**Transatlantic Mail: German States to the Americas**
	Erivan Haub
	Items from almost all German states to the U.S., British North America, the Caribbean and Mexico, showing different routes and rates. Includes several rarities and unique items.
106–110	**U.S. and Confederate States Postmasters' Provisionals**
	Erivan Haub
	Highlights of the 1845–46 and 1861–63 Provisionals, including some of the most important items of American philately such as the Alexandria "Blue Boy", the "Boscawen cover," the "Lockport cover," the "Grove Hill cover," the Livingston pair on cover and the Victoria 10¢ cover.
113	**The World's Earliest Known Postage Stamp**
	Alan Holyoake
	From the archives of leading postal campaigner Robert Wallace, the earliest example of the world's first stamp, the Penny Black, dated April 10, 1840.
167–168	**New York Postmaster's Provisional Issues of 1845**
	In memory of Leonard Kapiloff
	Congress enacted uniform U.S. postage rates in 1845, but did not authorize a national postage stamp issue until 1847. Robert H. Morris of New York was the first of the local postmasters who stepped in to fill the gap with their own issues.
152–153	**New York City Foreign Mail Fancy Cancels 1872–75**
	Nicholas Kirke
	On cover, 38 of the 56 fancy cancels produced in the New York City Foreign Mail Department between 1872 and 1875.
169	**Mobile, Alabama C.S.A. Provisional Issue**
	Van Koppersmith
	All aspects of the Mobile C.S.A. provisional issue, showing all of the rates and most of the important or unusual uses.
199	**Royal Mail Steam Packets Through Mobile, Alabama: January 1849–August 1850**
	Van Koppersmith
	A complete showing of R.M.S.P. covers through Mobile showing virtually all known origins, rates and destinations, including all recorded British Crown "Paid" markings from the route.
154–155	**The First Postal Issues of the Spanish Antilles (1855–65)**
	Yamil Kouri
	Highlights of a comprehensive exhibit covering all aspects of the first postage stamps used in the Spanish West Indies.
187–188	**U.S. Departmentals, 1873–84**
	Lester C. Lanphear III
	These stamps, for government use only, were the largest engraved set issued in a single day.
158	**Gems of China**
	King Yue Lee
	Four gems of China; treasures of the Republic of China; 1888 Taiwan Horses and Dragon Issues; Shanghai Local Post; Republic of China provisional neutrality.

Frame 213	**Local District and Company U.S. Narcotic Provisionals** *Ronald Lesher* Emergency measures were taken when stamps were not available from the Bureau of Engraving and Printing.
195	**The Rouletted Revenue Stamps of Finland, 1865–80: Rare Usages** *Jukka Mäkinen* Rare usages of the Finnish 1865 and 1866 rouletted revenues on fiscal documents: stock certificates, newspapers, stamped paper with mixed penny-kopeck frankings and high denominations.
137–144	**The Medallion Issues of Belgium, 1849–63** *Patrick Maselis* All aspects of the first Belgian stamps including their genesis, study of the printing plates, and use of the stamps on cover with unique international mixed frankings.
191–192	**Gems of Colonial Central America** *James Mazepa* Important letters from the Kingdom of Guatemala during the Spanish colonial period.
214–221	**Street Fighting: New York City Carrier and Local Mail, 1840–63** *Tom Mazza* Development of government carrier service in the United States, shown in New York City with the independent local posts that spurred that development.
189	**Desperate Times, Desperate Measures: Stamp Production in War-Torn Confederate States** *J. William Middendorf* Stamp printing methods of the Confederacy, including typesetting, lithography, typography and engraving.
222–229	**Japan: Etched Stamps, 1871–75** *Yigal Nathaniel* Japanese collection of etched stamps. Dragon and cherry-blossom stamps and covers from 1871 to 1875.
136	**July 4, 1776 Cover Addressed to John Hancock** *Smithsonian National Postal Museum* In 1775, the Revolutionary War began, and on July 4, 1776, the Continental Congress adopted the Declaration of Independence. That same day, a lawyer named William Bunt sent this letter to the declaration's most prominent signer, John Hancock.
205–209	**Mexico: The Guadalajara Provisional Issue of 1867–68, or How a Cancel Becomes a Stamp** *Omar J. Rodriquez* Stamps and postal history of this elusive issue created by the postmaster of Guadalajara during the ill-fated Maximilian Empire.
210	**Afghanistan Revenue Stamps** *Joseph Ross* Examples of early Afghanistan revenue stamps, such as bills of exchange and court fees (among many others) used between 1871 and 1899.

Top to bottom, from the William H. Gross exhibit of iconic United States rarities: Strip of eight of the U.S. 1855 10¢ Washington stamp; 1861 cover to Cape of Good Hope, bearing 1857 90¢ and four other stamps; largest recorded multiple of St. Louis "Bears" postmaster's provisional, including se-tenant pair of 5¢ and 10¢; unique unused example of Hawaii 2¢ "Missionary" stamp of 1851.

Frames 185–186	**The Vital Role of Waterways in the Carriage of Confederate Mail** *Steven M. Roth* The varied ways in which waterways were critical to the carriage of mail when land-based means were cut off or made impractical during the Civil War.
156–157	**Republican Campaign Covers in the 19th Century** *Karl Rove* Covers from G.O.P. presidential campaigns, from John C. Fremont (1856) to William McKinley (1896).
117	**United States Free Frank Covers** *Daniel Ryterband* Examples of various areas in which a philatelist may assemble a collection of free-franked covers.
200–204	**Music in Philately** *Spellman Museum of Stamps and Postal History* Theodore E. Steinway's collection showing postage stamps of the world connected with music, musical instruments, musicians and composers, presented as a document of contemporary human activity.
193	**Transcontinental Pony Express: April 1860 to October 1861** *Steven Walske* The rates and markings from all four Pony Express rate periods, in both eastbound and westbound directions.
190	**The United States 1869 Issue on Packet Mail to France, 1869–71** *Steven Walske* The 1¢ through 30¢ values on ten different route and rate combinations.
111–112	**One Cent Black on Magenta, British Guiana, 1856** *Stuart Weitzman* The only surviving one-cent stamp from British Guiana's provisional issue of 1856 was used at Georgetown, Demerara on April 4. Discovered in 1873, it has since become the world's most valuable stamp due in part to its history of wealthy, secretive and sometimes troubled owners.
159–166	**British Post Offices Abroad** *Hugh Wood* Illustrates the worldwide involvement of the British Post Office in the 19th Century. Areas shown include American Colonies, South America, Caribbean, Europe, Crimea and Mailboats.
230	**The Audrey Hepburn Semi-Postal Stamp** *Bruce Wright* Millions of this stamp were printed as part of a 2001 set honoring actors, but after Hepburn's son objected to her depiction with a cigarette, the print run was destroyed. Just three sheets of ten survived; how a handful came to be postally used has yet to be explained.
145–151	**"The Most Interesting U.S. Stamp" and Why: Relief Bruises on the 1¢ Stamp of 1857-61** *David Zlowe* A remarkable feature is rediscovered, and its significance explained, on a common early U.S. stamp by displaying its unique panes and important multiples.

At World Stamp Show...
Our Booth 1157 is Your
KEY SOURCE for all of these:

Outstanding
United States Essays & Proofs

Classic U.S. & Civil War
Postal History

Confederate States
Stamps & Postal History

Philatelic Literature

Drop by our booth for your copy of the Illustrated full color reprint of Clarence Brazer's **The Various Kinds of United States Essays & Proofs**. **Only $10.00**

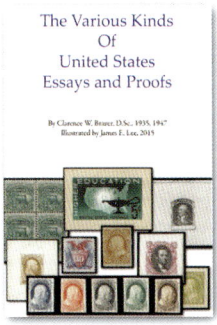

The Various Kinds Of United States Essays and Proofs
By Clarence W. Brazer, D.Sc., 1935-1947
Illustrated by James E. Lee, 2015

JAMES E. LEE
U.S. ESSAYS & PROOFS
U.S. 19TH CENTURY &
CIVIL WAR POSTAL HISTORY
P.O. Box 3876
Oak Brook, IL 60522-3876

P.O. Box 3876 • Oak Brook, IL 60522-3876

Phone: (847) 462-9130
Email: jim@jameslee.com

www.JamesLee.com

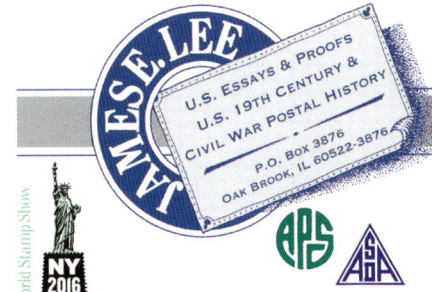

World Stamp Show NY 2016

NEW YORK, NY 10199
WORLD STAMP SHOW
MAY 28–June 4, 2016

UNITED STATES POSTAL SERVICE®
PRIORITY: YOU®
USA ★ Forever

★ THE WORLD STAMP SHOW — NY 2016 ★

World Stamp Show 2016 Show Cancels

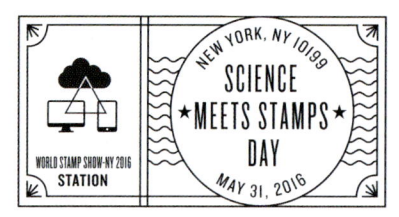

WORLD STAMP SHOW-NY 2016 STATION — NEW YORK, NY 10199 — THE WORLD OF STAMPS DAY — MAY 28, 2016	WORLD STAMP SHOW-NY 2016 STATION — NEW YORK, NY 10199 — U.S. STAMP DAY — JUNE 1, 2016
WORLD STAMP SHOW-NY 2016 STATION — NEW YORK, NY 10199 — LEARNING NEVER ENDS DAY — MAY 29, 2016	WORLD STAMP SHOW-NY 2016 STATION — NEW YORK, NY 10199 — BEAUTIFUL AMERICAS DAY & UNITED NATIONS DAY — JUNE 2, 2016
WORLD STAMP SHOW-NY 2016 STATION — NEW YORK, NY 10199 — ARMED FORCES DAY — MAY 30, 2016	WORLD STAMP SHOW-NY 2016 STATION — NEW YORK, NY 10199 — CHILDREN OF THE WORLD DAY — JUNE 3, 2016
WORLD STAMP SHOW-NY 2016 STATION — NEW YORK, NY 10199 — SCIENCE MEETS STAMPS DAY — MAY 31, 2016	WORLD STAMP SHOW-NY 2016 STATION — NEW YORK, NY 10199 — TOPICAL COLLECTING DAY — JUNE 4, 2016

Brought to you by
UNITED STATES POSTAL SERVICE®

Invited Class

THE FOLLOWING NON-COMPETITIVE EXHIBITS are shown by special invitation of the World Stamp Show–NY 2016 organizing committee. Listed alphabetically by exhibitor

First-day ceremony program for the 2009 U.S. issue honoring the popular Simpsons cartoon characters. The card is autographed by the Simpsons' creator, Matt Groening, as well as Dan Castellaneta, the actor who voices Homer Simpson. From the exhibit by Jay Bigalke.

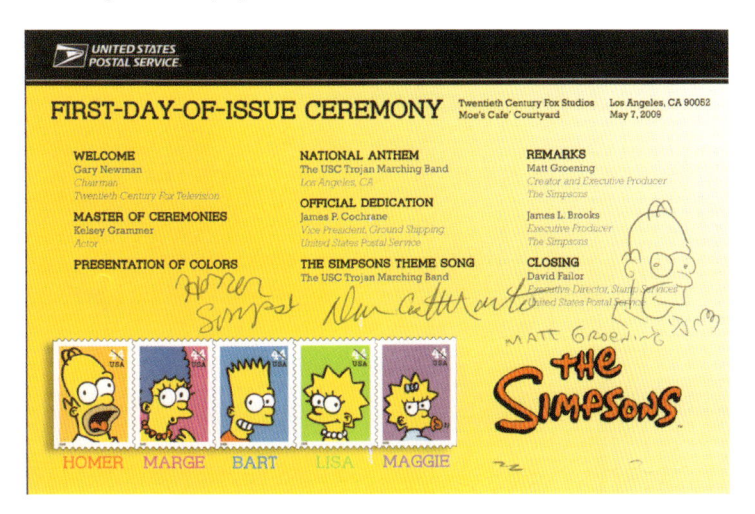

Frame 316   **Alta California**
Anonymous Collector
Alta California includes parts of the present states of California, Nevada, Utah and other states, from 1768 to statehood in 1850. The highlight is a 1776 autographed letter signed by the recently sainted Junipero Serra

318   **Abraham Lincoln**
Anonymous Collector
Covers that follow and celebrate the life of Abraham Lincoln, one of the most beloved American presidents. A Lincoln free frank, campaign and patriotic envelopes, and mourning envelopes published after his assassination are among the highlights

374–375   **Bootleg and Other Letters Carried Outside the U.S. Mails from the Colonial Period to 1851**
Clifford J. Alexander
Covers show the ways letters were carried from one city to another outside the official mail system from the Colonial Period to 1851 primarily because of limited postal service, high postal rates and convenience

Cover from New York governor Charles Whitman to U.S. President Woodrow Wilson, flown on May 15, 1918, the first day of regularly scheduled U.S. air mail service. The cover is exhibited by Robert A. Siegel Auction Galleries alongside a working Curtiss JN-4H biplane, the aircraft depicted on the stamp.

Original pencil sketch by Paul Calle for the 1969 U.S. 10¢ First Man on the Moon commemorative

Frame 313	**United States 1851–60 3¢ Rarities**	

James Allen

Earliest documented uses of the first nine 3¢ plates and the early and rarest colors of the imperforate and perforated series

356–360   **Walt Disney's First Superstar: Mickey Mouse**
Edward Bergen
Showcases some of the earliest Mickey Mouse postal and paper items to demonstrate Mickey's world-wide cultural significance right from the start, in 1930

325   **Terrorism: Impact on the Mails, 1922–89**
Steven Berlin
Terrorism postal history reveals early domestic to criminal, political, religious, to radical Islamic examples from Libyan and Palestinian sources. Featuring the Unabomber to the Lockerbie disaster

378   **A Birth, A Death, A Rebirth: Vignettes from Six Periods in Our Early Post**
Bernard Biales
Cover and original documents, and images from contemporary sources, highlight episodes in the birth of our post

301–308   **Springfield USA: The 2009 U.S. Simpsons Stamp Issue**
Jay Bigalke
The 2009 U.S. Simpsons stamps, showing how each of the 50 states truly has a connection to the television show

379–380   **United States First Issue Revenue Rarities**
Brian Bleckwenn
Selected United States first issue revenue rarities including rarities known only as singles, rare pairs and multiples with some still on original documents

376–377   **Florida Postal History, 1763–1865**
Deane Briggs
Florida postal history highlights from the British period through the end of the Civil War

309   **In Cahoots**
A fun-in-philately fabricated exhibit about the historic and dynamic role that the village of Cahoots played in the development of New York State and the nation.
Roger Brody

314–315   **First Man on the Moon**
Chris Calle
Through the use of original sketches and hand drawn First Day Covers, this exhibit tells the story of the 1969 moon landing commemorative (U.S. Scott C76) and its designer, Paul Calle

341–345   **The United Nations Precancel, 1952–1958**
Anthony Dewey
A comprehensive study of the only service stamp issued by the United Nations, with an emphasis on usage

346   **Mail Between Switzerland and Germany from April 1, 1945 to April 1, 1946**
Walter Farber
Shows how some mail crossed the border although regular international mail service to and from Germany was banned by the Allied Military Government

Frames 319–320	**Valentines—Expressions of Love** *Dale Forster* Eye-catching designs from the mid-1800's, and New York City delivery options
311	**Philadelphia Buildings on 19th Century Advertising Covers** *Helen M. Galatan-Stone* Philadelphia civic and commercial buildings pictured on pre-1900 covers
333–337	**The World's Capital—The United Nations Headquarters** *Greg Galletti* The story of the United Nations' struggle to find a permanent home, the decision to build in New York City, and the international effort to design the iconic UN Headquarters complex
338–340	**The League of Nations—The War Years** *Greg Galletti* Postal history about the League's struggle to maintain contact with the world during World War II, through study of the rates and routes used to move the mails
322–324	**New York Postmaster's Provisional, 1845–1847** *Stefan Heijtz* A study of this iconic stamp including essays and proofs, examples of the issued stamp unused, used and on cover to and from different U.S. states and a number of foreign destinations
326–328	**New York City, Illustrated—1845–1890** *Michael Heller* Illustrated lettersheets and envelopes depicting buildings and street scenes of 19th century New York City
352–353	**Danish West Indies Foreign Mail: 1748 to UPU** *Matthew Kewriga* Highlights of Danish West Indies foreign mail postal history showing destination, incoming and transit mails illustrating the importance of St. Thomas as a pre-Universal Postal Union transit hub
361–366	**For the Love of the Dog** *George Kramer* The importance of dogs in our society. What they do for us; what we do for them
367–368	**Domestic and International China Mail** *King Yue Lee* Large Dragon covers; customs mail matter covers; Formosa covers
354–355	**Pre-UPU United States–Breman Rates Highlights** *Dwayne Littauer* Examples of covers before the General Postal Union/Universal Postal Union, focusing on rates and accounting
329	**New York City—Early Mail** *Thomas Mazza* Stampless mail of New York, primarily 18th century

Above: Unique original drawing of an early design by Otto Wallish for the first Israeli stamps. He picked "Yehuda", an ancient name for the Jewish people, as a country name. From the exhibit by Robert Pildes.

Right: An illustrated letter sheet showing an early New York City street scene, from the exhibit by Michael Heller.

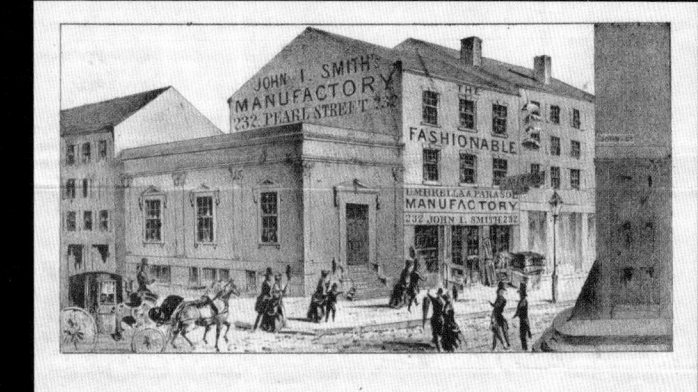

New York February 1st, 1847—

Dear Sir

The time being near when our merchants will be in this city to purchase their spring stock, it is desirable they should know where to select the richest styles & best goods at the very lowest market price.— With regard to New York, all are aware that every kind of manufactures & imports may be bought at a lower price than any city in the Union, and far larger stocks to select from, the difficulty with many of our merchants on their arrival is to know where such houses may be found & therefore make their selection from limited & inferior stocks previously purchased either from the manufacturer or importer & not unfrequently very dear. Permit me therefore as a wholesale manufacturer of Umbrellas Parasols &c. to call your attention to this establishment, which I think you will allow is the most extensive in the United States. It would be useless to go into a detail of the variety of patterns & elegance of styles which I am daily manufacturing & upon which very much depends in order to insure ready sales at a good profit & would respectfully solicit you

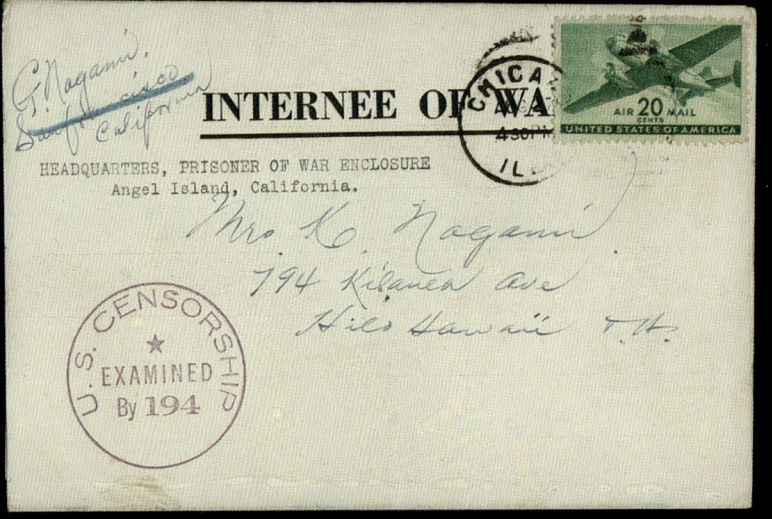

Censored cover mailed at Angel Island, Ca. in 1942 by Genichi Nagami, a Japanese-Hawaiian resident who was in transit after being shipped off to the mainland. He was interned as an "enemy alien" during the war. In Hawaii, Japanese were allowed to stay unless they were deemed to be "threats"—a category that included being a Japanese community group leader before the war. Ironically, Nagami's son, Hiroshi, joined the U.S. Army's celebrated 442nd Regiment, made up of Nisei citizens. In July 1944, Sgt. Nagami was killed in action in Italy. His father remained a captive until the war ended. From the exhibit by Scott R. Trepel.

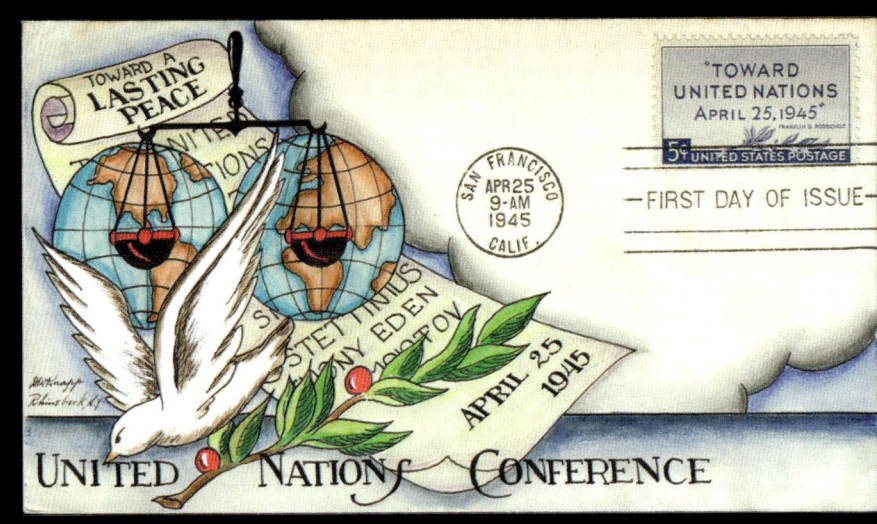

A first-day cover, hand-illustrated by Dorothy Knapp, for the United Nations commemorative stamp of 1945. The United Nations Conference on International Organization convened 61 nations in San Francisco, CA. on April 12, 1945, to develop the U.N. Charter. The Conference concluded with the signing of the charter on June 26. From the exhibit by Greg Galletti.

Frame 330	**New York City—1840s**
	Thomas Mazza
	Provisional and first general issue uses
331	**New York City—1850s**
	Thomas Mazza
	Selection of markings and uses primarily of second general issue
332	**New York City—1860s**
	Thomas Mazza
	Selection of experimental and war related covers
347–351	**The 1948 Doar Ivri and Dmei Doar Issue of Israel: Proofs and Essays**
	Robert Pildes
	Development and production for first issue of Israel, including Dmei Doar (Postage Due) as printed from same plates
369–373	**Every Ten Years for the Past 100: Welcome to World Stamp Show–NY2016**
	Steven J. Rod
	Starting with the first U.S. International Philatelic Exhibition in 1913, shown are covers, cinderellas and ephemera from the ten Shows preceding World Stamp Show–NY 2016!
317	**The "Special Arrangement" Between Liverpool and the United States, 1843–1848**
	Mark Schwartz
	The range of letters and markings that were sent on Cunard steamers under a "closed bag" agreement before the U.S.–U.K. Treaty of 1848
321	**Postal Markings of Newbury and Newburyport, Mass. during the Stampless Period, 1755–1855**
	Mark Schwartz
	An illustration of the markings used there until stamps became required in January 1856
312	**In Vino Veritas**
	Scott R. Trepel
	Exploring the philatelic and postal history aspects of wine and viniculture
310	**The Japanese-American World War II Experience**
	Scott R. Trepel
	The story of the Japanese in the United States during World War II

Nineteenth-century cover with the advertising corner card of a New York City wine merchant. From the exhibit by Scott R. Trepel.

— Booth K 956 —

LEONARD STAMPS
Where the Unusual is Usual

We specialize in Cinderellas, Ephemera, and Revenues, especially British Commonwealth Revenues, Unopened French, Italian and British Colonies Stamps

11001 Arroyo Dr.
North Bethesda, MD 20852
Phone: (301) 897-8588 • Fax: (301) 571-1739
E-mail: hkleonard@starpower.net

GEEZER'S TWEEZERS
The Best for the Least

Hundreds of Country Collections Reasonably Priced

1726 Reisterstown Rd
Pikesville, MD 21208
Phone: (410) 580-1607
Online: geezerstweezers.com

RUSHSTAMPS (ENGLAND)
Visit us at Booth 1164
BUYING AND SELLING
(We pay in U.S. $s on Citibank, New York)

**Great Britain • British Commonwealth
Cinderellas • First Day Covers • Locals
Omnibus Issues 1935–1966 • Proofs & Essays • More**

RUSHSTAMPS (RETAIL) LTD.
P. O. Box One, Lyndhurst, Hampshire • England SO43 7PP
Tel: +44 (0)23 8028 2044 • Fax: +44 (0)23 8028 2981
E-mail: enquiries@rushstamps.co.uk • Website: www.rushstamps.co.uk
Over 55 Years of Trading at Your Service (Est. 1958)
Members of PTS (London) and ASDA (New York)
VAT No. GB 411 7942 62

Est. 1958

Grand Duchy
Great Philately!

Discover the Grand Duchy of Luxembourg through its stamps

Visit us at booth 107

www.postphilately.lu

POST LUXEMBOURG

Auctions

May 29: Robert A. Siegel Auction Galleries

The series of auctions in conjunction with World Stamp Show–NY 2016 opens with a pair of very special collections: the William H. Gross collection of Hawaii and the Steve Walske collection of transatlantic mail to and from France, offered by the Siegel firm of New York. Highlights include:

- Hawaii 5¢ "Missionary" on cover.
- 13¢ "Hawaiian Postage" missionary, unused, the finest in existence.
- Hawaii 5¢-on-13¢ provisional surcharge, on cover to Persia.
- France 1849 1-franc dark carmine on yellowish paper, tête-bêche pair on cover.
- France 1849 1-franc dull vermilion on yellowish, strip of three on cover.

Catalogs and further information:

www.siegelauctions.com
stamps@siegelauctions.com
Tel. +1 212 753 6421

May 30: Auktionshaus Christoph Gärtner

The Gärtner firm, based near Stuttgart, Germany, will hold their CG Rarities Auction—Worldwide rarities, important classic stamps, postal history covers and collections, with a good offering of North American philately including important Confederate States. Highlights include:

- Goliad, Texas 10¢ black on dark blue Confederate postmaster's provisional.
- St. Louis 20¢ black on grey lilac "Bears" provisional, type II, position 3.
- Canada 12¢ Queen Victoria black on laid paper, imperforate, used.
- British Guiana 1856 4¢ black on blue, used on piece.
- Saxony 1850 3-pfennig brick red, margin example on piece.

Catalogs and further information:

www.auktionen-gaertner.de
info@auktionen-gaertner.de
Tel. +49 7241 789 400

May 31: Robert A. Siegel Auction Galleries

The Siegel firm returns for a second day of auctions with their 2016 Rarities of the World Sale—United States rarities, classics and postal history. Highlights include:

- United States 1918 24¢ Inverted Jenny (position 58), graded XF-Superb 95.
- 1908 imperforate 4¢ Grant with Schermack type III perfs, original gum single.
- 1861 "First Design" 12¢ Washington with original gum, ex-Lilly and A.T. Seymour.
- 1908 1¢ Franklin coil pair, perforated 12 horizontally, ex-Agris and Whitman.
- Unique set of plate blocks of eight of the 1869 Pictorial issue invert plate proofs

Catalogs and further information:
www.siegelauctions.com
stamps@siegelauctions.com
Tel. +1 212 753 6421

June 1: Schuyler Rumsey Philatelic Auctions

The Rumsey firm, based in San Francisco, is offering their worldwide Rarity Sale with over 650 lots and the specialized Large Gold-winning Robert L. Markovits collection of United States Special Delivery issues, 1885-1971 with 208 lots. Highlights include:

- United States 1858 5¢ Indian Red, original-gum, graded VF-80 by the P.S.E.
- 1918 24¢ Inverted Jenny (position 8).
- Newfoundland 1860 1s Orange Vermilion, ex Ferrary, Moody, Lilly, Cartier, Schneider.
- Falkland Islands 1964 6 pence HMS Glasgow vignette error, extremely fine.
- Unique, imperforate, top plate-number block of 1895 watermarked 10¢ special delivery.

Catalogs and further information:

www.rumseyauctions.com
srumsey@rumseyauctions.com
Tel. +1 415 781-5127

June 2: Daniel F. Kelleher Auctions

The Kelleher firm, of Danbury, Conn., will be offering the comprehensive mint collection of the world, 1840–1950, amassed over decades by the philatelist Adolph J. Capurro. The sale will consist of approximately 800 lots.

The Kelleher firm felt it was important to use the venue of this once-in-a-decade event to showcase what our firm actually does, rather than to offer the usual "rarities"-type auction that regularly surfaces at these events. The Capurro collection has enabled us to do just that.

This collection will touch the widest possible range of both collectors and dealers. For the mint singles collector, there are hundreds of popular sought-after sets from the British Empire, through A–Z general foreign. The collection lots which accompany nearly every country are outstanding and will undoubtedly please the collector looking to embark on a new collecting area or the dealer, who will rarely get the opportunity to acquire mint collections of this stature.

It is with great sadness that we note the passing of Mr. Capurro in mid-April during the final processing of his significant collections. Both his family as well as the Kelleher family had hoped he would live to witness the sale of his fine collections.

Please visit our super-booth to view this fine collection, as well as the Kelleher & Rogers Asia sale and several Kelleher sales taking place in June.

Catalogs and further information:
db.kelleherauctions.com
info@kelleherauctions.com
Tel. +1 203 297 6056

Kelleher Auctions
Daniel F. Kelleher Auctions, LLC
America's Oldest Philatelic Auction House
Established 1885

Kelleher & Rogers Fine Asian Auctions Ltd

Michael Rogers Online
Sharing Philately Worldwide

June 3: H.R. Harmer, Inc.

H.R. Harmer, of Tustin, Ca. is part of Global Philatelic Network, a consortium that includes Heinrich Kohler (Germany), Corinphila (Switzerland and Netherlands) and John Bull Auctions (Hong Kong). Highlights of this two-part sale include:

- The Don David Price exhibit collection of the "CIA" Invert
- The "Erivan" collection of U.S. and Confederate postal history, incl. Pony Express $2 red on westward cover and Nashville 10¢ on Adams Express cover
- U.S. Local and Private Posts incl. unique 1¢ black Swarts' City Dispatch Post on cover
- Philippines 1854 1r slate blue, "CORROS" error, in left margin pair (pos 21-26)
- New Zealand 1855 1d deep carmine red, London printing, postally used with manuscript cancel

Catalogs and further information:
hrharmer.com/en/ny2016/
info@hrharmer.com
Tel. +1 714.389.9178

Liane & Sergio Sismondo
The Classic Collector
— Booth 1060 —

If you are looking for the rare and valuable, this is your mandatory stop!

Come and browse through our inventory books and thousands of valuable and rare stamps, proofs, and covers of the world with emphasis on the classic period and first issues.

50-Years Experience Helping Collectors Build Important Collections

P.O. Box 10035
Syracuse, NY 13290-3301
Phone: 315 422 2331 Fax: 315 422 2956

www.sismondostamps.com
sismondo@dreamscape.com
Phone in Canada 613 722 1621

Members APS, ASDA, CSDA, PTS. CCNY, many others

PRINZ
Quality without compromise...

Harry Edelman Distributor
Numismatic
and
Philatelic Supplies

PRINZ does manufacture not only
High Quality Stamp Mounts,
PRINZ produces also the following items:

- ✓ stockbooks
- ✓ stockcards
- ✓ stockpages
- ✓ hinges

- ✓ stamp tongs
- ✓ cover albums

and now available:
- ✓ watermark fluid

Visit us at Booth N656.

website: www.harryedelmaninc.com

e-mail: harryedelmaninc@aol.com

SARATOGA COUNTY'S (NEW YORK)
COLLECTIBLES HEADQUARTERS

AZUSA COLLECTIBLES

World Stamp Show - NY Booth #657

Visit our Office/Gallery location at Northway Exit 10
258 Ushers Road, Suite 203, Clifton Park, NY I 2065
(518) 877-3027 azusacollectibles@yahoo.com

**THE BEST IN WORLDWIDE STAMPS "A" TO "Z" plus the U.S.A.
THAT'S AZUSA!**

Our 38th year of continuous stamp store operation!

A Great Selection of Sets, Singles and Souvenir sheets of:
Canada and Provinces – mint and used
Great Britain, including Channel Islands
British Colonies * France and Area
Germany and Area * Italy and Area
Other European
Asia, Central and South America
Topicals – Animals, Disney, Famous People, Flowers, Scouts,
Space, Sports, 3-D, World's Fair, etc.

Member:
American Philatelic Society – 38 years

*American Air Mail Society
*Adirondack Stamp Club
*Fort Orange Stamp Club
*New York State Postal History Society
*President, Federation of New York State Stamp Societies

Qualified Estate Appraisers
Experience includes 38+ years of store ownership on Long Island and New York's Capital District

Also:
Mint and Used U.S. Stamps
U.S. First Day Covers
U.S. Plate Blocks
U.S. Booklets and Booklet Panes
U.S. Revenues, including Ducks
U.S. Back-of-Book

New Issues

EIGHT NEW United States Postal Service stamp issues will be dedicated between May 28 and June 3 at World Stamp Show—NY 2016.

World Stamp Show—NY 2016 commemorative sheets

These souvenir sheet commemorate America's decennial philatelic event. The sheets feature intaglio-printed stamps in two color configurations and will be sold only as a set.

Their design is based on two stamps issued in August, 2015 to announce the show. Those stamps, printed by offset lithography, comprised large areas of solid color. The new stamps consist of finer detail, more suitable to the technique of line-engraving.

Michael Dyer of New York designed the sheet. Antonio Alcalá of Alexandria, Virginia, was the art director.

All images ©United States Postal Service. All rights reserved. Used by permission.

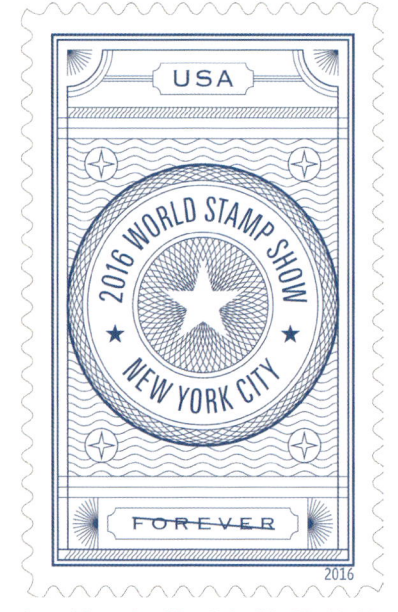

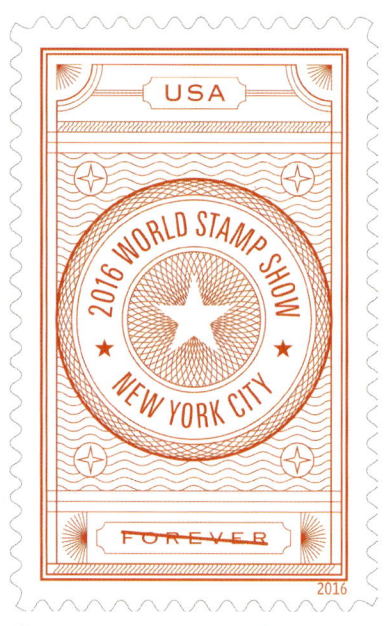

Issued Saturday, May 28th—The World of Stamps Day

Repeal of the Stamp Act, 1766

This issue commemorates the 250th anniversary of the repeal of the Stamp Act, British legislation that galvanized and united the American colonies and set them on a path toward revolution.

The act required payment of a tax on a wide array of paper materials, such as newspapers, pamphlets, legal documents, licenses, mortgages, contracts, and bills of sale. To indicate that the payment had been made, a stamp—not an adhesive, as in our modern understanding of the word, but rather an embossed imprint—would be applied to these papers.

The artwork on the new commemorative depicts a crowd gathered around a "liberty tree" to celebrate the repeal of the Stamp Act. In place of a denomination is the word "Forever", indicating that the stamp remains valid for first-class letter postage regardless of future rate increases (or decreases).

The sheet margin displays a proof print of a one-penny revenue stamp and includes a famous slogan from the era: "Taxation without representation is tyranny." Additional explanatory text appears on the back of the pane.

Greg Harlin of Annapolis, Maryland was the artist, working under the direction of Antonio Alcalá.

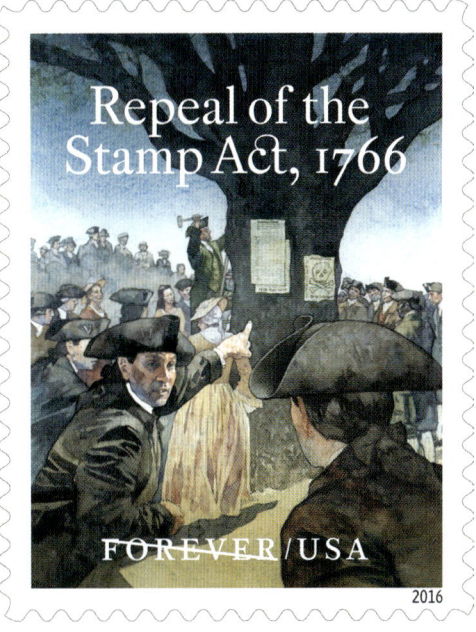

Issued Sunday, May 29th—Learning Never Ends Day

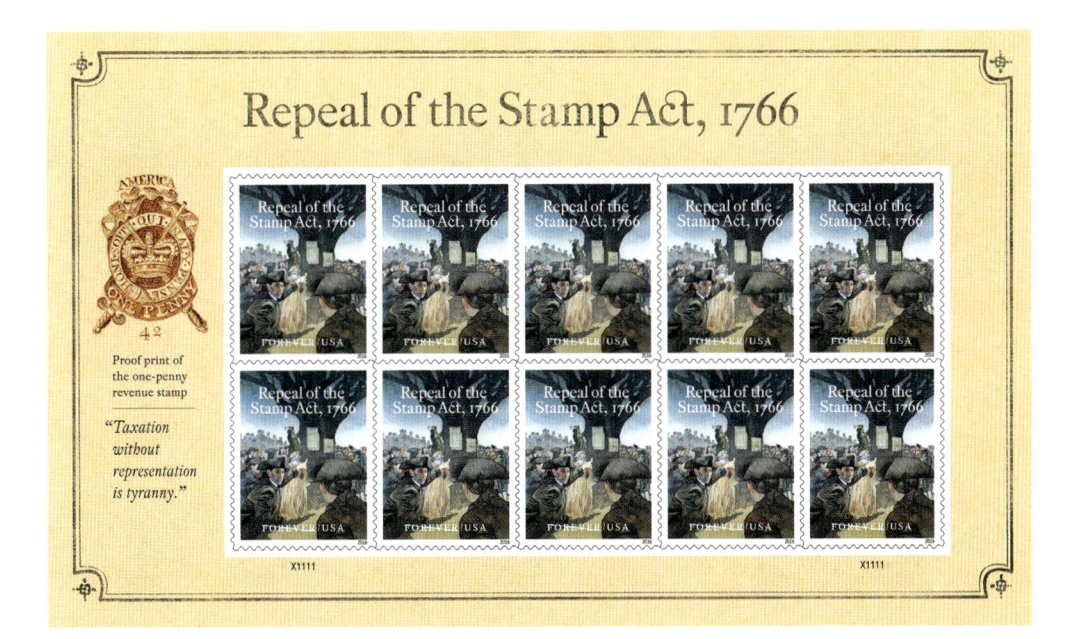

167

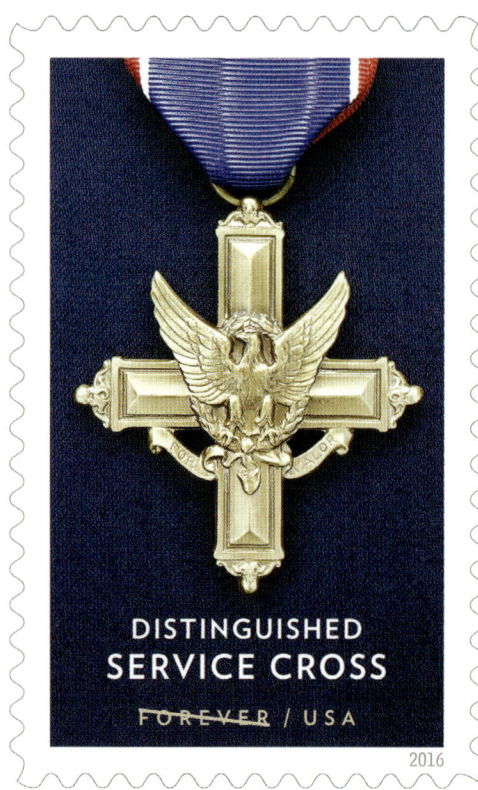

Honoring Extraordinary Heroism: The Service Cross Medals

This issuance continues a Postal Service™ tradition of honoring the bravery and achievements of members of the U.S. Armed Forces. Previous issuances have depicted the highest military decoration for valor in combat: the Medal of Honor. These new First-Class Forever® stamps recognize the second highest decoration: the Distinguished Service Cross (Army), Navy Cross (Navy and Marine Corps), Air Force Cross, and Coast Guard Cross. Each stamp consists of a photograph of one of the four medals suspended from a ribbon and shown against a dark blue backdrop. There are a total of 12 stamps on the sheet, shown in two rows. These decorations are awarded for acts of extraordinary heroism in which an individual braved enemy fire, made bold decisions, and took selfless actions to rescue or protect fellow service members. Art director Greg Breeding designed the stamps working with photographs of the medals by Richard Frasier.

Issued Monday, May 30th—Armed Forces Day

Views of Our Planets

With this pane of 16 "Forever" stamps, the Postal Service showcases some of the more visually compelling full-disk images of the planets obtained in the modern era of interplanetary exploration.

Eight colorful stamps, each shown twice, feature Mercury, Venus, Earth, Mars, Jupiter, Saturn, Uranus and Neptune. Some show the planets' "true color"—what we might see with our own eyes if traveling through space. Others use colors to represent and visualize certain features of a planet based on imaging data. Still others use the near-infrared spectrum to show things that cannot be seen in visible light.

Text on the back of the stamp pane explains what these images reveal and identifies the spacecraft and powerful telescopes that helped obtain them.

Antonio Alcalá was the art director and designer of the stamps.

Issued Tuesday, May 31—
Science Meets Stamps Day

169

Pluto—Explored!

In 1991, to celebrate the exploration of our solar system, the Postal Service issued a set of ten commemorative stamps. Eight of the planets, plus our Moon, were shown in detailed color images, complemented by illustrations of the space probes that had visited them.

The tenth stamp pictured a fuzzy, pinkish-white blob in the inky blackness of space—our best image to date of what was then regarded as the ninth planet. It bore the inscription "Pluto: Not Yet Explored."

In 2006, NASA placed one of these 29¢ Pluto stamps in its New Horizons spacecraft just before it was launched on a six-year voyage to visit Pluto. Ironically, that same year the International Astronomical Union downgraded Pluto to the status of dwarf planet—but the mission continued just the same. In 2015, the spacecraft zipped past Pluto and continued on towards the outer solar system.

With this stamp, the Postal Service recognizes the historic first reconnaissance of Pluto.

"The New Horizons project is proud to have such an important honor from the U.S. Postal Service," said Alan Stern, New Horizons lead scientist from the Southwest Research Institute in Boulder, CO. "Since the early 1990s, the old 'Pluto Not Yet Explored' stamp served as a rallying cry for many who wanted to mount this historic mission of space exploration. Now that NASA's New Horizons has accomplished that goal, it's a wonderful feeling to see these new stamps join others commemorating first explorations of the planets."

The souvenir sheet of four "Forever" stamps contains two new stamps appearing twice. The first shows an artists' rendering of the New Horizons spacecraft and the second shows the spacecraft's image of Pluto taken near its closest approach.

The view, which is color-enhanced to highlight surface texture and composition, is a composite of four images from New Horizons Long Range Reconnaissance Imager (LORRI), combined with color data from the imaging instrument Ralph that clearly reveals the now-famous heart-shaped feature.

Antonio Alcalá was the art director.

Classics Forever

Issued in celebration of the long history of U.S. postage stamps—and in appreciation of stamp collectors and philatelists everywhere—this souvenir sheet features new versions of six of America's earliest and most alluring stamps, now issued as Forever® stamp to make them easily distinguishable from the mid-19th-century originals. Art director Antonio Alcalá designed the issue and Eric Madsen created the selvage artwork. *Issued Wednesday, June 1—United States Stamp Day.*

Issued Tuesday, May 31—Science Meets Stamps Day

National Park Service Centennial

This miniature sheet of 16 stamps honors the timeless beauty of one of America's greatest public resources, our National Park system, with a mix of stunning photography and paintings.

The National Park Service, established through the efforts of visionary leaders including John Muir, Theodore Roosevelt and Stephen T. Mather, today manages a range of cultural sites including monuments, parkways, battlefields, cemeteries, and recreation areas. This rich variety has created a portfolio of over 390 parks, all with their own special contribution to the American story.

The 16 stamps use both horizontal and vertical formats to showcase their subjects. The featured parks are:
- Glacier Bay National Park and Preserve, Alaska
- Mount Rainier National Park, Washington
- Marsh-Billings-Rockefeller National Historical Park, Vermont
- Acadia National Park, Maine
- Grand Canyon National Park, Arizona
- Assateague Island National Seashore, Maryland
- San Francisco Maritime National Historical Park, California
- Arches National Park, Utah
- Theodore Roosevelt National Park, North Dakota
- Kenilworth Park and Aquatic Gardens, District of Columbia
- Bandelier National Monument, New Mexico
- Everglades National Park, Florida
- Haleakalā National Park, Hawai'i
- Yellowstone National Park, Wyoming
- Carlsbad Caverns National Park, New Mexico
- Gulf Islands National Seashore, Mississippi and Florida

Ethel Kessler of Bethesda, Md. was the art director.

Issued Thursday, June 2nd—Beautiful Americas Day & United Nations Day

Colorful Celebrations

This booklet of 20 Forever stamps includes 10 digitally created designs with eye-popping patterns that showcase geometric shapes, flowers, and birds. The stamp designs come in one of four colors: teal, orange, purple, and magenta. They are intended to send a cheerful, celebratory message for any kind of event, at any time of year.

Atzin Gaytan, the illustrator of these stamps, was inspired by the intricate art form known in Spanish as "papel picado", or pierced paper. It was originally developed in Mexico, but is now also popular in the United States and around the world. Crafted with sharp tools and layers of tissue paper, papel picado designs often include birds, flowers and, traditionally, religious iconography. The elaborate decorations are hung during holidays, weddings, birthdays, and other festivities.

Sally Andersen-Bruce designed the stamps and Derry Noyes served as the project's art director.

Issued Friday, June 3rd—Children of the World Day

172

Official Cachets

THE EIGHT CACHETS DEPICTED BELOW, designed by Chris Calle, are available throughout the show for those wishing to prepare First Day Covers of the new stamps being issued at World Stamp Show–NY 2016. They are available either plain or serviced with stamps and cancellations.

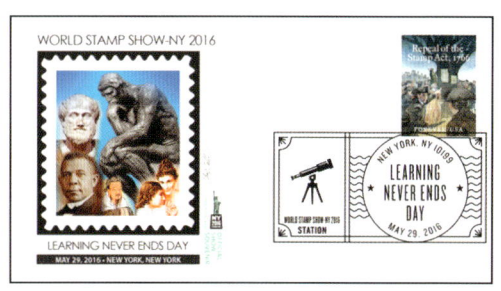

173

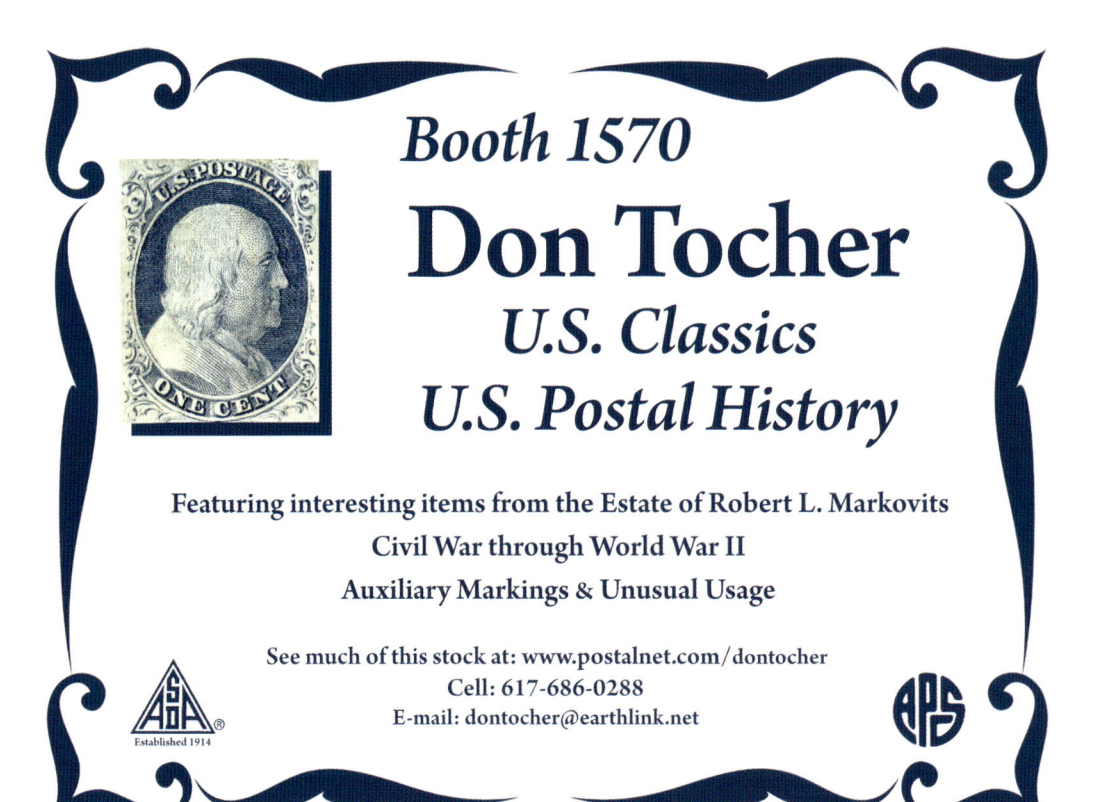

— FOR THE BEST OF BRITISH —
(stamps that is) go to the official website of

COLLECTORS EXCHANGE
www.BritishStampsAmerica.com

Visit us at Booth 757

*Buying & Selling STAMPS & POSTAL HISTORY
of Great Britain and the British Family of Nations*

We also stock Worldwide Topicals

1814A Edgewater Drive, Orlando, FL 32804
Phone: 407-620-0908

GREAT BRITAIN — GREAT BUYS!

Proud Member of Leading Philatelic Societies

Booth 1570
Don Tocher
U.S. Classics
U.S. Postal History

Featuring interesting items from the Estate of Robert L. Markovits
Civil War through World War II
Auxiliary Markings & Unusual Usage

See much of this stock at: www.postalnet.com/dontocher
Cell: 617-686-0288
E-mail: dontocher@earthlink.net

ASDA Established 1914

APS

ePost shop

www.posta.hr

With one click to the stamp!

We are presenting you our ePost shop, a new web page of Croatian Post aimed at philately fans. From now on you can search, see and buy Croatian postage stamps, albums, stamp collections, postcards and other products from our rich philatelic assortment directly from the comfort of your home.

Croatian Post Inc., Jurišićeva 13, HR-10000 Zagreb, Croatia
E-mail: filatelija@posta.hr
www.epostshop.hr

France International Stamps By Themes
Booths 569–571

Your best source for thematic philately. Over 30 years in business.

Original artwork, die proofs, trial colors, illustrated stationery, fancy cancels, specimens, errors, imperforates, deluxe sheets, meter cancels, maximum cards and much more.
Special show discounts.
Also view more than 30,000 items online at our website **www.stampsbythemes.com**

Contact information: PO Box 580, Gibsonia, PA 15044
E-mail: stamps@salsgiver.com • Phone: 724-443-8580 • Fax: 724-443-8599

Monaco artist proof — Jules Verne 20,000 Leagues under the Sea

Fancy cancel from Buffalo, Indiana.

Artwork from North Korea — Nautilus

What is the FIP?

THE FÉDÉRATION INTERNATIONALE DE PHILATÉLIE— or, to use the English variant of its name, the Federation of International Philately—isn't a club you can join. It is more like the United Nations of stamp collecting: a federation of 92 countries, represented by the primary national stamp organizations in each one. In the United States, for example, the FIP has one member, the American Philatelic Society (APS).

Each year, the FIP sponsors one or two international stamp exhibitions around the world. Because World Stamp Show–NY 2016 has been formally recognized by the FIP, the prizes and awards won by exhibitors competing here will be internationally recognized, and will count towards qualification for future competitions.

Peter P. McCann, RDP, is a past president of the American Philatelic Society, has served on the FIP board for the past 12 years, and is the president of the Jury of NY 2016. Here, he answers some questions about the role of the FIP.

What is its role at World Stamp Show–NY2016?

As a member of the FIP, the APS asked it nine years ago to grant patronage for an exhibition in New York in 2016. The Congress of FIP granted the request and appointed an FIP board member to act as a coordinating liaison between FIP and the organizing committee of World Stamp Show–NY 2016.

The role of the FIP before and during the exhibition is to help select the jury and to ensure international standards of choosing and judging competitive exhibits. The FIP has no role in any other aspect of the exhibition and is not involved in the finances.

Where did the FIP come from?

The FIP was founded in 1926. It grew from a primarily European-based organization in the first part of the 20th century to a worldwide organization today. Individual collectors cannot be members—only countries.

There is an FIP Congress held every two years, always at the end of a major world exhibition to minimize travel costs. At the Congress, all 92 countries meet to discuss and vote on any issues or resolutions put forward by member federations or by the FIP Board, which manages the organization on a day-to-day basis.

The FIP Board is comprised of seven members: two from each continent which has FIP members—Europe, the Americas, and Asia-Oceania—and a president, who can be from any continent. (Africa has two active members, South Africa and Egypt, which both group themselves with Asia). The current president, Tay Peng Hian, is from Singapore.

The FIP is a very small organization. Besides the seven board members, there is a full-time Secretary-General based in Switzerland. That's it.

What is the mission of the FIP? What does it do to promote philately in different countries, and how does it work with postal administrations?

The FIP's annual budget is small—much less than that of the APS, for example—so its activities to promote stamp collecting are limited to representing global philately in an official capacity. The FIP sits on several committees organized through the Universal Postal Union—which is part of the United Nations—in Basel, Switzerland. Often, FIP representatives are invited to participate in other meetings and conferences around the world, but such costs must be covered by the inviting party.

What does the FIP do to keep the future of philately vibrant?

The FIP has ten technical committees, called commissions, which represent the major collecting and exhibiting disciplines represented in exhibitions: Traditional, Postal History, Thematics, Aerophilately, Revenues, Postal Stationery, Youth, Literature, Astrophilately, and Maximaphily.

The boards running these commissions are made up of volunteers who are nominated and elected by the FIP members. The commissions are composed of philatelic exhibitors and jurors from all over the world and are extremely active, doing most of their work via email and at the bi-annual meetings at the FIP Congress.

By examining and testing new exhibiting ideas and trends, and turning them into formal concepts to be used by exhibitors and FIP judges, these commissions help ensure that organized philately remains in touch with and responsive to the needs of the collecting community around the world.

Pair of stamps issued by Saint-Pierre and Miquelon in 2014, honoring the Large Gold award won by native son Jean-Jacques Tillard at the FIP-sponsored exhibition in Thailand the year before as well as the Federacion Interamericana de Filatelia (FIAF) exhibition hosted by the islands that year. Tillard's prize-winning exhibit covered 19th-century surcharges on French stamps for use in the North Atlantic colony.

The American Philatelic Society

SUSTAINABILITY AND PASSION: These are two of the most enduring traits that drive the hobby of philately.

Stamps—from those costing mere pennies to rarities that only the wealthiest can afford—start with the purpose of moving documents across the world but also satisfy our inner need to grasp hold of a small piece of that world. These tiny, colorful slips of paper and the envelopes and documents they are attached to connect us to history, geography, art, technology, culture and more.

"The collecting of stamps brings untold millions of people of all nations into greater understanding of their world neighbors," said Francis Cardinal Spellman in 1972, while laying the foundation stone at the museum that bears his name in Weston, Massachusetts.

Since its founding in 1886 by 219 collectors, the American Philatelic Society has given collectors a community, and the hobby its esteemed status and professionalism.

Today the APS, with nearly 32,000 members worldwide, is one of the hobby's most important and viable societies, with modern facilities,

AMERICA'S STAMP CLUB
STAMPS.ORG

The American Philatelic Society booth at a 1926 collectors' convention.

Interior of the 19th-century Headsville, W.V. post office, on permanent display at the American Philatelic Center.

One of the most popular APS benefits is the circuit-book system, allowing members to buy and sell on approval from the comfort of home.

resources and paid staff, as well as the incomparable American Philatelic Research Library (APRL). Yet many of the services first offered 130 years ago remain cornerstones for which members gladly pay annual dues. These include:

- A code of ethics by which members are admitted and retained.
- An annual convention that includes two major stamp events: the summertime StampShow, the nation's largest yearly philatelic gathering, and wintertime AmeriStamp Expo. Both bring together dealers, seminars, workshops, society meetings, and exhibits. The APS also works closely with about 30 regional shows in a network called the World Series of Philately.
- The mail-order Circuit Sales Division and internet-based StampStore, which together move about $2 million of merchandise a year. All items sold are from APS members. Only APS members can buy from Circuit Sales books; the public can buy from StampStore, although APS members receive a discount.
- An Expertizing Division, with paid staff and more than 100 volunteers using top forensic techniques.
- A monthly journal, *The American Philatelist*, dating to 1887, and the APRL quarterly, the *Philatelic Literature Review*.
- A collection insurance program.
- Educational opportunities for youth and adults: seminars and workshops at stamp shows and online; a weeklong Summer Seminar on Philately at APS headquarters; a nationwide educational program for youths; youth areas at stamp shows; the All-Star Stamp Club; and a Young Philatelic Leaders Fellowship.
- Five hundred local chapters and 195 affiliate societies that bring APS benefits to specialty areas.
- Web-based reference material; a translation service; a dealer directory; a repository of literature, exhibits and postal artifacts; and free stamp album pages.

APS Executive Director Scott English says, "The original purpose of the APS remains central to what we do today: create a safe place for collectors to buy and sell stamps. Through education efforts, research, and sales and expertizing, we continue to protect the investments of collectors and promote a great hobby."

Janet Klug, a former APS president, author and exhibitor, explains the sustaining appeal of the hobby in her Guide to Stamp Collecting (2008): "You can collect stamps because they are beautiful, historically important, illustrate something that appeals to you, are a connection to the past, or any other reason that strikes your fancy."

APS Basics

The American Philatelic Society is the largest stamp collecting organization in the world with nearly 32,000 members. Founded in 1886, for the last 70 years it has been headquartered in and around State College, Pennsylvania.

The American Philatelic Research Library was incorporated in 1968 and serves as the library and archives for the APS. The non-profit educational organizations are associated, but are directed by separate boards of trustees.

Since 2004, the two organizations have been housed at the American Philatelic Center in Bellefonte, Pa. at a renovated complex that was a match factory from 1899 to 1947.

The center, which is on the National Register of Historic Places, includes 100,000 sq. ft. of space in 18 buildings on about six acres of land. The societies have spent $16 million renovating the property, of which nearly half is leased to other tenants.

The latest renovations at the center—a new, $3.5 million state-of-the-art space for the APRL—has just been completed, more than doubling the library's original space.

Between them, the APS and APRL have 30 paid staff members and about 15 volunteers who are regularly on site.

Cover of a recent issue of the American Philatelist, the APS monthly magazine for members.

American Philatelic Society
100 Match Factory Place
Bellefonte, PA 16823

Open 8:00–4:30, business days

814-933-3803

apsinfo@stamps.org
www.stamps.org

Tours are available afternoons. Please call ahead to ensure availability.

The American Philatelic Center, home of the APS and APRL, occupies a converted 19th-century match factory in Bellefonte, Pa.

Interesting artifacts

American Philatelic Research Library
STAMPLIBRARY.ORG

BESIDES THEIR ACTIVITIES IN SALES, education, research, exhibiting and expertizing, the APS and APRL have acquired several interesting philatelic artifacts over the decades, now on display in newly renovated spaces. Here are some of the many good reasons to visit Bellefonte, PA:

- An entire 19th-century rural post office and general store is housed within the American Philatelic Center. The former Headsville, W.V. wooden building has been on loan from the Smithsonian's Museum of American History since 2008 and operates as a contract post office. The building, a post office from 1860 to 1914, was the model for the 1972 U.S. 8¢ Mail Order Centennial stamp.
- The oldest known presidential free frank, a letter George Washington signed in May, 1789 to receive free postage just three weeks after he became president. It was donated to the APS in 2013.
- An Inverted Jenny, part of a block of four once belonging to Ethel McCoy, stolen at a stamp show in 1955 and recovered in 1977.
- A 1729 post map, showing postal routes in New England and adjoining colonies, that predates the United States. It was produced by Herman Moll and includes text descriptions of the routes.

A 1729 postal map, showing postal routes in New England and adjoining colonies

The American Philatelic Research Library

WHEN BRITAIN ISSUED THE WORLD'S FIRST postage stamp in 1840, it's doubtful that anyone could have foreseen that this humble piece of paper would launch a hobby enjoyed by millions worldwide.

Within 20 years, most countries were issuing their own postage stamps and there were tens of thousands of collectors around the world. As the number of stamp-issuing entities increased, the one thing collectors sought even more eagerly than stamps themselves was information.

The first stamp catalog appeared in France in 1861 and the first dedicated philatelic journal in Britain the following year.

Today, the American Philatelic Research Library is considered one of the philatelic world's most valuable resources, with 23,000 book titles and 6,000 journal titles on more than three miles of shelving: catalogs, general books on philately, monographs on single subjects, glossy magazines, specialist journals, dictionaries, government publications, indexes and unpublished notes and correspondences.

Much of the APRL's collection has arrived via donations over the decades, sometime just a volume or two, sometimes many box loads. This includes donations from the Boston Philatelic Society, William Reynolds Ricketts, and, in 2015, from the estate of George A. Atkins, weighing in at 7,000 pounds.

The nearly 32,000 American Philatelic Society members can use the library either on-site or long distance, with the aid of APRL Librarian Tara Murray and other staff members. Collections can be searched via the APS website and stamplibrary.org.

In the spring of 2016, the library moved to an airy, 19,500-sq.ft. space located on two floors of a historic, converted factory building at the American Philatelic Center in Bellefonte, Pa.

"The new library will provide visitors a more flexible and comfortable space to browse and research," noted Murray.

"It will also allow our staff and volunteers to provide better library services to researchers around the world and to carry out digitization, preservation, and indexing projects."

There is secure storage for the library's rare and unique collections, much-needed work space and a used-book and gift shop. A dedication is planned for Oct. 29, 2016.

From thin Scott catalogs of the 1890s to the modern ones compiling the world's stamps in six volumes (weighing over 50 pounds); from the eight

The Inverted Jenny, position 65 from the original sheet of 100, displayed at the library. It was once part of the block belonging to Ethel McCoy that was stolen in 1955.

The library's new, state-of-the-art interior.

volumes of *Cuba Filatelica* (1905) in Spanish to the *Western Stamp Collector* journal of the 1950s; from century-old auction catalogs to the newest from the most recent sales; from hundreds of government documents, such as the *U.S. Postal Bulletin* and *Domestic Mail Manual* to the private papers of famous philatelists of the past, visitors can find it all.

Special collections include the likes of the Daniel Hines airmail archives, which document pioneer U.S. air mail service; the Belmont Faries and John Stark files, which document U.S. stamp design and production of the 1950s–80s; and the Czeslaw Slania Collection, devoted to the work of the Polish-Swedish engraver.

Those who use the library are usually pleased.

Ken Lawrence, a widely respected philatelic writer who lives half an hour from the library, is one frequent user. He has collected and exhibited in areas as diverse as political protest material, Walt Disney topicals, Nazi Holocaust mail, plate number coils and the First Nesbitt Issue stamped envelopes of 1853-60.

He says his links to the APS and APRL have been vital.

"I began philatelic writing in 1983," Lawrence said. "When I lived in Mississippi, the APRL supplied references by mail, which was cumbersome."

He moved to Pennsylvania and became a more frequent user of the library. Access to Elliott Perry's correspondence in the archives enabled Lawrence's American Philatelic Congress Book article "The One-Cent Z Grill Mystery," while Ernest Kehr's files made possible articles on stamps and postal history of the independent Trucial States.

"I have written about every U.S. philatelic controversy, none of which would have been possible without those APRL resources, " Lawrence says.

Charles Posner, of England, is a newcomer to the APRL.

"I am a collector," said Posner, a University of London professor. "But I have become a writer largely to fill a void in our understanding of modern American postage stamps."

Though he collects Burma, France and the U.S. 3¢ Locomotive stamp of 1869 on cover, Posner is researching and writing a series of articles about U.S. stamp issues of the 1950s. His stories cover every stamp from concept to finished product, including proponents, politics, rejected designs, production, first-day ceremonies and controversies.

"I have had to do research in many libraries, like the British Library and the Bibliothèque Nationale in France, but never have I had the interest and support I receive from the APRL," Posner said. "The librarian goes the extra mile, as do the others on the staff."

CAMPAIGN FOR PHILATELY
Building for our PAST • PRESENT • FUTURE

2016 is a very important year for the American Philatelic Society. With your help, we can build on the 130-year legacy that has made the APS the flagship of the philatelic community.

A great way to start this exciting journey is to make a donation today. Even better, make a donation on behalf of a friend, a loved one, or someone you admire. You can also include a message to share your love of the hobby.

Your generous tax-deductible contribution will keep us building for our past, our present, and our future.

Building for the Past
The library is almost complete, bringing together the largest collection of philatelic research under one roof. Join us on October 29 to celebrate the opening. To donate, visit stamps.org/Library-Donations.

Building for the Present
APS joins the world collecting community in New York City for World Stamp Show-NY 2016. What better way to celebrate our birthday in September but to remind the world why the APS has been a leader for 130 years. To donate, visit **stamps.org/donate**.

Building for the Future
The Campaign for Philately begins a new effort to keep the APS a force for the hobby well into the future by growing our education programs for all collectors, increasing access to our philatelic resources in an ever-shrinking world, and attracting current and future collectors to join us in the mission.
stamps.org/userfiles/file/reports/Draft-StrategicPlan2016.pdf.

STAMPS.ORG/DONATE

American Philatelic Society
American Philatelic Research Library
100 Match Factory Place, Bellefonte, PA 16823
Phone: 814-933-3803 • Fax: 814-933-6128
E-mail: scott@stamps.org

American Philatelic Research Library

AMERICA'S STAMP CLUB

APS STAMP SHOWS 2016–2019

The American Philatelic Society's AmeriStamp and StampShow events have locations set through 2019. Attend the two largest annual stamp shows in the United States. Locations have been finalized for Oregon, Nevada, Virginia, Alabama, Ohio, and Nebraska. Show highlights include: public auctions, exhibits and rare stamp displays, meetings and seminars, stamp dealers and cachetmakers, a Stamp Zone for children, and more.

AMERICAN PHILATELIC SOCIETY STAMPSHOW
PORTLAND, OR
AUGUST 4–7, 2016

AMERICAN PHILATELIC SOCIETY AMERISTAMP
RENO, NEVADA
MARCH 3–5, 2017

AMERICAN PHILATELIC SOCIETY STAMPSHOW
RICHMOND, VA
AUGUST 3–6, 2017

AMERICAN PHILATELIC SOCIETY STAMPSHOW
OMAHA, NE
AUGUST 1–4, 2019

AMERICAN PHILATELIC SOCIETY STAMPSHOW
COLUMBUS, OHIO
AUGUST 9–12, 2018

AMERICAN PHILATELIC SOCIETY AMERISTAMP
BIRMINGHAM, AL
FEB. 23–25, 2018

STAMPS.ORG/STAMP-EXPO
STAMPS.ORG/STAMPSHOW

APS Shows and Exhibitions
100 Match Factory Place, Bellefonte, PA 16823
Phone: 814-933-3803, ext. 217 • Fax: 814-933-6128
E-mail: stampshow@stamps.org

AMERICAN PHILATELIC SOCIETY EST. 1886
AMERICA'S STAMP CLUB

The Philatelic Foundation Authenticates the Real McCoy!

ON MONDAY, APRIL 4, 2016, a representative of a leading rare stamp auction house, brought an enigmatic Inverted Jenny to The Philatelic Foundation's New York offices for authentication on behalf of a potential consignor.

The stamp appeared genuine, but it didn't match any known examples and the telltale penciled number on the back was missing.

The PF's experience and expertise in authenticating this iconic United States rarity is unrivaled. The Foundation has issued Certificates of Authenticity for 84 of the 100 stamps from the original sheet of the "upside down airplane stamp"—including all six of the existing blocks.

The PF's staff immediately began the expertization process, led by Executive Director Larry Lyons and Curator Lewis Kaufman. After careful examination to rule out forgery, the stamp—referred to as a "patient"—was matched against the PF's detailed records, photos and electronic scans of all the known inverts.

Despite signs of tampering, the evidence quickly pointed to the possibility that the patient was one of the two missing stamps from a famous block of four Jenny inverts, previously owned by Ethel McCoy, that had been stolen from its exhibition frame in 1955 during an American Philatelic Society convention in Norfolk, Virginia.

The long-lost position 76 Inverted Jenny, certified by the Philatelic Foundation on April 12, 2016.

The PF staff certified the patient as position 76 from the error sheet of 100—the lower right stamp from the McCoy block. At some time following the block's theft, it had been broken into four singles, each altered to disguise its identity as a stolen stamp. Upon close examination, position 76 was found to have been reperforated at its left side to remove traces of the vertical red guide line from the tips of its original perforations, and had a portion of the gum and identifying number removed from the back.

The American Philatelic Society and law enforcement were immediately notified of the identification of this long lost Jenny invert as the Real McCoy!

Collect with confidence—with a PF certificate.

The Philatelic Foundation
341 West 38th Street, 5th floor
New York, NY 10018
Tel. 212-221-6555
www.philatelicfoundation.org
philatelicfoundation@verizon.net

The Philatelic Foundation

Images from the website of Foster+Freeman, makers of the video spectral comparator, showing the famous British Guiana One Cent Magenta in both natural and infrared light.

The unique plate-number block of the Inverted Jenny error of 1918, certified genuine by the PF.

THE PHILATELIC FOUNDATION IS A not-for-profit educational organization established in New York in 1945. Since its beginnings, the foundation's most important role has been to issue certificates of authenticity for stamps and covers.

A PF certificate is one of the most widely accepted ways of establishing confidence in the genuineness of a valuable stamp or cover. With over 70 years of experience, and having issued over half a million certificates, the PF is recognized as the leading philatelic expertizing authority in the United States.

Its staff of in-house experts are lifelong collectors with many years of professional experience. They have ready access to the PF's world-wide reference collection of 240 volumes of stamps and covers as well as to a comprehensive research library filling over 1,000 feet of shelving.

The PF is also the only expert body in the United States with high-tech equipment to assist in the review process, including a video spectral comparator (VSC6000) and an x-ray spectrometer (Bruker XRF).

The VSC6000 uses high definition magnification, different wave lengths of light, and the application of direct light in a variety of modes. This device, on display at World Stamp Show–NY 2016, assists in confirming faults and repairs to both stamps and covers.

The Bruker XRF helps determine the elements of ink used to print stamps. It has proven invaluable to correctly identifying certain stamp issues of similar color but with inks of very different composition.

The PF has digitized a large portion of its database of certificates and made them available online to the collecting community through the PF Search feature on its website at philatelicfoundation.org

The PF has expertized 84 examples of the 24¢ Inverted Jenny—more than anyone else—including one of the most iconic pieces in all of United States philately: the unique plate block, which was issued PF Certificate No. 431538, stating "it is genuine."

In support of its educational mission, the PF website offers a wide variety of PF books, pamphlets and articles published over the years, all of which can be downloaded free. The most recent title in the PF's acclaimed *Opinions* book series is *Hawaii Foreign Mail to 1870*, a three-volume Grand Award-winning work by Fred Gregory, available for purchase at NY 2016.

The U.S. Philatelic Classics Society

- The largest specialty group devoted to the classic issues of the U.S.
- The *Chronicle*, a 104-page full color journal issued 4 times each year, recognized as one of the leading philatelic journals in the world by winning First Prize in the CG International Philatelic Promotion competition in 2014.
- The digital, fully searchable *Web Chronicle* which includes all issues since we began in 1948.
- An unrivaled and state-of-the art website containing a vast amount of philatelic information, including searchable books, exhibits, censuses, and other archives.

Please stop at our Superbooth
(opposite the USPS booth)
and learn more about the USPCS.

www.uspcs.org

UNITED STATES STAMP SOCIETY

www.usstamps.org

The largest organization dedicated to the research and study of U.S. postage and revenue stamps.

Since 1930 *The United States Specialist* has been the leading journal for modern U. S. philately and postal history.

Publisher of the *Durland Standard Plate Number Catalog* and *The Encyclopedia of United States Stamps and Stamp Collecting*

Outstanding website including the searchable *Specialist*, Research Papers, Publications, Philatelic Resources, and Exhibits

Visit us at our Superbooth #736

(Opposite the USPS booth)

A Brand New Stage for U.S. Stamps

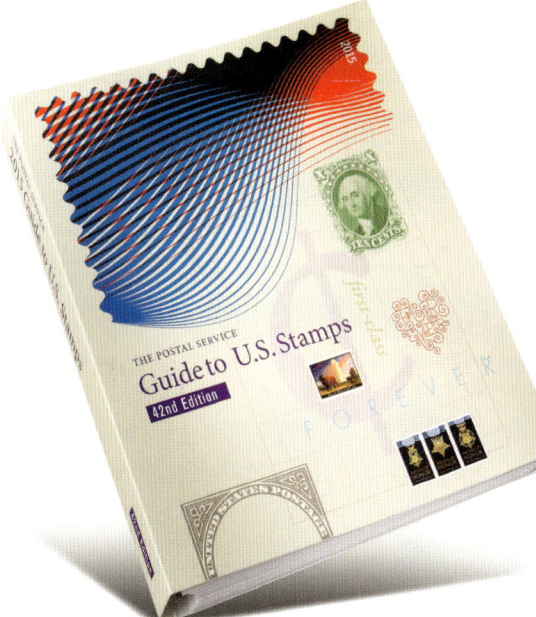

Up-to-date with recent stamp releases, high-quality images, and meticulous attention to detail, the 42nd edition of the *Postal Service™ Guide to U.S. Stamps* is every philatelist's friend. Collectors— beginners, experts, and everyone in between— are invited to enjoy and devour decades of philatelic features.

Available for $39.95 at
usps.com/SHOP or call
1-800-782-6724
Item# 891500

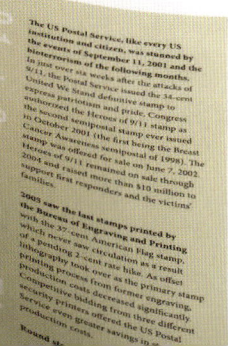

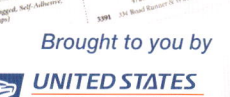

Brought to you by
UNITED STATES POSTAL SERVICE

The Collectors Club: Some notes on our heritage

By K. David Steidley, Ph.D.

THE SUMMER OF 1896 in New York City was the hottest in history and the number of heat stroke deaths was alarming Police Commissioner Theodore Roosevelt. It certainly wasn't improving the mood of 51-year-old John W Scott, America's premier stamp dealer, as he scurried about town to organize a private men's club for philatelists.

Nevertheless, by October 5 he was done and "The Collectors Club" had their first meeting in their newly rented house at 351 4th Avenue, now Park Avenue South, near 25th Street.

Alas, that building is no more. The Club had a library in a closet but a really spacious billiards room with a fine cigar assortment.

One hundred members had been persuaded to buy a $25 share in this new corporation. Sixty-six had New York metropolitan addresses while thirty-three more were scattered throughout the United States. There was one international member in Shanghai, China. Today we have 127 international members from 34 countries.

Scott and his cadre had recruited the cream of American philately for the Club. The names of many of the dealers and collectors are well known 120 years later: John Luff, Henry Duveen, Ernest Ackerman, Henry Crooker, Hiram Deats, Charles Mekeel, J.V. Painter, George Worthington, J.M. Bartels and many others.

The Roaring Twenties were a renaissance period for the Club as it once again reached a membership of one hundred under the leadership of collectors such as Alfred F. Lichtenstein and Theodore Steinway. The Club had changed locations six times by then and now had a fine library but no billiards room. Women collectors began to join in 1922 as the first issues of the *Collectors Club Philatelist* rolled of the presses under the editorship of Harry Lindquist.

Franklin D. Roosevelt joined in 1926 but his physical handicap and hectic schedule prevented his attendance at meetings. By 1930, membership was at about 700 and the Club was internationally known and respected for its scholarly approach to philately.

Needing a permanent home, the Club was able to purchase the former residence of a major art dealer, Thomas B. Clarke, for $36,600 in 1937. This fine old five story structure at 22 East 35th Street had been glamorized and modernized in 1902 by the famed architect Stanford White. After

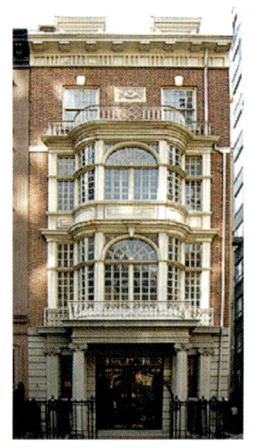

The Collectors Club at 22 East 35th Street.

Monaco stamp featuring Roosevelt collecting stamps with six fingers on his left hand.

A stock certificate from the Collector's Club.

Franklin D. Roosevelt's application to the club.

some modest improvements by the architect-collector Clarence W. Blazer in late 1937, this house has continued to serve us well for over 75 years.

Under President Thomas Mazza, the house was structurally rehabilitated and important modernizations were made in the early 2000s. This year, the house is again getting a facelift inside and out.

The modern era has seen the Club continue its tradition of important publications, displays of major and unique collections (now posted as videos on the web at CollectorsClub.org) and support of organized philately such as its co-sponsorship, with seed money and talent, of World Stamp Show–NY 2016.

The club's leadership foresees a great future for stamp collecting and are always looking for new members who have an intense interest in this hobby.

Kay & Company
Booth 1065

We have an extensive stock of mint British Commonwealth sets & singles, 1840–1952

More than 10,000 listings at
kaystamps.com

Kay & Company
P. O. Box 5545 • Bend, OR 97708
Phone/Fax: 541 312-4263
E-mail: kayandco@msn.com

APS • ASDA • PTS

PostalStationery.com
Philip & Henry Stevens

P. O. Box 1006
Alton, NH 03809
603.875.5550
const@tds.net

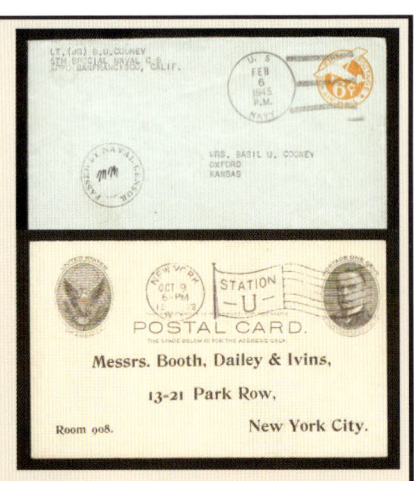

BOOTH 665

U275

U145

American Stamp Dealers Association, Inc.
Established 1914

ASDA Online
americanstampdealer.com

The ASDA website features:
- About the ASDA
- ASDA Member List • Find a Dealer
- Guide to Buying & Selling
- ASDA-Sponsored Stamp Shows
- Stamp Shows
- ASDA Hall of Fame
- General Articles • Dealer Articles
- Revenue Articles
- Confederate Articles
- Auction Calendar
- Collecting Interests
- Contact Us • And More!

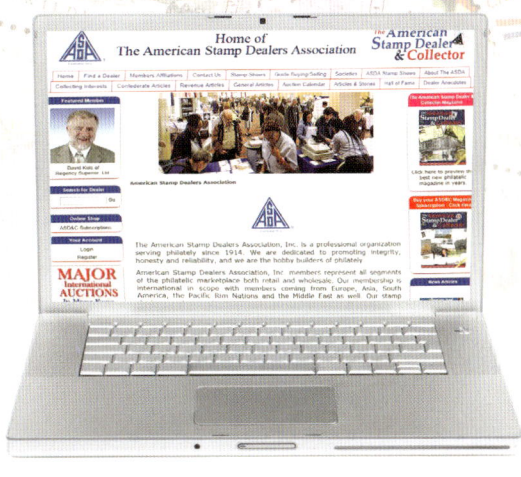

Looking for a dealer in your area?
Visit our website and
select "Find a Dealer"

Subscribe!

The American Stamp Dealer & Collector

America's Best Stamp Magazine!

10 printed issues per year • 80 pages per issue
Prior issues available to current subscribers
Online version only available for
$9.95 for 1 year, $17.95 for 2 years

View a sample copy and subscribe at AmericanStampDealer.com
or call 800-369-8207, select ext. 1 for subscription

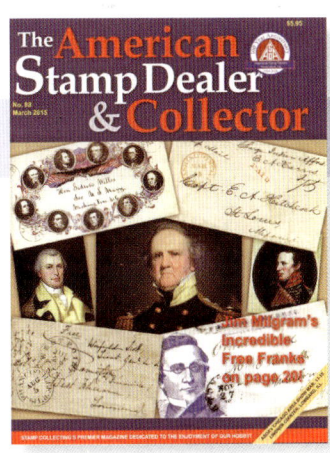

U.S. Rates
$21.95 for 1 year
$37.95 for 2 years

Foreign Rates
$61.95 for 1 year
$117.95 for 2 years

Jenny and the birth of air mail

THE FIRST THING to grab the attention of most visitors to World Stamp Show–NY 2016 would be the airplane in the atrium.

The Curtiss JN-4, a World War I-era biplane, is a monument to early 20th-century American innovation and resourcefulness. It is the craft that launched one of the world's first successful air mail services, and would become known to millions of stamp collectors and members of the general public alike as the "upside-down airplane".

Thousands of the JN-4 aircraft—nicknamed the "Jenny" since its earliest days—were manufactured in several variants for the United States Army and Navy by the Curtiss Aeroplane and Motor Company in and around Buffalo, N.Y., in 1916 and 1917. The aircraft was so successful that it was adopted by the militaries of several countries, including Britain, Canada, Argentina, Brazil, Cuba and China.

The restored, working Curtiss JN-4H on display at World Stamp Show–NY 2016 spends most summer weekends wowing audiences at

Trial color proof of a Chinese airmail stamp of 1921, showing a Curtiss JN-4, or "Jenny," flying over the Great Wall. Image courtesy the Smithsonian's National Postal Museum.

Weekend air shows at the Old Rhinebeck Aerodrome, north of New York City, feature a wide variety of restored, vintage aircraft. Image courtesy ORA.

Color-lithographed labels from a set of 18 produced by Curtiss to advertise its JN model biplane. Air mail contractors in Colombia converted some of the labels in this series into postage stamps in 1920 by overprinting them "Compañia Colombiana de Navegacion Aerea" and a value of 10 centavos.

vintage-aircraft shows at Old Rhinebeck Aerodrome in Dutchess County, N.Y., about two hours' drive north of New York City. The aerodrome graciously agreed to loan the plane for exhibition at the stamp show in return for a generous financial donation from Robert A. Siegel Auction Galleries of New York and the show's organizers.

During the pioneer air mail era, from 1910 to 1916, Curtiss gained attention as one of many aircraft makers trying to demonstrate the viability of carrying the post by air. The last of the so-called pioneer flights took place in a Curtiss Model R-7 biplane in late 1916.

Sponsored by The New York Times, the aviator Victor Carlstrom left Chicago on Nov. 2 of that year on an attempted non-stop flight to New York. Engine trouble forced him to land in Erie, Pa. and again in Hammondsport, N.Y., but he safely reached Governor's Island in New York harbor the following day, having set an American distance record of 452 miles on his first leg. Mail carried on Carlstrom's flight is prized by collectors of pioneer airmail memorabilia.

It was the Curtiss model JN, however, that convinced the U.S. Post Office Department of the viability of regularly scheduled "aerial mail" service. This was kicked off with much haste and fanfare on the morning of May 15, 1918, when two Jenny planes took off from Washington and New York, flying toward each other.

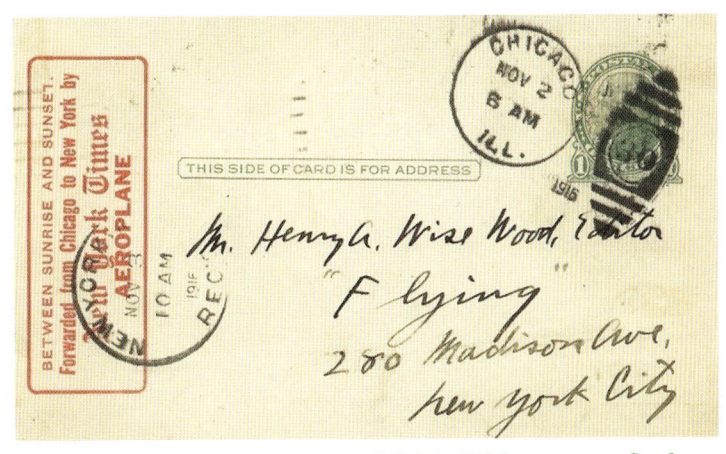

Postal card flown on the last pioneer air mail flight in 1916. Image courtesy Don Jones.

195

Each of the two-seaters carried a mail bag in the front with a pilot in the rear. Most of the letters were franked with the brand new, bi-colored 24¢ stamp hurriedly issued for the event. The stamp covered 2¢ postage, 12¢ air mail and 10¢ special delivery fee.

In the rush to prepare the new stamps in time, a few of the sheets were inadvertently printed with the airplane inverted in relation to its frame.

The stamps were printed on a hand-operated "spider" press at the Bureau of Engraving and Printing in Washington, D.C. The printing process required each sheet of paper to be few through the press twice, once for each color.

According to Scott R. Trepel, the president of the Siegel auction firm and an avid student of the stamp's history, the error might not necessarily have been the result of half-printed sheets being turned around, but of another, somewhat surprising happenstance.

To obtain the best results, the printers had to remove the printing plate from the press after each pass, reheat it, and put it back. It seems only natural that now and then, the hurried pressmen replaced it upside-down.

Only one sheet of 100 of the resulting error ever surfaced, but thanks to its all-American iconography and storied history, it is probably the most famous U.S. stamp ever issued. Pop-culture references to it abound, and it reliably fetches far more at auction than lesser-known stamps of comparable scarcity.

Though the actual Jenny used as a model for engraving America's first airmail stamp has been lost, the one at Rhinebeck is nearly identical. Its story, too, is worth retelling.

The Old Rhinebeck Aerodrome is a living museum of antique aviation, located in the historic town of Rhinebeck, N.Y. It holds one of the largest collections of early airplanes in the world, as well as automobiles, motorcycles, early engines and memorabilia spanning the period from 1900 to 1939.

At weekend air shows during summer months, the aerodrome turns back the hands of time and—weather permitting—relives the early years of aviation, bringing back that colorful era amidst the roar of rotary engines and thrill of watching

Cole Palen and his first Jenny. Image courtesy ORA.

delicate, hand-restored airplanes lift off into the blue yonder.

The aerodrome was founded by Cole Palen (1925-1993), a collector and lifelong aficionado of vintage aircraft.

Upon returning home from World War II, Palen entered the Roosevelt Aviation School at Roosevelt Field, Long Island, N.Y. to train as a mechanic. He was thrilled to discover a hangar full of vintage planes there, and when the airfield closed in 1951—to become a suburban shopping mall—Palen bid his life savings for them.

Somewhat to his surprise, he found himself the proud owner of a SPAD XIII, Avro 504K, Curtiss Jenny, Standard J-l, Aeromarine 39B and Sopwith Snipe. Given 30 days to remove the aircraft, he embarked on nine 200-mile round trips, towing the planes back to his family home, where they were stored at first in abandoned chicken coops.

On January 30, 1957, Palen received (by rail) 19 pieces of a wrecked aircraft from C.W. Adams, Jr. of Winter Haven, Fla. The aircraft had been advertised as a Standard J-1 but turned out to be an engine-less Curtiss JN-4H. No prior history was available for the airplane. Over the years, some of the missing original parts (wings, radiator) turned up, along with a 180-horsepower Hispano Suiza Model E engine, which was obtained from the Franklin Institute in Philadelphia, Pa.

Restoration of this Jenny began in 1967 and the aircraft was rebuilt from original parts and sections from other JN-4s. It is one of only three

Hisso-powered Jennys flying in the world today. It flew regularly at the aerodrome from 1969 through 1998; it was then stripped down for total restoration and returned to the skies in 2001.

Palen had begun conducting weekend air shows for the curious in 1960. His philosophy was that aircraft should not only be shown in their natural environment, but also provide a fun and entertaining day out for the whole family. His shows would include such zany melodramas as the daring Sir Percy Goodfellow doing battle with the Evil Black Baron for the hand of the lovely Trudy Truelove.

When faced with a mammoth restoration project, Palen's typical response would be "No problem, it'll fly." This would be followed by his trademark raucous laugh.

After Palen passed away in 1993, the aerodrome was transformed into a non-profit organization, run by a board of directors, and gradually expanded into what it is today.

Every summer, Saturday shows chronicle the history of flight, with pioneer-, World War I- and Lindbergh-era aircraft taking to the skies. If the air is calm, visitors are even treated to the 1909 Bleriot, the oldest flying aircraft in the United States, taking to the air. Sunday shows feature a World War I dogfight as well as barnstorming aircraft.

The Aerodrome also offers four museum buildings housing static displays of aircraft from these eras, which are open to the public seven days a week from June to October. Further information about the aerodrome, its programs and how to reach it are at www.oldrhinebeck.org

Instrument panel of the Old Rhinebeck Aerodrome's restored Jenny. Image courtesy ORA.

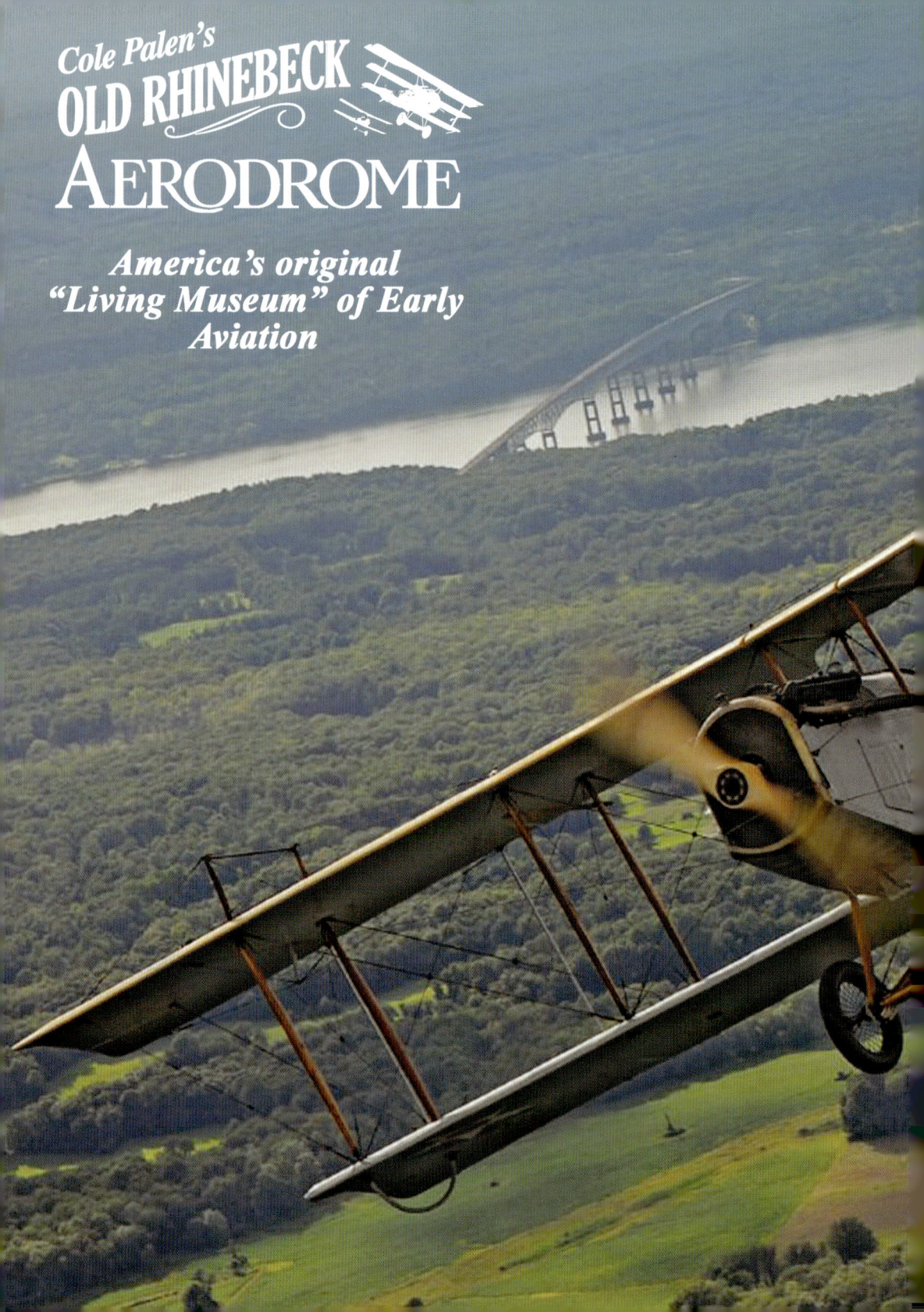

Cole Palen's OLD RHINEBECK AERODROME

America's original "Living Museum" of Early Aviation

The Old Rhinebeck Aerodrome's original 1918 Curtiss JN-4H "Jenny", above scenic Rhinebeck and the mighty Hudson River. The "Jenny" was used as a trainer during the First World War, and later as a mail-carrier and barnstorming aircraft through the 1920s. Photo: ©PhilipMakanna/GHOSTS

Just 100 miles North of New York City in beautiful Hudson Valley, scores of Antique Aircraft and Vintage Vehicles will transport you back in time to the early 1900s.

* Airshows Every Saturday & Sunday
(weather permitting) June 11 through October 9

* Museum open daily - May 14 through October 23

*Open-cockpit Biplane rides available

For more information please visit:
www.oldrhinebeck.org or call 845-752-3200

WALTER KASELL

Top Quality United States Stamps

• 19th Century Classics •
• 20th Century Gems •
• Mint & Used • Plate Blocks • Sheets •

We Buy Collections!

See us at Booth 757

Walter Kasell
175 Richdale Avenue • Cambridge, MA 02140
617-694-9360 • wbkasell@yahoo.com

World Stamp Show

NY 2016

BEJJCO
OF FLORIDA, INC.
Arnold H. Selengut

U.S. & WORLDWIDE
Stamps and Covers — All Continents, All Countries

Agent for the
WORLD TRAVELER COLLECTION
1840 to 1981, 99%++ complete *(including Scott listed varieties)*
Selections Available at the Show * Serious Want Lists Accepted

Let us help you fill those empty spaces.
See us at Booth #SB-1
E-mail: arnsel@verizon.net
P.O. Box 16681 Temple Terrace, FL 33687-6681   (813) 980-0734

Buying and Selling Worldwide Stamps and Covers
Mountainside Stamps

See Us at Booth 1156

United States: Single Stamps — used and unused, Plate Blocks, Booklet Panes and Booklets, BOB, Ducks, Revenues, Stationery, Sheets, FDCs, Confederate, Possessions, and United Nations

Canada: Singles, Booklets, Plate Blocks, and Revenues

British Commonwealth: All Areas — Great Britain and Offices, Australia, America, Oceana, Pacific, Africa, and Asia

Western Europe: Single Stamps and Booklets from Germany, France, Italy, Vatican, Greece, Switzerland, Liechtenstein, Belgium, Netherlands, Luxembourg, Portugal, Spain, and Scandinavia

Eastern Europe: Albania, Poland, and Russia

Asia: China, Hong Kong, Macao, Malaya, and Japan

Post Office Box 1116 • Mountainside, NJ 07092
Tel: 908-232-0539 • E-mail: tjacks@verizon.net
www.mountainsidestamps.com

TOMORROW

Detail of sculpture "Mail Delivery East" (1939) by Edmond Amateis, from a series at the Robert C. Nix Federal Building and U.S. Courthouse in Philadelphia. Photographed (2007) by Carol M. Highsmith for the General Services Administration. Obtained from the Library of Congress, Prints and Photographs Division.

The future of philately

by Matthew Healey and Alexander Haimann

FOR OVER A hundred and seventy-five years, the humble postage stamp has been king. Schoolchildren and royalty and everyone in between have found in philately a hobby that educates, elevates—and equalizes.

This "king of hobbies and hobby of kings" has also proven to be one of the world's most accessible and egalitarian leisure activities: anyone can take it up, spending little or no money, simply by saving the stamps that arrive on the day's mail.

In truth, famous philatelists have generally been millionaires: Philippe von Ferrary, Arthur Hind, Maurice Burrus, William H. Gross—or indeed, kings: George V of England, Carol II of Romania, Farouk of Egypt, not to mention presidents from Franklin D. Roosevelt to Nicolas Sarkozy.

Yet it has always been the millions of young collectors, many penniless, who have anchored our hobby in the popular imagination. From young Vernon Vaughan and John Lennon down to you and me, childhood has been the time when stamp collecting first gains its footing, fulfilling our desire for discovery, both of faraway lands and—one could dream!—rarities within our grasp.

Nowadays, though, children seem drawn to more instantaneous forms of gratification. So, can philately endure? Where will our hobby find itself by the time the bicentennial of the first U.S. stamps rolls around in 2047, three decades from now? Will nations even bother printing stamps by then? Is the postage stamp really dead?

To answer these difficult questions, let us examine what has happened over the past 30 years, to stamps and to how we buy and sell them, how we communicate, how we organize ourselves, and ultimately how we collect. Perhaps those trends can be extrapolated for some clues about what is to come in the next 30 years.

A look at stamps themselves

Stamps have always served a dual role: as tokens to account for pre-payment of postage and (to put it in academic terms) as signifiers of national identity and propaganda.

These days, we must accept that the postage stamp's role in paying postage is on the way out. First, there has been a huge decline in first-class mail volume, as email, texting, video chat and other instantaneous communication replaces letter-writing.

Matthew Healey, a member of Generation X, began collecting stamps at age 6, after becoming immersed in his father's old Minkus Master Global stamp album one rainy afternoon. He writes about stamp auctions for Linn's Stamp News *and occasionally about stamps and coins for* The New York Times.

Alexander Haimann, a member of Generation Y, had his stamp collecting gene activated at age seven. He was the youngest dealer at the Washington 2006 exhibition, and has been instrumental in launching the APS Young Philatelic Leaders Fellowship program and recruiting donors to the Liberty Club for World Stamp Show–NY 2016.

The opinions expressed in this article do not necessarily reflect the official position of World Stamp Show–NY 2016 or its sponsors.

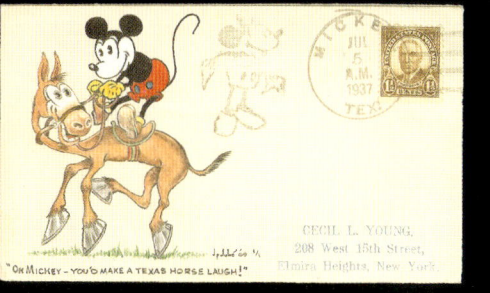

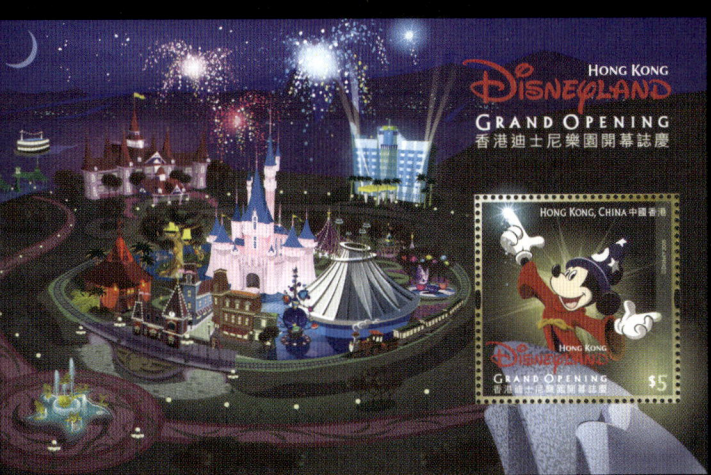

Items from Ed Bergen's exhibit, "Walt Disney's First Superstar: Mickey Mouse", here at NY 2016. Bergen's pursuit of this topic is not limited to Mickey Mouse on stamps. It includes cancellation markings, town names such as "Mickey, Texas", advertising covers featuring Mickey and of course mail sent to Walt Disney Studios with amateur versions of Mickey on the envelope.

Second, the classic adhesive and postmark are fast becoming functionally obsolete, analog relics outmoded by digital barcodes and electronic scanners that make every piece of important mail instantly trackable.

In fact, the good old-fashioned postage stamp is such an onerous and antiquated way of paying the postage that in 2014, the United States Postal Service essentially imposed a 1¢ penalty on using one: the first-class rate was set at 49¢ for letters franked with stamps, but 48¢ for letters bearing metered labels or barcodes (the metered-mail rate rose to 48.5¢ in 2015 and both rates dropped in tandem in April, 2016).

The number of stamps arriving on household mail is therefore smaller than ever. Children nowadays have less and less familiarity with stamps and their purpose. How can they grow up to be stamp collectors?

Astute observers have pointed out that it is rare for a new technology to completely displace an old one. Instead, the new becomes layered over the old, each serving new and different purposes. Think of elevators: we still build staircases. Think of cars: we still walk and (occasionally, at least) ride horses.

And we do still send letters. Anyone who has received a wedding invitation will have noted the enduring popularity of stamps and elegant calligraphy: far from being an anachronism, these remain tangible expressions of life's most important relationships. A stamp on a handwritten letter says "I care about you" in a way no email, text, or Facebook post ever can.

It is hard to imagine this vanishing in the next 30 years. The postage stamp may remain a niche product, but it will remain.

This will be thanks in no small part to stamps' other role: that of presenting a nation's culture, history, people, art, geography, tourism, sporting achievements and commercial resources to the world. Governments still produce stamps because they feel they still have something to say through stamps.

Being depicted on a postage stamp is universally seen as an honor and a privilege—a stamp of approval, if you will. Every year, tens of thousands of citizens clamor for recognition of their favorite subjects by the U.S. Postal Service, and the situation must be similar in many countries.

The 442nd Infantry Regiment was established as an all-Japanese-American unit in World War II. By the end the war, it was the most decorated unit for its size and length of service in U.S. history. More than two-thirds of the 14,000 men who served in the 442nd received the Purple Heart. Additionally, 21 Medals of Honor were awarded to members. This cover, accompanied by an original 442nd uniform shoulder patch, represents a tangible link to its history and legacy.

Stamps are marks of national sovereignty and legitimacy, a sign of national life: the only time a country ever ceases issuing stamps is when it ceases to exist.

This is why all 192 members of the Universal Postal Union keep turning out plenty of new stamps each year, and why an impressive one-third of the world's postal administrations have eagerly paid for the honor of presenting their latest wares at World Stamp Show–NY 2016. This is far from an activity in decline.

Back in 1986, advances in mechanical reproduction had made stamps more colorful and imaginative than ever—but also cheaper and quicker to produce, which tended to lower the quality of their design. The world was awash in ugly "wallpaper", and skeptics were right to question stamps' future.

Fortunately, that trend has been changing. One needn't look far (Mexico comes to mind) to find countries that produced some regrettable stamps in the 1970s and 80s, but have since returned to their fine design traditions of yore.

As the issuing of stamps becomes an increasingly discretionary activity aimed at a more discerning number of customers, countries will have to put maximum effort into making stamps as good as they can possibly be.

How will we buy and sell stamps in the future?

In 1986, the year of the great Ameripex exhibition in Chicago, which many still fondly remember as a high water mark for philately in the USA, most of the stamp trade happened either in brick-and-mortar shops, at shows of various sizes, or by mail. Dealers would send out printed price lists and auction catalogs on a regular basis. It was still possible to visit the old mecca of Nassau Street in lower Manhattan to buy stamps and supplies.

The stamp market had experienced a boom and bust in the late 70s and early 80s, driven by an ill-advised investment frenzy and general economic malaise. The lesson was unmistakable: stamps should be for fun, not profit. Stamps' real worth is intangible.

And yet, putting out new stamps remains highly profitable: the USPS earns hundreds of millions of dollars a year selling stamps to people who don't use them on mail.

Half a century ago, in 1966, a young collector of U.S. stamps could visit her local post office during the course of a year, buying all the new issues at face value, and her total cost—setting aside the $5 John Bassett Moore definitive stamp issued that year—would have been $1.15.

Adjusted for inflation, that's about $8.50 today. Compare that to the $102.26 that *Linn's Stamp News* reported collectors had to pay for new stamps in 2014, or even the more modest $52.81 for 2015.

Collectors may gripe about how expensive stamps have gotten, but as long as they keep buying and saving them, the post office will surely keep issuing them.

The Internet has revolutionized the stamp trade—along with everything else—by eliminating distance and leveling the playing field. If it is to blame for bringing about the demise of stamped mail, the web has, on the other hand, proven a boon to collectors.

Delegate ribbon from the 1904 World's Fair in St. Louis.

HOLD CARD TO LIGHT.
OFFICIAL SOUVENIR
WORLD'S FAIR
ST. LOUIS 1904.

Administration Building

AFTER 5 DAYS, RETURN TO
G. H. DIEDERICH FURNITURE CO.
CORNER SECOND AND TYLER STREETS,
ST. LOUIS.

WORLD'S FAIR ST LOUIS
1803 1904

MANUFACTURERS BUILDING

ST. LOUIS, MO
MAY 23
12 AM
1905

WORLD'S FAIR ST LOUIS

Mss. Tillman Bros.
La Crosse,
Wis.

The United States celebrated the 100th anniversary of the Louisiana Purchase with an international exhibition in St. Louis from Apr. 30 to Dec. 1, 1904. The exhibition hosted exhibits by 63 countries, including over 1,500 buildings across a 1,270 acre area (in present day Forest Park and Washington University in St. Louis). By the time the Fair closed, nearly 20 million people had passed through its gates. The U.S. issued

Gone are the days when collectors were obliged to purchase stamps, sight unseen, from a printed price list by catalog number alone. Everything can now be scanned and zipped around the world in the blink of an eye—see before you buy!

This has made the stamp business less like a stock exchange and more like a flea market. It lets buyers be better choosers: to spot unheralded gems, or to steer clear of things that seem "off".

Thanks to eBay and its ilk, anybody can now be a dealer and reach a global market. This has cut into the profits made by old-time dealers and sharp-eyed arbitragers, but allowed collectors access to a vastly broader selection. Many of the exhibitors competing at World Stamp Show–NY 2016 will readily admit they could not have formed their prize-winning collections as easily before the Age of the Internet.

The Internet has also made buying more effortless. Scott Trepel, the president of Siegel Auction Galleries, likes to spin the adage that "auction is theater" into the observation that nowadays, auctions are mostly home theater. Everyone can buy stamps in their pajamas.

In the future, one can only hope that the playing field will continue to flatten, as more and more historical price data becomes available and searching becomes even more efficient. Imagine looking at a stamp in 2047 and muttering "what's it worth?"—and having your wristwatch instantly provide the answer.

How has our communication and organization changed?

Back in 1986, hobbyists had three means of long distance communication: by phone, by letter or through society journals. Calling long-distance was expensive, though, while cell phones and email were virtually non-existent. There was no Web.

Most newspapers, including *The New York Times*, ran weekly columns about stamp collecting, with plenty of classified advertising from the stamp trade. Membership in stamp clubs, capped by national groups like the American Philatelic Society, was approaching an all-time high.

By today's standards, the exchange of ideas and information with fellow collectors and dealers tended to be slow and deliberate. Information-gathering was laborious: it could take weeks to answer a simple question. Serious collectors had to maintain files of clippings, or wait for a library to mail a desired book.

Now, communication is both faster and richer—color photos, online video and collaborative platforms such as stamp chat boards and Facebook are an integral part of our conversations. While newspaper columns about stamp collecting are mostly a thing of the past, and fewer and fewer public libraries keep stamp magazines or a set of Scott catalogs on the shelves, this has been more than replaced by the information available online.

Whether aiding in research, gaining access to libraries, exhibiting, translating, buying and selling from worldwide counterparts, or simply browsing other people's collections, the Internet has made collecting a less solitary and tedious affair than it used to be. It has also made some of the benefits of belonging to an organization less obvious—driving groups like the A.P.S. to undertake new initiatives that capitalize on technology and rethink philatelic activities for a new era.

Futurists promise us that in decades to come, we will wear our computers and be always-on, constantly plugged into one another and streaming our very consciousness around the clock.

It seems likely that the accumulated body of philatelic knowledge will also become more instantly accessible, whether through a Wikipedia-type platform or some great, unified philatelic library in the cloud. Joining a club or society will become as easy as joining any other online social network, and the benefits will be commensurate.

It will be possible to point-and-click a smart device at any stamp or cover and instantly learn all there is to know about it – its identity, who made it, its purpose and usage, what scarce varieties it may reveal on closer inspection. Far from robbing stamp collecting of its magic, this will make exciting discoveries more common and sleuthing easier to verify and share.

How has collecting changed?

To young collectors of Generation X, Ameripex was their first major stamp show. Nonetheless, there was already a sense that the golden age of the stamp hobby might be waning. Would Generation Y—the Millennials— follow them into philately at all?

As it turned out, they would. Perhaps not in the same masses as prior generations, but certainly enough to give the hobby fresh energy. And of course, millennials are discovering new ways to collect and experience stamps.

Back in the day, a child could grab his or her album and dash off to a friend's house to spend a happy afternoon absorbed in the world of stamps. Collections were typically organized by country, and the entire world fit comfortably into one volume.

Sometime in the 1960s, that ceased to be possible: there were simply too many stamps. Two, three and four volumes became necessary to accommodate them all. Philately grew cumbersome—and who could really get passionate about all those questionable issues from places like the uninhabited island of Redonda?

The Internet has changed how we buy and sell and learn about stamps. It has also begun to effect a change in what and how we collect. As a result, many collectors are moving away from striving to "fill spaces"—that is, collecting geographically and resigning themselves to empty holes for the items they'll never afford.

Instead, the last 30 years have seen a strong and steady rise in topical collecting—the pursuit of stamps by subject matter—as well as thematic collecting, which is the gathering of material around a unifying idea.

The maxim "collect what you like" now rings truer than ever. The new emphasis in competitive exhibiting is on building narratives, rather than showing one of everything or simply amassing rarities. The market reflects this trend, too: mid-priced stamps in middling condition are becoming harder to sell, while "better" items that tell a unique or compelling story are hotly fought over.

Here, too, technology is the philatelist's friend, as it has become easier than ever to produce polished, custom-made album pages on a home computer.

Another trend that will grow stronger is collecting material related to one's own life story, what we might call "bio-philately." There are endless

The 1924 British Empire Exhibition was opened on Apr. 23, 1924 by King George V. It hosted exhibits and attractions related to all the places around the world that made up the British Empire. The exhibition grounds were in Wembley, now part of Greater London. Britain issued two commemorative stamps, its first ever, for the event. Many more stamps and related postal items were produced by participating British colonies. Even more three-dimensional objects, souvenirs of every imaginable category and significant arrays of advertising materials were produced and sold before and during the event. The 1924 season was so popular that the Exhibi-

ways to take a family history, a personal connection or a non-collecting interest and explore its contours through philately, giving tangible manifestation to the vital moments of one's life.

In this way, for example, a personal interest in wine or medicine or a favorite cartoon character can be parlayed into a compelling personal tale, told through stamps and postal history. A Japanese-American or someone with a deep interest in World War II might treasure a cover sent from a member of the 442nd Infantry Regiment, deployed in Europe, even though the "value" of the cover might otherwise be modest.

The future will also see greater acceptance within our hobby of non-philatelic material. Collecting one thing, like stamps, has never limited the passionate collector from veering into other collecting areas: postcards, model trains, art, antiques and yes, even coins.

In all examples of thematic and "bio-collecting," where stamps and postal objects showcase the theme's central elements, objects from other collecting disciplines can be found to enhance the presentation even further. As the Internet shrinks the world and makes the body of available knowledge more accessible, there will be a growing interest in cross-pollinating with other collecting areas.

For example, if one has a passion for Worlds Fairs and Exhibitions, what better way to explore their magnificent landscapes than to collect the picture postcards, posters, advertisements, stereographs, and souvenirs sold at the events?

The collecting "bug" is endemic in modern society. Many future collectors of stamps and postal history are already collectors of something else; they simply have yet to discover how philatelic materials can complement their existing passions.

The notion of collecting with a personal interest is not a new one. Collectors of 19th century British stamps have long had a fondness for examples that bear their own initials in the lower-corner check letters—in this case, MH.

Philately will endure

There is no danger of collecting itself going away. As Warner Muensterberger wrote in his seminal 1994 book, *Collecting: An Unruly Passion*: "Collectors themselves—dedicated, serious, infatuated, beset—cannot explain or understand this all-consuming drive, nor can they call a halt to their habit."

As long as people grasp that stamps signify human stories and connections, as long as the world's postal administrations continue to produce well-designed stamps with subjects of genuine cultural, historical, artistic and geographic importance, we can be confident that stamp collectors, and stamp collecting, will be as vibrant in 2047 as they have ever been.

Our hobby is full of paradoxes. Stamp collectors like to be catered to, but we spurn pandering. We like our stamps to be beautiful, but we expect them to fulfill a prosaic postal need. We want them to be affordable, but we hope that one day some of them will be valuable. We are impatient with "snail mail" but we bemoan what is lost to digital technology. Philately, with its love of the old and authentic and tactile, must turn to mobile, digital technology to find better ways of connecting and sharing.

In short: collectors, like the very act of collecting, may not be entirely rational, but we are human.

Some say the postage stamp is dead. We say—long live the postage stamp!

The American Revenue Association

The ARA's mission is: to stimulate, encourage, create, sponsor, advance and guide the study and collection of fiscal or revenue stamps and related materials, both government and private issues, of the world, from an educational, informational and historical standpoint;

to establish and support study and research groups devoted to the various aspects and interests of such fiscal issues of the world;

and to prepare, publish and distribute literature of a philatelic nature and periodicals dealing with such material.

Membership includes a subscription to *The American Revenuer*, our quarterly magazine, discounts on our other publications, and the ability to bid in our member-only auctions.

Membership information is available at www.revenuer.org or by writing the Secretary, 473 E. Elm, Sycamore, IL 60178-1934.

STATE REVENUE SOCIETY

The SRS promotes the study and collection of revenue stamps and related materials of the states of the United States of America and their subdivisions. Member benefits include the full color, award-winning quarterly journal, **State Revenue News**, buying and selling in member-only auctions, buying certain current state-issued stamps at cost, and member prices on publications.

Membership applications may be found on the web site, http://staterevenue.org, or by writing the Secretary, Box 67842, Albuquerque, NM 87193.

Web Site   Application   Join Online

Welcome to NY2016

Visit us at Booth 681 to learn about

Ephemera and Paraphilately

The Ephemera Society of America

PLSG — POSTAL LABEL STUDY GROUP

American Philatelic Society Affiliates

SCOUTS ON STAMPS SOCIETY INTERNATIONAL

www.sossi.org

Come and See us! We are located in: Booth 783

On 5/29/2016 at 1:00 PM: Our General Meeting is in Room 1E19
Our Seminars/Presentations are also located in Meeting Room 1E19
- 5/29/2016 at 2:00 PM: Postal Autographs of the Baden-Powell's
- 5/30/2016 at 1:00 PM: Scout Philately a Many Faceted Hobby

For Information Contact: President - Lawrence E. Clay, PO Box 6228, Kennewick, WA 99336-0228
Or our Secretary - Jay Rogers, *secretary@sossi.org*

Society for Hungarian Philately

APS Unit #34 – Established in 1969

Invites you to visit us at the NY 2016 - WorldStampShow – Booth 779
General Meeting - Monday, May 30th, 1pm to 3pm, Room 1E16
Presentations by Robert Morgan and Karoly Szucs

We are an International Society whose benefits include:
- Award winning quarterly newsletter
- Reference Library with access to a wealth of philatelic material
- Quarterly Auctions

Share the experience – join your fellow collectors !!
USA Membership – only $18 / year
http://www.hungarianphilately.org/

American Air Mail Society

Dedicated to the research, study, documentation and preservation of aerophilately worldwide through education, study, research and services.

Benefits of Membership:

- Monthly gold-medal winning *Airpost Journal*

- Discounts on all AAMS publications, including the *AAMC*

- Exclusive bidding rights in the bi-monthly AAMS auction

Stop by Booth 777
at World Stamp Show NY 2016

and visit the AAMS website:
www.americanairmailsociety.org

The Royal Philatelic Society London

The Royal Philatelic Society London, the oldest philatelic society in the world, was established in 1869. It is the home of philatelic excellence, expertise and friendship.

We have over 2,200 members; 'The Royal' is a truly international society with philatelists from 78 different countries. It's a little known fact that there are more members overseas than in the UK, including over 250 in the USA.

Our libraries, collections and archives go back to the beginning of the postage stamp and beyond. The Society's website allows everyone to actively be involved in the Society, whether through research using our extensive online databases or by viewing our world-class presentations broadcast live to members via the internet.

Please come and visit us at Booth 775/874, where we would be delighted to explain the benefits of membership.

www.rpsl.org.uk

The entrance to the Society's premises at 41 Devonshire Place in London's prestigious Marylebone district.

Precancel Stamp Society

Visit the Precancel Information Booth # 878

COLLECT   ENJOY   LEARN   JOIN IN

Collect Stamps
Have Fun

Collect Precancels
Have More Fun

www.precancels.com
www.facebook.com/groups/Precancels
PSS Information: Box 10295   Rochester, NY 14160
APS Affiliate #0065

INTERNATIONAL SOCIETY FOR JAPANESE PHILATELY

Visit us at Booth 882

Covers all aspects of the philately of Japan.

Website: www.isjp.org
E-mail: secretary@isjp.org
Mail address: PO Box 230462, Tigard OR 97281 USA
Annual membership dues: US $16. Apply through the website or request an application form.

Bimonthly full-color journal JAPANESE PHILATELY typically running over 250 pages annually in 8½ x 11 format. Free sample provided on request to publisher@isjp.org. Cumulative index to the journal available on the website.

Services:
Extensive lending library for members
Expertization for members
Postal stationery new issue service for members
Monographs and back-issues of the journal available on paper or on CDs

Explore Canadian Philately

British No. America Philatelic Society	Royal Philatelic Society of Canada	Postal History Society of Canada
www.bnaps.org	www.rpsc.org	www.postalhistorycanada.net

Collect the Stamps and Postal History of Canada & British No. America; to find out more, visit us at NY2016 Booth Number 881

Collect Philippines

IPPS Benefits: Quarterly Journal, Yearly 350+ Lot Online Auction, Downloads, & Meetings

Join the:
International Philippine Philatelic Society (IPPS)
Information: www.theipps.info ◆ USA 1-301-834-6419

UNITED STATES POSSESSIONS PHILATELIC SOCIETY

(APS Affiliate #99)
A 501(c)(3) nonprofit organization for the study of stamps and postal history of the U.S. Possessions

Areas of interest include, all U.S. Possessions, Administrative Areas, and Post Offices Abroad, such as Canal Zone, Cuba, Danish West Indies/U.S. Virgin Islands, Guam, Hawaii, Marshall Islands, Micronesia, Palau, Philippines, Puerto Rico, Ryukyu Islands, American Samoa, U.S. Offices in China, AMG operations, Haiti, and other military expeditions.

For more information visit our website www.uspps.net or email us at USPPS.Possessions@gmail.com, and visit Booth 875/877 for a copy of our journal

Mexico Elmhurst Philatelic Society International

We are the Society that specializes in the philately of Mexico.

As a member you receive a copy of Mexicana, our quarterly journal, access to our library, sales of printed and digital publications on Mexico and our monthly circuit book sales.

Membership is affordable at $35 per year. Contact us on the Internet at www.mepsi.org or write Eric Stovner, PO Box 10097, Santa Ana, California 92711-0097.

APS Affiliate 42

World Stamp Show NY 2016

VISIT COVER COLLECTORS AT BOOTH 1280!

AMERICAN SOCIETY OF POLAR PHILATELISTS

WEBSITE: WWW.POLARPHILATELISTS.ORG
EMAIL: ALANWAR@COMCAST.NET

MILITARY POSTAL HISTORY SOCIETY

WEBSITE: WWW.MILITARYPHS.ORG
EMAIL: DUBINE@COMCAST.NET

UNIVERSAL SHIP CANCELLATION SOCIETY

WEBSITE: WWW.USCS.ORG
EMAIL: SHAYMUR@FLASH.NET

ATA

American Topical Association — Serving the World of Thematic Philately

World's Largest Thematic Collecting Organization
Stop By Booth 1276-1278
For Fun With Topicals, and Have Your Passport Stamped

FRIDAY, JUNE 3

11:00-12:00 – Informal gathering of worldwide topical/thematic collectors – Room 1E06

1:00 – 3:00 – ATA Annual Meeting – Room 1E06
  Presentation by Dr. Damian Läge, former president of FIP Thematic Commission: "Developing Your Story – The Key Concept of Thematic Philately"

3:00 – Dr. Damian Läge leading walk through thematic exhibits – Meet at the first thematic frame

www.americantopicalassn.org
PO Box 8 • Carterville, IL 62918-0008 • USA
americantopical@msn.com • Tel: 618.985.5100

Rocky Mountain Philatelic Library

Visit us in the society section at booth 1279.

We have something for every collector!

- Learn how easy it is to access the nation's philatelic libraries on a computer.
- You may win a philatelic book of your choosing.
- Get a special NY2016 edition of our newsletter, *Scribblings*.
- View (and buy) books and videos we have published.
- Kids will love our free stamp map kit.
- Pick up a souvenir sheet saluting NY2016 and the RMPL.
- Already a member? Drop by and say hello!

The cinderella in the souvenir sheet.

2038 S Pontiac Way, Denver CO 80224-2412 • (303) 759-9921 • rmpl@qwestoffice.net • www.rmpldenver.org

United Postal Stationery Society

The United Postal Stationery Society (UPSS) was formed July 1, 1945 from the merger of the Postal Card Society of America, in existence since 1891, and the International Postal Stationery Society, founded 1939. There were 164 members by the end of the inaugural year and we now have about 900 members worldwide. We are a society of philatelists devoted to the collection, research, and promotion of world wide postal stationery. Information about membership can be obtained at 1659 Branham Lane, Suite F-307, San Jose, Ca 95118-22291, via email at membership@upss.org or on our website, www.upss.org.

The Society has been active in producing postal stationery publications in the form of handbooks, catalogs and manuscripts since 1955, when the first United States Postal Card Catalog was published. The Society has since published numerous books and catalogs concerning U.S. and worldwide postal stationery that are updated periodically. These, and much more, are available to everyone one our website shown above.

As part of our effort to promote postal stationery, UPSS offers two exhibiting awards at each WSP show; the Marcus White Award for the best multi-frame exhibit of postal stationery ,and the UPSS Single Frame Award for the best single frame exhibit of postal stationery. Annually, we also give the UPSS Champion of Champions Award for the best of the Marcus White Award winners of the past several years and UPSS Single Frame Champion of Champions Award for the best of the UPSS Single Frame Award winners of the past several years. In addition, we offer the Lewandowski Literature Award annually to the best postal stationery publication. Past winners of C of C and Literature awards can be found on our website.

Join the Fascinating World of Confederate States Philately

The Confederate Stamp Alliance, founded in 1935, is a nonsectional, nonpolitical organization for fraternity, research and cooperation among collectors of Confederate stamps, covers, and postal history.

The CSA holds its annual convention and exhibition at World Series of Philately national stamp shows across the country. This event is the major annual gathering of Confederate collectors and features spectacular exhibits and the famous Southern Supper, where CSA awards are presented. Another Mid-Year meeting is a more casual weekend held in the fall.

The Confederate Philatelist Members receive four quarterly issues of one of American philately's oldest and most respected journals. The *CP* is the backbone of the collecting and study of Confederate philately.

For more information contact:
CSA Secretary
Col. Larry Baum
316 W. Calhoun Street
Sumter, SC 29150
Website: *www.csalliance.org*

*"If you're an expert, we'll learn from you;
if you're a beginner, we'll teach you all we know"*

Established in 1948, the Rhodesian Study Circle brings together over 400 philatelists from around the world interested in the areas of Rhodesia, Northern Rhodesia, Southern Rhodesia, British Central Africa and Nyasaland, and the present day republics of Malawi, Zambia and Zimbabwe.
Benefits for members include:

- Publications of the Rhodesian Study Circle including the Gold Medal award-winning 52 page quarterly, the *Rhodesian Study Circle Journal* (the 250th edition was published in March, 2014), and the renowned authoritative *Memoir* Series now numbering 29.
- Access to a Philatelic library
- Regular regional meetings in Africa, North America, Oceania, and UK.
- Postal auctions, and
- Exchange packets (UK only).

To join the RSC please contact the Secretary, Tony Plumbe, using email **ajplumbe@hotmail.com** or download a membership application form from: **www.rhodesianstudycircle.org.uk**

FREE CATALOG

New members receive a catalog of their choice (see below) with a three-year prepaid membership. US/Canada addresses only.

Look for this logo and visit our booth at NY2016, APS Stamp Show, Minnesota Stamp Expo and Chicagopex.

Scandinavian Collectors Club, Box 16213, St. Paul, MN 55116   www.scc-online.org

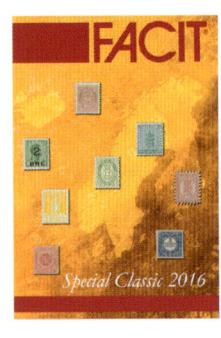

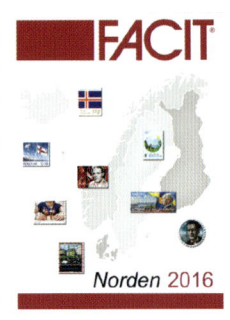

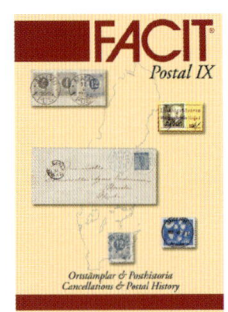

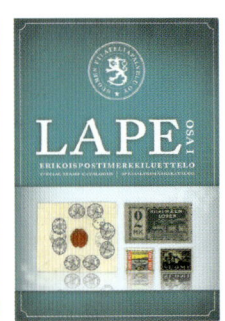

UKRAINIAN PHILATELIC AND NUMISMATIC SOCIETY

Союз Українських Філателістів і Нумізматиків

Since 1951

upns.org

Colombia/Panama & Canal Zone Study Groups
Booth 879

co|pa|phil

More information at
www.COPAPHIL.org
Annual Dues only
 $15-USA
 $17-Canada
 $20- other countries

COPAPHIL
c/o Allan Harris
26997 Hemmingway Ct, Hayward, CA 94542-2349
copaphilusa@aol.com

Colombia/Panama Philatelic Study Group Presentations

Sunday May 29, 10-11 AM, Room 1E08
SCADTA: The First Issues
Monday, May 30, 10-11 AM, Room 1E07 *Panama: The Path Between the Seas*
Wednesday, June 1, 10-11 AM, Room 1E08
Colombia: The Affair Michelesen and the Reprints of the 1868 Issue $5 & $10 Pesos

Canal Zone Study Group

Meeting-Open to Everyone
Sunday May 29, 11 AM-1 PM, Room 1E07

More Information at
www.CZSG.org
Annual Dues only
 $12 including Air Mail worldwide

CZSG c/o Mike Drabik
P.O. Box 281 Bolton, MA 01740
CZSGsecretary@gmail.com

The Key Resource

for Philatelic Exhibiting and Exhibitions. Founded in 1986

Publishers of *The Philatelic Exhibitor* magazine. A vigorously active international organization with myriad energetic activities and committees serving all elements of philatelic exhibiting. Presence at all World Series of Philately stamp shows. Sponsors of the Youth Champion of Champions. For 30 years the incubator for a wide range of innovations in the exhibiting world. Developing, nurturing and leading the exhibiting community in our hobby throughout our existence.

Available for purchase at our booth: Steven Zwillinger's terrific new book packed with wonderful, proven tips & techniques for preparing exhibits. **Only $39.95!**

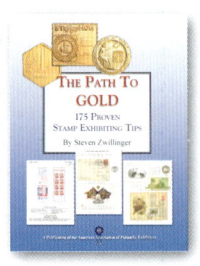

Join Us!
You'll find helpful information and people (and a membership application, too!)
at Superbooths 1664-1670

The American Association of Philatelic Exhibitors
Founded at AMERIPEX 1986
www.aape.org

Kelleher's
World Renowned Public Auctions Since 1885 • Online Auctions • Many Personalized Services

Here for you. Then and Now.
Since 1926—Ten Decades— A major presence at America's Historic International Exhibitions.

Grand Central Palace, N.Y.

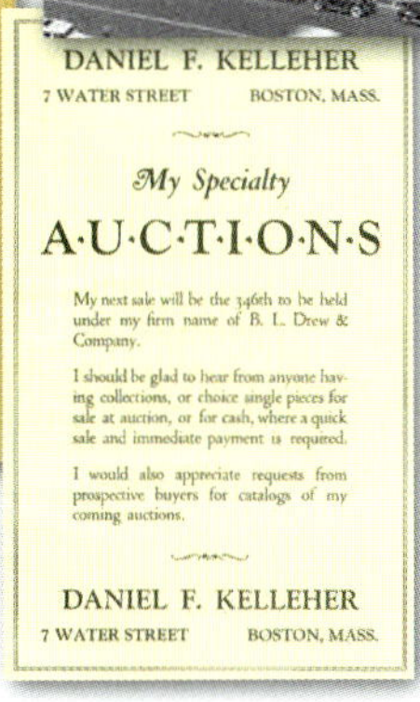

Daniel F. Kelleher

Our ad in the 1926 program (above) of America's 2nd International Exhibition at NY's Grand Central Palace.

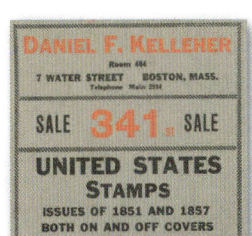

Continuing our 131-year historic tradition of service as the oldest continually-operated stamp auction house in the United States.

For much of the past half century **Stanley Richmond** carried forth the great history of the Kelleher firm with offices in its original home city of Boston. His sale of the firm to Coogle and Gibson ushered in a vibrant new era as a key worldwide firm.

In 1996, **David Coogle** co-founded the Nutmeg Stamp Sales auction firm. In 2004, Greg Manning purchased Nutmeg and later merged it with H.R. Harmer with David as President. In 2010, he joined with Laurence Gibson to acquire the Daniel F. Kelleher firm.

Our Kelleher & Rogers Hong Kong division is under the direction of **Laurence Gibson**, a respected authority on Asian philately. Mr. Gibson has handled numerous powerful China/Asia collections and major rarities over the past 20 years including the Varro Tyler estate.

Visit Us at Booth 1329
Here at World Stamp Show - NY 2016

Daniel F. Kelleher Auctions
America's Oldest Philatelic Auction House • Established 1885
4 Finance Drive, Suite 100 • Danbury, CT 06810
Phone: 203.297.6056 • Toll Free: 877.316.2895 • Fax: 203.297.6059
www.kelleherauctions.com
Email: info@kelleherauctions.com

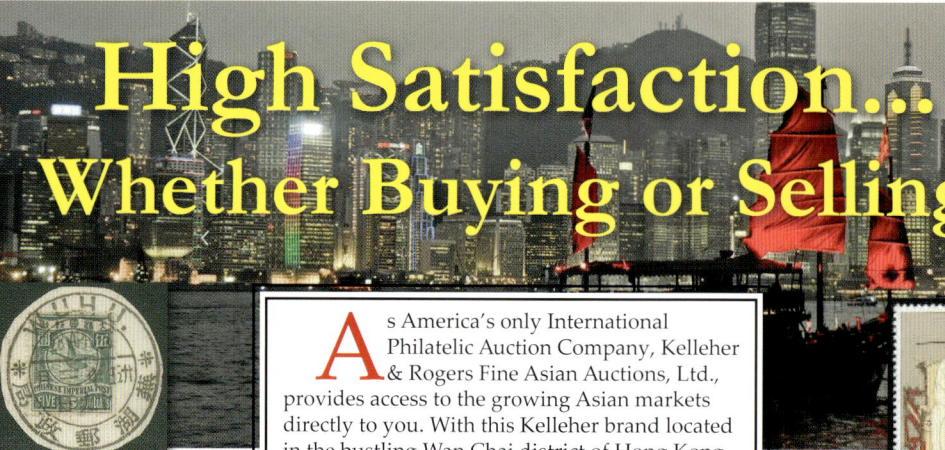

High Satisfaction...
Whether Buying or Selling.

As America's only International Philatelic Auction Company, Kelleher & Rogers Fine Asian Auctions, Ltd., provides access to the growing Asian markets directly to you. With this Kelleher brand located in the bustling Wan Chai district of Hong Kong, the markets of Hong Kong, Beijing, Shanghai, Tokyo, Bangkok, Malaysia and the rest of Asia are available to you now. Why sell locally when the Global markets provide better competition and realizations? This is the ultimate opportunity for selling at auction, direct sale, or private placement within the Asian marketplaces.

Deal with experts who are internationally acclaimed professional philatelists with over 70 years combined experience.

Consign now or enjoy Outright Sale for immediate payment or specialized Private Treaty placement. Liberal advances available.

Call or email us right now to arrange your consultation. **Do contact us today**.

Whether buying, selling or consigning, you will always receive our personal attention. We are just a phone call or e-mail away and **Michael Rogers** travels widely for larger philatelic holdings. He is now our Director of Acquisitions.

The Kelleher & Rogers firm in Hong Kong is under the direction of **Laurence Gibson**, Former director of John Bull Stamp Auctions, Hong Kong, and a respected authority on Asian philately. Mr. Gibson has handled numerous powerful Japan/China/Asia collections and major rarities over the past 20 years including the Varro Tyler estate.

Kelleher & Rogers
Fine Asian Auctions Ltd.

Malaysia Building, 50 Gloucester Road, 9th Floor, Wan Chai, Hong Kong
Email: stamps@kelleherasia.com
U.S. Offices: 4 Finance Drive, Suite 100, Danbury, CT 06810 USA
203.297.6056 • Fax: 203.297.6059
Website: www.kelleherauctions.com
info@kelleherauctions.com

THE LISTINGS

Illustration based on a detail of the U.S. 10¢ presorted-rate stamp issued in 2000, depicting the New York Public Library lions sculpted by Edward Clark Potter in 1911. The stamp was designed by Carl T. Herrman and illustrated by Nancy Stahl for the USPS.

Exhibits

PERHAPS EVEN MORE than the dealer bourse, the auctions, the array of worldwide postal administrations, the new issues or the society gatherings and seminars, the exhibits form the heart and soul of a major international philatelic exhibition.

Here one comes face-to-face with the superstars of our hobby: the great rarities, familiar to every child who has ever opened a book about stamps, as well as more common stamps presented in a novel context or well-researched narrative that lets us see familiar items with renewed wonder.

World Stamp Show–NY 2016 is pleased to present 4,500 frames—72,000 pages—of exhibits, not to mention nearly 200 literature entries and special displays.

The bulk of these—4,125 frames—are competitive entries from 700 individuals vying for awards. The rest comprise the Court of Honor, the Invited Class, the Society exhibits, and special presentations from the Universal Postal Union (UPU) and other organizations. There are even a couple of frames in the Youth and Beginner Area!

So learn. Be inspired. Above all—please enjoy.

Competitive Exhibits by Class
(Frames 1001–5125)
1: FIP Championship class
2: Traditional philately
3: Postal history
4: Postal stationery
5: Aerophilately
6: Astrophilately
7: Thematic (topical) philately
9: Revenues
10: Youth philately
12: One-frame exhibits
13: Modern philately
14: Open philately or display exhibits
15: First-day covers

Literature Exhibits (Class 11)
Reading Room

Index by Surname
Follows the main listing of competitive exhibits.

Court of Honor
(Frames 101–232)
Presented in detail on pages 127–146 of this catalog.

Invited Class
(Frames 301–380)
Presented in detail on pages 149–155 of this catalog.

Universal Postal Union (UPU)
(Frames 401–440)

Society Exhibits
(Frames 501–576)
See pages 310–311 of this catalog.

Competitive Exhibits

Class:	**2A**	1048-1094 →	← 1047-1001	**2A**
	2A/2B	1142-1188 →	← 1141-1095	**2A/2B**
	2B	1236-1282 →	← 1235-1189	**2B**
	2B/2C	1330-1376 →	← 1329-1283	**2B/2C**
	2C	1424-1470 →	← 1423-1377	**2C**
	2C	1518-1564 →	← 1517-1471	**2C**
	2C	1612-1658 →	← 1611-1565	**2C**
	2C/2D	1696-1732 →	← 1695-1659	**2C/2D**
	2D	1780-1826 →	← 1779-1733	**2D**
	2D	1874-1920 →	← 1873-1827	**2D**
	2D	1968-2014 →	← 1967-1921	**2D**
	2D/3A	2062-2108 →	← 2061-2015	**2D/3A**
	3A	2156-2202 →	← 2155-2109	**3A**
	3A	2250-2296 →	← 2249-2203	**3A**
	3A/3B	2344-2390 →	← 2343-2297	**3A/3B**
	3B	2428-2464 →	← 2427-2391	**3B**
Class:	**3B/3C**	2525-2584 →	← 2524-2465	**3B/3C**
	3C	2645-2704 →	← 2644-2585	**3C**
	3C	2765-2824 →	← 2764-2705	**3C**
	3C	2885-2944 →	← 2884-2825	**3C**
	3C	3005-3064 →	← 3004-2945	**3C**
	3C/3D	3125-3184 →	← 3124-3065	**3C/3D**
	3D	3245-3304 →	← 3244-3185	**3D**
	3D	3354-3402 →	← 3353-3305	**3D**
	3D	3463-3522 →	← 3462-3403	**3D**
	3D/4/1	3583-3642 →	← 3582-3523	**3D/4/1**
	1/4	3703-3762 →	← 3702-3643	**1/4**
	4	3823-3882 →	← 3822-3763	**4**
	4/5	3943-4002 →	← 3942-3883	**4/5**
	5	4063-4122 →	← 4062-4003	**5**
	5/6/7	4183-4242 →	← 4182-4123	**5/6/7**
	7	4293-4342 →	← 4292-4243	**7**
	7	4403-4462 →	← 4402-4343	**7**
	7	4523-4582 →	← 4522-4463	**7**
	7/9	4643-4702 →	← 4642-4583	**7/9**
	9/10	4763-4822 →	← 4762-4703	**9/10**
	10	4883-4942 →	← 4882-4823	**10**
	10/13/14	4990-5036 →	← 4989-4943	**10/13/14**
	14/15	5082-5115 →	← 5081-5037	**14/15**

Dealers and Societies

Dealers

Entrance

Class 1—FIP Championship

For exhibits that have been awarded three Large Gold medals, in three different years, at World Exhibitions held under FIP patronage over the last ten years (2006–2015). A Grand Prix counts as a Large Gold medal.

3583–3590	**The "Kassandra Collection"—Greece Large Hermes Heads, 1861–1886** *Stavros Andreadis, Greece* A collection of the first stamps of Greece, which were circulated between 1861 and 1886. (8)
3591–3598	**The Statues of Knight Roland: Medieval Symbols of Civic Rights in Central Europe** *Alfred Schmidt, Germany* The exhibit tells the story about the origin and meaning of medieval Roland Statues. (8)
3599–3606	**Greece: Incoming and Outgoing Mail from the Pre-Stamp Period to the UPU, 1828–1875** *Wolfgang Bauer, Germany* Covering the different possibilities for countries and routes with covers without stamps in the pre-stamp period, stamps only in one country, and later in both countries, and with combination covers and Large Heads of Greece. (8)
3607–3614	**Large Hermes Heads of Greece, 1861–1867, and Combination Frankings** *Wolfgang Bauer, Germany* The first three issues as Paris Prints, Provisional Athens, and Definitive Athens. Printings are shown in their immense varieties of colors, printings, control figures, papers, etc., followed by some combination frankings. (8)
3615–3622	**Saint Vincent: The Printings of Thomas De La Rue & Co., 1882–1932** *Russell Boylan, Australia* A detailed study, including essays, proofs, color trials, issued stamps, specimens, and usage, of the De La Rue printings for the period 1882 to 1932. (8)
3623–3630	**Round About September 1871 (in the French Internal Rate)** *Francis Carcenac, France* After the Franco-Prussian War, many internal rates changed. The new stamps were not ready in time, resulting in many combinations: provisional frankings, mixed frankings, with previous and new stamps, errors, varieties, in territorial and local mail. (8)
3631–3638	**Panama: First Issues as a State of Colombia and their Forerunners** *Alvaro Castro-Harrigan, Costa Rica* This is the history of the postal development of Panama beginning with the colonial period, the consular agencies of European and Central American countries before the first issue came into existence, and the nuances of the 1887–88 "Map Issue." (8)
3639–3646	**Postal History of Hungary, 1867–1871** *Géza Homonnay, Hungary* The exhibit guides us through the four-year validity of the first issue of Hungary. (8)
3647–3654	**Ludvig van Beethoven—His Life in Historical Context and His Legacy** *Yukio Onuma, Japan* The exhibit describes Beethoven's life and legacy in five chapters. The first three describe his life. The fourth describes his influences on succeeding generations. The fifth, quotations from and on Beethoven. Finally, a tribute to him is made. (8)

3655–3662	**Japanese Post Offices and Foreign Postal Activities in Korea, 1876–1909** *Kazuyuki Inoue, Japan* Postal history exhibit of Japanese post and foreign postal activities in Korea, from opening of the Japanese post office in Fusan to invalidity of Korean Empire stamps. (8)
3663–3670	**Iraq: 1917–1918 Occupation Issues of Baghdad and Iraq** *Alfred Khalastchy, U.K.* This exhibit shows all the British occupation issues of stamps for various parts of Iraq between 1917 and 1923. (8)
3671–3678	**The History of Taste** *Kim Ki-Hoon, Korea* A meditational, theoretical, historical, and lifestyle study on transcendental epicurism. (8)
3679–3686	**Vignettes of Western Trails and Routes, 1849–1870s** *George Kramer, U.S.A.* A study of private western express companies, government authorized routes, and combinations therein. (8)
3687–3694	**Uruguayan Air Mail, 1910–1930** *Enrique Lewowicz, Uruguay* Evolution of Uruguayan airmail from the pioneer period, including first airmail transport stages until 1930, when airmail services had been developed and were consolidated in Uruguay. Included are covers, postcards, newspapers, and first air stamps. (8)
3695–3702	**New Zealand Postal Stationery, 1876–1940** *Stephen D. Schumann, U.S.A.* A comprehensive showing of the significant items of New Zealand postal stationery from 1876 to 1940. (8)
3703–3710	**Iceland until 1901** *Douglas Storckenfeldt, Sweden* The first two stamp issues, the 1873 Skilling and the 1876 Aur values, in original without overprints, including the official issues and forerunners from the prephilatelic and Danish periods. (8)
3711–3718	**The Eagle-Shield Stamps Sent to Foreign Destinations, 1872–1875** *Jan-Olof Ljungh, Sweden* The exhibit shows items with the German eagle shield stamps sent to foreign destinations during 1872 to 1875, when the stamps were used. (8)
3719–3726	**Land Cultivation from the Beginning of Agriculture to the Present Time** *Joshua Magier, Israel* Land cultivation technological development and its socioeconomic implications are described, from the beginning of growing crops (before about 12000 years) till the present time. (8)

Class 2—Traditional Philately

For exhibits about the inception, design, production, varieties and uses of postage stamps.

Class 2A   United States of America

1001–1005	**The First United States 12¢ Stamp of 1851–1861** *James Allen, U.S.A.* Traditional exhibit illustrating all aspects of the stamp—rarities, plating, markings, uses, preproduction, and later printings from the 1851 die. (5)

1006–1010   **Jamestown, 1907**
Roger Brody, U.S.A.
A traditional study of the stamps celebrating the tercentenary of the 1607 English settlement of Jamestown and the 1907 World's Fair at Hampton Roads, Virginia. Includes stamp development, production, and domestic, foreign, and exposition mail use. (5)

1011–1018   **United States 10¢ Issue of 1861**
Kenneth Gilbart, U.S.A.
This exhibit tells the story of the versatile 10-cent value of the 1861 issue by showing essays, proofs, overprints, issued types, various cancels, domestic usages, and uses to and from countries all over the world. (8)

1019–1026   **Confederate States of America: The Lithographed General Issues**
Leonard Hartmann, U.S.A.
The lithographed general issues of the Confederate States of America with emphasis on original research on the stamps along with a selection of usages. (8)

1027–1034   **United States 10¢ Postage Stamp of 1869**
Michael Laurence, U.S.A.
Traditional survey exhibit of this fascinating stamp: essays, proofs, stamps, covers. (8)

1035–1039   **The 2¢ Stamp of the United States 1869 Pictorial Issue**
Stephen Rose, U.S.A.
A traditional exhibit of the two-cent 1869 stamp showing essays, proofs, printing varieties, cancels, plus domestic and international uses on cover. (5)

1040–1047   **Washington and Franklin Coils—Third Bureau Perforated Issues, 1908-1922**
Gregory Shoults, U.S.A.
The exhibit includes production material and uses for flat plate, rotary press, and coil-waste issues of the Third Bureaus. (8)

1048–1052   **United States Special Handling, 1925–1959—The Stamps and the Service**
Robert Rufe, U.S.A.
The forerunner of Priority Mail: the proofs, production, complexity, and uses of America's Special Handling stamps. (5)

1053–1060   **The U.S. Imperforate Issues of 1851–1856 and their Importance in an Expanding Postal System**
Gordon Eubanks, U.S.A.
A comprehensive study of the five imperforate stamps issued between 1851 and 1856. It shows a diverse range of uses: how the stamps were treated by the post office, the innovative uses patrons found for the mails, and how the post office met needs. (8)

1061–1065   **Canal Zone Overprints on Panama's 1909 ABNC Portrait Designs, 1909–1924**
Thomas Brougham, U.S.A.
A study of the Canal Zone overprint types and their settings applied to Panama's 1909 American Bank Note Co. portrait designs, together with their varieties and errors, their booklet panes and booklet covers, and their use on covers. (5)

1066–1070   **United States Vended Postal Insurance, 1965–1985—A Failed Experiment**
Alan Moll, U.S.A.
The production, sale, usage, and demise of U.S. Postal Insurance stamps and booklets from 1965 to 1985. (5)

1071–1078   **20¢ United States Flag of 1981**
Tim Lindemuth, U.S.A.
Study of sheet, coil, and booklet formats, including varieties, usages, and errors, some of which are unique to U.S. philately. (8)

1079–1083   **United States Special Delivery Stamps and Service, 1885–1954**
Colin Beech, Australia
Stamps and mail associated with the U.S. Special Delivery service from 1885 to 1954. (5)

1085–1089   **The Development and Use of the 3¢ Washington, 1861–1869**
Jan Hofmeyr, South Africa
The exhibit chronicles the patents and experiments aimed at the prevention of fraud against the backdrop of the genesis and ongoing use of the stamp. (5)

1090–1094   **The Flat Plate Printings of the Fourth Bureau Issue, 1922–1938**
Kunihiko Tamura, Japan
This exhibit shows the differences of gutter spacing, star plate and grain running, using stamps with plate numbers of the flat-plate printings of the Fourth Bureau Issue. (5)

Class 2B   The Americas except the USA

1098–1102   **Republica Argentina Classic Issues**
Pablo Reim, Argentina
Traditional exhibit of the first two classic issues of Republica: Escuditos and Rivadavia issues. (5)

1103–1110   **Argentina: Serie Próceres y Riquezas Nacionales, 1935–1958**
Guillermo Agustín Pettigiani, Argentina
Study of the 26 issues, the different papers used, artist's original artworks, die proofs, essays, plate proofs, samples, booklets, postal forgeries, and use in different frankings. (8)

1111–1118   **Argentina: Rivadavia, Belgrano and San Martin, 1892–1899**
Juan Martin Dagostino, Argentina
Die proofs, essays, studies of paper, watermarks, and perforated stamps, varieties and postal history. (8)

1119–1123   **Chile: First Issues of Postage Stamps, 1853–1867**
Oscar Schublin, Chile
Chile first issues of postage stamps, 1853 to 1867, in unused and used conditions, singles, blocks, strips, etc. (5)

1124–1128   **Ecuador: Postal Tax Stamps, 1920–1958**
Juan Pablo Aguilar, Ecuador
First study of Ecuador postal tax stamps, with additional information, unknown to this day, about what postal taxes have existed, how they were used, and the quantities in which they were produced. (5)

1129–1133   **Haiti: First Issues, 1881–1887**
Guy Dutau, France
Haiti joined the UPU and issued its first series of postage stamps. The postal rates remained unchanged during the period covered by this exhibit, which concerns liberty heads perforated and imperforate, and post Salomon issue, 1887. (5)

1134–1141   **Emision Primer Centenario de la Revolucion de 1810**
Miguel José Casielles, Argentina
Description of the complete collection: essays, stamps, postcard-bulletins especially maximum cards from the ½c to the 20 pesos. (8)

1142–1146   **Mexico Exporta, 1975–1993**
Michael Rhodes, Australia
This definitive series was issued over a period when Mexico had very high inflation, particularly in the late 1980s and the early 1990s. At the beginning of the series, the highest value was $.60 pesos and at the end, 7200 pesos. (5)

1147–1154	**Drafts, Essays, Tests and Proofs of Brazilian Commemorative Stamps**
	Noely Luiz Orsato, Brazil
	Brazilian commemorative stamp sketches, essays, tests, and proofs, with printing stages, various colors and papers, initial works, one-of-a-kind pieces, watermark varieties, perforates and imperforates, artist-signed pieces, specimens, etc. (8)
1155–1162	**Canada: The Small Queens of 1870–1897**
	Guillaume Vadeboncoeur, Canada
	A traditional exhibit of the issue covering essays, die proofs, plate proofs; the issued stamps, including errors and varieties and their use, with a focus on the pre-UPU period and unusual destinations. (8)
1163–1170	**Saint-Pierre and Miquelon: Colonial Series Through First Pictorial**
	James Taylor, Canada
	Pre-stamp covers from St. Pierre and French Shore Concession Newfoundland, French colonial general issues from St. Pierre 1859, scarce 1855 "SPM" surcharges, "tablet" and "pictorial" proofs, overprints, surcharges, varieties, issued stamps, covers. (8)
1171–1178	**The Maple Leaf Issue of Canada, 1897–1898**
	David McLaughlin, Canada
	This is a traditional exhibit of the 1897–98 Maple Leaf issue, featuring pre-production and production material and usages of the issue. (8)
1179–1183	**Essays and Proofs of the Stamps of Mexico**
	Enrique Trigueros, Mexico (COFUMEX)
	Essays, die proofs, color proofs, and specimen stamps of Mexico. (5)
1184–1188	**Mexico: The 1868 Issue**
	Eladio Garcia Prada, Mexico (COFUMEX)
	Study of the most outstanding aspects of the stamps with thick numbers of the issue of 1868. (5)
1189–1196	**Canada: The Large Queens, 1868–1896—The First Stamps Printed in Canada**
	Fred Fawn, Canada
	The dominant key items: the rarest die essays and die proofs; the only full, intact sheet of Large Queens; unique postal history destinations. Plate varieties, old and newly recorded by this exhibitor, watermarks, postmarks, unique multiples. (8)
1197–1204	**Colombia Classic Issues, 1859–1868**
	James Johnson, Colombia
	Exhibit of the eight stamps issued during the 10 years of geopolitical changes of governments. (8)
1205–1212	**Classic Colombia—The First Six Issues, 1859–1863**
	Ricardo Botero, Colombia
	The first 27 stamps with all relevant aspects: colors and shades, different printing stones, conformation of the stamps on the stones, main errors and varieties with their positions on the stones, constant plate flaws, and town cancellations. (8)
1213–1217	**The Fisherman's Head, First Type Stamp of Saint-Pierre and Miquelon**
	Fabrice Fouchard, St.-Pierre and Miquelon
	Different values of the first type stamp of Saint-Pierre and Miquelon are exhibited in this collection. (5)
1218–1222	**Saint-Pierre and Miquelon Viewed by France in Its Philately, 1982**
	Eric Resseguier, St.-Pierre and Miquelon
	The only French issue related to Saint-Pierre and Miquelon during the time it had Department status (1976–1985), when the territory issued no stamps of its own. (5)

1223–1230	**Founding of the University of Costa Rica Issue, 1941**	

Alexander Romero, Costa Rica

This collection shows essays of non-approved designs, photographic drafts, artist's proofs, vignettes, die proofs, specimens, varieties, and postal use in uncommon and rare destinations for surface and airmail issues. (8)

1231–1235 **A Study of Bermuda King George V Key Plates**
David Cordon, Bermuda
This exhibit includes one frame of printings followed by four frames showing the head plate flaws by position and printing on the "Nyasa" design used for the Bermuda King George V high value stamps. (5)

1236–1243 **Colonial Cuba, 1855–1898**
Leonardo Palencia, Cuba
Cuba colonial issues from 1855 to 1898. (8)

1244–1248 **Haiti's 1902 Provisional Issue**
Peter Jeannopoulos, U.S.A.
A comprehensive traditional exhibit of the genuine issue and the 29 different forgeries. (5)

1249–1253 **The Early Sailing Ship Stamps of British Guiana, 1852–1882**
Richard Maisel, U.S.A.
Traditional exhibit of sailing ship stamps issued by British Guiana 1852 to 1876. (5)

1254–1258 **The Spanish-American War and the U. S. Postal Administration in Cuba**
Jack Thompson, U.S.A.
This exhibit provides a comprehensive view of the Spanish American War of 1898 and the U.S. postal administration in Cuba. (5)

1259–1266 **Classic Peru, 1857–1873**
Antonello Fumu, Italy
The collection describes and studies the first 18 stamps of Peru in 1855–73: "Pacific Steam Company" provisional issue, Peruvian "Coat of Arms" lithographic issue, "Lecocq" issue, and the "Llamas" issue printed by the American Bank Note Company. (8)

1267–1274 **Peru: Study of Lithographed Stamps, 1858–1862**
Carlos Brenis, Peru
Study based on investigation of the lithographic stamps of Peru, including newly discovered and identification of the plate position in the different issues. (8)

1275–1282 **The Peruvian Security Seal for Certified Mail of 1916**
Henry Marquez, U.S.A.
A comprehensive study of one of the most elusive postal items issued by Peru Post in the 20th century. (8)

1283–1290 **Overprints of Saint-Pierre and Miquelon in the 19th Century**
Jean-Jacques Tillard, St.-Pierre and Miquelon
The most important study of the classics of Saint-Pierre and Miquelon. (8)

1291–1298 **Classic Costa Rica to the 1889 "Correos" Overprint Issue**
Roland Nordberg, Sweden
A deep study of the first issues of regular stamps and fiscals printed by the American Bank Note Company and allowed for postage all over the country. (8)

1299–1306 **Mexico: The Hidalgo in Profile Issue, 1872–1874**
Fritz A. Aebi, Switzerland
The most interesting and challenging issue of classic Mexico, presenting in a cross-section the largest units, the famous errors of color, rare districts, and fancy cancellations. (8)

1307–1314	**Guatemala: The Small Quetzal Issues, 1879–1881**
	Arthur Woo, U.K.
	An in-depth study with an unrivalled assembly of proofs, issued stamps with multiples, plate blocks, and inverted centres, plus a fine array of usages on cover, including all the largest recorded frankings. (8)
1315–1322	**Uruguay: "Escuditos" Issues, 1864–1866**
	Eduardo Boido, Uruguay
	In 1864 were issued the first stamps with decimal currency, the "Escuditos," used until the end of 1865, then surcharged for use in 1866, but with a validity of only 10 days. This issue is rare because of the short time used and the small number printed. (8)
1331–1338	**Classic Mexico: The First Issues from Colonial Mail and First Hidalgo Issues to 1867**
	Omar Rodriguez, U.S.A.
	Stamps and postal history of the earlier issues of Mexico. Starts with colonial mail as a forerunner of the postal system and includes first Hidalgos (1856–1861), issues during the French Intervention (Eagles, Maxis), and provisional issues and Gothics. (8)
1339–1346	**British Columbia and Vancouver Island, 1858–1871**
	Robert D. Forster, U.S.A.
	A traditional exhibit arranged chronologically by postal frank and stamp issue. (8)
1347–1354	**Chile Correos: Presidente Adhesives With Legend, 1911–1936**
	William Lenarz, U.S.A.
	Chilean Presidente definitive series with strong showing of preproduction material and errors. (8)
1355–1362	**Mexico: The Provisional Period, 1867–1868**
	Marc E. Gonzales, U.S.A.
	The provisional stamps and stampless franks of Mexico used in the interim after the fall of the Maximilian regency and prior to the issuance of the national issue of 1868. (8)
1363–1370	**St. Thomas, La Guaira, Puerto Cabello**
	Eduardo Borberg, Venezuela
	Local mail of Venezuela to St. Thomas and the rest of the world, rare covers, routes, study of plates and settings, reconstruction of sheets. (8)
1725–1732	**First Hand: Bolivian Presidential Philately**
	Ariel Kwacz, Peru
	Postal history, stamps and fiscal/revenue documents, all signed by Presidents of the Republic of Bolivia (8)

Class 2C Europe

1371–1375	**Denmark's Wavy Line Design: The Surface Printed Issues**
	Donald Brent, U.S.A.
	This exhibit shows the development and use of stamps with Denmark's wavy-line design from the design contest of 1902 until the change in printing methods in 1933. (5)
1377–1384	**Classic Germany**
	Takashi Yoshida, Japan
	Traditional collection of classic Germany imperforate stamps. (8)

1385–1392	**The Last Issues of Albert I: Kepi and Allegory** *Mark Bottu, Belgium* The genesis, definitive issues, and specific use of the "Albert with Kepi" stamps issued in 1931, including their use in the development of international airmail lines in Europe and overseas areas, such as the Congo, the Americas, and other continents. (8)
1393–1400	**Multistamp Flat Printing From Steel Engraving** *Miloš Hauptman, Czech Republic* Study of stamps printed by flat plate printing, arranged chronologically, documenting trial of procedures toward multi-colour printing. Extremely rare material of this period is presented. (8)
1401–1405	**Britain's Marvelous Machins** *Stephen McGill, U.S.A.* This exhibit of stamps documents the evolution of the denominated Machin series. (5)
1406–1410	**Sweden: The Medallion Series, 1910–1919** *Ross V. Olson, U.S.A.* Complete series of Medallion issues: essays, proofs, entire production process, each stamp in all its sub-varieties, and each denomination on cover, illustrating uses where that value paid correct postage. (5)
1411–1415	**Bosnia and Herzegovina: Austro-Hungarian Occupation, 1878–1908** *Alfonso Zulueta, U.S.A.* A traditional exhibit which documents the Austro-Hungarian occupation of Bosnia-Herzegovina by showing the proofs, stamps, and usages. (5)
1416–1423	**The Swedish Postage Reform in the 1850s: The Coat of Arms Type I Skilling Banco, 1855–1858** *Gustaf Douglas, Sweden* The most comprehensive exhibit ever formed on the first stamps from Sweden, including the famous 3 skilling banco yellow. (8)
1424–1431	**Great Britain: Line Engraved and Embossed Issues** *Ake Rietz, Sweden* The world's first issues of stamps and stationery: Mulready stationery and line-engraved and embossed items. (8)
1432–1436	**Irish Coil Stamps, 1922–1940** *Robert Benninghoff, U.S.A.* Two major coil designs were produced for use in Ireland from independence in 1922 to 1940. This exhibit illustrates the use of these stamps for both postage and revenue purposes. (5)
1437–1441	**The First Perforated Postage Stamp: Great Britain Penny Red Stars, 1850–1864** *Juan Farah, U.S.A.* The development of the first perforated stamp, from the Archer perforation trials of the 1850s through the use of reserve plates in the 1860s; perforations, colors, varieties, plate repairs, imprimaturs, early usages, and foreign destinations. (5)
1442–1446	**The Half-Penny (Decimal) Machin** *Lawrence Haber, U.S.A.* The lifecycle of the Great Britain Machin: from the onset of decimal currency to withdrawal in 1985, and a bit beyond. (5)
1447–1454	**The 1920 Schleswig Plebiscite Stamps** *Göran Persson, Sweden* This exhibit describes the referendum stamps from Schleswig with reference to main events and prominent individuals. (8)

1455–1462	**Finland: The 1875 and 1885 Series** *Erkki Toivakka, Finland* This exhibit displays the stamp emissions of the three printing houses and illustrates characteristics and postal use of stamps by showing different perforations, tete-beches, multiples, different frankings, and postmarks in domestic and foreign mail. (8)
1463–1470	**Kingdom of Saxony Post** *Michael Schewe, Germany* The King John issue (1855–1860) with emphasis on printing plates, anomalies, and usage, including foreign country covers. (8)
1471–1475	**Sweden: Official Stamps—First Issue, 1874–1884** *Valter Skenhall, Sweden* The first Swedish official stamps in large size, perforation 14, from 1874 to 1884, concentrating on cancelled stamps and stamps on cover. The first section describes common features, and the second section describes individual values. (5)
1476–1480	**Finland: Model Saarinen, 1917–1930** *Pekka Rannikko, Finland* The first definitive stamp issue of independent Finland. (5)
1481–1488	**Schleswig-Holstein before 1868** *Rolf Beyerodt, Germany* The employed mail free stamps from 1850 at Schleswig-Holstein, with peculiarities such as mini sheets, changing colors, and letters of different postal rates and overseas destinations. (8)
1489–1496	**The Stamps of South East Europe and Levant, 1850–78** *Georg Störmer, Norway* The purpose of the exhibit is to show how the different stamp-issuing authorities took advantage of the rather unclear situation resulting from the gradual Ottoman withdrawal from their 16th-century southeast European and Levanthine empire. (8)
1497–1504	**The Small Hermes Heads of Greece, 1886–1901** *Anestis Karagiannidis, Canada* This collection represents the second classical period of Greece (1886 to 1901) with all printing issues: Belgium and Athens for the small Hermes heads. (8)
1505–1509	**Production and Postal Usage of the Large Hermes Heads' Paris Printings** *Louis Fanchini, France* Die proofs, plate proofs, "Galvanos," stamps, and covers of the "Cérès 1858," "Cérès without inscription," and "large Hermes head" of Greece, all of the Paris printings, with an in-depth study of the fabrication process. (5)
1510–1517	**Austria and Lombardy-Venetia: The 1850 Issues** *Tamaki Saito, Japan* Traditional philatelic collection of the 1850 issues of Austria and Lombardy-Venetia. (8)
1518–1522	**Norway Coat of Arms, 1855–68** *Klaas Biermann, Norway* Norway coat of arms stamps from 1855 to 1868. (5)
1523–1530	**Switzerland: Cantonal & Early Federal Issues, 1843–1854** *Joseph Hackmey, U.K.* The Cantonal issues of Zurich, Geneva, and Basel, and the first Federal issues, with unused, used, covers, rates, and routes. (8)

1531–1535	**Great Britain: King George V Commemorative Stamp Issues** *Mary Pugh, Canada* A detailed study of the three commemorative stamp issues of George V's reign, including the reasons for their issue, pre-production material, production process, issued formats, varieties, and usage. (5)
1536–1540	**The Story of The Penny Black—The Plates, Varieties and Usage** *Graham Locke, Canada* The history of the Penny Black, from its introduction in May 1840 until its final printing in February 1841. (5)
1541–1548	**Great Britain: The "£sd" Machin Definitives, 1967–1971** *Tony Walker, U.K.* A comprehensive study of this short-lived pre-decimal currency issue, examining early artwork and essays; sheet, booklet, and coil printings; and a range of errors and varieties, many unique. (8)
1549–1556	**The Stamps of the Italian Kingdom Issued during the Reign of Victor Emanuel II** *Eric Werner, Switzerland* This collection shows a partial view of the development of the postal activity during the Kingdom of Victor Emanuel II, king of Italy from 1861 to 1878. (8)
1557–1564	**Spain: The Black of 1850** *Luis Domingo, Spain* All aspects of the first adhesive stamp from Spain, such as essays, first and last day of usage, first world forgery, usages contrary to regulations, varieties, printing faults, mail abroad, plating, largest multiple known, cancellations, postmarks. (8)
1565–1569	**Grand Duchess Charlotte, 1921–1939** *Guy Jungblut, Luxembourg* Stamps of Luxembourg depicting Grand Duchess Charlotte issued from 1921 to 1939. (5)
1570–1574	**Russian Stamps, 1858** *Marina Mandrovskaya, Russia* The first issues of Russian stamps and their types, varieties, and essays. (5)
1575–1582	**Switzerland, 1 Mar. 1843 to 14 Sept. 1854** *Hugo Goeggel, Colombia* The classic stamps of Switzerland issued from 1 March 1843 to 14 September 1854. (8)
1583–1590	**Stamps of the Government of the Grand National Assembly of Turkey (Ankara Government), 1920–1923** *Kayhan Akduman, Turkey* Collection studies and exhibits the stamps and postal documents of the Ankara government, issued during the Turkish War of Independence between 1920 and 1922. (8)
1591–1598	**Rural Post Stamps of Russian Empire, 1865–1917** *Evgeniy Bogomolny, Russia* Postage stamps of Russian Zemstvo Post. More than 3000 main stamps with their types. (8)
1599–1606	**Zemstvo Stamps of Perm Governorate, 1871–1919** *Yuri Obukhov, Russia* Zemstvo stamps of the districts of the Perm Governorate are not an ordinary event in Russian postal history. (8)
1607–1611	**Bulgaria, 1877–1895** *Nikolay Mandrovskiy, Russia* The first issues of Bulgarian stamps and their types, varieties, and essays. (5)

1612–1619	**Zemstvo Postage Stamps of Kharkov Province, 1868–1918** *Vitaliy Katsman, Ukraine* Stamps and postal items of Zemstvo Post from 7 districts of Kharkov province: Ahtyrka, Kharkov, Lebedin, Starobelsk, Sumy, Valki, and Wolchansk, with types and varieties, with well-known and previously unknown rarities. (8)
1620–1624	**Carpatho-Ukraine, 1945** *Martin Jurkovič, Slovakia* Exhibit documents stamps and covers issued in the territory of Carpatho-Ukraine in 1945. The first and second issue, with unique strips, tete-beche pairs, and special plate positions. (5)
1625–1632	**Ukraine, 1918: The Trident Overprints on Stamps of the Russian Empire** *Petro Borukhovych, Ukraine* Stamps of the Ukrainian State, classified by types of the Trident overprints, with rare items (overprints on the 1902 issue, local issues) and overprint varieties (inverted, doubled, missed, etc.). Usages illustrated by various mailings in 1918 to 1920. (8)
1633–1640	**Slovenia: Kron and Dinar Ordinary Post Stamps, 1919–1920** *Bojan Kranjc, Slovenia* Exhibit presents the diversity of Slovenian stamps. (8)
1641–1648	**Kingdom of Serbia, 1880–1903** *Predrag Antić, Serbia* Exhibit shows stamps of the Kingdom of Serbia issued from 1880 to 1903. (8)
1649–1653	**German Feldpost—World War II** *Helmut Zodl, Austria* The use of the Feldpost stamps, used and on letters. (5)
1654–1658	**Cyprus Stamps: The Victorian Issues, 1880–1896** *Costas Athanasion, Cyprus* Including all issues since the establishment of the British post office in Cyprus since 1st April 1880. (5)
1659–1666	**Sweden: The First Five Stamp Issues, 1855–1872** *Peter Wittsten, Denmark* The exhibit shows the various phases of a classic period of Swedish philately in brief facts regarding production and design, main postal uses, and all shades, including many covers. (8)
1667–1674	**The "In British Occupation" Provisionals of Baghdad and Mosul** *Akthem Al-Manaseer, U.S.A.* Exhibit on the British occupation provisionals of Baghdad and Mosul during World War I. (8)
1676–1680	**Norway Stamp Issues, 1872–1885** *Jon Fladeby, Australia* Norwegian stamp issues of 1872 to 1885, commencing with the last pre-decimal issue, followed by the "shaded posthorn," the bi-coloured King Oscar II, and the "large die" issue, demonstrating printings, plates, papers, colour shades, and later surcharges. (5)
1681–1685	**British Heligoland, 1866–1890** *Lawrence R. Mead, U.S.A.* Heligoland postal history and stamps from the British era, 1866 to 1890. (5)

Class 2D　　Asia, Oceania and Africa

1696–1703　　**Japan Earthquake Emergency Issue, 1923–1924**
Tatsutoshi Kamakura, Japan
Stamps were issued on and after Oct. 25, 1923, due to damage to postal facilities by the earthquake and fire on Sept. 1. There were 9 denominations of Osaka and 7 of Tokyo printings. Shows details of secondary and tertiary flaws with early usages. (8)

1704–1708　　**Israel First Airmails, 1950**
Brian Gruzd, South Africa
The exhibit traces the planning, development, printing, and usage of the first airmail stamps of Israel in 1950. (5)

1709–1713　　**Japan: Hand Engraved Issues, 1871–1876**
Yuji Yamada, Japan
This collection includes the earliest series of Japan stamps, Dragon and Cherry Blossom issues. (5)

1717–1724　　**The British South Africa Company—Rhodesia, 1913: The George V "Admiral" Issue**
Patrick Flanagan, South Africa
The exhibit shows the designs, die proofs, plate proofs, issued stamps, and varieties through the Die I, Die II, Die IIIA, and Die IIIB printings together with usage in a comprehensive display of the issues. (8)

5201–5205　　**Tibet: The Stamps and Their Usage, 1912–1960**
Rainer Fuchs, Germany
The exhibit describes in chronological order the stamps of Tibet and their use, with proofs and essays, single stamps, multiples, and complete sheets. The commercial usage of the stamps is represented by covers from various post offices. (8)

1733–1737　　**Palestine, 1865–1948**
Syed Imtiaz Hussain, Pakistan
A very specialized and comprehensive study of stamps of Palestine, including the study of foreign consular and mission mail in Palestine during this period. (5)

1738–1742　　**Japanese Occupation of the Philippines, 1942–1945**
Akira Kaburaki, Japan
All 64 kinds of stamps issued during the Japanese occupation of the Philippines with imprint blocks, errors, varieties, and usages. Rarity and uniqueness were taken into account when selecting materials for the exhibit. (5)

1743–1750　　**Madagascar, 1825–1935**
Øystein Grøntoft, Norway
Extracts of an extended catalog collection, supplemented with letters, cards, stationery, imperforate stamps, proofs, etc. (8)

1751–1758　　**Bhopal, 1868–1903**
Salman Qureshi, Pakistan
A highly researched full exhibit of stamps from Bhopal, from 1868 to 1903, including the study of stones/plates, shades, varieties, and errors through stamps, covers, etc. (8)

1759–1766　　**Australia: Kangaroo-and-Map Design Postage Stamps**
Hironobu Nagashima, Japan
First, I show all kinds of mint stamps. Next I display proofs, specimens, imprints, varieties, used stamps, covers, parcel tags, and perfins. (8)

1767–1774	**Private Printing Period in Victoria, 1850–1859**
	Masayasu Nagai, Japan
	From first stamps in Victoria, half-length of 1850, printed by Thomas Ham, Melbourne, to "Emblems" printed by Calvert Brothers and others until 1859. Between 1850 and 1859, the colonial government ordered various local printers to print stamps. (8)
1775–1779	**Chefoo Local Post, China, 1893–1896**
	Sammy Chiu, Canada
	Exhibit aims to show that there was an actual demand and need for the stamps and services of Chefoo local post by foreign residents. (5)
1780–1787	**Ryukyus, 1945–52**
	Tsukasa Ishizawa, Japan
	Traditional collection of the stamps and related items issued in the Ryukyu Islands from 1945 to 1952. Stampless covers and postcards are also exhibited because they comprise an important part of a traditional collection of the Ryukyus. (8)
1788–1792	**Classic India Used from Burma**
	Santpal Sinchawla, Thailand
	Traditional, comprehensive exhibit starting with the history of Burma and how it came under British rule. Then first set of lithography stamps of India used in Burma, showing the four values, their printing, and usage on cover. (5)
1793–1800	**The Zuid Afrikaansche Republiek-Transvaal, 1869–1885**
	Lars Jørgensen, Belgium
	The early stamps with the main focus on the Arms issue printed from the same plates over a 16-year period. Classified by printers, papers, colours, and separation, and plated on the basis of varieties and wear. Unusual postmarks and usage on covers. (8)
1801–1808	**Siam: King Rama IV and King Rama V, 1832–1904**
	Ayuth Krishnamara, Thailand
	Descriptive usage of royal mails, prestamp, and first issue of Siam stamp up to King Rama V Jubilee. (8)
1809–1816	**China: Coiling Dragon and Its Overprints, 1897–1912**
	Lin Tzu-Mu, Chinese Taipei
	Both Coiling Dragon issues, starting with the design, varieties, and usage of original stamps, then various styles of surcharge, including in the Imperial Qing Dynasty and in the Republic era, with varieties of overprints. (8)
1817–1821	**The Victoria Stamps of Tasmania**
	Lars Peter Svendsen, Denmark
	The exhibit shows the four Queen Victoria issues from printer's proofs to issued stamps and usage. (5)
1822–1826	**Republik Indonesia, 1945–1949, under Netherlands Indies Civil Adminstration**
	Avie Wijaya, Indonesia
	The Republik Indonesia stamps issued in 1945 to 1949 under the Netherlands Indies Civil Administration. (5)
1827–1831	**Ethiopia: Empress Zauditu and Ras Tafari, 1928–1931**
	Daryl Reiber, U.S.A.
	An in-depth look at the Ethiopian 1928 definitive used from September 1928 to June 1931. (5)
1832–1836	**Johore—The Classic Period**
	Nestor Nunez, U.S.A.
	Stamp issues from first overprint on Straits Settlement stamps to 1940. (5)

Frames	Exhibit
1837–1844	**Study of the Early Lion Issue, 1st and 2nd Portrait** *Massoud Novin Farahbakhsh, Iran* A special, well-collected 1865–1880 first Lion issue of Persia and first and second Shahs' portrait issues. (8)
1845–1852	**Egyptian Government Post, 1814–1922** *Mahmoud Ramadan, Egypt* A study of the history of the stamps of the Egyptian Government Post since its inception during the reign of Mohamed Aly (1805–1848) up to the declaration of the Egyptian Kingdom in 1922. (8)
1853–1860	**Afghanistan in the Reign of Amir Abdur Rahman, 1881–1899** *Usman Ali Isani, Pakistan* A very specialized study of stamps of Afghanistan in the reign of Amir Abdur Rahman (1881–1899) through stamps, proofs, and covers, including my original research. (8)
1861–1868	**Afghanistan—19th Century, 1871–1880** *Sultan Mahmud, Pakistan* A highly specialized research study of the first issue of Afghanistan (Tiger Heads), large and small. It includes the study of covers of the first Anglo Afghan War (1837–42) as forerunner. (8)
1869–1873	**New Zealand: The Chalon Issues, 1855–1873** *David Patterson, U.S.A.* This exhibit is a study of the first postage stamp issue of New Zealand. The exhibit shows the different printings, papers, separation methods, and shade variations with unused, used, multiples, and covers. (5)
1874–1881	**Ottoman (Turkish) Empire Issue, 1876–1890** *Iqbal Nanjee, Pakistan* Exhibit of Turkish "Empire Issue" stamps and related provisionals represents a comprehensive study of the subject, with die proofs, plate proofs, colour trials, major errors, rarities, provisional bisects, usages, postmarks, forgeries, and new research. (8)
1882–1886	**The British Military Administration of Malaya** *Peter Cockburn, U.K.* The exhibit demonstrates the interesting complexity of a small issue of stamps produced under difficult circumstances in three different locations thousands of miles apart. (5)
1887–1894	**Persia: 1902 Provisional Typeset Issue of Teheran** *Behruz Nassre-Esfahani, U.S.A.* This exhibit studies the 1902 provisional typeset issue of Teheran, which was prepared due to depletion of existing stock. All various types of basic stamps, control overprints, varieties, and usages are shown. (8)
1895–1902	**Classic Persia, 1865–1882** *K. Joe Youssefi, U.S.A.* Exhibit begins in pre-stamp era, covers the initial development of the postal system in Persia, and ends with the joining of the UPU. Focus is on historic events and technical analysis. Features top three most important items in all Persian philately. (8)
1903–1910	**The 1948 Doar Ivri and D'mei Doar Issues of Israel and their Usage** *Robert Pildes, U.S.A.* Development of design and production for first issue of Israel, including Dmei Doar (postage due) as printed from same plates. (8)

1911–1915	**Post Liberation Provisional Issues of Bangladesh** *Mannan Zarif, Bangladesh* A study of Bangladesh overprints on Pakistan stamps. (5)
1916–1920	**Union of South Africa: 1935 Silver Jubilee of King George V** *A. Du Plessis, South Africa* The exhibit describes the production, major and minor flaws of the four values (½d, 1d, 3d and 6d), isolated errors and plating. (5)
1921–1928	**New South Wales Centennials—World's First Commemoratives** *Ben Palmer, U.K.* A study of the eight values that constitute the world's first commemorative stamps, which includes multiples, unadopted essays, proofs, colour trials, perforation errors, marginal imprints and monograms, overprints, and use on cover. (8)
1929–1936	**Ryukyu Islands: "Heavenly Maiden" Air mail Issues, 1951–1972** *Iris Adair, U.S.A.* Traditional exhibit of airmail postage stamps bearing the "Heavenly Maiden" motif, issued under authority of two Ryukyu governments during United States administration. (8)
1937–1944	**British King George V Definitive Stamps, 1915–1923, Overprinted for Use in Nauru** *Robert C. Stein, U.S.A.* An original research report about the variations in Profile Head and Seahorse definitives overprinted for Nauru. Material includes archives and specimens, definitions, and a catalog of variations within each value. (8)
1945–1949	**Development of the 2d and 3d Large Format Pictorial Printings of the Union of South Africa, 1925–1951** *Eddie Bridges, U.S.A.* A traditional exhibit illustrating the various printings of the first issues. Shown are the printings from Bradbury Wilkinson through the domestically produced stamps, including roll and booklet issues. (5)
1950–1954	**Cape of Good Hope, 1853–1864** *Richard Debney, U.S.A.* A traditional study of the classic triangular stamps, encompassing both the London printings and locally produced provisionals. (5)
1955–1959	**The Hong Kong "China" Overprinted Stamps, 1917–1930** *Ian Gibson-Smith, U.S.A.* This exhibit shows the stamps of Hong Kong overprinted "China" for use in Treaty Ports from 1917 to 1930. (5)
1960–1967	**Victorian Natal, 1857–1899** *Keith Klugman, U.S.A.* The Victorian stamps of Natal and their usage from 1857 to 1899. (8)
1968–1972	**Egypt's Fourth Issue, 1879–1913** *Trenton Ruebush, U.S.A.* This exhibit traces the design, production, and use of Egypt's fourth issue of definitive stamps from 1878 to 1913, showing original artwork, essays, color recipes, proofs, and examples of the wide variety of postal rates in use during that period. (5)
1973–1980	**Scouting on Stamps "Classics"—The Three Earliest Issues** *Frederick P. Lawrence, U.S.A.* The formation and development of the international scouting movement told through the first three issues of scouting on stamps: 1900 Cape of Good Hope Mafeking Besieged "blues," 1918 Czechoslovakia Scout Post, and 1920 Siam "Scout's Fund" overprints. (8)

1981–1988	**Keeping Pace With Inflation: The Post-War Chinese National Currency Issues** *H. James Maxwell, U.S.A.* Illustrates the postal administration's difficulties in dealing with the rampant inflation following World War II. (8)
1989–1996	**The Missionary Stamps of Uganda, 1895–1899** *John Griffith-Jones, U.K.* A study of the typewritten and typeset stamps that marked the birth of Uganda's postal system. The exhibit features unused and used stamps, many errors and varieties, and an extensive range of covers demonstrating internal and external usage. (8)
1997–2004	**Egypt: The First Issue, 1866** *Gregory Todd, U.K.* The genesis of the first issue, from the government post of 1865 followed by essays, proofs, trials. Thereafter with a study of the first seven stamps with multiples, varieties, and usages on and off cover. (8)
2005–2009	**Saudi Arabia: The Nejd Takeover of Hejaz, 1925–1926** *Sarah Saud Mohd. Al-Thani, Qatar* The exhibit shows rare and unique postage stamps, errors, and covers used in Hejaz from 1925 to 1926. (5)
2010–2014	**Benin/Dahomey** *Paul Barsdell, Australia* Benin/Dahomey from forerunner and Dubois French general colonial material and then Benin and Dahomey issues up to about 1913, with a selection of proofs, specimens, varieties, and usages. (5)
2015–2022	**New Zealand: The Second Sideface Issue, 1882–1900** *Paul Wreglesworth, U.K.* A study of the evolution, development, production, and postal usage of this complex issue, the first full issue to be entirely designed, engraved, and printed within the colony and the first specifically intended for both postal and revenue purposes. (8)
2023–2030	**New Zealand Postage Dues, 1899 to 1951—1st, 2nd and 3rd Issues** *James Shaw, Australia* The first series of 11 values includes major varieties and errors. The second series of four stamps continues this pattern with a complex array of printings. Comprehensive and original research on the underpaid usage of covers has enhanced this exhibit. (8)
2031–2038	**Hong Kong: Designs, Proofs, Specimens and Other Archival Materials** *William Kwan, Hong Kong* From Queen Victoria (first issue) in 1862 (De La Rue had been the official printers of Hong Kong stamps) to Queen Elizabeth II of the Hong Kong issues. (8)
2039–2043	**Chinese Post Silver Dollar Period Mail Postage Stamps, April–December 1949** *Lu Shusheng, China* Examples of mail bearing silver dollar postage stamps from different postal zones, the rate adjustment and charges, and the application of stamps and postmarks in different postage values following the implementation of silver dollar postage. (5)
2044–2048	**Metered Mail, 1897–1922** *Luc Legault, Canada* This exhibit is a stamp and cover presentation on the postal history of metered mail covering the first 25 years, from the first world trial in New York City in 1897 to 1922, the year the UPU agreement normalized the use of meters. (5)

2049-2053	**A Study of the First Issues of India, 1852-1854**
	Pragya Jain, India
	The exhibit aims to study the first postal issues of India and their die variations, designs and flaws starting from Scinde Dawks in 1852, the 1854 lithographs and the 1854 2 Anna typograph. (5)
2054-2061	**The Crown Issue and Surcharges of Macau, 1884**
	Cheong-Too Choi, Hong Kong
	This is original study and research of the issue, focusing on the first and second series, colour shade, perforations, multiples, in complete sheets, printing plates, proofs, specimen varieties, reprints, overprints, surcharges, and postal usages. (8)
2062-2069	**King Carlos Issues of Macau**
	Stephen Chan, Hong Kong
	A detailed study of the King Carlos issues of Macau and related postal history. (8)
2070-2077	**Unit, Basic and Silver Yuan Stamps of China**
	Patrick Choy, Singapore
	The exhibit illustrates how the Communist government achieved a stabilized transition of postal administration by allowing a temporary usage of gold/silver stamps in the newly liberated areas. (8)
2078-2085	**Soruth (Indian Feudatory State)**
	Dhananjay Desai, India
	Stamps of Soruth (Indian Feudatory State). (8)
2086-2093	**The Philately of the New Hebrides, 1842-1941**
	Martin Treadwell, New Zealand
	An exhibit tracing the development of New Hebrides philately, from the pre-stamp era, through the use of British, NSW, and New Caledonian stamps, to the condominium post office and the development of gold currency. (8)

Class 3

For exhibits of covers—including folded letters, envelopes, postcards, wrappers, printed matter and other mailed pieces—examining services, rates, markings, routes and destinations.

Class 3A	**United States of America**
2094-2098	**The Marcophily of Hudson, N.Y., 1793 to the UPU**
	George DeKornfeld, U.S.A.
	Traces the evolution of the various postal markings used in Hudson beginning in 1793, the earliest known use. (5)
2099-2103	**Postal Uses of the U.S. 12¢ 1861 Issue**
	Chip Gliedman, U.S.A.
	A study of the uses of the 12-cent 1861 issue to show the breadth, depth, and complexity of postal services and global mail transit during the period. (5)
2104-2108	**The U.S. Local Posts Handled the City Mail**
	Larry Lyons, U.S.A.
	A showing of the eastern local posts which handled the mail and set an example for the U.S. Carrier Department. (5)

2109-2116	**Philadelphia-Great Britain Mails** *John Barwis, U.S.A.* The evolution of letter mails to, from, or through Great Britain from early colonial times until the General Postal Union. (8)
2117-2124	**The Development of Adhesive Stamp Usage on Transatlantic Mail** *Carol Bommarito, U.S.A.* The development of postage prepayment using adhesive stamps on transatlantic mail to and from the U.S., 1840 to 1975. (8)
2125-2132	**Mail Between the U.S. and Germany Before the Universal Postal Union** *Robert Boyd, U.S.A.* Describes the evolution of US-German mail transit and postage rates from the early 19th century to 1875. (8)
2133-2137	**Postal History of the Thirteen Colonies, 1675-1781** *Timothy O'Connor, U.S.A.* The exhibit chronicles the rise of a postal service in early America during the period of British rule. We choose 1675-1781, beginning with and ending with a military event. Commerce and war are the drivers of growth. (5)
2138-2142	**A Country Divided: Effects of the American Civil War on the Mails** *Daniel Ryterband, U.S.A.* Exhibit shows changes to the Union postal system, formation of the Confederate postal system, and impact on wartime correspondence. (5)
2143-2147	**San Francisco Postal History, 1849-1869** *Rick Mingee, U.S.A.* Displays postal history of San Francisco from the beginning of the post office through the first 20 years of operation. (5)
2148-2155	**External Mail Routes of the United States, 1854-1875** *Armando Grassi, U.S.A.* This exhibit illustrates the network of external mail routes from and to the United States between 1854 and 1875. The exhibit focuses on route changes within a broad historical context that includes wars, political changes, diseases, and other factors. (8)
2156-2163	**Fighting the Fed in Philadelphia: Carrier, Local Posts and Independent Mails, 1835-1868** *Vernon Morris, U.S.A.* Intense competition from private enterprise caused the federal government to significantly reduce postal rates and provide greatly improved service. (8)
2164-2168	**The U.S. Forces and Postal Censorship by General Headquarters in Japan** *Gensei Ando, Japan* 2015 was the 70th anniversary of the end of World War II. Examine defeat of Japan, display U.S. Army and GHQ mail. (5)
2169-2176	**New Jersey Stampless Covers: Handstamp Postal Markings, 1775-1855** *Robert G. Rose, U.S.A.* The various types of handstamped postal markings used in New Jersey on prestamp and stampless covers from the time of the Revolutionary War in 1775 until postage stamps were required at the end of 1855, representing those used throughout the early U.S. (8)
2177-2184	**Boston Postal History to 1851** *Mark Schwartz, U.S.A.* The evolution of the rates and services of the American postal system from early colonial times through the rate simplification of 1851, as shown through the window of the Boston Post Office. (8)

2185–2192	**Pioneer Arizona Area Classics, 1783–1870**
	John Birkinbine II, U.S.A.
	Development of mail communication during the pioneer and classical periods. Outgoing, incoming, and internal covers showing routes, rates, and stamps available. Includes few early documents and revenue usages. Over 80% are one to five known. (8)
2193–2200	**Post Office Forms, Including Envelopes Created for Conducting the Registered Mail Process, 1842–1929**
	Fumiaki Wada, Japan
	The objective of this exhibit is to demonstrate the development of the procedures that the U.S. Post Office Department used to handle registered mail from the inception of the service. (8)
2203–2210	**The Origin and Evolution of America's First Express Company—Harnden's Express**
	Roland H. Cipolla II, U.S.A.
	This exhibit tells the story of the three distinct elements of Harnden's Express Company as it evolved within the United States and overseas between its start in March 1839 until its disappearance in 1878. (8)
2211–2218	**The United States 1869 Pictorial Issue Used in International Mails**
	Jeffrey Forster, U.S.A.
	This exhibit displays covers addressed to foreign destinations or originating from abroad bearing U.S. 1869 pictorial issue stamps and mailed when this issue was available. (8)
5206–5210	**Gold Rush Days**
	Dennis Hassler, U.S.A.
	The prelude to the Gold Rush days and the aftermath with foreign connections. Exemplified through stampless covers, 1842 to 1859. (5)
2227–2234	**United States 1870–1888 Bank Note Issue Postal History**
	Matthew Kewriga, U.S.A.
	Domestic and foreign postal history of the U.S. 1870–88 Bank Note issue during its period of general use from 1870 to 1890. This issue was the longest lasting issue of the 19th century and therefore shows a wide coverage of rates, routes, and markings. (8)
2237–2244	**United States Penalty Clause Mail: The Classic Period, 1877–1909**
	Lester C. Lanphear III, U.S.A.
	Extensive study of U.S. penalty clause mail from its beginnings in 1877 to 1909. (8)
2245–2249	**German, Austro-Hungarian and U.S. Civilians Interned in the U.S. During World War I**
	Ed Dubin, U.S.A.
	The World War I (1914–1920) postal history of the U.S. internment of citizens (judged disloyal), along with German and Austro-Hungarian military and foreign nationals in the United States. (5)
2250–2257	**Hawaiian Foreign Mail**
	Richard Malmgren, U.S.A.
	Outgoing and incoming Hawaiian foreign mail from earliest missionary covers in 1820 to United States territorial status in 1900. (8)
2258–2265	**North American Blockade Run Mail, 1775–1865**
	Steven Walske, U.S.A.
	This exhibit shows blockade run mail from the American Revolutionary War, the Anglo-American War of 1812, and the American Civil War. (8)

2266–2273	**The Progression of New York City Foreign Mail Cancels, 1845–1878** *Nicholas Kirke, U.K.* Plots the development of obliterating cancels used on outbound New York City foreign mail from 1845 to 1878. (8)
2275–2282	**The First Four Decades of U.S. Railroad Contract Mails** *Hugh Feldman, U.K.* The development of the carriage of mails by railroad within the U.S. from the early POD contracts of 1838 to the laying of railroads in the southwest in the late 1870s. The information displayed was obtained from original records at the National Archives. (8)
2283–2290	**Southern Mail** *Daniel Warren, U.S.A.* The postal service of the Confederate States of America. (8)
2291–2295	**United States RRR and AR Service to 1945** *David Handelman, Canada* United States return receipt requested (RRR) and avis de reception (AR). (5)
2296	**Postal Markings of Waterbury, Connecticut, 1865–1890** *Bruce Wakeham, Mexico (COFUMEX)*
2297–2304	**New Orleans Postal History—Stampless Mail** *Geoffrey Lewis, Australia* The city's postal history reflects its political history. Being the port near the mouth of the Mississippi meant there was much commercial mail. Includes covers from the Spanish colonial period, pre-statehood period, and to Europe. (8)
2305–2309	**Postal Services in the 1946 Atomic Tests—Operation Crossroads** *James Johnstone, Australia* The exhibit shows the use of postal services during the first major atomic bomb testing program—Operation Crossroads. Covers and postmarks to and from Bikini Atoll describe the location of target and support ships and the nature and use of postal items. (5)
2310–2314	**Rates and Uses of the 3¢ Circular-Die Stamped Envelopes, 1917–1960** *Stephen Suffet, U.S.A.* A postal history exhibit showing how the 3-cent circular die stamped envelopes were used in their day. (5)
2315–2322	**Expansion of U.S. Airmail to Foreign Destinations, 1922–1941** *Murray Abramson, U.S.A.* Examines the expansions of U.S. airmail to foreign destinations, 1922–1941. (8)
Class 3B	**The Americas except the USA**
2324–2328	**Argentina Certified Mail from 1892 to 1920** *Carlos Chaves, Argentina* The collection shows the evolution, variety of marks, routes, and rates of certified mail within the period of 1892 to 1920, a time of many changes in the Argentine mail. (5)
2329–2333	**Marcophilie de La Ville de Quebec, 1763–1851** *Gregoire Teyssier, Canada* Postmarks and postal history of Quebec City Main Post Office from the beginnings of postal service to 1851. (5)
2334–2338	**A Postal History of the Yukon** *Kevin O'Reilly, Canada* Provides an overview of the postal history of the Yukon Territory. Material is organized chronologically and geographically into twelve parts reflecting economic trends. (5)

2339–2343	**Postal Usages in the Province of Quebec and Lower Canada until 1831** *Christiane & Jacques Faucher-Poitras, Canada* The exhibit presents the beginnings of the postal system. (5)
2344–2351	**Navigation Lines Serving South America** *Everaldo Santos, Brazil* To show the postal activities of the navigation lines serving South America, starting with the first postal regulated lines for each country up to the moment they joined the GPU/UPU. (8)
2352–2356	**Chile: Postage Due, 1853–1924** *Cristian Mouat, Chile* Correspondence from 1853 to 1925 that applies the due marking, which includes postage due stamps used on incoming and outgoing covers as well as different postmarks used. (5)
2357–2364	**The Long Way to the Bull's Eyes** *Peter Meyer, Brazil* Postal history letters (1648 to 1843) from kings, queens, and regents, conflicts letter, Brazilian independence, and pre-philatelic cancellations. (8)
2365–2372	**Brazilian International Mail: 1798 to UPU** *Marcos Chusyd, Brazil* This collection includes many destinations, postal rates, routes, and marks under the most important postal conventions during 1798 to UPU. (8)
2373–2380	**In Defense of the Border: Canadian Military Mails, 1667–1885** *David L. Hobden, Canada* Examination of the military use of posts in the evolution of Canada from 1667 to 1885. (8)
2381–2385	**Postmarks of Main Offices in the Carrera General from Cartagena to Tuquerres** *Dario Diez, Colombia* Evolution of postmarks of the main offices in the "Carrera General" that connected Cartagena to Lima within today's Colombia. (5)
2386–2390	**Bermuda Postal History: Forerunners to the UPU—Internal, External and Transit Mail** *David Pitts, U.S.A.* A comprehensive postal history of Bermuda: all routes from, to, and through her, the internal and external rates, and her markings. (5)
2391–2398	**Colombia Pre-Philatelic Letters with Contents** *Jorge Enrique Arbelaez, Colombia* Pre-philatelic letters from Colombia from 1531 to 1859. (8)
2399–2406	**Panama—The Path Between the Seas** *Alfredo Frohlich, U.S.A.* Development of the Panama postal system from colonial times to the first issue of the sovereign state of Panama. (8)
2408–2412	**Cancel Styles and Standardization of Postmarks in 19th Century Mexico** *Peter Taylor, U.S.A.* This exhibit shows the development and use of canceling devices by post offices within the General Postal Administration of Mexico from 1821 to 1900. (5)
2413–2417	**Mexican Postal Districts: The "Reforma" Years, 1856–1864** *Jaime Benavides, Mexico (COFUMEX)* Choice examples showing 46/47 of the Postal Districts in Mexico during this period (Mexican first issue). (5)

2418–2422	**Nova Scotia Cancellations on Saint-Pierre and Miquelon Mail** *Loic Detcheverry, St.-Pierre and Miquelon* Large study of the different Canadian cancellations used on the postage stamps of Saint-Pierre and Miquelon. (5)
2423–2427	**The Postal History of Uruguay, 1779–1880** *Walter Britz, Uruguay* The postal history of Uruguay up to 1880 (when Uruguay joined the UPU), including different frankings, routes, and the evolution of rates. Includes scarce franked items, unique covers, rare destinations, and array of postmarks. (5)
2428–2435	**Costa Rica: Railway Mail from 1873 to the Mid-20th Century** *Alvaro Castro-Harrigan, Costa Rica* This is the postal history of the railway system in Costa Rica, which begins with the first attempts of mail transportation, the main traveling post office routes, and ending with the last postmarks reported before the train stopped its service. (8)
2436–2443	**The Pre-Stamp Period of Costa Rica** *Giana Wayman, Costa Rica* Development of the postal service from the first post offices to the issue of stamps. Includes rates, routes, marks, and destinations. Includes 56 of the 59 reported postal marks, all of the rate handstamps, and all of the receptarias marks. (8)
2444–2448	**Pre-Stamp Mexico: Routes, Rates and Postal Markings** *David Braun, Mexico (COFUMEX)* Study of the routes, rates, and postal markings of Mexico before 1856, when the first stamp was issued. (5)
2449–2456	**Postal Rates, Regulations, and Uses in the Small Queen Era, 1870–1897** *William Averbeck, U.S.A.* Study of Canadian domestic and foreign postage and registration rates and postal regulations during this period. (8)
2457–2464	**Falklands or Malvinas?** *Mark A. Butterline, U.S.A.* The philatelic contest for the islands. (8)
2465–2472	**Postal History of the Cayman Islands, 1829–1945** *Graham Booth, U.K.* There was no post office until 1889, then use of Jamaican stamps was allowed. Under the UPU from 1900, growth was very rapid. Service improved in the 1930s by an increase in the number of post offices, and in 1935, air transit from Jamaica to the USA. (8)
2473–2480	**Canadian Participation in the South African War, 1899–1902** *Joachim Frank, U.K.* The exhibit documents the preparations in Canada and the involvement of the Canadian volunteers who served in the Canadian contingents, British, and colonial units, and the South African constabulary in the war and its aftermath. (8)
2481–2488	**Falkland Islands: A Postal History until 1945** *Mike Roberts, U.K.* Postal communications to, from, and within the islands, the first ship letters, the Royal Navy, and the beginning of packet services. The post offices and their markings, rates, and special treatments. (8)
2489–2496	**The Route of the UPU, Mexico's Foreign Mail Issues and Their Postal History** *Salomon Rosenthal, Mexico(FIP)* Postal history of the Juarez issue, used during the transition of the postal system to adjust to the UPU. (8)

2497–2504	**Maritime Mail of Spanish Colonies in America**
	Jesus Sitja Prats, Spain
	The exhibit shows the postal history of the mail of the Spanish colonies in America from 1509 to the middle 1800s. (8)
2505–2512	**Puerto Rico Postal History, 1778–1900**
	Stefan Heijtz, Sweden
	This is a study of the postal history of Puerto Rico, from the pre-stamp and Spanish period through the U.S. occupation. (8)
2513–2520	**Honduras Pre-Philately**
	Maria Beatriz Bendeck, Honduras
	This exhibit presents a study of the pre-philatelic postmarks, routes, and fares of the Honduran post during the Spanish colonial era and the postcolonial era until the introduction of the first Honduran postage stamps in 1865. (8)
2525–2529	**The Pre-Stamp Period of El Salvador**
	Guillermo Gallegos, El Salvador
	A selection of Salvadoran items that provide an overview of its pre-stamp era throughout its three major historical periods (Colonial, Central American Federation, Republic), with a special emphasis on seldom seen markings and routes. (5)
2531–2535	**Ferrocarriles de la Provincia de Buenos Aires Marcos Postilos Ambulantes**
	Hector DiLalla, Argentina
	Development of different railroads and postmarks. (5)

Class3C — Europe

2537–2544	**Accountancy Markings Associated with the 1857 Franco-British Postal Convention**
	Jeffrey Bohn, U.S.A.
	A comprehensive exhibit that attempts to show examples of all the "GB" and "FR" accountancy markings introduced for use under the 1857 Franco-British Postal Convention. (8)
2545–2552	**Faroe Islands Mail, 1751–1948**
	Geoffrey Noer, U.S.A.
	This exhibit examines classic Faroe Islands postal history from the earliest known cover through the end of World War II. (8)
2553–2557	**Austrian Lloyd Steam Navigation Company, 1839–1917**
	William Sandrik, U.S.A.
	The postal history of the company from its early beginnings until 1917. (5)
2558–2562	**Switzerland Registered Mail, 1785–1863**
	Michael Peter, U.S.A.
	This exhibit examines the wide variety of Registration markings in Switzerland from prephilately though their classic Federal stamps period. (5)
2563–2570	**Austrian Post Offices in Bulgaria**
	Idor Gatti, U.K.
	The postal history of the Austrian post offices in Bulgaria prior to the formation of Bulgaria in 1879. (8)
2571–2578	**The British Postal Reforms of 1839–1840**
	James Grimwood-Taylor, U.K.
	The postal history study of Rowland Hill's great reforms, tracing the origins of the world's first postage stamp from 1694, the postal rate inflation that caused the campaign for cheap postage and the process/effects of reform. (8)

2579–2583	**Great Britain: The Franking System and Official Mail from Queen Elizabeth I to 1840** *Robert Galland, U.K.* This exhibit shows official letters up to 1652, early letters of the franking system and development of handstamps associated with the franking system. (5)
2585–2589	**The British Recorded Delivery Service, 1961–2010** *John Sussex, U.K.* A study of the Great Britain recorded delivery service from its inception in 1961, following its development until 2010. (5)
2590–2594	**Stampless Maritime Overweight Mail in Pre-UPU Times, 1765–1876** *Paul Wijnants, Belgium* A study of stampless maritime overweight mail before the introduction of the UPU, subdivided into nonconventional and conventional mail, as well as direct mail and mail in transit. (5)
2595–2602	**Postal Services in the Habsburg Kingdom of Hungary to 1900** *Bill Hedley, U.K.* This exhibit traces the development of postal services in Hungary from the 1530s until the currency change in 1900. (8)
2603–2610	**Secured Delivery Leading to Introduction of U.K. Registration of Internal, External and Transit Mail, 1201–1862** *Alan Holyoake, U.K.* Though a formal system of registration was introduced on January 6, 1841, the need for a secure system of delivery had long been recognized. This exhibit traces the complex story that led to registration. (8)
2611–2618	**The Posts in the City of Lübeck before 1868** *Chris King, U.K.* Postal services in the city from the introduction of the Thurn and Taxis postal handstamps of 1784, including early mail items showing the Hanseatic and Princely posts, to the creation of the North German Confederation on January 1, 1868. (8)
2619–2626	**Ottoman Railway Postal History** *Atadan Tunaci, Turkey* This exhibit presents the postal history of the Ottoman Railways, which is the beginning of the railway post. (8)
2627–2634	**The Postal Correspondence of the Russian Navy Personnel, 1901–1918** *Vladimir Berdichevskiy, Israel* This exhibit shows the history of postal correspondence of Russian Navy Personnel until 1918 (including periods of the Russian-Japanese War and World War I), including correspondence from all fleets and flotillas. (8)
2635–2639	**Express Service in Italy, 1890–2001, and Its Precursors from the 15th Century** *Claudio Ernesto Manzati, Italy* This collection documents the history of the express service in Italy from the prephilatelic through service establishment in the Kingdom of Lombardy Veneto in 1860 and the Kingdom of Italy in 1890 until its suppression in the late twentieth century. (5)
2640–2644	**Tuscany's Worldwide Postal Relationships, 1849–1863** *Vittorio Morani, Italy* This exhibit illustrates the domestic mail of Tuscany as well as the mail to and from the Old Italian and the Foreign States, including the Overseas States. (5)

2645–2652 **The Perforated Cérès: Rates, Routes & Postmarks, 1871–1878**
Yacov Tsachor, Israel
A study of France 1871–1878 Cérès local and foreign rates, insured mail, destinations, maritime and consular mail, mixed frankings, redirected mail, foreign post offices, etc. (8)

2653–2660 **Principality of Monaco, 1704–1898**
Nicola Posteraro, France
The postal markings and postage rates for letters from Monaco under the French postal administration and during the period of the protectorate by the Kingdom of Sardinia. (8)

2661–2668 **Postal Exchanges to and from Foreign Countries with the Perforated Cérès Issue**
Daniel Paulin, France
1870–1875 Perforated Cérès issue: a selection of franking, destination, printed matter, ballons montes, seapost, and mail to or from abroad. (8)

2669–2676 **Hermes, The First Issue of Hellenic Stamps on International Mail, 1861–1882**
Michèle Chauvet, France
The use of large Hermes head on all international mail, including prepaid mail from Greece to abroad, taxes of Greece on unpaid mail from abroad, and combination covers with partial frankings and taxes. (8)

2677–2684 **Mail with the Stamps of Umberto I of Italy, Aug. 15, 1879 to Sept. 20, 1902**
Giovanni Nembrini, Italy
This exhibit shows mail franked with the 31 definitive and 20 special stamps issued during the reign of Umberto I, including usages with earlier issued and later issued postage stamps, until the end of their validity period. (8)

2685–2689 **The Use of Austrian Stamps in the Hungarian Half of the Empire, 1850–1867**
Adriano Bergamini, Switzerland
This exhibit will show the use of the first five issues of Austria in the Hungarian part of the Empire. (5)

2690–2694 **The Anglo-American Postal Convention of Dec. 15, 1848**
Lars Boettger, Luxembourg
Development of the Anglo-American convention of 1848. (5)

2695–2702 **Venice: The Contagion, Quarantine, Disinfection and Quarantine Hospitals**
Franco Rigo, Italy
Postal history of the health office from the 16th Century to the 19th Century (8)

2705–2712 **Italian Express Mail**
Alessandro Agostosi, Italy
This exhibit shows the different ways of Express Courier since 1489 (Old Italian States). (8)

2713–2720 **Geneva Postal Services, 1839–1862**
Jean Voruz, Switzerland
From Cantonal Post to Federal Post: postal links in Geneva locally and with major neighboring countries in the context of the birth of the Swiss Franc. (8)

2721–2728 **The Postal History of the Wynental, Switzerland**
Jürg Roth, Switzerland
A selection of postal marks and frankings of the Wynental valley in Switzerland from 1813–1907, showing prephilately and postal-route marks on letters, as well as cancellations of the first Swiss federal stamps in red. (8)

2729–2736	**Swedish Postal Rates, 1920–1970**
	Kjell Nilson, Sweden
	This exhibit shows all existing kinds of postal items and services paid for with stamps; the development of important rates and fees during this period; and includes scarcer single franked items. (8)
2737–2744	**The Eagle-Shield Stamps—Domestic Mail, 1872–1875**
	Jan-Olof Ljungh, Sweden
	This exhibit shows different domestic postal rates during the first years of the German Empire, when the Eagle Shield stamps were used. (8)
2745–2752	**Cancellations from Swedish Steamship Mail Post Offices, 1869–1951**
	Gunnar Lithén, Sweden
	Cancellations from Swedish post offices on board Swedish steamships operating in Sweden, to Norway and Finland, from 1869 up to 1951. (8)
2753–2760	**Swedish Military and Volunteers in Wars, Campaigns or Active Service Abroad, 1582–1905**
	Richard Bodin, Sweden
	This exhibit shows postal and special communication arrangements for Swedish militaries during war and volunteers in foreign services abroad. (8)
2765–2772	**Postal Services in Rural Areas in the Netherlands before 1850**
	Hotze Wiersma, Netherlands
	This exhibit shows the development of postal possibilities at the countryside. (8)
2773–2780	**The Netherlands: Postmarks from the First to 1813–1814**
	Peter Heck, Germany
	Netherlands postmarks from the first to 1813–1814 (8)
2781–2788	**Correspondence of Saxony with the Old Italian States**
	Arnim Knapp, Germany
	Illustrates the period from 1730 (Reich Post time) until the beginning of the German-Austrian mail in 1850 and the end of sovereignty of the Kingdom of Saxony at the end of 1857. (8)
2789–2796	**Prussia as the Main Link of the Russian-Polish Mail with the West**
	Karlfried Krauss, Germany
	This exhibit shows the postal relations and conventions for carrying mail between Russia and Prussia, and beyond Prussia to and from foreign countries from the beginning until the General Postal Union became effective. (8)
2797–2804	**Hungary: Hyperinflation, 1945–1946**
	Robert Morgan, U.S.A.
	This is a study of the hyperinflation period's 27 rate changes and postal usages. Discoveries, unusual and elusive usages and destinations are included. (8)
2810–2814	**Kingdom of Poland: Study of Rates for Stampless Mail, 1815–1871**
	Wieslaw Kostka, U.S.A.
	This exhibit illustrates the complex system used to determine postal tariffs of various classes of mailing. (5)
2815–2819	**The Principality of Serbia**
	William Maddocks, U.S.A.
	The expansion of the post and postal routes in the prephilatelic period. (5)

2820–2824	**Mail Routes and Rates between France and Foreign Countries by Sail and Steam, 1828–1849**
	Robert Abensur, France
	A study of maritime connexions between France and overseas from January 1, 1828, to August 1, 1849. (5)
2825–2832	**From Angora to Ankara**
	Koray Özalp, Turkey
	A study of postal history in Ankara from 1840 to 1940, a period that includes its development into a city and its rise and fall in the period following the establishment of the Turkish Republic. (8)
2833–2840	**Beginnings of the Post in Independent Poland, Nov. 1918–1920**
	Julian Auleytner, Poland
	This exhibit documents the process of Polish Post's unification after a long period of partitions, showing short-time applied solutions by Post in different areas of Poland. (8)
2841–2848	**Postal Rates and Frankings of Slovenia, Croatia, and Bosnia and Herzegovina, 1918–1921**
	Henk Buitenkamp, Netherlands
	This exhibit illustrates the problems and developments of the Post during the tumultuous days after World War I. In 2½ years, the old Austrian-Hungarian/Bosnian postal systems are transformed into a new national postal system. (8)
2849–2856	**Military Mail in the Netherlands in the Napoleonic Era**
	Frederik Boom, Netherlands
	This exhibit shows the use of postal markings on military mail in the Netherlands in the so-called French or Napoleonic Era from 1793–1813. (8)
2857–2864	**Serbia in World War I, 1914–1918**
	Aleksandar Krstić, Serbia
	Development of the postal system through first war days through Albania, Thessilonika Front, Corfu, Liberation. All cancels, few uniques, rates, occupation. (8)
2865–2869	**Austro-Hungarian Field Post, 1914–1918**
	Lubor Kunc, Czech Republic
	This exhibit shows the key elements of the field postal system through postal documents and philatelic material. (5)
2870–2874	**Madrid Royal Post and Public Correspondence, 1561–1856**
	Ramón Cortés de Haro, Spain
	A study of the creation of the postal service in Madrid, initially for exclusive use of the Royal House, later becoming a public service, showing its evolution using postmarks until the obligatory use of adhesive postage stamps in 1856. (5)
2875–2879	**Foreign Mails from the Netherlands during World War II**
	Hans van der Horst, Netherlands
	This exhibit shows the impact of censorship and other restrictions on postal senders to and from the Netherlands during World War II. (5)
2880–2884	**Serbia Postal History, 1840–1915**
	Aleksandar Boričić, Serbia
	The development of postal history from forerunners, Austrian Post, First Emission Mihailo and Milan Kingdom, with all known rarities. (5)
2885–2892	**Bosnia and Herzegovina, 1826–1918: The Cancellations Study**
	Zoran Stepanović, Serbia
	This exhibit illustrates chronological postal cancellations from forerunners through the occupation period, including introduction and development of the B and H postmark up to 1918. (8)

2893–2900	**The Norwegian Skilling Issues on Postal Items** *Knut J. Buskum, Norway* Use of Norwegian stamps on postal items from 1855 until the late use of skilling stamps when the öre stamps were put in use in 1877. (8)
2901–2908	**Cunard Line: The Ships and the Transatlantic Mail in the Monopoly Years, 1846–1867** *Eigil Trondsen, Norway* Cunard, the Steamship Line that transformed the communication between between the Old and New Worlds. (8)
2909–2916	**History of Postal Services in the Děčín Region** *Miloš Červinka, Czech Republic* This exhibit illustrates the development of the postal services in the Děčín region from the 17th to 19th centuries mainly by showing usage of posting and receiving postmarks on Austrian stamps and entires. (8)
2917–2924	**Postmarks of the Kingdom of Valencia, 1566–1875** *Juan Antonio Llácer Gracia, Spain* A study of the evolution and development of postmarks in the Kingdom of Valencia, including pre-philatelic postmarks of origin, certificate postmarks, pre-postage, franchises, among others. (8)
2925–2929	**Plain and Numbered Star Cancels on Mail from Paris Central and 39 District Offices, 1852–1876** *Ted Nixon, Canada* A study of mail from Paris showing plain and numbered star cancels and related varieties from Paris Central Office 1852–1876 and 39 district offices 1863–1876. (5)
2930–2934	**Foreign Frankings from Hungary, 1926–1944** *Péter Dunai, Hungary* The foreign frankings of the Pengö-fillér period to different destinations. (5)
2935–2939	**Postal Censoring Challenges: Dealing with World War II Mail Violations** *Michael Deery, Canada* This exhibit illustrates how many postal regulations were violated by Allied and Axis countries, including civilian, military and POW correspondence, and the actions taken, usually directed to the sender of the mail. (5)
2940–2944	**Transnistria: Civilian and Military Censorship, 1941–1944** *Alexandru Săvoiu, Romania* The postal history of Transnistria under Romanian occupation. (5)
2945–2952	**Free Hanseatic City of Bremen—Letters of the Various Postal Administrations** *Friedrich Meyer, Germany* The flexibility of a Free Trading City with worldwide commercial connections from the first overseas postal agreements during the 1840s until the end of the city's sovereignty on December 31, 1867. (8)
2953–2960	**Bokelian Seamen's Letters from and to Sailing Vessels, 1830–1890** *Djordje Katurić, Montenegro* Bocca di Cattaro during Austrian Empire until 1867. Correspondence to and from sailors, captains, families, shipowners, agents and brokers. (8)
2961–2968	**Postal History of Bocca di Cattaro, 1809–1875** *Tomo Katurić, Montenegro* This exhibit shows the postal history of Bocca di Cattaro from the Napoleonic period through the Austro-Hungarian Empire to the Universal Postal Union. (8)

2969–2976	**Railway Postmarks of the RSFSR and USSR** *Valentin Levandovskiy, Russia* Railway postmarks of the Russian Soviet Federative Socialist Republic and the Soviet Union (8)
2977–2984	**Classic Postal System of Romania, 1858–1872** *Constantin Milu, Romania* The development of Courier Postal System in Moldavia, Wallachia, United Principalities and Romania, illustrating the succession of postal routes and postal rates in the classic period. (8)
2985–2989	**Postal History of Finland until the UPU** *Risto Pitkänen, Finland* Great rarities of Finnish postal history. (5)
2990–2994	**Moscow Postal History** *Alexey Strebulaev, Belarus* This exhibit illustrates the origin, development and, particularly, postal stationery in Moscow. (5)
2995–2999	**The Pre-Philatelic Period of the Hellenic Postal Service** *Thomas Arvanitis, Greece* The establishment and the development of the Hellenic postal service. The post offices, postal routes and postal rates. Post offices abroad and the postal conventions. Auxiliary marks and services. (5)
3000–3004	**Provisional Cancellations of Latvia, 1919–1921** *Vesma Grinfelds, U.S.A.* A detailed macrophilatelic study of post-World War I cancellations used in Latvia prior to standardized postmarks. (5)
3005–3012	**North Atlantic Mail by Steamship until the UPU** *Seppo Talvio, Finland* The story of the development of the scheduled mail service across the north Atlantic Ocean and the competition between ship lines in the 19th century. (8)
3013–3020	**Irish Postal History** *Des Quail, Ireland* Tracing the development of the postal system in Ireland from 1591–1891, including handstamps, rates, routes for each period. (8)
3021–3028	**The Austrian Post in the Levant—200 Years of Habsburg Interests in the Orient** *Werner Schindler, Austria* The development of the Austrian Post in the Ottoman Empire from the beginning of the first land routes in 1719 up to the termination of "Capitulations" in 1914. (8)
3029–3036	**Kingdom of Lombardy-Venetia, 1815–1866** *Heinrich Stepnizka, Austria* All postal activities in Lombardy and Venetia between 1815 and 1866, except parcel mail, covering the transition from the Napoleonic Italian postal system to the Austrian and later to the Sardinian mail systems. (8)
3037–3044	**Letter-Mail from Austria to Italy during the Risorgimento, 1848–1870** *Klaus Schoepfer, Austria* This exhibit illustrates routes and rates from the First War of Unification in 1848 to the Annexation of the Papal States in 1870. (8)
3045–3049	**The Slovenes in the Camps of the Duce** *Veselku Guštin, Slovenia* The Slovenes from occupied territories confined in different parts of Italy as soldiers in BSL, internees, or political prisoners. (5)

3050–3054	**Germany: Mail Postilion on Postcards**
	Herwig Kussing, South Africa
	This exhibit presents official postcards and reply postcards issued by the German Empire with the mail postilion as imprinted value. (5)
3055–3059	**Field Post of the Estonian Army, 1918–1920**
	Mati Senkel, Estonia
	This is an exhibit of letters and postcards sent by different soldiers in different units of Estonia. (5)
3060–3064	**Descent into the Abyss**
	Bruce Chadderton, Australia
	This exhibit uses predominately philatelic material to trace the events that unfolded as Germany persecuted Europe's Jews, actions now known as the Holocaust. (5)
3065–3072	**Postal History of Bosnia and Herzegovina, 1813–1900**
	Nikola Nino Marakovic, Austria
	The Turkish and Austro-Hungarian Occupation of Bosnia and Herzegovina. (8)
3073–3080	**French Naval Mail to America: The "RF" Period and Lead-Up, 1943–1945**
	Lewis Bussey, U.S.A.
	Postal history, including cancels and censoring of mail sent to the Americas by French sailors from their ships and bases, with key and/or unique usages plus a short comparison of legitimate U.S. forgeries. (8)
3081–3088	**Norwegian Skilling Covers—Domestic and Abroad**
	Tom Komnæs, Norway
	This exhibit illustrates the rates, routes and destinations on Norwegian skilling covers. (8)
3089–3096	**The Universal Postal Union and Its Impact on Global Postal Services**
	James Peter Gough, U.S.A.
	How the UPU influenced the development of worldwide postal services. (8)
3097–3104	**Early Postmarks of Russia, 1765–1815**
	Alexander Mramornov, Russia
	In 1764, Empress Ekaterina Velikaja has begun reorganization and improvement of postal business in Russia. (8)
3105–3112	**Polar History of Russia**
	Lev Safonov, Russia
	This exhibit shows the history of development of the northern regions of Russia, the Northern Sea Route. (8)
3113–3117	**Belgian, British and American Restrictions on Civil Mail in the Rhineland, 1918–1925**
	Robin Pizer, U.K.
	Censorship of mail and restrictions on postal services are illustrated for the Belgian, British and American occupation zones of Germany. (5)
5211–5218	**World War II: Effect on Mail in Holland and the East Indies**
	Kees Adema, U.S.A.
	This exhibit sheds light on the causes for distribution and delay while placing mail in its historical context. (5)

Class 3D — Asia, Oceania and Africa

3118–3122	**A Study of Persian Native Postmarks, 1876–1926**
	Tamouchin K. Shahrokh, Iran
	This exhibit examines the very first postmarks used in villages and small towns, all irregular in shape with no or limited dates displayed on them. (5)

3125-3132   **Turkish Post in the Holy Land, 1841-1918**
Shaula Alexander, Israel
Turkish postal routes and rates for domestic and foreign mail, army post and Jewish settlements. (8)

3133-3140   **Israel: 1948 Transition Period—Cities under Emergency Conditions**
Itamar Karpovsky, Israel
This exhibit shows selected pages of official local post services during the 1948 War of Independence, from the towns of Jerusalem, Safad, Nahariya and Rishon-lezion. (8)

3141-3148   **The Japanese Couriers, 1601-1873**
Yoshiyuki Yamazaki, Japan
Three times couriers have been started since 1615. The Japanese government established postal services in Tokaido on April 20, 1871, then the courier was closed on June 1, 1873. (8)

3149-3156   **Prompt Delivery in Japan from the Pre-Adhesive Period to 1937**
Kenzaburo Ikeda, Japan
This exhibit is a specialized Japanese postal history collection including many important or unique items. (8)

3157-3164   **Postal History of Great Joséon and Imperial Daehan, 1884-1905**
Young Kil Kim, Korea
The postal history of Great Joséon and Imperial Daehan from 1884 to 1905. (8)

3165-3169   **Postal History of Internees and POWs Held in Australia during World War II**
Sybrand Jitse Bakker, Netherlands
The postal history of internees and prisoners of war held in Australia during World War II (5)

3170-3174   **The Civil Censorship Process in Australia, 1939-1945**
Monica M. Comrie, New Zealand
This exhibit examines the development of the Civil Censorship process during the war years with examples from all seven censorship regions. (5)

3175-3179   **Kenya, Uganda, Tanganyika: Postal History, 1933-1961**
Susan Vernall, New Zealand
"Internal mail, surface mail, airmail, short paid mail and traveling post offices, along with examples of civilian and military censorship during World War II. " (5)

3180-3184   **Postal Development of the Malayan Post Union, 1934-1942**
Henry Ong, Singapore
This exhibit examines issues faced by the Malayan Postal Union from its inception until February 15, 1942, when the surrender of the British to the Japanese army in Singapore ended British rule of the Malaya peninsula. (5)

3185-3192   **Postal History of Mongolia, 1863-1933**
Chuluundorj Enkhbat, Mongolia
This exhibit examines the Mongolian courier relay horse mail, the Russian branch post offices, the Chinese branch post offices and the independent postal service. (8)

3193-3200   **Destination Insulinde**
Gerard Louis van Welie, Netherlands
Mail sent to the Dutch East Indies from all parts of the world, with an emphasis on the 19th century. (8)

3201-3208   **Prisoner-of-War Correspondence, Japanese Occupation of the Far East, 1942-1945**
Lindsay Chitty, New Zealand
A postal history study of prisoner-of-war mail during the Japanese occupation, providing information on the prisoners, the postal history, routes, rates and marcophily, organized by region. (8)

3209–3216	**Postal History of Nyasaland—African Postal Union to Federation** *Ross Wood, Australia* The African Postal Union commenced on 1 April 1936, with a reduction in postal rates between the members. The exhibit begins on this date and continues until Nyasaland becomes part of the federation of Rhodesia and Nyasaland in 1953. (8)
3217–3224	**Bahrain Postal History** *Mardyya Wahab Hussain, Qatar* Bahrain postal history from the Indian administration to independence, with examples of stamps, covers and aerogrammes and cancellations. (8)
3225–3229	**Sharjah Postal History** *Nasser Bin Ahmad Al Serkal, U.A.E.* This exhibit examines the development of the postal system in Sharjah from 1914. (5)
3230–3234	**Postal History of Ethiopia, 1895–1909** *Ulf Lindahl, U.S.A.* Ethiopia's postal history during its organizing period from the first mail in January 1895 to UPU membership in November 1908 and the issuance of the second set of stamps in January 1909. (5)
3235–3239	**India: Postal Markings and Rates of King Edward VII** *Khalid Naeem, U.A.E.* A study of postal markings and postal rates through examples of ordinary and registered covers. (5)
3240–3244	**Postal History of South Georgia** *Hugh Osborne, U.K.* A postal history of South Georgia. (5)
3245–3252	**Jerusalem, 1655–1917** *Mihael I. Fock, Slovenia* The development of postal communications to and from Jerusalem during the Ottoman occupation from 1655–1917. (8)
3253–3260	**Official Mail of the Cape of Good Hope, 1806–1910** *Hugh Amoore, South Africa* This exhibit traces the postal treatment of official mail during the colonial period. (8)
3261–3268	**Russian (Caucasus)-Persian Interpostal Relations** *Björn Sohrne, Sweden* This exhibit examines the importance and effects of Russian political, economic and military pressure and presence in Persia related to Persia postal development and communication. (8)
3269–3276	**Dutch West Indies: Postal Routes and Rates, 1695–1918** *Sven Påhlman, Sweden* This exhibit examines the development of postal services between Europe/America and the Dutch West Indies, including West Africa, Curaçao and Suriname, with an emphasis on postal routes and route marks. (8)
3277–3284	**Japanese Military and Prisoner of War Mail of the Thai-Burma Railway** *Terence Pickering, U.K.* Mail of the Japanese military and prisoners of war engaged in the construction of the Thai-Burma Railway during World War II, including American prisoners of war mail. (8)

3285-3292	**Netherlands East Indies Mail, 1789-1877** *Richard Wheatley, U.K.* This exhibit examines the inland mail service and mail to and from overseas, including development of the overland route with the world's first postage due label. (8)
3293-3300	**Foreign Postal Operations in the Holy Land, 1852-1914** *Michael Bass, U.S.A.* This exhibit examines the development of formal European postal services for France, Austria, Germany, Russia and Italy in the Holy Land, 1852–1914. (8)
3305-3312	**Morocco Foreign Post Offices and Agencies** *Larry Gardner, U.S.A.* A postal history chronology of the four foreign post offices and agencies that opened in Morocco prior to the one opened and operated by the Sultanate of Morocco. (8)
3313-3320	**The Four Siege Cities of 1948: Rishon Lezion, Safad, Nahariya, Jerusalem** *Henry Nogid, U.S.A.* Despite being surrounded and cut off, these four cities continued mail services and produced their own stamps. (8)
3322-3329	**Victorian Outgoing Indian Mail to Great Britain, Europe and the U.S., October 1854–July 1876** *Paul Allen, U.S.A.* A study of the rates and routes by which Indian mail reached the stated destinations. (8)
3330-3337	**The Postal History of Tahiti Through the First Pictorial Issue** *Ralph DeBoard, U.S.A.* This exhibit traces the philatelic history of the South Pacific islands centered around Tahiti from the earliest philatelic artifact through the usage period of the 1913 pictorial issue. (8)
3338-3345	**Australian Colonies-U.S. Mail** *Dale Forster, U.S.A.* A postal history study of the various routes for mail in both directions between Australia and the U.S.A. (8)
3346-3353	**The Russian Post at the Chinese Eastern Railways** *Alexey Timofeev, Belarus* This exhibit examines mailings on train traveling post offices (TPOs) and also railway stations on the Chinese Eastern Railways. (8)
3354-3361	**Imperial Postmarks of the Trans-Siberian Railroad from Chelyabinsk to Manchuria** *Edward Laveroni, U.S.A.* The rates, routes, and a representation of the postmarks of the various railroad lines, large stations, and small stations of the Trans-Siberian Railroad from Chelyabinsk to Manchhyria. (8)
3362-3369	**The Foreign Postal System in Great Joséon during the Treaty Ports Era, 1876-1899** *Oh Byung Yoon, Korea* Survey of foreign postal systems in the Korean peninsula from 1876–1899 (8)
3370-3377	**The Conquest and British Military Administration of Palestine and (Greater) Syria, 1914-1920** *Jonathan Becker, U.S.A.* This postal history exhibit shows the period of richest diversity and scarcest surviving material in Palestine philately. Military and civilian mails are shown to illustrate the range of unorthodox and conventional postal policies and practices. (8)

3378–3385	**China: The Postal History of Mongolia, 1841–1921** *Wei Gang, China* This exhibit is divided into four parts: The Qing Dynasty courier mail system and early missionary mail (1755–1910), Russian post office (1872–1917), Chinese Imperial Post Office (1910–1912) and the Chinese Republic post office. (8)
3386–3393	**A Postal History of British & Qajar Dynasty Persia, 1857–1924** *Ali Raza Nanjee, Pakistan* A study of the postal history of Persia, comprising the British Indian administration period from the Field force 1857, Queen Victoria, King Edward VII and King George V periods. (8)
3394–3401	**Turkey: The Ottoman Post in Lebanon, 1841–1918** *Robert Stuchell, U.S.A.* The wide variety of Ottoman postal markings from towns within the present borders of Lebanon. (8)
3402–3406	**Interrupted and Delayed Mail of the Arab-Israeli Conflict** *Daryl Kibble, Australia* Important interrupted/delayed mail and instructional markings from the Arab-Israeli conflict beginning in 1848, focusing on mail that did not reach its intended destination and/or addressee, was returned to sender, or was significantly delayed. (5)
3407–3414	**The Postal History of New South Wales, 1801–1849** *Stephen Browne, Australia* This exhibit traces the development of postal services in the colony of New South Wales from first settlement, covering the establishment of the post office in 1810 and the major postal acts of 1825 and 1835. (8)
3415–3422	**"Postage to Collect" for Australian Colonial Mail** *Alan Grey, Australia* Postal history including deficient postage, returned for postage, insufficient postage for designated route, unpaid postage, overweight letters, unstamped letters, redirection, damaged/invalid stamps, among others. (8)
3423–3430	**Mission Mail—Central Africa** *Paul Peggie, Australia* A study of the mail routes that linked the missions to the postal system, predominantly in the territories of northern Rhodesia and central Africa from 1891 to 1924. (8)
3431–3438	**Forces Mail in Western Australia During World War II** *Glen Stafford, Australia* The postal history of the Western Australian Forces defending Western Australia during World War II. (8)
3439–3446	**The Military Posts of the Chinese People's Volunteers, 1950–1958** *Kang Yongchang, China* The military posts of the Chinese People's Volunteers, showing different types of military postmarks related to "CPVA Military Post" and special postal services for CPVA. (8)
3447–3454	**The Postal History of Imperial China, 1897–1911** *Tsai Wen-Lung, Chinese Taipei* Domestic and overseas postage rates, including rates to special destinations such as Korea, Sinkiang, Mongolia, Tibet, and Yunnan, as the Chinese Imperial Post started to service the border areas with special postal routes. (8)

3455–3462	**Egypt: Maritime Mail Routes of the 19th Century** *Hany Salam, Egypt* The role of Egypt as an important link in the network of 19th century maritime mail routes, showing the progress in speed and regularity of communication between Europe mail routes that transited or served Egypt. (8)
3463–3470	**Forwarding Mail from and inside Ethiopia, from the 1840s to 1936** *Juha Kauppinen, Finland* This exhibit shows how mail was forwarded by foreign posts inside Ethiopian territory prior to 1835, by the Ethiopian private posts, how Ethiopia entered the UPU, and how postal services became available in the countryside in the early UPU years. (8)
3471–3478	**Life and Conditions in Mauritius, 1680–1870, Illustrated by Its Postal History** *Robert Marion, France* The historical aspects of Mauritius postal history. (8)
3479–3486	**Morocco Postal History, 1852–1925** *Maurice Hadida, France* This exhibit consists of a selection of covers from the four foreign post offices (British, French, German and Spanish), including mixed frankings with the local and Cherifian posts. (8)
3487–3494	**Postal History of Sinkiang** *Kin Chi Danny Wong, Hong Kong* Heavily influenced by Russia, semi-independent from China in modern history and troubled by internal unrests, this exhibit examines the colorful postal history of Sinkiang (Xinjiang) up to the founding of the People's Republic in 1949. (8)
3495–3502	**China-America Mail** *Francis Au, Hong Kong* This exhibit is a study of 19th century China-America mail, including early mail, transatlantic and transpacific mail, route and rate changes due to military activities and international postal conventions. (8)
3503–3507	**Postal History of Huadong (East China) Liberated Area, 1946–1950** *Dao Wenjin, China* The Huadong Liberated Area was formed in September 1946, with Shandong and Huazhong sub-bureaus, and expanded continuously with the progress of the Liberation War, promoting the unification of national postal affairs. (5)
3508–3512	**The Development of Yunnan's Postal System, 1901–1949** *Mah Lang-Moe, Chinese Taipei* This exhibit focuses on the public mails of Yunnan Province, including the opening of individual post offices, the introduction of postal rates, routes and cancellations, and the different services provided by the post office. (5)
3513–3517	**Mongolia Postal History, 1878–1941** *Stefan Petriuk, Germany* This exhibit shows, with letters and postal cancellations, the development of the post in Mongolia, with the Russian post starting from 1878, the Chinese post starting from 1909 and the Mongolian post from 1924 until 1941. (5)
3518–3522	**Selangor, 1935–1969** *Muhammad Azharuddin Md Azmi, Malaysia* Selangor, 1935–1969 (5)

3523-3530	**Postal History of Cochin** *K. S. Mohan, India* This exhibit examines 17th, 18th and 19th century Dutch, Portuguese and British letters to and from Cochin, Cochin prepost letters, the one and only temple seal cancellation letter and the very rare manuscript date stamp and registration letter. (8)
3531-3538	**Study of Postal Cancellation During Japanese Occupation of the Netherlands Indies, 1942-1945** *Asroni Harahap, Indonesia* This is a study of the postal cancellations used during the Japanese occupation of the Netherlands Indies, 1942-1945. (8)
3539-3546	**Netherlands Indies Postal Cancellations, 1789-1917** *Fadli Zon, Indonesia* The postal history of V.O.C. stamps until Squared Circle Cancellation at the documents. (8)
3547-3554	**Kuwait Postal History—Indian Era, 1902-1949** *Khaled Abdul Mughni, Kuwait* Kuwait postal history under the Indian era, before the opening of the Kuwait post office under Pakistani administration in 1947 until 1948. (8)

Class 4

For exhibits about envelopes, postcards, wrappers aerogrammes and other items pre-printed with an indication of postage paid.

3557-3561	**Post Cards of the Russian Empire with Multiple Advertisements** *Valery Krepostnov, Belarus* Postcards of the Russian Empire with multiple advertisements (5)
3562-3566	**People's Republic of China: Stamped Letter Sheets of 1952** *Chen Yue, China* China postal stationery issue of 1952 (5)
3567-3574	**New South Wales Postal Stationery** *Michael Blinman, Australia* This exhibit examines the development and usage of different types of postal stationery from the first issue of 1838 to the early years of the Australian commonwealth. (8)
3575-3582	**Leeward Islands Postal Stationery** *Darryl Fuller, Australia* Federal issues of postal stationery of the Leeward Islands, including archival material together with usage in the individual islands, together with personal research. (8)
3727-3734	**Envelopes and Postcards of Canada** *Ian McMahon, Australia* The postal stationery envelopes and postcards of Canada from the first issues to those of King George V. (8)
3735-3742	**Gold Coast Postal Stationery** *Philip Levine, Australia* The postal stationery of this most important British colony, featuring usage and precursor material. (8)
3743-3747	**AQ Letter Sheets of the Republic of Venice—First 40 Years, 1608-1648** *Wang Zhigang, China* Taxed postal stationery in the Republic of Venice (5)

3748-3752 **Postal Stationery of the Kingdom of the S.H.S. and the Kingdom of Yugoslavia, 1921-1941**
Damir Novaković, Croatia
This exhibit examines all postal stationery issued within the stated time frame, with mint and used examples. Used examples have been selected with a particular reference to destinations and handling. (5)

3753-3757 **Postal Stationery of the Pneumatic Post of Paris, 1879-1901**
Hervé Barbelin, France
This exhibit examines postal stationery of the pneumatic post of Paris during its first period from May 1, 1873, to December 31, 1901, when the rate was based on the stationery type (card, letter-card or cover). (5)

3758-3762 **Postcards of the British Territories in Central Africa**
Johan Diesveld, Netherlands
Postcards issued between 1893 and 1938 follow the development of the area from a privately owned territory to three separate countries. (5)

3763-3770 **Panama Republic Postal Stationery to 1940**
John Sinfield, Australia
Originally a state of Colombia, from November 1903 independence until June 1940, Panama issued a small range of stationery forms, all shown here as proof, mint and used examples. Personal research has identified several separate printings. (8)

3771-3778 **The World's First Correspondence Card**
Johannes Haslauer, Austria
Its use in Austria, Liechtenstein, Hungary and Austrian post offices of the Levant (8)

3779-3786 **The Postal Stationeries of the Brazil Empire**
José Carlos Vasconcellos dos Reis, Brazil
All the forms and types of postal stationery issued by Brazil during the Imperial Era (1869-1889), including envelopes, postal cards, letter-cards and wrappers, with essays, proofs, varieties and plates. (8)

3787-3794 **Nigeria Postal Stationery**
Peter Hørlyck, Denmark
Various items of postal stationery issued by Nigeria and the preceding colonial administrations: Lagos, Oil Rivers/Niger Coast Protectorate and Southern Nigeria. (8)

3795-3802 **Postal Stationery of Egypt, 1865-1930**
Khaled Mustafa, Egypt
A comprehensive study of postal stationery issued in Egypt from 1879 until 1930, showing different usages of stationery, postal routes and rates. Early essays, proofs, die proofs and varieties are shown. (8)

3803-3807 **Ceylon, 1857-1901**
Nadeem Akhtar Syed, Pakistan
A comprehensive study of the postal stationery of Ceylon in the reign of Queen Victoria (1857-1901) including envelopes, post cards, wrappers, registration envelopes and letter-cards. (5)

3808-3812 **Wells Fargo Conquers Mexico**
Peter Bamert, Switzerland
The development of Wells Fargo Mexico from 1863 to 1909. (5)

3813-3817 **Fifty Years of Uruguay's Postal Stationery**
Rogelio Charlone, Uruguay
Postal stationery issues and usages from 1866 until 1916, including proofs, printing varieties and scarce usages. (5)

3818–3822   **The Postal Stationery Cards of Bechuanalands**
Peter Thy, U.S.A.
A survey of the postal stationery cards of British Bechuanaland, Bechuanaland Protectorate and Botswana (5)

3823–3830   **The First Postal Stationery Issues of Independent Finland, 1917–1929**
Jussi Tuori, Finland
A traditional postal stationery exhibit treated by cardboards and colors, including all known proofs in private hands and major existing varieties. (8)

3831–3838   **Hong Kong Queen Victoria Postal Cards, 1879–1901**
Kok Ying Kei, Hong Kong
After Hong Kong's ascension to the UPU, 18 different types of formula post cards were issued from 1897–1901, before the arrival of postal stationery cards. This exhibit shows mint and used examples from Hong Kong and Treaty Ports. (8)

3839–3846   **UPU Post Cards of Japan, 1877–1940**
Masaki Sugihara, Japan
This exhibit examines the manufacture and usage of Japanese post cards for foreign rate post (stating "Koban 3–5-6" until "Himeji castle 10sen"). (8)

3847–3854   **Postal Stationery of the Russian Empire**
Arnold Ryss, Russia
2015 marks the 170th anniversary of the stamped envelopes issued issued by the Russian Empire. Duke of Finland, ordered the release of private correspondence stamped envelopes priced at 10 and 20 cents. (8)

3855–3862   **United States Postal Cards, 1873–1913**
Hans van Dooremalen, Netherlands
A study of the postal cards of the United States of America issued between 1873 and 1913, emphasizing rates and usages, and including essays, proofs and specimens. (8)

3863–3870   **Romania Postal Stationery to 1918**
Emanoil-Alexandru Săvoiu, Romania
Varieties of Romanian postal stationery from 1870 to 1918, including unique and rare usages from the period. (8)

3871–3878   **Argentina Postal Stationery of the "Ribadavia" Issue**
Arturo Ferrer Zavala, Spain
This exhibit examines the "Ribadavia" postal stationery issue of Argentina. (8)

3879–3886   **The Postal Stationery of Peru**
German Baschwitz, Spain
This exhibit examines envelopes, post cards, letter-cards and wrappers issued by Peru, including cataloged items and some discovered by the exhibitor, with errors, rare destinations and spectacular enfranchises. (8)

3887–3894   **The Second Period of Postal Stationery in Sweden, 1890–1942**
Lennart Daun, Sweden
After the end of the first period (1872–1897), new sizes, layouts and printing dates for postal stationery in Sweden for the basis of the second period (1890–1942). (8)

3895–3902   **The System of International Reply Coupons**
Otmar Lienert, Switzerland
This exhibit examines the purposes of the International Reply Coupon and includes descriptions and examples of each, as well as an annex with different national reply coupons. (8)

3903–3910	**Bahamas Postal Stationery, 1881–1965**
	Keith Hanman, U.K.
	Unused and used examples of Bahamas postal stationery issued from 1881–1965, including artist's drawings, die proofs and essays. (8)
3911–3918	**Great Britain Postal Stationery Stamped-to-Order Issues, 1855–1901**
	Alan K. Huggins, U.K.
	This exhibit examines the introduction of the stamping to order service in 1855 and the changes in the embossed dies used up to 1901, with each value treated separately and showing proofs, specimens and issued items. (8)
3919–3926	**Great Britain Queen Victoria Stamped-to-Order Envelopes, 1855–1901**
	Neil Sargent, U.K.
	This exhibit examines the full range of stamped-to-order envelopes in value order, with mint and used examples of all dies shown, together with multiple compound printings. (8)
3927–3934	**Postal Stationery of the Ottoman Empire, 1869–1922**
	"Levantine", U.S.A.
	This exhibit examines the postal stationery of the Ottoman Empire before its collapse on November 16, 1922, showing different designs and usages, and including die proofs, essays, proofs, errors, specimens, printing and paper varieties. (8)
3935–3942	**British India: Queen Victoria Postal Stationery**
	Sandeep Jaiswal, U.S.A.
	A study of all Victorian postal stationery with special emphasis on dies, paper, preproduction items and unusual usages. (8)
2219–2226	**Ottoman Postal Stationery**
	Timur Kuran, Turkey
	Issues from forerunners to late provisional issues. Emphasis on printing varieties and diversity of usages. (8)

Class 5

For exhibits about the history and development of various forms of air mail.

3946–3950	**Argentina Airmail Issues, 1928–1936**
	Domingo Antonio del Fabbro, Argentina
	A complete display of the series and usage of all values. (5)
3951–3958	**Argentina Airmail Services, 1912–1939**
	Jorge Eduardo Moscatelli, Argentina
	This exhibit examines the airmail evolution from its inception until 1939 (the beginning of World War II). (8)
3959–3966	**Austrian Civil Airmail to America in the First Republic**
	Peter Huethmair, Austria
	This exhibit examines the efforts of the very young Austrian Posts & Telegraphs to link into the newly developing international network of civil mail travelling by air in the European interbellum. (8)
3967–3971	**Development of Delivery of Airmail in the USSR, 1941–1960**
	Sergey Tkachenko, Belarus
	Airmail mailings illustrating the development of major local routes. (5)
3972–3976	**Bulgaria—Airmail Abroad, 1928–1945, and Forerunners**
	Boncho Bonev, Bulgaria
	This exhibit is completely renovated and a lot of new covers to rare destinations have been added. (5)

3977–3984	**Netherlands East Indies Airmail from 1920 to 1942** *Lin Mao-Hsin, Chinese Taipei* This exhibit traces the development of Netherlands East Indies airmail from 1920 to 1942, and is divided into four periods: the Pioneer period, the Experimental period, the Development period and the World War II period. (8)
3985–3989	**Airmail from and to New Caledonia, 1929–1949** *Jean-Daniel Ayache, France* The development of airmail services from and to New Caledonia during the first 20 years of its aviation history through flown covers from the first attempted flight in 1929 to the first regular air service between Paris and Noumea in 1949. (5)
3990–3997	**The Air Field Post Admission Stamp of the German Empire** *Claus Petry, Germany* The Air Field Post admission stamp of the German Empire (8)
3998–4002	**Haiti Airmail Development through 1948** *Barbara Levine, Israel* The development of airmail from pioneer flights of U.S. Marines occupation up through 1948, including inbound/outbound flights, airmail rates, and World War II censorship. (5)
4003–4010	**Hong Kong Airmails** *Anna Lee, Hong Kong* A study of the development of airmail routes and rates out of Hong Kong from 1924 to 1952, and her contribution as an air hub of worldwide importance in the Far East, organized by topic in chronological order. (8)
4011–4018	**Graf Zeppelin LZ 127: The Postal Globetrotter** *Brian Callan, Ireland* Details the early pioneering flights of this airship followed by the first Europe-to-South America commercial airmail service. (8)
4019–4026	**The Postal History of Latvian Air Mail, 1921–1940** *Yehoshua Eliashiv, Israel* Different aspects of the airmail connections of Latvia, including study of routes and tariffs, Zeppelin, catapult and rare destination items. (8)
4027–4034	**Souvenir du Siège de Paris, 1870–1871: Private Mail by Ballons-Montés Out of Paris during the Siege** *Ferdinando Giudici, Italy* Different kinds of private mail transported out of Paris by Ballons-Montés during the Prussian Siege of 1870–1871, leading to the birth of the first airmail post service held by an official authority. (8)
4035–4039	**Austrian Imperial and Royal Aviation in the First World War** *Ladislav Fekete, Slovakia* The types of stamps and correspondence in the Fort of Przemysl of the Austrian Imperial and Royal Aviation division. (5)
4040–4047	**Airmail within, from and to the Nordic Countries, 1809–1924** *Fredrik Ydell, Sweden* Tracing the chronological development of the Nordic countries' airmail routes from 1809 to 1924. (8)
4048–4052	**The French Influence on Airmail Development in South America** *Henry Pillage, U.K.* The development of the French air mail routes to West Africa and Latin America to October 1933. (5)

4053–4057	**Uruguay: Air Mail until 1930**
Gabriel Martinez, Uruguay
Evolution and development of Uruguayan airmail, including first flight covers and the study of routes and rates. (5)
4058–4062	**U.S. Aerial Mail, 1910–1924**
James O'Bannon, U.S.A.
The early development of transporting mail by plane in the United States in two sections: the "Pioneer" period (1910–1916) and the "Governmental" period (1918–1923). (5)
4063–4070	**Swiss Airmail**
Roger Muller, Switzerland
The Swiss airmail from 1910 in departure from Switzerland. (8)
4071–4078	**Hindenberg Mail**
Eckhard Foerster, Switzerland
The chronological structure from the first mail-carrying flight until the Hindenburg disaster, with selected treaty states, postal rates, frankings, flight combinations and other specialities. (8)
4079–4086	**International Airmail in Russia, RSFSR and USSR, 1870–1941**
Dmytro Frenkel, Ukraine
This exhibit the development of the delivery of air mail with the help of flying devices from the territory of Russia. (8)
4087–4094	**A Postal History Study of Air Mail from Iraq, 1919–1945**
Ahmad Bin Eisa Al Serkal, U.A.E.
This exhibit studies the rates and routes of airmail from Iraq from 1919 to 1945, the first 30 years including R.A.F. flight, special flight, crash mail and some feeder services. (8)
4095–4102	**Establishing the U.S. Transcontinental Air Mail Service, May 15, 1918 to June 30, 1924**
Allen Jones, U.S.A.
This exhibit examines how the Post Office Department formed a transcontinental air mail route by establishing short segments between cities and then tying them together. (8)
4103–4110	**Airmail in the Polish Territories, 1914–1939**
Jerzy Kupiec-Weglinski, U.S.A.
This exhibit examines the development of domestic and international airmail services in Poland; the siege of Premysl, the Vienna-Krakow-Lvow-Kiev line, pioneer flights, Expansion period, LOT Polish Airline, Zeppelin flights from Poland/Gdansk. (8)
4111–4118	**Lebanon Air Mail, 1919–1950**
Lucien Toutounji, U.S.A.
This exhibit is a detailed examination of the development of Lebanon air mail from the earliest recorded cover to 1950. (8)
4123–4130	**The United States Governmental Flights, 1918–1927**
Patrick Walters, U.S.A.
This exhibit is a comprehensive presentation of flown postal items and related ancillary materials carried by U.S. government planes during the formative years of the establishment of U.S. airmail routes. (8)
4131–4138	**Momotombos: The First Airmail Definitives of Nicaragua**
John Allen, U.S.A.
This exhibit is a study of the Momotombo airmail definitives. (8)

4139–4143	**The Development of International Airmail in the Kingdom of Yugoslavia, 1923–1941**
	Ratomir Živković, Serbia
	This exhibit examines the role of the Kingdom of Yugoslavia in the development of airmail service between western and southeastern Europe, and the connection to North America via Pan Am transatlantic service and to South America via LATI. (5)

Class 6—Astrophilately

For exhibits about mail in space.

4145–4152	**From Rocket Mail to Space Mail**
	Walter Hopferwieser, Austria
	"This exhibit shows examples of rocket mail from 1931 to satellite mail, lunar mail and present day space station mail " (8)
4153–4157	**The First Space Rocket and Its Heirs in East and West**
	Jaromir Matejka, Austria
	This exhibit examines the development of the first space rocket and its heirs. (5)
4158–4162	**From Science-Fiction to Science–Fact**
	Sandra Matejka, Austria
	This exhibit examines the development of space flight. (5)
4163–4170	**Americans in Space: Project Mercury, Gemini and Apollo**
	David S. Ball, U.S.A.
	This exhibit traces the odyssey of the first Americans in space, from the 1959 NASA programs to put a man into orbit, to the high water mark of man walking on the moon. (8)
4171–4175	**Spacemail**
	Alexander Matejka, Austria
	This exhibit shows covers flown by rocket into space and held onboard Soviet space stations. (5)
4176–4180	**Shenzhou Spaceship and Space Envelope**
	Wang Ruowei, China
	Shenzhou spaceship and space envelope (5)
4181–4188	**From the Early Period of Space Exploration to Space Mail**
	Lin Da'An, China
	Space in philately (8)

Class 7—Thematic Philately

For exhibits of stamps, postal stationery and postal history on a particular topic or theme. Exhibits are classified under Nature, Culture or Technology.

Class 7A   Nature

4415–4422	**Flower Magic**
	Linda Lee, Australia
	With ancient links to the supernatural, flowers cast their spell on all our senses, as messengers and medicines, and by enhancing our environment. (8)
4423–4430	**May We Introduce You To…**
	Helmuth Hiessboeck, Austria
	A conversation about wine in six parts between two friends, touching on the first cave finds by ancient cultures, folklore, a look into the Bible, grape varieties, vineyards and, vintages, as well as marketing. (8)

4431-4935	**Dog**	
	Zhang Guolzang, China	
	The dog in philately (5)	
4436-4440	**The Butterfly Effect**	
	Greg Herbert, U.S.A.	
	Butterflies and humanity have coexisted since antiquity, and they have inspired and affected humanity in countless ways. Unfortunately, humanity's effect on butterflies has been much less positive. (5)	
4441-4448	**Pigeons: Great Diversity in the Wild—Domesticated and Admired by Man**	
	Lutz König, Germany	
	The history of the pigeon and its relationship with humanity, including its evolutionary and environmental history, its role in civilian and military communication, religion, sports and philately. (8)	
4449-4456	**The Palm, A Royal Plant**	
	Giovanni Licata, Italy	
	A short history of the palm tree, the "Prince of Trees," its natural environment, symbols and the use of its products. (8)	
4457-4461	**A Trip to the Alps**	
	Bruce Marsden, U.S.A.	
	A thematic exhibit featuring both the natural and human history of Europe's alpine mountain region. (5)	
4463-4470	**Hunting: Necessity, Sport or Extermination?**	
	Ruth Ordoñez Sanz, Spain	
	Hunting, its evolution, as well as the possible causes of the extinction of some animal species. (8)	
4471-4478	**A Whale's Tale**	
	Lesley Marley, U.K.	
	This tale explores the world of whales, whose families collectively are known as cetaceans, and shows their origins and remarkable adaptation for lives in water, their influence in human history and the steps now taken to protect them. (8)	
4479-4486	**The Coconut Palm**	
	Phillip Stager, U.S.A.	
	A study of the coconut palm (Cocos nucifera) and its relation to humanity and the world. (8)	
Class 7B	**Culture**	
4190-4194	**In the Footsteps of "Impeesa"—Scouting**	
	Christian Gabriel Pérez, Argentina	
	The scout movement: symbology, rationale, activities, branching and major events. (5)	
4195-4202	**Sun, Sea, Surf and Sand—The Discovery of the Beach**	
	Luiz Paulo Rodrigues Cunha, Brazil	
	The use of the beach, as well as the changing attitudes toward them over the centuries. (8)	
4203-4210	**Liquid Bread—Beer**	
	Luo Daoguang, China	
	Beer in philately (8)	

4211–4218	**Advertzine**	

François Krol, France

Pubzine/Advertzine is a collection whose design is based on that of a magazine and whose aim is to demonstrate present knowledge commercial advertising on all types of documents issued or authorized by postal administrators. (8)

4219–4226 **Life and Fate of the American Natives**

Wolf Hess, Germany

This exhibit follows the life and fate of indigenous people showing the opening of their human history. It also encompasses the existence (culture), way of life, and the contacts/conflicts with the "white man." (8)

4227–4234 **One World, One Promise**

Gita Noviandi, Indonesia

This history of scouting, scout movement activities and the final meeting at World Scout Jamboree. (8)

4235–4242 **The Jewish Homeland, Our Struggle for Survival**

Lawrence Fisher, Israel

The struggle of Israel, the Jewish homeland, for survival and recognition, through wars, isolation and terrorism, while looking for peace. (8)

4243–4247 **Peruvian Prehistory**

Roger van Laere, Belgium

A timeline showing archaeological artifacts, monuments and buildings of the pre-Inca and the cultures of Peru. (5)

4248–4252 **Watercolor of Brazil: Essay of History and Culture, from Its Origins to 1889**

Ginaldo Bezerra da Silva, Brazil

The history and cultural development in the process of Brazil's formation. (5)

4253–4260 **The History of Cartography—Mapping the World and Its Regions**

Takao Nishiumi, Japan

The history of mapping not only tells the stories of exploratory history, but also examines how we have moved from stick chart to woodcut map to satellite maps. This exhibit examines the history of cartography showing the known regions of each age. (8)

4261–4268 **A History of Hong Kong**

Yosuke Naito, Japan

This exhibit is a historical and philatelic reconstruction of Hong Kong and its surrounding areas from the prehistoric era to its handover to China in 1997. (8)

4269–4276 **The History of Artist's Portraits: Tracing 600 Years Hand-in-Hand with Muses**

Kiyoshi Emura, Japan

Portraits produced by artists from the Renaissance, when artists were unseen craftsmen, to periods when artists were almost revered as God. Changes in artists' portraits through absolute monarchy, revolution and world wars. (8)

4277–4284 **The German-Austrian Romantic Music in the 19th Century**

Kim Seong Kwon, Korea

This exhibit introduces German-Austrian Romantic music within the flow of western music history. (8)

4285–4292 **Albrecht Dürer: Product and Model of His Time**

Bjørn Gunnar Solaas, Norway

The German artist Albrecht Dürer (1471–1528) in his time. (8)

4293–4297	**The History of Church Architecture**	
	Chen Pu, China	
	This exhibit is made up of six different administrative regions of the Liberated Area, displaying stamps of different plating and setting, prints and paper, and various varieties errors and mailed covers. (5)	
4298–4302	**Gold & Golden**	
	Julije Maras, Croatia	
	Since the beginning of history, humanity has had a fascination with gold and its suppleness and sensuality. (5)	
4303–4307	**Hunting and Fishing**	
	Leif W. Rasmussen, Denmark	
	Man's hunting and fishing from prehistoric to present times. (5)	
4308–4312	**The Philatelic Footprint of the University of Tartu, 1632–2012**	
	Kaido Andres, Estonia	
	A philatelic history of Tartu University and people related to the university, with letters, postage stamps, proofs, stamp designs and errors, both foreign and domestic. (5)	
4313–4317	**Freemasonry**	
	Jean Luc Joing, France	
	What is free-masonry? Symbols, history. (5)	
4318–4325	**My Life as a Bicycle**	
	Vojtech Jankovič, Slovakia	
	An autobiographical story of a bicycle's life through its curriculum vitae in four stages: personal data, professional record, professional experience and hobbies. (8)	
4326–4330	**Gold Story**	
	Jean-Pierre Gabillard, France	
	A story of the precious metal, the subject of unceasing pursuit, its uses and symbolic worth. (5)	
4331–4335	**Children—Adorable Treasure**	
	Shin Sang Man, Korea	
	Children are adorable treasures. (5)	
4336–4340	**Illuminated Guards, for a Safe Sea Journey**	
	E.M.A. Limmen-Stegemeijer, Netherlands	
	Started as fires on beaches to lead fishing boats back to harbor, these fires were later moved atop towers, and thus the name lighthouse was born. (5)	
4341–4345	**A City Wall of Water—The Defense Line, or "Stelling", of Amsterdam**	
	John Dehé, Netherlands	
	Over history, the Dutch developed a defense system based on inundations, which included a defense line ("Stelling") around the capital, Amsterdam. In 1996, this defense line was added to the UNESCO World Heritage List, because of its value to humanity. (5)	
4346–4350	**Our Little Sister, The Moon**	
	Jean-Marc Seydoux, Switzerland	
	From the night of time, the moon has seduced humanity. This study allows us to treat the progression of thought during time, first by redrawing its use in mythology and religion, then by reflecting its perceptible picture in the course of generations. (5)	
4351–4358	**The Conquest of the Horizon**	
	Francisco Piniella, Spain	
	Columbus's voyage from a global perspective. (8)	

4359-4366	**The Scouting Adventure**
	Estanislao Pan de Alfaro, Spain
	The scout movement as an adventure for kids, with educational and moral principles explained. (8)
4367-4371	**Sport in Art**
	Vitaliy Bankov, Ukraine
	This exhibit examines chronologically the development of physical culture and sports in art. (5)
4372-4376	**The Magic of Cinema**
	Eloy Orlando Corres, Argentina
	The cinema in philately (5)
4377-4384	**The American Civil War, 1861-1865—Background, Course of Events and Aftermath**
	Anders Olason, Sweden
	A thematic exhibit using mostly contemporary material that will show reasons why the Civil War erupted, how the "old" war changed into modern warfare by development of communications, armaments and mustering of troops, and glimpses of the aftermath. (8)
4385-4392	**Olympic Games**
	Phairot Jiraprasertkun, Thailand
	The Olympic Games in philately (8)
4393-4400	**The Bayeux**
	Jack André Denys, U.S.A.
	The Bayeux Tapestry, really an embroidery, a 950-year-old artistic and historic treasure that has survived fire, revolution and war, shows William the Conqueror's invasion of England and the Battle of Hastings. (8)
4401-4405	**Romanian Sports**
	Paul Vasile, Romania
	History of Romanian sports, from popular sports to the Olympic Games. (5)
4406-4413	**The Summer Olympic Games**
	Mehmet Edip Agaogullari, Turkey
	A study of the history of the Olympic Games from ancient Greece to its revival by Coubertin, covering the modern Olympiads from Athens 1886 until Berlin 1936, before the start of World War II. (8)
Class 7C	**Technology**
4487-4494	**AAA—All About Automobiles**
	Rudolf Spieler, Austria
	The automobile in philately (8)
4495-4502	**The Life Beat**
	Rogerio Dedivitis, Brazil
	The anatomy, physiology, diseases, diagnosis and treatment of the heart and blood vessels are shown. (8)
4503-4507	**Photographer—Camera—Picture**
	Arieh Favell Lavee, Israel
	The history of photography, including cameras, films, pictures, slides, inventors, photographers and manufacturers. (5)
4508-4512	**The Information Age**
	Menachem Lador, Israel
	The development of calculation, [tele]communication and information media until their current fusion in the Information Age. (5)

4513-4517	**The Allure of Diamonds**
	Frank Friedman, South Africa
	Diamonds in philately (5)
4518-4522	**Paper—Past and Present**
	Wendy Buckle, U.K.
	The history and technology of papermaking, how it is used today and whether it has a future. (5)
4523-4530	**From Abacus to Phablet**
	Johann Vandenhaute, Belgium
	The full history of the computer, starting with the early abacus to the latest product in the computer world, the phablet, a handheld thin personal computer. (8)
4531-4538	**Better Oral Health for Better Life—Dentistry**
	Hsiao Shish-Cheng, Chinese Taipei
	This exhibit examines dental history, diseases and treatments, and also provides a guide to better dental health through the extension of oral hygiene. (8)
4539-4546	**Drawing the World: A Story of Cartography**
	Søren Juhl-Hansen, Denmark
	The origin of our universe and earth are the fixed starting points of this story, which will examine the concepts of cartography and the fascinating tale of mapmakers and their magnificent ships exploring and charting the world. (8)
4547-4554	**The Development of the United Nations**
	Thomas Radzuweit, Germany
	This exhibit examines the history of the League of Nations and United Nations. (8)
4555-4562	**Mathematics, a Science between Theory and Application**
	Joachim Maas, Germany
	This exhibit examines how both pure and applied mathematics have supported humanity's social, cultural and technical evolution from the era of early civilizations up to today. (8)
4563-4570	**A History of the Telephone—Telegraph to Digitalization**
	Akinori Katsui, Japan
	This is a six-chapter, thematic exhibit examining the birth of the telephone and its subsequent technological development, until digital technology enabled its widespread use on a global scale. (8)
4571-4578	**Records of the Sea**
	Kim Heesung, Korea
	This exhibit examines the history of ships and navigation, naval history, sea exploration, fishing, etc. (8)
4583-4590	**Bitter Pills and Strong Drops**
	Turid Veggeland, Norway
	This exhibit is a story about drugs and humanity's incessant search for new and better drugs to combat our illnesses and pain. (8)
4591-4598	**The History of Chemistry**
	Bengt-Göran Österdahl, Sweden
	This exhibit examines the history of chemistry from humanity's learning to use nature in prehistoric times to today's contemporary chemistry, including the significant problems caused to our environment. (8)

4599–4606 **Liquid of Life: Blood, from Ancient Myth to Modern Medicine**
Peter Weir, U.K.
A study of blood and the circulatory system, from ancient myths and legends to the development of the modern day sciences of cardiology and hematology, including diseases and the role of philately in the appeal for blood donors. (8)

4607–4614 **Go By Cycle!**
Brian Sole, U.K.
A crude invention by Karl von Drais in 1818 leads to the start of the cycling industry, cycle racing and utilitarian cycling. (8)

Class 9—Revenues

For exhibits about stamps that pay a tax or fee, rather than postage.

4617–4624 **The Fiscal Stamps of Western Australia**
John Dibiase, Australia
Study of fiscal stamps issued by Colonial Government of Western Australia and later during state commonwealth period (8)

4625–4632 **Revenues of Bolivia in the 19th Century**
Martha Villarroel de Peredo, Bolivia
Revenues used during the 19th century; proofs, specimens, documents, rates, and services (8)

4633–4637 **Study of Indian Fiscal Stamps Used in East Bengal, 1712–1890**
Sheikh Shafiqul Islam, Bangladesh
Study of Indian fiscal stamps used in East Bengal, 1712–1890 (5)

4638–4642 **The Consular Service of Chile**
Heinz Junge, Chile
Chile consular revenues since 1905, with artist's original composite model (1907–1996); includes proofs, essays, technical facts and rates (5)

4643–4650 **The Fiscal Stamps Issued and Used in North China Border Areas and Liberated Areas**
Liu Yongxin, China
Fiscal stamps issued and used in north China (border and liberated areas) (8)

4651–4658 **Revenues of Colombia, 1858–1904**
Manuel Arango Echeverri, Colombia
Comprehensive study showing the development of fiscal stamps in Colombia, 1858–1904. Colombia is the first Latin American country to introduce revenue stamps (8)

4659–4666 **The Leaf Underprint Revenues of the Austrian Empire and Its Countries, 1854–1875**
Ralph Ebner, Germany
Sheet of under print revenues from Austrian empire and areas, 1854–1875 (8)

4667–4674 **Fiscals of Cochin**
Anil Suri, India
Wide range of archival material; new discoveries of several issues, whole series, and printers (8)

4675–4682 **The Hand Etched Documentary Revenue Stamps of Japan, 1873–1874**
(Stephen) Jun Hasegawa, Japan
Original study of 28 different hand-etched revenue stamps includes errors, blocks, specimens, official verification forms, reconstruction sheets, etc. (8)

4683-4687	**Fiscals of Jodhpur**
	Angeet Suri, India
	Fiscal stamps of Jodhpur (5)
4688-4692	**Indian Princely State Kishangarh**
	Ajay Kumar Mittal, India
	Kishangarh State revenue stamps (court fees, etc.) using essays and specimens (5)
4693-4697	**Hungary's First Documentary Revenues During the Forint-Krajczar Currency Period, 1868-1898**
	Károly Szücs, Hungary
	50 years of study and research has culminated in a complete display of Hungary's first documentary revenue stamps, including the rarest stamps issued by the Hungarian State (5)
4698-4702	**U.S. Postal Notes & Postal Note Stamps, 1945-1951**
	Theo van der Caaij, Netherlands
	Complete collection of Postal Notes, 1945-1951; includes original press release form, trial color proof stamps, 3 colors of specimen Postal Note cards, and 72 plate blocks (5)
4703-4710	**Nepal Revenues**
	Dick van der Wateren, Netherlands
	Nepal revenues (8)
4711-4718	**Indian Fiscal Stamps**
	Safdar Mohammed Kamal, Saudi Arabia
	Indian revenue fiscal stamps, 1820–1900; including stamp papers of East India & Queen Victoria period (8)
4719-4726	**Fiscal Stamps of the Indian States of Indore and Jaora**
	Sebah Fatima Abdullah, Saudi Arabia
	Consists of court fee and revenue stamps (including first stamp papers of Indore 1844–1855 and handstruck Jaora first stamp paper) (8)
4727-4731	**The Peruvian Revenue Stamps of 1866-1885**
	Guillermo Llosa, Peru
	Covers Peruvian fiscal revenue stamps (first emissions during bonanza of the guano boom) (5)
4732-4736	**Cuba: Judicial Law Issues, 1856-1864**
	Fernando Cabello, Spain
	1st issue of judicial law emissions (1856–1864); specialty collection (5)
4737-4744	**South West African Revenues and Allied Tax Stamps**
	Howard Green, South Africa
	Includes 1900 German SWA revenues, South African Administration revenues (1915–1923), along with South Africa's first Gemsbok revenues (8)
4745-4749	**Norwegian Revenue Stamps and Papers**
	Finn Aune, Norway
	Classic revenues of Norway, commencing with stamped papers from 1600s, including different monograms of successive kings, and documentary tax stamps (8)
4753-4757	**Guernsey Adhesive Revenue Stamps**
	Jon Aitchison, U.K.
	Focusses on reveue and emergency wartime sales tax stamps (die proofs, plate proofs); includes personal research (5)

4758–4762 **Cyprus: Stamps for Revenue, King George VI to the Republic**
Christopher Podger, U.K.
Cyprus stamps used for revenue KGVI QE2 & Republic to 2014; includes examples of documentary usage (5)

4763–4770 **Telegraph Stamps of Chile, 1883–1893, and Their Postal Use**
Martyn Cusworth, U.K.
Survey of development of telegraph stamps, including die and plate proofs; includes postal use of large format 1883 issues during 1891 revolution (8)

4771–4778 **U.S. Civil War-Era Fiscal History Panorama**
Michael Mahler, U.S.A.
Intact documents bearing U.S. Revenue stamps of the Civil War era (8)

4779–4783 **The ABCs of Patent Medicines: United States Private Die Proprietary Medicine Revenue Stamps**
Albert Briggs, U.S.A.
Traces patent medicine companies issuing tax stamps pursuant to Revenue Act of 1862; includes essays, proofs, stamps, and related collateral advertising material (5)

4784–4788 **A License and Stamp System for Waterfowl Conservation in the 20th Century U.S.**
Will and Abby Csaplar, U.S.A.
Shows how licenses and stamps played vital role in waterfowl conservation in the United States during the 20th century (5)

4789–4793 **Newfoundland Legal Documents: Stampless Precursor and 1898 Queen Victoria First Revenue Types**
John M. Walsh, Canada
Presents the known Newfoundland revenue document types; discovery research corrects all reference books (5)

Class 10—Youth Philately

For exhibits by young collectors, aged as of Jan. 1, 2016.

Class 10A   10–15 Years

4795–4797 **The Usage of Liberation Areas Stamps in the People's Republic of China**
Zhang Ningnan, China
Usage of liberation area stamps in People's Republic of China (3)

4798–4799 **A Visit to the Farm**
Harold Fernandez, Cuba
Visit to the farm (2)

4800–4800 **Los Vehiculos, Ruedan, Corren Impactan**
Brian Morera, Cuba
Vehicles in philately (1)

4801–4803 **Navigating, a Fascinating Journey**
Christian Nunez, Cuba
Navigation (journeys, travel) (3)

4804–4805 **Safari Photo in Massai Mara**
Maxence Muller, France
Safari photos (Massai Mara) (2)

4806–4808	**Gliding at Winter Sports Is So Cool!**	

4806–4808 **Gliding at Winter Sports Is So Cool!**
Nicolas Cosso-Hoedt, France
Portrays use of gliding in winter sports; includes Olympic Winter Games (3)

4809–4811 **Herbivorous Dinosaurs**
Pascal Koehler, Germany
Herbivorous dinosaurs (3)

4812–4812 **The Waterfall, One of Nature's Wonders**
Levente Bánás, Hungary
Collection introduces formation, shapes, and utilization of waterfalls (1)

4813–4815 **Netherlands Indies Airmail, 1927–1942**
Mayong Bibakkati Kalua, Indonesia
Focuses on development of airmail route in Netherlands Indies (experimental beginning, development of regular services), from 1927 until end of operations in 1942 (3)

4816–4818 **Growth and Development of Revenues in Republican Java, 1945–1949**
Mauritania Wibawanto, Indonesia
Specialized collection concentrating on the growth and development of wage revenues in area under Republic of Indonesia authority, Java Island, 1945–1949 (3)

4819–4822 **The War in 1941–1945, as Viewed by Children**
Kirill Levandovskiy, Russia
Perspectives of World War II, from the eyes of children (4)

4823–4825 **Horses**
Aurelie Jungblut, Luxembourg
Categorizes horses according to sports, war, transportation, etc. (3)

4826–4828 **Poland Olympic Chronicle**
Jagoda Gałusińska, Poland
Olympic movement in Poland, 1919–2014; includes rebirth of Olympic idea; Polish Olympic Committee, and Olympian Club community activities (3)

4829–4831 **Rail Transport**
Łukasz Wierzbicki, Poland
Development of rail transport (infrastructure, rolling stock railway organizational activity) over the past 2 centuries (3)

4832–4834 **Thailand: King Rama IX Eighth Definitive Issue**
Chatchaya Karnasuta, Thailand
Specialized study of King Rama IX, 1988–1996 (8th definitive issue, including proofs of different printings, varieties, booklets) (3)

4835–4837 **China: The Great Country**
Maria Fotiou, Cyprus
Description of China from several aspects, including carving, constructions, fauna, flora, marine life, mountains, and printings (3)

Class 10B 16–18 Years

4838–4840 **Silent Hunters of the Night**
Stefan Wallner, Austria
Philatelic description of night birds of prey (3)

4841–4844 **France: The Rooster of Decaris Issue, 1962–1967**
Tanguy Pron, France
Rooster of Decaris issue (France 1962–1967) (4)

4845–4847	**Save The Tiger**
	Petra Findenig, Austria
	A philatelic description of the tiger (3)
4848–4849	**Bangladesh Postal Stationery with Errors and Varieties**
	Ashrar Hussain, Bangladesh
	Bangladesh postal stationary history, 1972–2006, focusing on major error varieties (2)
4850–4852	**The Bear Family**
	Laure Michiels, France
	Bear family (3)
4853–4856	**Technology in Agriculture**
	Niklas Koehler, Germany
	Use of technology in agriculture (4)
5034.1–5034.2	**We Go To School**
	Johann-Romain Meheu, France
	Going to school (2)
4858–4861	**French Airmail Stamps from 1984 to 1997**
	Achille Hamelin, France
	French airmail stamps, 1984–1997 (4)
4862–4864	**Space: from Observation to Conquest**
	Xavier Espy, France
	Observation and conquest of Space (3)
4865–4867	**French Republic: Postage Stamps of the Semeuse Type**
	JBF Bruschsal, Germany
	French republic postage stamps (postally used) (3)
4868–4870	**Elephants**
	Marcel Tampe, Germany
	Elephants in philately (3)
4871–4873	**Indonesia's Locally Issued Stamps in Java Island, 1945–1950**
	Christopher Tampenawas, Indonesia
	Stamps and postal materials used in Java Island, 1945–1950 (includes Dutch East Indies and Japanese occupation stamps used before and after first issues, commemorating independence) (3)
4874–4877	**Olympic Games**
	Avinash Sharma, India
	Describes history of Olympic Summer Games (ancient-modern) (4)
4878–4880	**Pre-Philatelic Valencian Markings of the 18th and 19th Centuries**
	Miriam Gisbert Llácer, Spain
	Prephilatelics marks and franchises collection of the Kingdom of Valencia, 18th–19th centuries (3)
4881–4882	**The American Dream**
	Toby Asson, U.K.
	History of America and how the American Dream has been realized (2)
4883–4886	**Revenue Gathering Stamps of New Zealand**
	Warrick Wright, New Zealand
	Describes adhesive stamps for gathering revenue for New Zealand government (first issued in 1867); use reflects economy, industry, and law of New Zealand for nearly a century (4)

4887–4890	**The Postal Stationery of Mexico's "Serie Mulitas"** *José Carlos Rodriguez Pinero, Spain* Postal collection, 1895–1900 (includes envelopes, postcards, wrappers, with specimens, varieties, and samples) (4)
4891–4894	**In the Magic World of Harry Potter** *Mathilda Larsson, Sweden* Presents principal characters from the Harry Potter books (focuses on episodes from Harry Potter and the Philosopher's Stone, the first book in the series) (4)
4895–4898	**Dubai: Errors and Varieties** *Eisa Bin Ahmad Al Serkal, U.A.E.* Full collection of errors (printing, overprints) and rare varities (color variations, etc.) (4)
4899–4902	**Building a Nation…One State at a Time** *Adam Mangold, U.S.A.* Showcases individual territories admitted into the United States of America (adhesives and covers) (4)
4903–4906	**Turnhout, A Lively City** *Binkse Jeugd, Belgium* Story of Turnhout, capital of the Green Campine (Kempen) (4)
4907–4908	**Olympic Games Beijing, 2008** *Alexandru Negrea, Romania* The Beijing Olympics of 2008 (2)
4909–4911	**Violin Lessons** *Carolina Mujica, Argentina* Violin lessons (3)
4912–4913	**Iron Giants** *José Julian Baujin, Cuba* Iron giants (2)
4914–4916	**The Universe** *Darren Corapcioglu, U.S.A.* Presents facts and details on the Universe (includes stamps, souvenir sheets, booklets, postal stationary, covers) (3)
4921–4925	**"Pakistan" Overprints on British Indian Stamps & Postal Stationery, 1947–1950, Used in East Bengal** *Ajme Sheikh Nafisa Anjum, Bangladesh* Features "Pakistan" overprints on British Indian stamps and postal stationary, 1947–1950, used in East Bengal (5)

Class 10C 19–21 Years

4917–4920	**The Most Important Postal Services in the Town of Hornstein** *Bernhard Gaubmann, Austria* Describes history of postal services in the Town of Hornstein (includes single, registered, express, and insured letters, along with cash remittance) (4)
4926–4930	**My Friend's Dog** *Daiana Aylen Casielles, Argentina* Friend's dog (5)

4931–4934	**The Čertoryje National Nature Reserve and Its Flora** *Pavlína Ondrejková, Czech Republic* Exhibit represents the Čertoryje National Nature Reserve and the flora that can be found there (4)
4935–4938	**Monkeys** *Alexandra Michiels, France* Monkeys (4)
4939–4942	**The Bear** *Amandine Grellier, France* Bear (4)
4943–4946	**Heraldry (The Art of the Blazon)** *Wilfried Grellier, France* Heraldry (Art of Blazon) (4)
4947–4949	**Dinosaurs: And if We Had Lied to Ourselves** *Sylvan Espy, France* Dinosaurs (3)
4950–4952	**The Fine Arts in Our Lives** *Lee Ga Hwa, Korea* Fine arts (3)
4953–4957	**The Hungarian Field Post during World War II** *János Károly Manz, Hungary* Demonstrates main actions of Hungarian field post during World War II (5)
4958–4962	**The Charms of Polish Motorization** *Konrad Andraczek, Poland* Focuses on the reconstruction of Poland's economy after World War II, namely on the production of personal cars, trucks, tractors, and motorcycles (5)

Class 11—Philatelic Literature

Literature entries appear in a separate section following. Entries may be viewed in the reading room.

Class 12—One-Frame Exhibits

Exhibits in this class should be based on a narrow subject that is best treated in a single frame of 16 pages. An extract from a past International award-winning multiple frame exhibit (5 to 8 frames) to one frame is not allowed. Exhibits are classified under the following headings, and within those heading further grouped by U.S., Americas except U.S., Europe and Asia–Oceania–Africa:

Class 12A   Traditional

1084	**Wheat Ridge: The Other Christmas Seal** *Alan Moll, U.S.A.* Production and usage of the Wheat Ridge Christmas Seal in booklet format, 1910–1942 (1)
1095	**How Errors and Varieties Arose on Flat Press U.S. Stamps Overprinted CANAL ZONE** *Richard Bates, U.S.A.* Mistakes that created errors and varieties on Canal Zone stamps produced by the Bureau of Engraving and Printing during overprinting of Fourth Bureau Issues (1)

1096	**The 50¢ Zeppelin Issue: A Study in Design**	
	Cheryl R. Ganz, U.S.A.	
	Exhibit traces the POD & BEP design process in 1933 through original research and rare production objects (1)	
1097	**Saint Louis Bears Postmaster's Provisional Stamps**	
	Barry K. Schwartz, U.S.A.	
	Exhibit comprises stamps and covers from each of the 3 plates (1)	
1323	**Bolivia, 1925: Centenary of the Republic Issue**	
	José Luis Zeballos, Bolivia	
	Complete collection of 1925 Centenary of the Republic issue (photo proofs, drawings, proofs, covers) (1)	
1324	**Argentina, 1892: The World's First Columbians**	
	Wolf Spille, U.S.A.	
	First commemorative stamp issue of the Americas, from conception to production and emission (one day only postal use) (1)	
1325	**The Bermuda Dock Issue**	
	David Cordon, U.S.A.	
	Exhibit covers production of stamps issued in Bermuda during reign of King Edward VII (1)	
1326	**The Bolivia Sports Issue of 1951**	
	Elizabeth Hisey, U.S.A.	
	1951 commemorative Bolivia sports issue (1)	
1327	**Haiti's 50-Centime Nord-Alexis Stamp of 1904**	
	Peter Jeannopoulos, U.S.A.	
	Exhibit identifies the genuine, reprints, and two types of forgeries (1)	
1328	**Canada: The 1¢ Quebec Tercentenary Stamp of 1908**	
	John McEntyre, Canada	
	Exhibit emphasizes inclusion of previously unrecorded constant plates; organized with a proposed original classification scheme (1)	
1329	**Saint-Pierre and Miquelon: "Le Frigorifique", 1955–1956**	
	Jean-Louis Desdouets, St.-Pierre and Miquelon	
	Study of a series of four stamps representing refrigeration 1955–1956 (1)	
1376	**Essays and Proofs of Hungary's 1919 Issues**	
	Fred Fawn, Canada	
	Designers' original artworks, die essays, 4 types of die proofs, archival, full-colour die proofs, plate proofs, etc. (1)	
1675	**Fiume 1918—Provisional Issues with the Fiume overprint on Hungarian Postage Stamps**	
	Nenad Rogina, Croatia	
	Exhibit features machine and hand-overprinted Hungarian stamps used in Riseka (Fiome), December 1918-April 1919 (1)	
1686	**Stamps of the Hungarian Revolution, 1956 (The 1956 Sopron overprint)**	
	Ferenc Kostyál, Hungary	
	Collection presents the complete issue set with printing errors (1)	
1687	**Denmark's Third Issue: 2 Skilling**	
	Paul Clemmensen, U.S.A.	
	Exhibit showcases Denmark's third stamp and includes development and production, plating varieties, cancellations during 10-year period of Danish postal history (1)	

1688	**Latvia: The Rising Sun Stamp of 1919**
	Vesma Grinfelds, U.S.A.
	Traditional study of a single stamp issue; proofs; errors, varities and uses (1)
1689	**The First Day: 6th of May, 1840**
	Alan Holyoake, U.K.
	Exhibit presents account of Penny Black (world's first postage stamp) and Mulready stationary (1)
1690	**Essays and Proofs of the Postwar Lublin Issue**
	Dariusz Grochowski, Poland
	Exhibit details all stages of preparation essays and proofs of the Lublin Issue (1)
1691	**1897 Provisionally Overprinted Egyptian Stamps in the Sudan**
	Ahmed Yousef, Egypt
	Provisionally overprinted Egyptian stamps in the Sudan, 1897 (1)
1692	**The Mafeking Siege "Blue" Issue of Cape of Good Hope, 1900**
	Cheong-Too Choi, Hong Kong
	Detailed study, focussed on printing of colour shades, paper shades, watermarks, setting varities, production varieties, and postal usage (1)
1692.1	**Cave Overprints on Ceylon Stamps, Covers and Cards**
	Graham Winters, U.K.
	Comprehensive study of privately produced pre-cancels of Ceylon postage stamps, covers, and postal stationary, 1878–1909 (1)
1692.2	**Western Australia: 1854 Lithographed Issue**
	Richard Debney, U.S.A.
1693	**Designing the 1938 King George VI Issue of Burma**
	Michael Ley, U.S.A.
	Design and approval process (1)
1694	**The Mafeking Blues**
	MaryAnn Bowman, U.S.A.
	3 different stamps, their usage and varities which were produced locally by a photographic process (1)
1695	**Egypt: The 3-Milliemes Army Post Stamps, 1936–1941**
	Richard Wilson, U.S.A.
	Exhibit shows the various forms of these 4 stamps (royal printings, control blocks), and their use (1)
1703.1	**New Zealand's First Pictorials overprinted for use in The Pacific Islands**
	Jeff Long, New Zealand
	Aitutaki, Niue and Samoa all used some issue from the New Zealand first pictorial issue of 1898, overprinted for local and international purposes (1)
1703.2	**The Humble Farthing—To What Purpose**
	George Stewart, New Zealand
	Nine colonies using the British Sterling farthing stamps, proving they were mostly produced for postal usage. Includes covers and postal stationary (1)
1714	**The 1961 Decimal Overprints of Basutoland**
	Avi Barit, South Africa
	In 1961, Basutoland converted its currency from sterling to decimal. This resulted in the overprinting of stamps and consequent errors and varieties (1)
1715	**Iraq Under British Occupation, 1918–1921**
	Alla-Ud-Din, Pakistan
	Comprehensive exhibit in 1st definitive series of Iraq, under British occupation through stamps, covers, and specimens etc. (1)

1716   **The First Issue of Jaipur**
Sandeep Jaiswal, U.S.A.
In-depth study of the various printings of the 1904 provisional issue of Jaipur (1)

Class 12B   Postal History

2201   **Handstamped Rates on Confederate Mail**
Howard Green, U.S.A.
Exhibit covers all Confederate rates that were hand stamped or combination hand stamped (1)

2202   **The Huguenot Walloon Issues: A Study of Rates to Domestic Destinations, 1924–1928**
Keith E. Maatman, U.S.A.
Covers showing how these stamps were used to accommodate major postal usages of this period (1)

2235   **New York City Foreign Mail Fancy Cancels, 1873–1875**
Nicholas Kirke, U.K.
Discusses complete range of New York foreign mail fancy cancels, 1873–1875 (1)

2236   **The War Rate, 1815–1816**
Anthony Dewey, U.S.A.
Exhibit showcases rates in effect from February 1, 1815—March 30, 1816, known as the War Rate (1)

2274   **World War I Censorship of Mail in the Canal Zone**
David Zemer, U.S.A.
Exhibit commemorates 100th anniversary of opening of Panama Canal and start of WWI (1)

2323   **Jundiahy/SP-Brazil: Postal Reform to the Republic, 1829–1889**
Almir Bufalo, Brazil
Exhibit portrays items circulated between the Postal Reform of 1829 and the proclammation of the Brazilian Republic in 1889 (1)

2407   **Canadian Military Hospitals at Sea**
Jon Johnson, Canada
Exhibit displays material from Canadian military hospital ships and ambulance transports (1)

2521   **French Military Mail During the Mexican Intervention, 1862–1867**
Jaime Benavides, Mexico (COFUMEX)
Correspondence from all 12 "Corps Expeditionaire du Mexique" (CEM) fighting units on Mexican soil (1)

2522   **Maritime Mail from Guayaquil, 1780–1865**
Eivind Lund, Norway
Exhibit showcases maritime mail used in the pre-philateic period of Quito and Guayaquil (1)

2523   **Peru-Postal Rates, 1858–1874**
Aldo Samame y Samame, Peru
Exhibit showcases the Peruvian postal rates evolution during first 2 decades after implementation (1)

2524   **Mail Carried by the Cunard Line Between Halifax and the United States**
David D'Alessandris, U.S.A.
Mail carried by the Cunard Line between Halifax, Nova Scotia, and the United States from 1840 until service to Halifax eliminated in 1867 (1)

2530   **The 1838–42 Wilkes Antarctic Expedition: Its Many (Often Unfavorable) Facets**
Hal Vogel, U.S.A.
History of the Wilkes Antarctic Expedition (1838–1842) from its posted mail, related documents, and other contemporaneous Antarctic expeditions with which it was linked (1)

2536   **The First Postal Convention between Great Britain and the Kingdom of Hanover**
Friedrich Meyer, Germany
Exhibit portrays different counties of origins and markings of an 8-year agreement, before being outdated by the Anglo-Prussian agreement of 1847 (1)

2584   **The Saxon Military Post and Field Post of the Napoleonic Era, 1806–1818**
Renate Springer, Germany
Exhibit portrays stationary field post offices in territories occupied by the Grand Armée during the Napoleonic Wars (1)

2703   **Saxony Letters during the Thirty Years' War, 1618–1648**
Christian Springer, Germany
Exhibit portrays Saxony as the strongest military territorial state of central Germany during the 30 year war (1)

2704   **The Serbs in Corfu during World War I**
Georges Sotiropoulos, Greece
Exhibit showcases remainder of Serbian army who were transported by English and French ships to Corfu after defeat and fall of Belgrade (1)

2761   **The Postal History of the French "Armee de Moree", 1828–1833**
Alexandre Galinos, Greece
The presence of the French army and navy in Peloponnese Greece during the Hellenic Independence War (1)

2762   **Russia via Vardo**
Jan Lauridsen, Norway
The postal history connected to the steamship line between Archangelsk in northern Russia and Vardo in northern Norway (1)

2763   **Letters of Hope**
Piotr Zubielik, Poland
Exhibit presents a lesser-known area of Polish philately concerning letters (1)

2764   **Aerial Formations of the Gen. Haller "Blue" Army and the French Military Mission in Poland 1917–1925**
Jacek Kosmala, Poland
Exhibit showcases the correspondence between the Blue Army and the French Military Mission in Poland (1)

2805   **The Collection of Postage Due Fees in Ireland, 1914–1926**
Robert Benninghoff, U.S.A.
Review of the labels and stamps used to collect additional monies due to the post office and customs for delivery of postcards, letters, and parcels, 1914–1926 (1)

2806   **Petite Messages: Development of the Carte de Visite Mail in 19th Century France**
Thomas Broadhead, U.S.A.
Essays, proofs, and postal uses illustrate the diverse and distinctive nature of French visiting card mail (1)

2807   **The Railroad Post Offices in Adelsberger/Postumia Grotto, 1899–1945**
Thomas Lera, U.S.A.
Exhibit examines underground post offices local in Adelsberger/Postumia Grotto serviced by their own railroad (1)

2808   **The World War II Ordeal of One Polish Family**
Jan Niebrzydowski, U.S.A.
Exhibit outlines war story of a Polish family whose fates interlaced with major events affecting WWII history of what used to be Eastern Europe (1)

2809   **The 1944 Gross Born POW Olympics**
Andrew Urushima, U.S.A.
Varieties and usages of the 1944 "Olympic" series from the World War II Gross Born POW camp in Poland (1)

3123   **India Used in Chandernagore (French Settlement), Postmarks from 1816–1954**
Uttam Reddy, U.S.A.
Exhibit focuses on postmarks and stamps (British India) used abroad in the French settlement of Chandernagore (1)

3124   **When Mail Stopped Coming**
Mannan Mashhur Zarif, Bangladesh
Postal history on the role of ICRC in Bangladesh between 1971 and 1974 (1)

3301   **Shibin El-Kom Postmarks, 1870–1922**
Tarek Mokhtar, Egypt
Exhibit is aimed at identifying postmark cancellation types and relevant usage from 1870–1922 (1)

3302   **Pre-Philatelic Postal History of Jerusalem**
Les Glassman, Israel
Display illustrates the development of postal communications to and from Jerusalem during the pre-philatelic period (1)

3303   **The 1914 Rebellion in South Africa**
James Findlay, South Africa
After the outbreak of World War I, British Imperial troops garrisoned in Union after Anglo-Boer War returned to England (1)

3304   **Nepalese Classic Official Mail from Locations without a Post Office**
Edward Gosnell, U.S.A.
Comprehensive study of Classic Era (1881–1911) official mail from government offices in locations not directly serviced by the regular postal system (1)

3321   **Late Mail Strikes on 19th Century Indian Mail**
Richard Hanchett, U.S.A.
Display of all known types of late mail strikes applied to 19th century Indian mail (1)

Class 12C   Postal Stationery

3555   **Luxembourg Formular Cards, 1870–1874**
Edward H. Jarvis, U.S.A.
Evolution of Luxembourg formular cards, beginning to end (1)

3556   **The Servicio Postal Fluvial Envelopes of Colombia**
Deborah Friedman, U.S.A.
Colombia's special envelopes for mail posted on Magdalena river boats from 1891–1899 (1)

3943   **The 10¢ U.S. Envelopes of 1870–1874**
Richard Taschenberg, U.S.A.
Exhibit of the completely redesigned 10 cent stamped envelope issue of 1870 (1)

3944 **Aerogramme at Bahrain Postal History**
Jassim K. Behzad, Bahrain
Discusses beginnings of aerogramme, overprinted at Jorge 6th and last print of postal stationary, 1986 (1)

3945 **London Design of Candian International Reply Coupons**
JJ Danielski, Canada
Typology and varieties of London design coupons printed for Canada; contains proofs and usage of coupons as postage on mail (1)

Class 12D Aerophilately

1330 **Three Months in '31**
Carlos Vergara, U.S.A.
Brief service life of Chile's elusive Vermillion 2 Peso Airmail Provisional (1)

4119 **Canadian Pioneer Airmails, 1918–1922**
Raymond Simrak, Canada
Canadian Flying Corps were the first to carry mail between Toronto and Ottawa on June 24, 1918; 19 additional pioneer mail carry flight shade in Canada from Lethbridge, Alberta to Ottawa on June 22, 1922 (1)

4120 **Graf Zeppelin LZ 127: Egypt Flight, 9–13 April, 1931**
Amr Laithy, Egypt
Comprehensive philatelic overview on Graf Zeppelin LZ 127 Flight to Egypt and Palestine, April 9–13, 1931 (1)

4121 **Airmail of the Caucasus, 1922–1939**
Dzhanguli Gvilava, Russia
Exhibit presents airmail correspondence illustrating the development of local routes (1)

4122 **Airmails from New Zealand to the United States, 1930–1953**
Bob Watson, New Zealand
Exhibit illustrates the development of airmail routes and letter rates from New Zealand to the United States from 1930 to 1953 (1)

4144 **The "1944" Overprint on the 1934 One Colon Official Airmail Stamp**
Pablo Sauma, Costa Rica
In-depth study of the 1 colon official airmail stamp of 1934 with a "1944" overprint. (1)

Class 12E Astrophilately

4189 **A Study of NASA VIP Cards**
Ray E. Cartier, U.S.A.
NASA gave five free souvenir postcards to each guest at VIP launch site from Apollo 7 through Skylab 2 (1)

Class 12F Thematic

4414 **I Am Nothing**
Michael Rhodes, Australia
I have been a difficult concept for man to comprehend. I was however needed as a way to account for the absence of anything to make use of man's ideas but I am still nothing. (1)

4462 **Twinkle, Twinkle, Little Star**
Margaret Morris, U.K.
Exploration of the first verse of the famous nursery rhyme. Each line has astronomical significance (1)

4579	**Who Is Liberty? What Is She?** *Masaru Kawabe, Japan* The anthropomorphic thought of Liberty that has been created by Delacroix and Bartholdi (1)
4580	**Men's Gymnastics: Dressed to Win** *Mark Maestrone, U.S.A.* Examines the historical development of men's gymnastics attire as a function of competition rules, mechanics of the sport, and political forces in the gymnastics movement (1)
4581	**Go: The World's Oldest Board Game** *Lester C. Lanphear III, U.S.A.* The story of the word's oldest board game Go is told in this exhibit (1)
4582	**The Charter of the United Nations (A Document for World Peace, San Francisco, 1945)** *Francis Adams, U.S.A.* Exhibit focuses on the Charter of the United Nations and its development based on Four Freedoms (1)
4615	**Fear Runs over the Tracks** *Paolo Guglielminetti, Italy* Collection traces the theme of fear related to transport by train (1)

Class 12H   Revenue

4616	**Cuba: Documentos Oficiales de Policia, 1865–1883** *Nuncio Cusati, Venezuela* Sample of different stamps and documents for the use of people, blocks, sets, high values, over 18 years, 1865–1883 (1)
4794	**French Revenue Stamps Taxing Pharmaceutical Specialties, 1918–1934** *Frank Guillotin, U.S.A.* Taxation rates and rules are clearly presented. Only about 3% of pharmaceutical specialties were taxable. Documents presented are extremely scarce, only a few known. (1)

Class 13—Modern Philately of the Past 20 Years

The objectives of this class are to encourage collectors of modern philatelic materials to exhibit at the highest level and to demonstrate to Postal Administrations that there is an extensive body of philatelists who collect and study materials issued in the present day. This class is available for exhibits complying with FIP regulations for (A) Traditional Philately, (B) Postal History and (C) Postal Stationery.

Qualifying exhibits for Modern Philately must contain philatelic materials issued by Postal Authorities primarily in the past 20 years. The allocation of points for this class recognizes that modern philatelic material is in many instances difficult to acquire, treat and present given that the short passage of time since their issue may not have provided an accurate indication of importance or rarity.

4963–4967	**Supplement Stamps of Austria to the Euro Introduction** *Ernst Krondorfer, Austria* Perforated and self-adhesive supplement stamp from the first design to printing and use (5)
4968–4972	**Novydux HB—A Private Port in Mullajo, Sweden** *JJ Danielski, Canada* Exhibit presents stamp issues of private post in Sweden since 1996 (5)

4973–4977	**The Hologram in Philately** *Nilo Dizon Jr., New Zealand* Exhibit traces the development of the hologram and its use on stamps and other philatelic products by governments for postal, postal-related, and revenue services (5)
4978–4982	**Modern Swedish Stamp Forgeries, 2003–2016** *Gunnar Dahlstrand, Sweden* Discussion of how one can determine the difference between genuine and forged Swedish stamps (5)
4983–4987	**Machine Vended Postage Labels of USA, 1989–2004** *Deepak Haritwal, U.S.A.* Study and display of all designs of machine (computer) vended postage labels issued by the United States Postal Service (USPS), from 1989 to 2004 (5)

Class 14—Open Philately or Display Exhibits

For exhibits that include non-philatelic material or material that would exempt the exhibit from one of the previous classes.

4988–4992	**Movers and Shakers of the Millennium** *Charles Bromser, Australia* A tribute to 100 people who, over the course of the last millennium, shaped the world, for better or worse (5)
4993–5000	**A Jubilee Reminiscence: The 1890 Penny Postage Jubilee** *John Davies, U.K.* Material produced to celebrate 50 years of Great Britain's uniform penny postage (1890) (8)
5001–5001	**The League of Nations Refugee Organization** *Greg Galletti, U.S.A.* The League of Nations and its role in supporting efforts to aid refugees (1)
5002–5006	**The Rise, Fall and Rebirth of the Murray River Trade** *Anthony Presgrave, Australia* Exhibit uses a variety of philatelic and non-philatelic material to relay the story of the Murray River Trade and its tributaries (5)
5007–5011	**The Portrayal of Living People in Australian Philately** *Martin Walker, Australia* Revealing the people portrayed on Australia's stamps, stationary, booklets, postmarks, etc. (5)
5012–5016	**The Birth of a Nation** *John Guldborg Hansen, Denmark* The story of the birth of the United States of America, from colonies to states (5)
5017–5021	**Victoria Regina, Her Life, Times and Legacy** *Patrick Casey, Ireland* Exhibit illustrates aspects and topics of the life of Victoria Regina, times, and legacy (5)
5022–5029	**A Good Walk Spoiled** *Graham Winters, U.K.* A humorous study of the game of golf, from early themes to recent (8)
5030–5034	**A Celebration of Christmas Traditions** *John Fitzsimons, Ireland* Exhibit covers some of the seasonal traditions of the annual Christmas festival (5)

5035–5039　**Tonga Tin Can Mail History, 1882–1947**
Kazuyuki Inoue, Japan
Exhibit showcases Tonga tin can mail history, 1882–1947 (5)

5040–5044　**Memories from Mexico**
Carlos Urzua Barbosa, Mexico (COFUMEX)
Collection of Mexico from 19th and 20th centuries with philatelic material showing people and historic moments (5)

5045–5049　**The South African Border War, Including the Involvement of the Cubans, 1966–1989**
Gawie van der Walt, South Africa
Exhibit showcases philatelic and other material of the war fought on the border of Southwest Africa and Anglo including the involvement of Cuban forces (5)

5050–5054　**James William Denver—The Man and His Times**
William J. Johnson, U.S.A.
Exhibit uses postal history, documents, letters, and other related items in order to tell the story of James William Denver (1817–1892), who had a long career of public service (5)

Class 15—First-Day Covers

A new class at the international level. Exhibits in this class are based on the rules of the American Philatelic Society and will be judged on this basis.

5055–5062　**Baseball Centennial**
Jeff Bennett, U.S.A.
Traditional first-day cover exhibit for the 1939 U.S. stamp commemorating the 100th anniversary of baseball (8)

5063–5067　**The 2¢ Hardings: Their First-Day Usage and the Birth of Modern Cacheted First-Day Covers**
James Hering, U.S.A.
Exhibit portrays the design, printing, perforations, cachets, and cancellations of the 2¢ Harding stamp (5)

5068–5075　**The Walt Disney Postal Commemoration of 1968**
Edward Bergen, U.S.A.
Exhibit centers around stamps and cacheted first-day covers for the 1968 U.S. Disney commemoration (8)

5076–5083　**The 3¢ Connecticut Tercentenary Issue of 1935 and Its First-Days**
Anthony Dewey, U.S.A.
Exhibit showcases the "Charter Oak" stamp commemorating the 300th anniversary of the settling of Connecticut (8)

5084–5091　**New York World's Fair, 1939**
Charles O'Brien III, U.S.A.
First-day cover exhibit presents a traditional study of the stamp, first-day postmarks, cachets, and usage (8)

5092–5099　**The U.S. 1948 Harlan F. Stone Stamp and Its First-Day Covers**
Harlan Stone, U.S.A.
Traditional exhibit for first-day subjects: creation of the stamp, designs of first-day cachets, and later uses of the stamp (8)

5100–5107 **The 1964 New York World's Fair Commemorative**
Ronald Klimley, U.S.A.
First-day cover exhibit studies the design and production of the stamp, the cachets produced, first-day and commercial usage (8)

5108–5115 **The 3¢ Oregon Territory Issue of 1948**
Ralph Nafziger, U.S.A.
Stamp development from design to production, first-day cancellations and cachets, and stamp usages (8)

Philatelic Literature
Entries may be viewed in the reading room.

Class IIA   Handbooks

IIA-001 **Argentinian Railways—Tracks, Stations & Postal History. 2 Volumes**
Martin Horacio Delprato, Argentina
Postal history of Argentinian Western Railway, 1857/8–1872 (book in 2 volumes)

IIA-002 **A Study of the Colours and Printings of the Rhodesia Bi-Colored Admirals**
Stephen Reah-Johnson, Australia
Rhodesia bi-colored admirals

IIA-003 **Mauritius Philatelic Society 25th Anniversary Souvenir Magazine**
Mico W.Antoine and Karl Patrick Kwan Cheung, Australia
Mauritius Philatelic Society (25th anniversary souvenir magazine)

IIA-004 **Postmarks on the Rhodesia "Admiral Issue", 1913–1925**
R.M.Gibbs, Jenifer Barry, Stephen Reah-Johnson and Sean Burke, Australia
Provides guide to the postmarks found in this iconic issue (product of many years of research, extensively illustrated)

IIA-005 **The 1836 Anglo-French Postal Convention**
Geoffrey Lewis, Australia
250 Stampless covers from all parts of the world described in detail (book analyzes effects these covers had on the international mail system)

IIA-006 **The Arab-Israeli Conflict: No Service, Returned and Captured Mail**
Daryl Kibble, Australia
Postal history of civilian No Service, Returned, and Captured Mail resulting from the Arab-Israeli conflict

IIA-007 **Post Office Rubberprint "Bangladesh" on Pakistan Stamps and Postal Stationery, 1971–1974**
Sheikh Shafiqul Islam, Bangladesh
Bangladesh rubber print varities with different post offices and rubber prints (book)

IIA-008 **Basic Classification of Brazilian Meter Stamps**
Mario Xavier Jr., Brazil
Complete listing of first classification of Brazilian meter stamps, 1925-present (includes illustrations of all types and subtypes)

IIA-009 **Academician Dr. N.I. Pirogov—"A Legend in Surgery"**
Dimitaz Radenovski and Boris Kalinkov, Bulgaria
Life of academician Dr. N.I. Pirogov (text, photos, stamps, etc.)

IIA-010	**Canadian Stamps with Perforated Initials, Fifth Edition (Electronic Handbook on Memory Sticks)** *Jon Johnson, Canada* Handbook lists Canadian Official and company perforations used to deter pilferage of office postage
IIA-011	**Mail from the French Shore of Newfoundland** *James Taylor, Canada* Exhibit discusses mail from the French shore of Newfoundland
IIA-012	**Postal History Research Vol. 32** *Yu Tzau-Nien, Chinese Taipei* Collaboration of research articles of distinguished authors. Articles are of Chinese classics and postal history areas
IIA-013	**Croatian Philatelic Almanac 2014** *Berislav Pervan, Croatia* Annual 2014 Croatian almanac (bilingual - Croatian and English)
IIA-014	**NATO in Philately** *Radovan Vukadinović, Croatia*
IIA-015	**Mail of French Prisoners of War in England, 1744–1815** *Jacques Renollaud, France* Study and analysis of transmission of recorded letters addressed to or from French Prisoners of War in England during Anglo-French wars
IIA-016	**A Contribution to the History of Competitive Philatelic Exhibition Activity in the Halle/Saale Region 1955–1990** *Hubert Tretner and Peter Laub, Germany* Describes history of competitive philatelic exhibition activity in the Halle/Saale region, 1955–1990
IIA-017	**Edition d'Or Vol. XL: Classic Peru, 1857–1873—The Julio Lugon Badaraco Collection** *Heinrich Koehler Auktionshaus, Germany* Includes biography of the collector, introduction to collecting field, list of awards, and index of the collection
IIA-018	**Edition d'Or Vol. XLI: Schleswig: From Danish Duchy 1625 to Plebiscite 1920—The Christopher King Collection** *Heinrich Koehler Auktionshaus, Germany* Includes biography of the collector, introduction to collecting field, list of awards, and index of the collection
IIA-019	**Edition d'Or Vol. XXXII: Brazil: The "Bull's Eye" Stamps of 1843—The Dr. Hugo Goeggel Collection** *Heinrich Koehler Auktionshaus, Germany* Includes biography of the collector, an introduction to the collecting field, and a list of awards
IIA-020	**Fiscal Legislation and Taxes in Baden from 1628 to 1952** *Steffen Eckert, Germany* Fiscal legislation and taxes in Baden, 1628–1952
IIA-021	**Fiscal Legislation and Taxes in Saxony from 1682 to 1952** *Steffen Eckert, Germany* Fiscal legislation and taxes in Saxony, 1682–1952

IIA-022   **Fundamentals of AM POST Stamps in Germany, American Print**
Andreas M. Wehner, Germany
Summarizes fundamentals of American print (70 years after issue of first AM-POST stamps); based on new archive material

IIA-023   **Greetings from the United Nations—Personalized Stamps, 2003–2015**
Klaus Guhl, Germany
Personalized sheets (souvenir sheets) of the United Nations Post Office

IIA-024   **Postfreimarken in Schleswig-Holstein, 1850–1867**
Rolf Beyerodt, Germany
Description of historical events in Schleswig-Holstein, 1850–1967; consists of essays, proofs, color variations of the German-Austrian Postal Union, as well as Danish authorities in the Dutch colonies, 1851–1864

IIA-025   **The Stamps of the Saxon Post Handbook and Catalogue**
Jurgen Herbst, Germany
Entire system of tariffs presented, inlustrated by examples of letters and postmarks (includes drafts, essays, stamp descriptions, proofs, and the printing process)

IIA-026   **Bilingual Sticker Labels of Post Savings Bank Account, Transcarpathia, 1939–1945**
László Perneczky, Hungary
Study of Post Bank bilingual labels in Transcarpathia by comparing the wording to text on postal R labels

IIA-027   **Horváth Lajos: Postal History of Lower Carpathians Region from the Beginning to 2014**
Lajos Horváth and Péter Gidófalvy, Hungary
Describes the postal history of the Lower Carpathians Region from initiation to 2014

IIA-028   **Collector's Guide to British India Bazaar Post Cards—Edwardian & Georgian Period**
Praful Thakkar, India
Book on private Bazar postcards during the British India period

IIA-029   **Collector's Guide to First Day Covers and Folders of India with Set of Stamps, Se-Tenant Stamps and Miniature Sheets**
Praful Thakkar, India

IIA-030   **India 1929 Airmail Stamps: A Study of Constant Varieties**
Rohit Prasad, India
In-depth study of India's first airmail stamps to document constant varities

IIA-031   **Indian Antarctic Expedition—Philatelist's Guide**
Abhai Mishra, India
Reference book on Indian Antarctic postal history; documents caches, labels, letterheads, cards, envelopes, and postcards used during the expedition)

IIA-032   **Mahatma Gandhi Memorial Issues of 1948**
Pradip Jain, India
Book investigates various aspects of Gandhi Memorial issue of 1948; in-depth research

IIA-033   **Stamps on Sikhs: A Thematic Tribute**
Chander Dev Singh, India
First authentic literature on the Sikhs (history, art, culture and valor of Skihs on worldwide stamps)

IIA-034   **The History of Olympic Games through Philately**
Dinesh Chandra Sharma, India
Book describes the history of the Olympic Games from origins in Olympia, Greece to the London 2012 Olympic Games (illustrated with philatelic material)

IIA-035	**150 Years Stamps in Indonesia, 1864–2014** *POS Indonesia, Indonesia* Describes 150 years, 1864–2014 of stamps in Indonesia
IIA-036	**Illustrated Postmarks of Iran, 1876–1924 (Digital Interactive Book and Specimen Hard Copy)** *Farzin Mossavar-Rahmani, Iran* Complete interactive presentation of Iran postmarks, 1876–1924 in digital eBook format (includes gallery of some of the rarest postmarks)
IIA-037	**Irish Free State—Plates, Controls & Overprint Settings** *Barry Cousins, Ireland* Working guide to aid the identification of GB printer's plates, sheet controls and overprint settings associated with stamps overprinted for use in Ireland
IIA-038	**The Postal History of the Transition Period in Israel 1948—Official Postal Services: Postal Administrations of British Mandate, Minhelet Ha'am and Israel** *Zvi Aloni, Israel*
IIA-039	**France Unadopted Proofs and Essays** *Giorgio Leccese, Italy* France unadopted proofs and essays in 4 volumes
IIA-040	**Granducato di Toscana: I francobolli e le variet· di ClichÈ** *Unificato-CIF Publisher, Italy* Describes stamps and varieties of Grand Duchy of Tuscany
IIA-041	**Monaco Unadopted Proofs and Essays** *Giorgio Leccese, Italy* Monaco unadopted proofs and essays
IIA-042	**Priority Mail History, Stamps, Postal Rates and Collectable Aspects** *Claudio Ernesto Mario Manzati, Italy* Describes the history, stamps, and postal rates of priority mail in Italy
IIA-043	**120th Anniversary of Japanese Commemorative Stamps** *Japan Philatelic Society Foundation, Japan* Describes 120th anniversary of Japanese commemorative stamps
IIA-044	**Handbook of the Roman Letter Machine Cancellations of Japan** *Stampedia Inc., Japan* Specialized handbook of marcophily with original study and research on Roman letter machine date stamps used in Japan, 1920–1968
IIA-045	**Hiroyuki Kanai: "Classic Japan, 1871–1876"** *The Philatelic Culture Museum Japan* Collections of Hiroyuki Kanai, Classic Japan, 1871–1876
IIA-046	**International Exhibition History, 1965–2004** *Yukihiro Shoda, Japan* Describes history of international exhibitions, 1865–2004
IIA-047	**Japan Definitive Stamps, 1871–1937** *Stampedia Inc., Japan* General collection of Japanese definitives a (bilingual, full-color)
IIA-048	**Postal History of the Japanese Military Mail, 1894–1921** *Jun-ichi Tamaki, Japan* This book is a full-colour collection of all leaves of the Postal History of the Japanese Military Mail, 1894–1921

IIA-049   **The History of the Red Cross**
Kim Do Hee, Korea

IIA-050   **Wagner in Philately**
Kim Seong Kwon, Korea
Set of philatelic articles from monthly philatelic magazine

IIA-051   **Beginning of Postal Services in Kuwait, 1896–1923**
Khaled Abdul Mughni, Kuwait
Study of early postal services before the printing of the Kuwait post office

IIA-052   **Coronation Stamps of Her Majesty Queen Elizabeth II, 1953**
Essa Dashti, Kuwait
Book discusses Queen Elizabeth coronation stamps (includes overprints, FDCs, covers, air letters, etc.)

IIA-054   **Baseball + Philately**
Museo de la Filatelia de Oaxaca (COFUMEX), Mexico

IIA-055   **Mexico Exporta Postal Design and International Trade**
Museo de la Filatelia de Oaxaca (COFUMEX), Mexico
Exporta series (includes preliminary sheets of all stamps issued)

IIA-056   **Mexico Turistico-Definitive Stamp Series**
Eugenio Treviño Aleman, Mexico (COFUMEX)
In-depth study of modern Mexican definitive stamp series, 1993–2002

IIA-057   **Practical Guide By Theme/Mexico Exporta (1975–1993)**
Carlos J. Alvarez Regalado, Mexico (COFUMEX)
A guide for young collectors and beginners to understand and collect this definitive stamp series

IIA-058   **The Chinese presence in Mexico through the mail**
José Gilberto Chong, Mexico (FIP)
Discusses China's presence through correspondence with countries such as the United States and Mexico

IIA-059   **War Hospitals in Brünn During the Great War**
Hans van Dooremalen, Netherlands
Monograph describing war hospitals in Brünn (Brno, Czech Republic) during and shortly after World War I.

IIA-060   **"Pakistan" Overprints on Service Post Cards of British India with Forms Used by North Western Railways. 2 Volumes**
Usman Ali Isani, Pakistan
Book in 2 volumes, providing a comprehensive study of service postcards of King George VI overprinted Pakistan; used by Pakistan Northwestern Railways

IIA-061   **Jammu & Kashmir: The Postage Stamps & Postal History (1866–1877): Volume 1**
Iqbal Nanjee, Pakistan
Discusses 19th century Indian Feudatory State

IIA-062   **Jammu & Kashmir: The Postage Stamps & Postal History (1878–1898): Volume 2**
Iqbal Nanjee, Pakistan
Discusses 19th century Indian Feudatory State

IIA-063   **Formation Cancels of the Polish Legions, The Polish Auxiliary Corps and the Royal Polish Army On Field Post Mail 1914–1918 and Their Historical Background**
Janusz Adamczyk, Poland
Discusses Polish Legions, Polish Auxiliary Corps, and Polish Armed Forces on Field Post Mail, 1914–1918

IIA-064   **Firefighters in Portuguese Philately**
Francisco de Oliveira Matoso Galveias, Portugal
Book describes history of firefighters in Portugal through stamps, postal stationery, postage stamp label printing, mechanical franking, all on the theme of fire

IIA-065   **Handstamps used in Portugal and in the Portuguese Overseas Territories in the Pre-stamp Period (1799–1886)**
Luis Frazao, Portugal
Book in 2 volumes discussing the use of hand stamps in Portugal and Potuguese Overseas Territories, 1799–1880

IIA-066   **Collections Reflect History. St. Petersburg, 2012**
The A.S. Popov Museum of Communications, Russia
Edition dedicated to 100th anniversary of Russian empire; series of postage stamps devoted to Tercentenary of Romanov dynasty

IIA-067   **Postal Stationery and Postal History. Almanac No. 20, 21 (2015)**
Union of Philatelists of Russia, Russia

IIA-068   **Postage Stamp as an Object of Cultural Heritage. St. Petersburg. 2014**
The A.S. Popov Museum of Communications, Russia
Edition consists of 4 sections, discussing postage stamp as object of cultural heritage (42 pages of colour illustrations of stamps and stationary)

IIA-069   **The Great Patriotic War on Postage Stamps and Postal Stationery, St. Petersburg**
The A.S. Popov Museum of Communications, Russia
Collection of articles on the Great Patriotic War (includes stamps, postal stationary, souvenir sheets, covers, postcards)

IIA-070   **The Muhammed Kamal Safder Collection of Indian State Revenues**
Safdar Mohammed Khatab, Saudi Arabia
Introduction to Indian state revenue stamps, according to duties paid

IIA-071   **Yilin Philatelic Study No. 10**
Been Yen Teo, Singapore

IIA-072   **The Most Beautiful Slovak Postage Stamps, 2005–2014**
Slovensk· Poöta, a. s. / POFIS, Slovakia

IIA-073   **Swaziland Philately to 1968 (e-book edition)**
Peter van der Molen, South Africa

IIA-074   **Swaziland Philately to 1968 (printed book edition)**
Peter van der Molen, South Africa
Handbook detailing postage stamps and their forgeries, postmarks, postal stationary, postal history, and revenues of Swaziland to Independence, 1968

IIA-075   **The Legend of the Nude Maja—Study of the Issue "Quinta of Goya", 1930**
Eugenio De Quaseda, Spain
Study of the issue Quinta of Goya, the Legend of the Nude Maja, 1930

IIA-077   **Manual of Postal rates of Spain and Its Overseas Territory**
José Antonio Herraiz, Spain
Manual of postal rates of Spain and its overseas territory

IIA-078   **Mountains of Santander, Approximation to Its Postal History, 1570–1870**
Rafael Angel Raya Sanchez, Spain
Summarizes key works of postal Spanish bibliography, referred to as the Cantabila.

IIA-079	**The Certified Mail with Stamps of Alfonso XIII, Pelon Type, 1889–1901** *EDIFIL, Spain* Study of letters of national and foreign registered mail with postage stamps
IIA-080	**Edition d'Or Vol. XLII: Belgium: Medallions, 1849–1866—The Patrick Maselis Collection** *Corinphila Auktionen AG, Switzerland* Includes biography of the collectors, an introduction to the collecting field, and a list of awards
IIA-082	**About Philately for Everyone** *Valerii Cherednychenko, Ukraine* Book for beginning philatelists
IIA-083	**The Zemstvo Post of Kharkov Province, 1868–1918** *Vitaliy Katsman, Ukraine* Zemstvo post, Kharkov province, 1868–1918
IIA-084	**Switzerland: The Cantonal Stamps—March 1, 1843 to September 30, 1854—Rare Frankings** *Corinphila Auktionen AG, Switzerland* Rare frankings of each stamp produced during this time period
IIA-085	**Stamp Collecting—A New Vision** *Nasser Bin Ahmed Bin Eisa Alkserkal, U.A.E.* Pertaining to new vision of stamp collecting
IIA-086	**Conflict: The Falkland Islands Postal Service, 30 March–14 June 1982—Falkland Islands Study Group Monograph 16** *William Featherstone, U.K.* Describes the postal services operated within the Falkland Islands by all combatants during 1982 invasion
IIA-087	**Evacuee Mail in the Falkland Islands—Falkland Islands Philatelic Study Group Monograph 17** *William Featherstone, U.K.* Describes rare postal history of Falkland Islands (WWI Evacuee Stamps)
IIA-088	**Stamps and Stamp Collecting in Popular Culture** *Howard Summers, U.K.* Book descibes the fictional and dramatic representation of philately in worldwide literature, theatre, movies, television, radio, music, art, and games
IIA-089	**The Mulready Postal Stationery** *Alan Holyoake and Alan Huggins, U.K.* Book covers the genes, production, and usage of Mulready postal stationary
IIA-090	**The Postage Dues of Zanzibar, 1875–1964: The Stamps, The Covers and Their Story** *John Griffith-Jones, U.K.* Comprehensive study of postage due stamps and handstamps of Zanzibar, including postal history, from opening of Indian post office in Zanzibar, 1875 to revolution in 1964
IIA-091	**University Mails of Oxford and Cambridge, 1490–1900** *David Sigee, U.K.* Book describes unique aspects of University posts (includes long-distance carrier mails, local college mails and special postal arrangements for University societies

IIA-092	**UPU Specimen Stamps, 1878-1961** *James Bendon, U.K.* UPU specimen stamps 1878–1961
IIA-093	**Collector's Guide to Confederate Philately, Second Edition** *John Kimbrough, U.S.A.* Guide to Confederate philately
IIA-094	**Encyclopedia of United States Stamps and Stamp Collecting** *Rodney Juell, U.S.A.*
IIA-095	**Every Stamp Tells a Story** *Cheryl R. Ganz, U.S.A.*
IIA-096	**Going...'Postal' Towards Space** *Randy Moore, Sr., U.S.A.*
IIA-097	**Hard Copy' Communication** *Randy Moore, Sr., U.S.A.*
IIA-098	**Hawaii Foreign Mail to 1870** *Fred F. Gregory, U.S.A.* Three-volume book analyzing and describing foreign mail to/from Hawaii to 1870
IIA-099	**Line Engraved Security Printing** *Gary Graznow, U.S.A.*
IIA-100	**Mails of the Westward Expansion, 1803-1861** *Western Cover Society, U.S.A.* Book describes evolution of U.S. Transcontinental mails across Rocky Mountains during 19th century American westward migration
IIA-101	**Postal Evidence of the American Civil War** *Randy Moore, Sr., U.S.A.*
IIA-102	**Soviet Clandestine Mail Surveillance, 1917-1991** *The Collectors Club of Chicago, U.S.A.*
IIA-103	**Spanish Philippine Postal Issues Genuine Surcharge Types of 1881-1888: Illustrated Guide** *Peterson, Gooding and Lera, U.S.A.*
IIA-104	**The Prestamp History of El Salvador 1525-1866** *The Collectors Club of Chicago, U.S.A.*
IIA-105	**The Sultanate of Nejd, A Philatelic Manual. A Study of Early Saudia Arabian Philately** *Ghassan Riachi, U.S.A.* Comprehensive reference guide for early Saudi Arabian stamps and their postal history
IIA-106	**USPS Automated Postal Centers, 2012-2014 (Electronic Book on DVD)** *Peter Elias, U.S.A.* Describes changes and development in postage labels of the APC (Automated Postal Centers) in U.S. Post Offices, 2012–2014
Class IIB	**Periodicals**
IIB-001	**Revista de la Asociacion de Filatelica y Numismatica de Rio Grande** *Asociacion de Filatelica y Numismatica de Rio Grande, Argentina*
IIB-002	**Postal Stationery Collector, Vol 21, 2015** *Ian McMahon, Australia* Journal of the Postal Stationary Society of Australia

IIB-003 **The Journal of the Rhodesian Study Circle**
Sean Burke, Australia
Published quarterly, this journal is the official publication of the specialist society (Rhodesian Study Circle)

IIB-005 **Filacap**
Filacap A.C., Brazil
Magazine for collectors

IIB-006 **SPP Bulletin (Philatelic Magazine)**
Paulista Philatelic Society, Brazil
Magazine gives emphasis to the Brazilian Philately news and publishes technical articles on Brazilian Philately

IIB-007 **The Flagstaff—Journal of the King George V Silver Jubilee Study Circle**
Neil Donen, Canada
Flagstaff publishes philatelic articles related to 1935 George V Silver Jubilee issue

IIB-008 **Chile Filatelico. No. 290**
Sociedad Filatelica de Chile, Chile
Chilean magazine since 1929 (published twice per year)

IIB-009 **Chinese Taipei Philatelic Magazine Vol. 91**
Lin Mao-Hsin, Chinese Taipei
Magazine consists of collection of research articles; published by the Chinese Taipei philatelic society

IIB-010 **Collectors' Philatelic Annual Report (2015), Vol. 27**
Chiu Chen-Lung, Chinese Taipei
Annual report—3 parts, including essays on philatelic studies

IIB-011 **Seminars and Activities Proceedings (2014)**
Ho Huei-Ching, Chinese Taipei
Annual proceedings (collection of monthly seminars and activities)

IIB-012 **"Zadarski Filatelist" Philatelic Magazine**
Croatian Philatelic Society, Croatia
Philatelic magazine (produced by members of the Croatian Philatelic Society)

IIB-013 **Hrvatska Filatelija 1–4. 2014**
Croatian Philatelic Society, Croatia
Newsletter of Croation Philatelic Society (2014)

IIB-014 **NFT—Nordish Filatelistisk Tidsskrift-Year 2015—the 122 edition**
Niels Kristian Hansen, Denmark
Official journal for Copenhagen Philatelic Club; main source for research of Danish stamps and postal history

IIB-015 **Irish Philately**
Brian Warren, Ireland
Quarterly journal of the Irish Philatelic Circle

IIB-016 **Indice Analitico**
Vaccari SRL Publisher, Italy
Analytical index

IIB-017 **Vaccari Magazine #53**
Vaccari SRL Publisher, Italy
Vaccari SRL magazine

IIB-018	**Stamp Club**	
	Stampedia Inc, Japan	
	Full-colour magazine free of charge, aiming to promote philately to youths	
IIB-019	**Stampedia Philatelic Journal**	
	Stampedia Inc., Japan	
	Bilingual philatelic magazine	
IIB-020	**AL Posta Magazine**	
	Kuwait Philatelic Society, Kuwait	
	Magazine of the Kuwait Philatelic Society (stamps, research news, history of the post, etc.)	
IIB-021	**The Malta Philatelic Society Journal**	
	Dr. Alfred Bonnici, Malta	
	Journal covering the Malta postal system, and a detailed account of all philatelic items issued by the Malta Post	
IIB-022	**Amexfil Magazine**	
	Alejandro Grossmann, Mexico (COFUMEX)	
	Quarterly magazine with new issues from Mexico as well as studies from classic issues	
IIB-023	**filatelia peruana**	
	Asociacion Filatelica Peruna, Peru	
IIB-024	**Journal "RUS" N. 7–8 (in Ukrainian)**	
	Dmytro Frenkel, Russia	
	Research journal on Russian, Ukrainian, and USSR philately for professionals	
IIB-025	**Philately 2015 Magazine**	
	"Marka," Russia	
	Monthly philatelic magazine	
IIB-026	**The World of Stamps and Coins**	
	Andrey Strygin, Russia	
	Quarterly magazine of stamps and coins	
IIB-027	**Revista No. 14 Espana Coleccionista**	
	Philatelic Society of Madrid, Spain	
	Magazine of the Philatelic Society of Madrid	
IIB-028	**RF Philately Magazine**	
	EDIFIL, Spain	
	Monthly philatelic magazine	
IIB-029	**Upland Goose: Journal of the Falkland Islands Philatelic Study Group**	
	Bill Featherstone, editor, U.K	
	Journal of the Falkland Islands Philatelic Study Group	
IIB-030	**Forerunners, Official Journal of the Philatelic Society for Greater Southern Africa**	
	Peter Thy, U.S.A.	
	Society journal of the Philatelic Society for Greater Southern Africa	
IIB-031	**Journal of Cuban Philately**	
	Ernesto Cuesta, U.S.A.	
IIB-032	**Journal of Sports Philately**	
	Mark Maestrone, U.S.A.	
	Quarterly full-colour magazine published by Sports Philatelists International; covers world of Olympic and sports philately for all levels of collectors	

IIB-033	**Menelik's Journal** *Ulf Lindahl, U.S.A.*
IIB-034	**Mexicana, The Journal of the Mexico Elmhurst Philatelic Society International** *Michael Roberts, U.S.A.* Journal of Mexican Philatelic Society
IIB-035	**Stamping Around (2015, Volume 28)** *Peter Elias, U.S.A.* Monthly newsletter of the Mid-CIties Stamp Club (Dallas/Ft. Worth, Texas)
IIB-036	**The American Philatelist** *American Philatelic Society, U.S.A.* Oldest continuously published philatelic journal in the world.
IIB-037	**The Cuban Philatelist** *Fernando Iglesias, U.S.A.*
IIB-038	**The Israel Philatelist** *Donald Chafetz, U.S.A.* Journal covering all aspects of postal history of Israel from 18th century to modern day, including Judaica material and the Holocaust
Class IIC	**Catalogs**
IIC-001	**Catalogo Especializado de Perforados—Rep. Argentina** *Miguel Casielles, Hugo Lencina and Juan Pablo Miri, Argentina*
IIC-002	**Advertising Postal Cards of the Russian Empire (II edition)** *Valery Krepostnov, Belarus* Exhibit presents airmail mailings illustrating the development of major local routes
IIC-004	**Taiwan Rarity—Illustrations of the Variants in Taiwan Philatelic Items (1888–2014)** *Chang Chien-Ping, Chinese Taipei* First catalogue in Taiwan to illustrate errors and varieties
IIC-005	**Catalogue of Estonian Stamp Errors and Varieties, 1991–2014** *Hubert Jakobs, Estonia* Catalogue features varities, errors, and specimens of stamps issued in Estonia from 1991–2014.
IIC-006	**Se-tenant stamps of the DDR, Printing plate flaws and printing errors** *Eberhard Richter, Germany* Discusses indexing and evaluation of se-tenant stamps with printing plate flaws and printing errors
IIC-007	**Specialized catalogue of Se-tenant stamps and stamp booklets of the DDR (part 1,2,3)** *Eberhard Richter, Germany* Discusses indexing and evaluation of se-tenant stamps and stamp booklets
IIC-008	**Catalogue of the Postage and Revenue Stamps of Hungary 2016–2017** *Philatelia Hungarica Philatelia Hungarica LLC, Hungary* 61st edition of the Hungarian stamp catalogue
IIC-009	**The Stamps of Iran—Qajar, Pahlavi, Islamic Republic (Electronic Web Site)** *Novin Farahbakhsh, Iran*
IIC-010	**Visual Japanese Stamp Catalog Vol. 1, Vol. 2, Vol. 3, Vol. 4** *Japan Philatelic Society Foundation, Japan* Visual Japanese stamp catalogue (4 volumes)

IIC-011	**The Catalogue of Polish Stamps, Vol. I, II** *Andrzej Fischer, Poland* Volume 1 includes all stamps issued in the Polish territory 1860–2009; volume 2 includes civic and municipal posts
IIC-012	**Romanian Postal Stationery Specialized Catalog 1870–1927** *Emanoil-Alexandru Săvoiu, Romania* Elaborate presentation of Romanian postal stationary
IIC-013	**Catalogue—Signs of Postal Payment of Russian Federation, 2014** *The Publishing and Trading Centre "Marka," Russia* Catalogue of postal payments
IIC-014	**Catalogue of Stamped Souvenir Sets, 1963–1991** *Valery Ivashkin, Russia* Catalogue of stamp souvenir sets, 1961–1991
IIC-015	**Definitive Postage Stamps of the USSR, 1923–1991** *ZAO "Publisher Centropoligraf," Russia* Definitive postage stamps of the USSR, 1923–1991
IIC-016	**Philatelic Geography** *Andrey Strygin, Russia* Philatelic geography
IIC-017	**ROSSICA: All About Russian Philately & Stamps** *Olga Ivanova, Russia* Comprehensive discussion of Russian philately and stamps
IIC-018	**Signs of Postal Payment of the USSR, 1961–1974** *The Publishing and Trading Centre "Marka," Russia*
IIC-019	**Specialized Catalogue of Postage Stamps of Russian Empire, RSFSR and USSR, 1857–1940. 2nd Edition** *Alexander V. Zverev, Russia* Specialized catalogue of postage stamps of the Russian Empire, RSFSR and USSR, 1857–1940 (2nd edition)
IIC-020	**The World of Stamps (Annual Almanac)** *Olga Ivanova, Russia* Annual almanac of worldwide stamps
IIC-021	**Catalog of Spain Stamps and Its Colonies. 2016** *EDIFIL, Spain* Catalogue of Spain stamps and colonies (Andorra, Equatorial Guinea, etc.)
IIC-022	**Cuba Stamp Catalog. Volume III. 2005–2015** *EDIFIL, Spain* Cuba stamp catalogue, 2005–2015
IIC-023	**Estudio De Los Sellos De Telegrafos De Cuba 1868/1896** *Federation Espanola De Sociedades Filatelicas, Spain*
IIC-024	**Specialized Catalog Cuba Stamps. Volume I. 1855–1958. With Supplement 2015** *EDIFIL, Spain* Specialized catalogue of Cuba stamps, 1855–1958
IIC-025	**Specialized Catalog of Spain Stamps. Volume III. Spanish State. 1936–1975** *EDIFIL, Spain* Specialized catalogue of stamps dedicated to the period of the government of the Spanish state, 1936–1975

IIC-026	**Specialized Catalog of Spain Stamps. Volume IV. Juan Carlos I. 1975–2000** *EDIFIL, Spain* Specialized catalogue of stamps dedicated to Juan Carlos I, King of Spain
IIC-027	**Facit Norden 2016** *Gunnar Lithén, Sweden* Specialized catalogue covering Nordic countries from 1951 and onwards
IIC-028	**Facit Special Classic 2016** *Gunnar Lithén, Sweden* Specialized catalogue covering the Nordic countries up to 1951
IIC-029	**Airmail Guide Switzerland** *Rene Koller, Switzerland* Switzerland airmail guide
IIC-030	**Czechout Interactive Indexes 1975–2015 (DVD)** *Czechoslovak Philatelic Society of Great Britain, U.K.* Interactive DVD of Indexes 1975–2015 of the Journal of the Czechoslovak Philatelic Society of Great Britain, CZECHOUT
IIC-031	**Croatia 1941–1945 Revenue Issues** *Philip J. Hughes, U.S.A.* Handbook/catalogue for revenue issues of World War II Croatia (national, district, and municipal issues included); bi-lingual
IIC-032	**International Postage Meter Stamp Catalog** *Richard Stambaugh, U.S.A.*
IIC-033	**Ngo's 2014 Catalogue of Philippine Republic Stamps & Postal Stationeries** *Tiong Tak Ngo, U.S.A.*
IIC-034	**USA: Variable Denomination Stamps (1989–2015)** *Karim Roder, U.S.A.*
IIC-035	**Worldwide Reply Coupon Catalog, Vol-I The UPU** *Jack Yao, U.S.A.* Catalogue of international reply coupons issued by all countries in the world

Exhibitors by last name

Exhibitor by last name	Class	Frame #s
Fritz A. Aebi	2B	1299-1306
Sebah Fatima Abdullah	9	4719-4726
Robert Abensur	3C	2820-2824
Murray Abramson	3A	2315-2322
Iris Adair	2D	1929-1936
Francis Adams	12F(B)	4582
Kees Adema	3C	5211-5218
Mehmet Edip Agaogullari	7B	4406-4413
Alessandro Agostosi	3C	2705-2712
Juan Pablo Aguilar	2B	1124-1128
Jon Aitchison	9	4753-4757
Kayhan Akduman	2C	1583-1590
Shaula Alexander	3D	3125-3132
Estanislao Pan de Alfaro	7B	4359-4366
Alla-Ud-Din	12A(D)	1715
James Allen	2A	1001-1005
Paul Allen	3D	3322-3329
John Allen	5	4131-4138
Akthem Al-Manaseer	2C	1667-1674
Sarah Saud Mohd. Al-Thani	2D	2005-2009
Hugh Amoore	3D	3253-3260
Predrag Antić	2C	1641-1648
Gensei Ando	3A	2164-2168
Konrad Andraczek	10C	4958-4962
Stavros Andreadis	1	3583-3590
Kaido Andres	7B	4308-4312
Ajme Sheikh Nafisa Anjum	10B	4921-4925
Jorge Enrique Arbelaez	3B	2391-2398
Thomas Arvanitis	3C	2395-2999
Toby Asson	10B	4881-4882
Costas Athanasion	2C	1654-1658
Francis Au	3D	3495-3502
Julian Auleytner	3C	2833-2840
Finn Aune	9	4745-4749
William Averbeck	3B	2449-2456
Jean-Daniel Ayache	5	3985-3989
Muhammad Azharuddin Md Azmi	3D	3518-3522
Sybrand Jitse Bakker	3D	3165-3169
David S. Ball	6	4163-4170
Peter Bamert	4	3808-3812
Levente Bánás	10A	4812
Vitaliy Bankov	7B	4367-4371
Hervé Barbelin	4	3753-3757
Avi Barit	12A(D)	1714
Paul Barsdell	2D	2010-2014
John Barwis	3A	2109-2116
German Baschwitz	4	3879-3886
Michael Bass	3D	3293-3300
Richard Bates	12A(A)	1095
Wolfgang Bauer (Pre-UPU mail)	1	3599-3606
Wolfgang Bauer (Hermes heads)	1	3607-3614
José Julian Baujin	10B	4912-4913
Jonathan Becker	3D	3370-3377
Colin Beech	2A	1079-1083
Jassim K. Behzad	12C	3944
Jaime Benavides ("Reforma")	3B	2413-2417
Jaime Benavides (French Military Mail)	12B(B)	2521-2521
Maria Beatriz Bendeck	3B	2513-2520
Jeff Bennett	15	5055-5062
Robert Benninghoff (Coil stamps)	2C	1432-1436
Robert Benninghoff (Postage Due)	12B(C)	2805
Vladimir Berdichevskiy	3C	2627-2634
Adriano Bergamini	3C	2685-2689
Edward Bergen	15	5068-5075
Rolf Beyerodt	2C	1481-1488
Klaas Biermann	2C	1518-1522
John Birkinbine II	3A	2185-2192
Michael Blinman	4	3567-3574
Evgeniy Bogomolny	2C	1591-1598
Richard Bodin	3C	2753-2760
Lars Boettger	3C	2690-2694
Jeffrey Bohn	3C	2537-2544
Eduardo Boido	2B	1315-1322
Carol Bommarito	3A	2117-2124
Boncho Bonev	5	3972-3976
Frederik Boom	3C	2849-2856
Graham Booth	3B	2465-2472
Eduardo Borberg	2B	1363-1370
Aleksandar Boričić	3C	2880-2884
Petro Borukhovych	2C	1625-1632
Ricardo Botero	2B	1205-1212
Mark Bottu	2C	1385-1392
MaryAnn Bowman	12A(D)	1694
Robert Boyd	3A	2125-2132
Russell Boylan	1	3615-3622
David Braun	3B	2444-2448
Carlos Brenis	2B	1267-1274
Donald Brent	2C	1371-1375
Eddie Bridges	2D	1945-1949
Albert Briggs	9	4779-4783
Walter Britz	3B	2423-2427
Thomas Broadhead	12B(C)	2806
Roger Brody	2A	1006-1010
Charles Bromser	14	4988-4992

Exhibitor by last name	Class	Frame #s
Thomas Brougham	2A	1061–1065
Stephen Browne	3D	3407–3414
JBF Bruschsal	10B	4865–4867
Wendy Buckle	7C	4518–4522
Almir Bufalo	12B(B)	2323
Henk Buitenkamp	3C	2841–2848
Knut J. Buskum	3C	2893–2900
Lewis Bussey	3C	3073–3080
Mark A. Butterline	3B	2457–2464
Fernando Cabello	9	4732–4736
Brian Callan	5	4011–4018
Francis Carcenac	1	3623–3630
Ray E. Cartier	12E	4189–4189
Patrick Casey	14	5017–5021
Miguel José Casielles	2B	1134–1141
Daiana Aylen Casielles	10C	4926–4930
Alvaro Castro-Harrigan (Costa Rica)	3B	2428–2435
Alvaro Castro-Harrigan (Panama)	1	3631–3638
Miloš Červinka	3C	2909–2916
Bruce Chadderton	3C	3060–3064
Stephen Chan	2D	2062–2069
Rogelio Charlone	4	3813–3817
Michèle Chauvet	3C	2669–2676
Carlos Chaves	3B	2324–2328
Chen Yue	4	3562–3566
Chen	7B	4293–4297
Lindsay Chitty	3D	3201–3208
Sammy Chiu	2D	1775–1779
Cheong-Too Choi (Mafeking)	12A(D)	1692
Cheong-Too Choi (Macau)	2D	2054–2061
Patrick Choy	2D	2070–2077
Marcos Chusyd	3B	2365–2372
Roland Cipolla II	3A	2203–2210
Paul Clemmensen	12A(C)	1687
Peter Cockburn	2D	1882–1886
Monica M. Comrie	3D	3170–3174
Darren Corapcioglu	10B	4914–4916
David Cordon (George V Key Plates)	2B	1231–1235
David Cordon (Dock Issue)	12A(B)	1325
Eloy Orlando Corres	7B	4372–4376
Nicolas Cosso-Hoedt	10A	4806–4808
S. Will and Abby Csaplar	9	4784–4788
Luiz Paulo Rodrigues Cunha	7B	4195–4202
Nuncio Cusati	12H	4616–4616
Martyn Cusworth	9	4763–4770
David D'Alessandris	12B(B)	2524
Ginaldo Bezerra da Silva	7B	4248–4252
Juan Martin Dagostino	2B	1111–1118
Gunnar Dahlstrand	13	4978–4982
JJ Danielski (IRC)	12C	3945–3945
JJ Danielski (Novydux)	13	4968–4972
Wenjin Dao	3D	3503–3507
Lennart Daun	4	3887–3894
John Davies	14	4993–5000
Richard Debney	2D	1950–1954
Ralph DeBoard	3D	3330–3337
Rogerio Dedivitis	7C	4495–4502
Michael Deery	3C	2935–2939
John Dehé	7B	4341–4345
George DeKornfeld	3A	2094–2098
Jack André Denys	7B	4393–4400
Dhananjay Desai	2D	2078–2085
Jean-Louis Desdouets	12A(B)	1329

Exhibitor by last name	Class	Frame #s
Loic Detcheverry	3B	2418–2422
Anthony Dewey (War Rate)	12B(A)	2236
Anthony Dewey (3¢ Connecticut)	15	5076–5083
John Dibiase	9	4617–4624
Johan Diesveld	4	3758–3762
Dario Diez	3B	2381–2385
Hector DiLalla	3B	2531–2535
Nilo Dizon Jr.	13	4973–4977
Luis Domingo	2C	1557–1564
Hans van Dooremalen	4	3855–3862
Gustaf Douglas	2C	1416–1423
A. Du Plessis	2D	1916–1920
Ed Dubin	3A	2245–2249
Péter Dunai	3C	2930–2934
Guy Dutau	2B	1129–1133
Ralph Ebner	9	4659–4666
Manuel Arango Echeverri	9	4651–4658
Yehoshua Eliashiv	5	4019–4026
Kiyoshi Emura	7B	4269–4276
Chuluundorj Enkhbat	3D	3185–3192
Xavier Espy	10B	4862–4864
Péter Espy	10C	4947–4949
Gordon Eubanks	2A	1053–1060
Domingo Antonio del Fabro	5	3946–3950
Louis Fanchini	2C	1505–1509
Juan Farah	2C	1437–1441
Massoud Novin Farahbakhsh	2D	1837–1844
Christiane & Jacques Faucher-Poitras	3B	2339–2343
Fred Fawn (Large Queens)	2B	1189–1196
Fred Fawn (Hungary 1919)	12A(C)	1376
Ladislav Fekete	5	4035–4039
Hugh Feldman	3A	2275–2282
Harold Fernandez	10A	4798–4799
Petra Findenig	10B	4845–4847
James Findlay	12B(D)	3303
Lawrence Fisher	7B	4235–4242
John Fitzsimons	14	5030–5034
Jon Fladeby	2C	1676–1680
Patrick Flanagan	2D	1717–1724
Mihael I. Fock	3D	3245–3252
Eckhard Foerster	5	4071–4078
Robert D. Forster	2B	1339–1346
Jeffrey Forster	3A	2211–2218
Dale Forster	3D	3338–3345
Maria Fotiou	10A	4835–4837
Fabrice Fouchard	2B	1213–1217
Joachim Frank	3B	2473–2480
Dmytro Frenkel	5	4079–4086
Deborah Friedman	12C	3556–3556
Frank Friedman	7C	4513–4517
Alfredo Frohlich	3B	2399–2406
Rainer Fuchs	2D	5201–5205
Darryl Fuller	4	3575–3582
Antonello Fumu	2B	1259–1266
Jean-Pierre Gabillard	7B	4326–4330
Alexandre Galinos	12B(C)	2761
Robert Galland	3C	2579–2583
Guillermo Gallegos	3B	2525–2529
Greg Galletti	14	5001–5001
Jagoda Gałusińska	10A	4826–4828
Cheryl R. Ganz	12A(A)	1096
Eladio Garcia Prada	2B	1184–1188

305

Exhibitor by last name	Class	Frame #s
Larry Gardner	3D	3305–3312
Idor Gatti	3C	2563–2570
Bernhard Gaubmann	10C	4917–4920
Ian Gibson-Smith	2D	1955–1959
Kenneth Gilbart	2A	1011–1018
Ferdinando Giudici	5	4027–4034
Frank Guillotin	12H	4794
Les Glassman	12B(D)	3302
Chip Gliedman	3A	2099–2103
Hugo Goeggel	2C	1575–1582
Marc E. Gonzales	2B	1355–1362
Edward Gosnell	12B(D)	3304
James Peter Gough	3C	3089–3096
Armando Grassi	3A	2148–2155
Howard Green (Confederate Mail)	12B(A)	2201
Howard Green (SWA Revenues)	9	4737–4744
Amandine Grellier	10C	4939–4942
Wilfried Grellier	10C	4943–4946
Alan Grey	3D	3415–3422
John Griffith-Jones	2D	1989–1996
James Grimwood-Taylor	3C	2571–2578
Vesma Grinfelds (Rising Sun)	12A(C)	1688
Vesma Grinfelds (Cancellations)	3C	3000–3004
Dariusz Grochowski	12A(C)	1690
Øystein Grøntoft	2D	1743–1750
Brian Gruzd	2D	1704–1708
Paolo Guglielminetti	12F(B)	4615
Veselku Gustin	3C	3045–3049
Dzhanguli Gvilava	12D	4121–4121
Lawrence Haber	2C	1442–1446
Joséph Hackmey	2C	1523–1530
Maurice Hadida	3D	3479–3486
Achille Hamelin	10B	4858–4861
Richard Hanchett	12B(D)	3321
David Handelman	3A	2291–2295
Keith Hanman	4	3903–3910
Søren Juhl-Hansen	7C	4539–4546
John Guldborg Hansen	14	5012–5016
Asroni Harahap	3D	3531–3538
Deepak Haritwal	13	4983–4987
Ramón Cortés de Haro	3C	2870–2874
Leonard Hartmann	2A	1019–1026
(Stephen) Jun Hasegawa	9	4675–4682
Johannes Haslauer	4	3771–3778
Dennis Hassler	3A	5206–5210
Miloš Hauptman	2C	1393–1400
Peter Heck	3C	2773–2780
Bill Hedley	3C	2595–2602
Stefan Heijtz	3B	2505–2512
Greg Herbert	7A	4436–4440
James Hering	15	5063–5067
Wolf Hess	7B	4219–4226
Helmuth Hiessboeck	7A	4423–4430
Elizabeth Hisey	12A(B)	1326
David L. Hobden	3B	2373–2380
Jan Hofmeyr	2A	1085–1089
Alan Holyoake (6th May)	12A(C)	1689
Alan Holyoake (Secured Delivery)	3C	2603–2610
Géza Homonnay	1	3639–3646
Walter Hopferwieser	6	4145–4152
Peter Hørlyck	4	3787–3794
Hans van der Horst	3C	2875–2879
Hsiao Shish-Cheng	7C	4531–4538
Peter Huethmair	5	3959–3966

Exhibitor by last name	Class	Frame #s
Alan K. Huggins	4	3911–3918
Syed Imtiaz Hussain	2D	1733–1737
Ashrar Hussain	10B	4848–4849
Kenzaburo Ikeda	3D	3149–3156
Kazuyuki Inoue (Japan in Korea)	1	3655–3662
Kazuyuki Inoue (Tin Can Mail)	14	5035–5039
Usman Ali Isani	2D	1853–1860
Tsukasa Ishizawa	2D	1780–1787
Sheikh Shafiqul Islam	9	4633–4637
Pragya Jain	2D	2049–2053
Sandeep Jaiswal (Jaipur)	12A(D)	1716
Sandeep Jaiswal (Postal Stationery)	4	3935–3942
Vojtech Jankovič	7B	4318–4325
Edward H. Jarvis	12C	3555
Peter Jeannopoulos (1902 Provisional)	2B	1244–1248
Peter Jeannopoulos (50c Nord Alexis)	12A(B)	1327
Binkse Jeugd	10B	4903–4906
Phairot Jiraprasertkun	7B	4385–4392
James Johnson	2B	1197–1204
Jon Johnson	12B(B)	2407
William J. Johnson	14	5050–5054
James Johnstone	3A	2305–2309
Jean-Luc Joing	7B	4313–4317
Allen Jones	5	4095–4102
Lars Jörgensen	2D	1793–1800
Guy Jungblut	2C	1565–1569
Aurelie Jungblut	10A	4823–4825
Heinz Junge	9	4638–4642
Martin Jurkovič	2C	1620–1624
Akira Kaburaki	2D	1738–1742
Mayong Bibakkati Kalua	10A	4813–4815
Tatsutoshi Kamakura	2D	1696–1703
Safdar Mohammed Kamal	9	4711–4718
Kang Yongchang	3D	3439–3446
Anestis Karagiannidis	2C	1497–1504
Chatchaya Karnasuta	10A	4832–4834
Itamar Karpovsky	3D	3133–3140
Vitaliy Katsman	2C	1612–1619
Akinori Katsui	7C	4563–4570
Djordje Katuric	3C	2953–2960
Tomo Katuric	3C	2961–2968
Juha Kauppinen	3D	3463–3470
Masaru Kawabe	12F(B)	4579
Kok Ying Kei	4	3831–3838
Matthew Kewriga	3A	2227–2234
Alfred Khalastchy	1	3663–3670
Daryl Kibble	3D	3402–3406
Kim Ki-Hoon	1	3671–3678
Kim Young Kil	3D	3157–3164
Kim Seong Kwon	7B	4277–4284
Kim Heesung	7C	4571–4578
Chris King	3C	2611–2618
Nicholas Kirke (NYFM Fancy Cancels)	12B(A)	2235
Nicholas Kirke (NYFM 1845–78)	3A	2266–2273
Ronald Klimley	15	5100–5107
Keith Klugman	2D	1960–1967
Arnim Knapp	3C	2781–2788
Pascal Koehler	10A	4809–4811
Niklas Koehler	10B	4853–4856
Tom Komnæs	3C	3081–3088
Lutz Komnæs	7A	4441–4448

Exhibitor by last name	Class	Frame #s
Jacek Kosmala	12B(C)	2764
Wieslaw Kostka	3C	2810-2814
Ferenc Kostyál	12A(C)	1686
George Kramer	1	3679-3686
Bojan Kranjc	2C	1633-1640
Karlfried Krauss	3C	2789-2796
Valery Krepostnov	4	3557-3561
Ayuth Krishnamara	2D	1801-1808
François Krol	7B	4211-4218
Ernst Krondorfer	13	4963-4967
Aleksandar Krstić	3C	2857-2864
Lubor Kunc	3C	2865-2869
Jerzy Kupiec-Weglinski	5	4103-4110
Timur Kuran	4	2219-2226
Herwig Kussing	3C	3050-3054
William Kwan	2D	2031-2038
Ariel Kwacz	2B	1275-1732
Menachem Lador	7C	4508-4512
Amr Laithy	12D	4120
Lester C. Lanphear III (Go)	12F(B)	4581
Lester C. Lanphear III (Penalty Clause)	3A	2237-2244
Mathilda Larsson	10B	4891-4894
Michael Laurence	2A	1027-1034
Jan Lauridsen	12B(C)	2762
Arieh Favell Lavee	7C	4503-4507
Edward Laveroni	3D	3354-3361
Frederick P. Lawrence	2D	1973-1980
Anna Lee	5	4003-4010
Linda Lee	7A	4415-4422
Lee Ga Hwa	10C	4950-4952
Luc Legault	2D	2044-2048
William Lenarz	2B	1347-1354
Thomas Lera	12B(C)	2807
Valentin Levandovskiy	3C	2969-2976
Kirill Levandovskiy	10A	4819-4822
"Levantine"	4	3927-3934
Philip Levine	4	3735-3742
Barbara Levine	5	3998-4002
Geoffrey Lewis	3A	2297-2304
Enrique Lewowicz	1	3687-3694
Michael Ley	12A(D)	1693
Giovanni Licata	7A	4449-4456
Otmar Lienert	4	3895-3902
E.M.A. Limmen-Stegemeijer	7B	4336-4340
Lin Tzu-Mu	2D	1809-1816
Lin Mao-Hsin	5	3977-3984
Lin Da'An	6	4181-4188
Ulf Lindahl	3D	3230-3234
Tim Lindemuth	2A	1071-1078
Gunnar Lithén	3C	2745-2752
Yongxin Liu	9	4643-4650
Jan-Olof Ljungh (Domestic)	3C	2737-2744
Jan-Olof Ljungh (Foreign)	1	3711-3718
Miriam Gisbert Llacer	10B	4878-4880
Juan Antonio Llacer-Gracia	3C	2917-2924
Guillermo Llosa	9	4727-4731
Graham Locke	2C	1536-1540
Jeff Long	12A(D)	1703.1
Lu Shusheng	2D	2039-2043
Eivind Lund	12B(B)	2522
Luo Daoguang	7B	4203-4210
Larry Lyons	3A	2104-2108
Joachim Maas	7C	4555-4562

Exhibitor by last name	Class	Frame #s
Keith E. Maatman	12B(A)	2202
William Maddocks	3C	2815-2819
Mark Maestrone	12F(B)	4580
Joshua Magier	1	3719-3726
Mah Lang-Moe	3D	3508-3512
Michael Mahler	9	4771-4778
Sultan Mahmud	2D	1861-1868
Richard Maisel	2B	1249-1253
Richard Malmgren	3A	2250-2257
Marina Mandrovskaya	2C	1570-1574
Nikolay Mandrovskiy	2C	1607-1611
Adam Mangold	10B	4899-4902
János Károly Manz	10C	4953-4957
Claudio Ernesto Manzati	3C	2635-2639
Nikola Nino Marakovic	3C	3065-3072
Julije Maras	7B	4298-4302
Robert Marion	3D	3471-3478
Lesley Marley	7A	4471-4478
Henry Marquez	2B	1275-1282
Bruce Marsden	7A	4457-4461
Gabriel Martinez	5	4053-4057
Jaromir Matejka	6	4153-4157
Sandra Matejka	6	4158-4162
Alexander Matejka	6	4171-4175
H. James Maxwell	2D	1981-1988
John McEntyre	12A(B)	1328
Stephen McGill	2C	1401-1405
David McLaughlin	2B	1171-1178
Ian McMahon	4	3727-3734
Lawrence R. Mead	2C	1681-1685
Johann-Romain Meheu	10B	5034.1-5034.2
Peter Meyer	3B	2357-2364
Friedrich Meyer (GB-Hanover)	12B(C)	2536
Friedrich Meyer (Bremen)	3C	2945-2952
Laure Michiels	10B	4850-4852
Alexandra Michiels	10C	4935-4938
Constantin Milu	3C	2977-2984
Rick Mingee	3A	2143-2147
Ajay Kumar Mittal	9	4688-4692
K. S. Mohan	3D	3523-3530
Tarek Mokhtar	12B(D)	3301
Alan Moll (Vended Postal Insurance)	2A	1066-1070
Alan Moll (Wheat Ridge)	12A(A)	1084-1084
Vittorio Morani	3C	2640-2644
Brian Morera	10A	4800-4800
Robert Morgan	3C	2797-2804
Vernon Morris	3A	2156-2163
Margaret Morris	12F(A)	4462
Jorge Eduardo Moscatelli	5	3951-3958
Cristian Mouat	3B	2352-2356
Alexander Mramornov	3C	3097-3104
Khaled Abdul Mughni	3D	3547-3554
Carolina Mujica	10B	4909-4911
Roger Muller	5	4063-4070
Maxence Muller	10A	4804-4805
Khaled Mustafa	4	3795-3802
Khalid Naeem	3D	3235-3239
Ralph Nafziger	15	5108-5115
Masayasu Nagai	2D	1767-1774
Hironobu Nagashima	2D	1759-1766
Yosuke Naito	7B	4261-4268
Iqbal Nanjee	2D	1874-1881

Exhibitor by last name	Class	Frame #s
Ali Raza Nanjee	3D	3386-3393
Behruz Nassre-Esfahani	2D	1887-1894
Alexandru Negrea	10B	4907-4908
Giovanni Nembrini	3C	2677-2684
Jan Niebrzydowski	12B(C)	2808
Kjell Nilson	3C	2729-2736
Takao Nishiumi	7B	4253-4260
Ted Nixon	3C	2925-2929
Geoffrey Noer	3C	2545-2552
Henry Nogid	3D	3313-3320
Roland Nordberg	2B	1291-1298
Damir Novaković	4	3748-3752
Gita Noviandi	7B	4227-4234
Nestor Nunez	2D	1832-1836
Christian Nunez	10A	4801-4803
James O'Bannon	5	4058-4062
Charles O'Brien III	15	5084-5091
Timothy O'Connor	3A	2133-2137
Kevin O'Reilly	3B	2334-2338
Yuri Obukhov	2C	1599-1606
Oh Byung Yoon	3D	3362-3369
Anders Olason	7B	4377-4384
Ross v. Olson	2C	1406-1410
Pavlina Ondrejková	10C	4931-4934
Henry Ong	3D	3180-3184
Yukio Onuma	1	3647-3654
Noely Luiz Orsato	2B	1147-1154
Hugh Osborne	3D	3240-3244
Bengt-Göran Österdahl	7C	4591-4598
Koray Özalp	3C	2825-2832
Sven Påhlman	3D	3269-3276
Leonardo Palenca	2B	1236-1243
Ben Palmer	2D	1921-1928
David Patterson	2D	1869-1873
Daniel Paulin	3C	2661-2668
Paul Peggie	3D	3423-3430
Martha Villarroel De Peredo	9	4625-4632
Christian Gabriel Pérez	7B	4190-4194
Göran Persson	2C	1447-1454
Michael Peter	3C	2558-2562
Stefan Petriuk	3D	3513-3517
Claus Petry	5	3990-3997
Giullermo Agustin Pettigiani	2B	1103-1110
Terence Pickering	3D	3277-3284
Robert Pildes	2D	1903-1910
Henry Pillage	5	4048-4052
Francisco Piniella	7B	4351-4358
Risto Pitkänen	3C	2985-2989
David Pitts	3B	2386-2390
Robin Pizer	3C	3113-3117
Christopher Podger	9	4758-4762
Nicola Posteraro	3C	2653-2660
Jesus Sitja Prats	3B	2497-2504
Anthony Presgrave	14	5002-5006
Tanguy Pron	10B	4841-4844
Mary Pugh	2C	1531-1535
Des Quail	3C	3013-3020
Salman Qureshi	2D	1751-1758
Thomas Radzuweit	7C	4547-4554
Mahmoud Ramadan	2D	1845-1852
Pekka Rannikko	2C	1476-1480
Leif W. Rasmussen	7B	4303-4307
Uttam Reddy	12B(D)	3123
Daryl Reiber	2D	1827-1831

Exhibitor by last name	Class	Frame #s
Pablo Reim	2B	1098-1102
José Carlos Vasconcellos dos Reis	4	3779
Ake Rietz	2C	1424-1431
Eric Resseguier	2B	1218-1222
Michael Rhodes (Exporta)	2B	1142-1146
Michael Rhodes ("I Am Nothing")	12F(A)	4414
Franco Rigo	3C	2695-2702
Mike Roberts	3B	2481-2488
José Carlos Rodriguez Pinero	10B	4887-4890
Omar Rodriguez	2B	1331-1338
Nenad Rogina	12A(C)	1675
Alexander Romero	2B	1223-1230
Stephen Rose	2A	1035-1039
Robert G. Rose	3A	2169-2176
Salomon Rosenthal	3B	2489-2496
Jürg Roth	3C	2721-2728
Trenton Ruebush	2D	1968-1972
Robert Rufe	2A	1048-1052
Arnold Ryss	4	3847-3854
Daniel Ryterband	3A	2138-2142
Lev Safonov	3C	3105-3112
Tamaki Saito	2C	1510-1517
Hany Salam	3D	3455-3462
Aldo Samame y Samame	12B(B)	2523
William Sandrik	3C	2553-2557
Everaldo Santos	3B	2344-2351
Ruth Ordoñez Sanz	7A	4463-4470
Neil Sargent	4	3919-3926
Pablo Sauma	12D	4144
Emanoil-Alexandru Săvoiu	4	3863-3870
Alexandru Săvoiu	3C	2940-2944
Michael Schewe	2C	1463-1470
Werner Schindler	3C	3021-3028
Alfred Schmidt	1	3591-3598
Klaus Schoepfer	3C	3037-3044
Oscar Schublin	2B	1119-1123
Stephen D. Schumann	1	3695-3702
Barry K. Schwartz	12A(A)	1097
Mark Schwartz	3A	2177-2184
Mati Senkel	3C	3055-3059
Nasser Bin Ahmad Al Serkal	3D	3225-3229
Ahmad Bin Eisa Al Serkal	5	4087-4094
Eisa Bin Ahmad Al Serkal	10B	4895-4898
Jean-Marc Seydoux	7B	4346-4350
Tamouchin K. Shahrokh	3D	3118-3122
Avinash Sharma	10B	4874-4877
James Shaw	2D	2023-2030
Shin Sang Man	7B	4331-4335
Gregory Shoults	2A	1040-1047
Raymond Simrak	12D	4119-4119
Santpal Sinchawla	2D	1788-1792
John Sinfield	4	3763-3770
Valter Skenhall	2C	1471-1475
Björn Sohrne	3D	3261-3268
Björn Gunnar Solaas	7B	4285-4292
Brian Sole	7C	4607-4614
Georges Sotiropoulos	12B(C)	2704
Rudolf Spieler	7C	4487-4494
Wolf Spille	12A(B)	1324
Renate Springer	12B(C)	2584
Christian Springer	12B(C)	2703
Glen Stafford	3D	3431-3438
Phillip Stager	7A	4479-4486

Exhibitor by last name	Class	Frame #s
Robert C. Stein	2D	1937–1944
Zoran Stepanović	3C	2885–2892
Heinrich Stepnizka	3C	3029–3036
George Stewart	12A(D)	1703.2
Georg Störmer	2C	1489–1496
Harlan Stone	15	5092–5099
Douglas Storckenfeldt	1	3703–3710
Alexey Strebulaev	3C	2990–2994
Robert Stuchell	3D	3394–3401
Stephen Suffet	3A	2310–2314
Masaki Sugihara	4	3839–3846
Anil Suri	9	4667–4674
Angeet Suri	9	4683–4687
John Sussex	3C	2585–2589
Lars Peter Svendsen	2D	1817–1821
Nadeem Akhtar Syed	4	3803–3807
Károly Szücs	9	4693–4697
Seppo Talvio	3C	3005–3012
Marcel Tampe	10B	4868–4870
Christopher Tampenawas	10B	4871–4873
Kunihiko Tamura	2A	1090–1094
Richard Taschenberg	12C	3943
James Taylor	2B	1163–1170
Peter Taylor	3B	2408–2412
Gregoire Teyssier	3B	2329–2333
Jack Thompson	2B	1254–1258
Peter Thy	4	3818–3822
Jean-Jacques Tillard	2B	1283–1290
Alexey Timofeev	3D	3346–3353
Sergey Tkachenko	5	3967–3971
Gregory Todd	2D	1997–2004
Erkki Toivakka	2C	1455–1462
Lucien Toutounji	5	4111–4118
Martin Treadwell	2D	2086–2093
Enrique Trigueros	2B	1179–1183
Eigil Trondsen	3C	2901–2908
Yacov Tsachor	3C	2645–2652
Tsai Wen-Lung	3D	3447–3454
Atadan Tunaci	3C	2619–2626
Jussi Tuori	4	3823–3830
Andrew Urushima	12B(C)	2809
Carlos Urzua Barbosa	14	5040–5044
Theo van der Caaij	9	4698–4702
Gawie van der Walt	14	5045–5049
Roger van Laere	7B	4243–4247
Guillaume Vadeboncoeur	2B	1155–1162
Johann Vandenhaute	7C	4523–4530
Paul Vasile	7B	4401–4405
Turid Veggeland	7C	4583–4590
Carlos Vergara	12D	1330–1330
Susan Vernall	3D	3175–3179
Hal Vogel	12B(B)	2530
Jean Voruz	3C	2713–2720

Exhibitor by last name	Class	Frame #s
Fumiaki Wada	3A	2193–2200
Mardyya Wahab Hussain	3D	3217–3224
Bruce Wakeham	3A	2296
Tony Walker	2C	1541–1548
Martin Walker	14	5007–5011
Stefan Wallner	10B	4838–4840
John M. Walsh	9	4789–4793
Steven Walske	3A	2258–2265
Patrick Walters	5	4123–4130
Wang Zhigang	4	3743–3747
Wang Ruowei	6	4176–4180
Daniel Warren	3A	2283–2290
Dick Vander Wateren	9	4703–4710
Bob Watson	12D	4122
Giana Wayman	3B	2436–2443
Wei Gang	3D	3378–3385
Peter Weir	7C	4599–4606
Gerard Louis Van Welie	3D	3193–3200
Eric Werner	2C	1549–1556
Richard Wheatley	3D	3285–3292
Mauritania Wibawanto	10A	4816–4818
Hotze Wiersma	3C	2765–2772
Łukasz Wierzbicki	10A	4829–4831
Avie Wijaya	2D	1822–1826
Paul Wijnants	3C	2590–2594
Richard Wilson	12A(D)	1695
Graham Winters (Ceylon)	12A(D)	1692.1
Graham Winters ("Good Walk Spoiled")	14	5022–5029
Peter Wittsten	2C	1659–1666
Kin Chi Danny Wong	3D	3487–3494
Arthur Woo	2B	1307–1314
Ross Wood	3D	3209–3216
Paul Wreglesworth	2D	2015–2022
Warrick Wright	10B	4883–4886
Yuji Yamada	2D	1709–1713
Yoshiyuki Yamazaki	3D	3141–3148
Fredrik Ydell	5	4040–4047
Takashi Yoshida	2C	1377–1384
Ahmed Yousef	12A(D)	1691
K. Joe Youssefi	2D	1895–1902
Mannan Zarif	2D	1911–1915
Mannan Mashhur Zarif	12B(D)	3124
Arturo Ferrer Zavala	4	3871–3878
José Luis Zeballos	12A(B)	1323
David Zemer	12B(A)	2274
Zhang Guolzang	7A	4431–4435
Zhang Ningnan	10A	4795–4797
Ratomir Živković	5	4139–4143
Helmut Zodl	2C	1649–1653
Fadli Zon	3D	3539–3546
Piotr Zubielik	12B(C)	2763
Alfonso Zulueta	2C	1411–1415

Society exhibits

501	Allied Military Government Collector's Club
502	American Air Mail Society
503	American Association of Philatelic Exhibitors
504	American First Day Cover Society
505	American Philatelic Congress, Postal History Society, & Spellman Museum of Stamps & Postal History
506	American Philatelic Research Library
507	American Philatelic Society
508	American Revenue Association & State Revenue Society
509	American Topical Association
510	American Society of Polar Philatelists
511	Bermuda Collectors Club, British Caribbean Philatelic Study Group & British West Indies Study Circle
512	British North America Philatelic Society
513	Canal Zone Study Group
514	Carriers and Locals Society
515	CartoPhilatelic Society
516	Christmas Seal and Charity Stamp Society
517	Collectors Club
518	Colombia-Panama Philatelic Study Group
519	Confederate Stamp Alliance
520	Cuban Philatelic Society of America & Puerto Rico Philatelic Society
521	Ebony Society of Philatelic Events & Reflections
522	Ephemera Society of America
523	Falkland Islands Philatelic Study Group
524	Fellowship of Samoa Specialists, Papua Philatelic Society, Pacific Islands Study Circle, & Society of Australasian Specialists/Oceania
525	France and Colonies Philatelic Society, Society for Thai Philately, & Society of Indo-China Philatelists
526	G.B. Overprints Society & Bechuanalands and Botswana Society
527	Germany Philatelic Society
528	Haiti Philatelic Society
529	India Study Circle and Nepal & Tibet Philatelic Circle
530	International Cuban Philatelic Society
531	International Philippine Philatelic Society
532	International Society for Japanese Philately
533	International Society of Worldwide Stamp Collectors
534	Iran Philatelic Study Circle

535 Machine Cancel Society
536 Meter Stamp Society
537 Metropolitan Air Post Society
538 Mexico-Elmhurst Philatelic Society International
539 Military Postal History Society
540 National Duck Stamp Collectors Society
541 Ottoman and Near East Philatelic Society
542 Perfins Club
543 Peru Philatelic Study Circle
544 Philatelic Foundation
545 Philatelic Society for Greater Southern Africa & West Africa Study Circle
546 Pitcairn Islands Study Group
547 Plate Number Coil Collectors Club
548 Polonus Philatelic Society
549 Post Mark Collectors Club
550 Postal History Foundation
551 Postal Label Study Group
552 The Postal Museum
553 Postal Order Society
554 Poster Stamp Collectors Club
555 Precancel Stamp Society
556 Rhodesian Study Circle
557 Rocky Mountain Philatelic Library
558 Rossica Society of Russian Philately
559 Royal Philatelic Society London
560 Royal Philatelic Society of Canada
561 Scandinavian Collectors Club
562 Scouts on Stamps Society International
563 Society for Czechoslovak Philately
564 Society for Hungarian Philately
565 Society of Israel Philatelists
566 South African Collectors Society
567 Sports Philatelists International and AICO
568 St. Helena, Ascension and Tristan da Cunha Philatelic Society
569 U.S. Philatelic Classics Society
570 Ukrainian Philatelic and Numismatic Society
571 United Postal Stationery Society
572 United States Stamp Society
573 Universal Ship Cancellation Society
574 Wreck & Crash Mail Society

Dealers

843	**A & D Stamps & Coins** Jim & Sue Dempsey Walnut Creek, CA *www.aanddstampsandcoins.com*	
1268	**A Grand Alliance** Richard Shelley Washington, DC *www.grandalliance.org*	
756	**AAA Stamp & Coin** Marc Achterhof Lansing, MI	
1067	**aGatherin'** Diane DeBlois & Robert Dalton Harris West Sand Lake, NY	
1264	**Albert's Stamps** Albert Curulli Brooklyn, NY	
1257	**Willard S. Allman** Willard Allman Ridgewood, NJ	
1165	**Argyll Etkin Ltd** Patrick Frost London, U.K. *www.argyll-etkin.com*	
657	**Azusa Collectibles** Thomas & Gail Auletta Clifton Park, NY	
1061	**Bardo Stamps** James Bardo Buffalo Grove, IL *www.bardostamps.com*	
1356	**Bill Barrell Ltd.** Bill Barrell Grantham, Lincs, U.K. *www.barrell.co.uk*	
737	**Behr** Pascal Behr Paris, France *www.behr.fr*	

1137	**Bejjco of Florida Inc.** Arnold Selengut Temple Terrace, FL	
831	**Mark Bloxham Stamps Ltd.** Mark Bloxham Newcastle Upon Tyne, U.K. *www.philatelic.co.uk*	
957	**Bolaffi SPA** Alberto Bolaffi Torino, Italy *www.bolaffi.it*	
1558	**Frederic S. Boatwright** Fred Boatwright Hawk Point, MO	
665	**Britannia Enterprises** Michael Mead Orleans, MA	
771	**Burstamp** Stewart Robbins Caboolture, QLD, Australia *www.burstamp.com*	
1070	**Canada Stamp Finder** Maxime Herold Brampton, ON, Canada *www.canadastampfinder.com*	
667	**Candlish McCleery Ltd.** Ross Candlish Worcester, U.K. *www.candlishmccleery.com*	
1566	**Carmichael & Todd Philatelists** Gregory Todd Lymington, Hants, U.K.	
870	**Castlerock Stamps** Jorge Castillo Coral Gables, FL *www.castlerockstamps.com*	
930	**Cavendish Philatelic Auctions Ltd.** James L. Grimwood-Taylor Derby, U.K. *www.cavendish-auctions.com*	

621	**Champion Stamp Company** Arthur Morowitz New York, NY *www.championstamp.com*	
1337	**Cherrystone Philatelic Auctioneers** Joshua M. Buchsbayew New York, NY *www.cherrystoneauctions.com*	
943	**Michael Chipperfield** Michael Chipperfield London, U.K.	
1060	**The Classic Collector** Sergio & Liane Sismondo Syracuse, NY *www.sismondostamps.com*	
757	**Collectors Exchange** John Latter Orlando, FL *www.britishstampsamerica.com*	
857	**Colonial Stamp Co.** George Holschauer Los Angeles, CA *www.colonialstamps.com*	
1230 & 1232	**Columbian Stamp Co.** Harry Hagendorf New Rochelle, NY *www.columbianstamp.com*	
1261	**Compustamp** Gary DuBro Santa Fe, NM *www.compustamp.com*	
729	**Corinphila Auctions, Switzerland** Antoine Clavel Zürich, Switzerland *www.corinphila.com*	
729	**Corinphila Auctions, The Netherlands** Gerard Garritsen *www.corinphila.nl*	

1343	Cover Story Philip Newby London, U.K.	943	Galerie Dreyfus Basel, Switzerland www.galerie-dreyfus.com	729	John Bull Auctions, Hong Kong Philip Cheng Hong Kong, China www.jbull.com
668 & 666	Coverman Alan Tohn Oceanside, NY	931	Auktionshaus Christoph Gärtner GmbH & Co. Christoph Gärtner Bietigheim-Bissingen, Germany www.auktionen-gaertner.de	1065	Kay & Company Malcolm S. Batchelor Bend, OR www.kaystamps.com
936	D & P Stamps Patricia McElroy Chula Vista, CA www.dpstamps.com				
836	Davo Paul Bartolomei Elk Grove Village, IL www.paloalbums.com	956	Geezers Tweezers Phillip Sager Baltimore, MD www.geezerstweezers.com	1344	Argyrios-Karamitsos Argyrios Karamitsos Thessaloniki, Greece www.karamitsos.com
860	Delcampe International Sebastien Delcampe Tubize, Belgium www.delcampe.net	971	Wayne Gehret Wayne Gehret Ephrata, PA www.usmintsheets.com	757	Walter Kasell Walter Kasell Cambridge, MA
		1051	Stanley Gibbons Ltd. London, U.K. www.stanleygibbons.co.uk	1365	Patricia A. Kaufmann Trish Kaufmann Lincoln, DE www.trishkaufmann.com
871	Dutch Country Auctions— The Stamp Center Russell Eggert Wilmington, DE www.dutchcountryauctions.com	1136	Henry Gitner Philatelists, Inc Henry L. Gitner Middletown, NY www.hgitner.com	1329	Daniel F. Kelleher Auctions LLC David Coogle Danbury, CT www.kelleherauctions.com
750	Michael Eastick & Associates P/L Michael Eastick Forest Hill, VIC, Australia www.michaeleastick.com	1170	The Gold Mine Geri & Gil Celli Massapequa, NY	729	Heinrich Koehler Auktionshaus GmbH & Co. Dieter Michelson Wiesbaden, Germany www.heinrich-koehler.de
		1459	Hamiltons for Stamps Steve Hamilton Forster, NSW Australia www.ham4stamps.com		
1037	Eric Jackson Eric Jackson Leesport, PA www.ericjackson.com			1042	George H. LaBarre Galleries Inc. George Labarre Hollis, NH www.glabarre.com
1171	etradegoods Alejandro Jaime Andover, MA	729	H.R. Harmer Tom Mills Tustin, CA www.hrharmer.com		
1237	The Excelsior Collection Robert Zatorski Scotch Plains, NJ www.theexcelsiorcollection.com	671	Harmers International Inc. Keith Harmer Yorktown Heights, NY www.harmersinternational.com	1150	William Langs William Langs New Milford, NJ www.wlangs.com
743	David Feldman SA David Feldman Geneva, Switzerland www.davidfeldman.com	765	Honegger Philatelie AG Gottfried Honegger St. Gallen, Switzerland www.ghonegger.ch	1057	James E. Lee, LLC James Lee Oak Brook, IL www.jameslee.com
1360	Filat AG Richard Johnson Zürich, Switzerland www.filat.ch	559	House of Zion Edward Rosen Redwood City, CA www.houseofzion.com	956	Leonard Stamps Harris Leonard Rockville, MD
569 & 571	France International Michael Shefler Gibsonia, PA www.stampsbythemes.com	752	Hunt & Co Brian Hunt Austin, TX www.huntstamps.com	837	Leuchtturm— Lighthouse Eric Werner Fairfield, NJ www.lighthouse.us
766	Richard Friedberg Stamps Richard Friedberg Meadville, PA www.friedbergstamps.com	833	Interasia Auctions Ltd. Rob Schneider Hong Kong, China www.interasia-auctions.com	836	Lindner Paul Bartolomei Elk Grove Village, IL www.paloalbums.com

951	**Linn's Stamp News—Scott Catalogue** Charles "Chad" Snee Sidney, OH *www.amospublishing.com*	
1469	**London Philatelists** David Wrigley Bangkok, Thailand	
1243	**Long Island Philatelics** Paul Weiser Smithtown, NY	
1342	**Gary L. Lyon (Philatelist) Ltd.** Gary Lyon Bathurst, NB Canada *www.garylyon.com*	
1236	**Markest Stamp Co.** Mark Eastzer Lynbrook, NY *www.markest.com*	
1036	**James T. McCusker Inc.** James McCusker Raynham, MA *www.jamesmccusker.com*	
1458	**MCXI Philatelics** Ralph Greenhut Libertyville, IL *www.mcxistamps.com*	
1571	**The Media** Mosharaf Husain Dhaka, Bangladesh *www.mediabd.com*	
937	**Miller's Stamp Company** Irving Miller Waterford, CT *www.millerstamps.com*	
1467	**MN Auction Russia** Raimonds Miskinis St. Petersburg, Russia *www.mnauctions.ru*	
1160	**Momen Stamps Inc.** Mostafa Momen Cary, NC *www.momenstamps.com*	
964	**Brian Moorhouse** Brian Moorhouse Peterborough, U.K. *www.brianmoorhouse.com*	
1261	**David Morrison** David Morrison Malmesbury, Wilts, U.K. *www.forpostalhistory.com*	

1056	**Mountainside Stamps, Coins & Currency** Thomas Jacks Mountainside, NJ *www.mountainsidestampsandcoins.com*	
1056	**Mowbray Collectables** John Mowbray Wellington, New Zealand *www.mowbrays.co.nz*	
842	**Gert Müller GmbH & Co.** Holger Thull Ettlingen, Germany *www.gert-mueller-auktion.de*	
629	**Mystic Stamp Company** Donald Sundman Camden, NY *www.mysticstamp.com*	
767	**Negev Holyland—Button Stamp Co.** Sid Morginstin Trenton, NJ *www.negev.stampcircuit.com*	
1357	**Newport Harbor Stamp Co.** David Cobb Newport Beach, CA	
836	**Palo Albums Inc.** Paul Bartolomei Elk Grove Village, IL *www.paloalbums.com*	
1071 & 1069	**Paradise Valley Stamp Co. Inc.** Torbjorn Bjork Concord, NH *www.stamp-one.com*	
1561	**Ian Perry Stamps** Ian Perry Newport, Telford, U.K.	
1559	**Philangles Ltd.** Simon Carson Warrington, Ches., U.K. *www.philangles.co.uk*	
1221	**Philasearch** Franz Fedra Munich, Germany *www.philasearch.com*	
769	**Hellman Auctions Ltd. / Philatelic Services of Finland Ltd.** Tatu Untinen Turku, Finland *www.filateliapalvelu.com*	
1131	**Stanley M. Piller & Assoc.** Stanley Piller Alamo, CA *www.smpiller.com*	

1043 & 1142	**Gary Posner Inc.** Gary Posner Rockville Centre, NY *www.garyposnerinc.com*	
665	**Postalstationery.com** Philip Stevens Alton, NH *www.postalstationery.com*	
960	**Postiljonen AB** Lars-Olow Carlsson Malmö, Sweden *www.postiljonen.com*	
656	**Prinz Verlag GmbLH** Gary Edelman South Ozone Park, NY *www.harryedelmaninc.com*	
1336	**Raritan Stamps Inc.** Nikolai Kondrikov Dayton, NJ *www.raritanstamps.com*	
565	**Mark Reasoner** Mark Reasoner Columbus, OH	
942	**Regency Superior Ltd.** David Kols St. Louis, MO *www.regencystamps.com*	
670	**REW Stamps-Coins LLC** Ross Wiessmann Augusta, NJ	
1161	**Richardson & Copp** Malcolm Richardson Oxted, Surrey, U.K. *www.richardsonandcopp.com*	
970	**Rising Sun Stamps** Haruyo Baker Marshalls Creek, PA	
1271	**Robin Philatelics** Robin Ko Oakland Gardens, NY *www.stores.ebay.com/robinphilatelics*	
864	**Roy's Stamps** Roy Houtby St. Catharines, ON, Canada	
561	**Royal William Stamps Ltd.** Robert Graham Edmonton, AB Canada *www.lornatstamps.com*	
1360	**Doreen Royan & Assoc. [Pty] Ltd.** Doreen Royan Johannesburg, South Africa *www.doreenroyan.com*	

ID	Name	ID	Name	ID	Name
1031	Schuyler J. Rumsey Philatelic Auctions Inc. Schuyler Rumsey San Francisco, CA www.rumseyauctions.com	1567	Stamps Inc./India & Indian States Exclusively Sandeep Jaiswal Cranston, RI	764	Vidiforms Inc. James Michalek Congers, NY www.showgard.com
1164	Rushstamps (Retail) Ltd. Eric Friedman Lyndhurst, Hants, U.K. www.rushstamps.co.uk	1564	Sukhani Europhil Limited Raj Sukhani Kolkata, India	1242	Vogt Stamps & Coins Pam Vogt Burlingame, CA www.caminocompany.com
1150	Martin Shupe Stamps Martin Shupe Vista, CA www.allstamp.net	753	James F. Taff James Taff Sacramento, CA	937	Volovski Rarities Lawrence Volovski Thomaston, CT
1229	Robert A. Siegel Auction Galleries Inc. Scott Trepel New York, NY www.siegelauctions.com	1568	Stephen T. Taylor Stephen Taylor Surbiton, U.K. www.stephentaylor.co.uk	1064	Weisz Covers Douglas Weisz McMurray, PA www.douglasweisz.com
1466	Steve Sims Steve Sims Anchorage, AK	1570	Don Tocher Donald Tocher Sunapee, NH www.postalnet.com/dontocher	751	Torsten Weller Torsten Weller Caulfield South, VIC Australia www.torstenweller.com
1364	Soler y Llach Xavier Llach Barcelona, Spain www.soleryllach.com	1157	Toga Associates Thomas Bansak Fairfield, CT www.togaassociates.com	1265	WIP International Inc. Ariel Hasid Surfside, FL www.wipstamps.com
1321	Spink & Son Olivier D. Stocker London, U.K. www.spink.com	1066	David R. Torre Co. David Torre Santa Rosa, CA	1451	Hugh Wood, Inc. Hugh Wood New York, NY www.hughwood.com
1250	StampArt Thomas Kinberg Lincoln City, OR	1467	Antonio Torres Antonio Torres London, U.K. www.antoniotorres.com	856	YPLF Stamps & Postal History Alex Haimann Bellefonte, PA www.stampfellowship.org
659	StampAuctionNetwork Tom Droege Durham, NC stampauctionnetwork.com	965 & 967	Triple S. Postal History Inc. Tom Gates Urbana, OH www.triple-sonline.com	961	Yvert et Tellier Gervais Benoit Amiens, France www.yvert.com
1569	Stampbay, Inc./India & Indian States Exclusively Deepak Jaiswal Palo Alto, CA www.stampbay.com	770	Van Dieten Stamp Auctions Roermond, Netherlands www.vandieten.nl	1166	Zhaoonline.com Shanghai, P. R. China english.zhaoonline.com
851	Stampfinder Richard Lehmann Miami Lakes, FL www.stampfinder.com/	865	Vance Auctions Ltd. Christopher Carmichael Smithville, ON Canada www.vanceauctions.com	658	Zirinsky Stamps Steven Zirinsky New York, NY www.zirinskystamps.com
643 & 645	Stampmen Inc. Kevin Custis Belle Mend, NJ	758	Victoria Stamp Co. Phoebe A. MacGillivary Sharon Springs, NY www.VictoriaStampCo.com	1359	Zurich Asia Louis Mangin Hong Kong, China www.zurichasia.com

A Walk Around the World

Countries

328	**Aland Post Ltd** *www.posten.ax*	
417	**Antigua & Barbuda** *www.igpc.com*	
428	**HayPost CJSC—National Postal Operator of Armenia** *www.haypost.am*	
525	**Aruba** *www.herrickstamp.com*	
325	**Australia Post** *auspost.com.au*	
115	**Austrian Post** *www.post.at*	
525	**Bermuda Post** *www.herrickstamp.com*	
417	**Brunei** *www.igpc.com*	
429	**Canada Post—Stamp Services** *www.canadapost.ca*	
320	**Cape Verde** *www.stamperija.eu*	
320	**Central African Republic** *www.stamperija.eu*	
425	**China National Philatelic Corporation** *www.chinapost.com.cn*	
525	**Congo** *www.herrickstamp.com*	
104	**Croatian Post** *www.posta.hr*	
525	**Curaçao** *www.herrickstamp.com*	
525	**Dutch Caribbean** *www.herrickstamp.com*	
417	**Gambia** *www.igpc.com*	
105	**Georgian Post** *www.gpost.ge*	
115	**German Post** *www.deutschepost.de*	
417	**Ghana** *www.igpc.com*	
417	**Gibraltar** *www.igpc.com*	
113	**Gibraltar Stamps** *www.gibraltar-stamps.com/*	
417	**Grenada and the Grenadines** *www.igpc.com*	
113	**Guernsey Post** *www.gernseypost.com*	
320	**Guinea** *www.stamperija.eu*	
320	**Guinea-Bissau** *www.stamperija.eu*	
417	**Guyana** *www.igpc.com*	
328	**Iceland Post Postphil** *www.stamps.is*	
525	**Ireland** *www.herrickstamp.com*	
417	**Israel** *www.igpc.com*	
525	**Japan** *www.herrickstamp.com*	
525	**Jersey Post** *www.herrickstamp.com*	
109	**Korea Post** *www.koreapost.go.kr*	
417	**Liberia** *www.igpc.com*	
525	**Liechtenstein** *www.herrickstamp.com*	
420	**Macau Post** *www.macaupost.gov.mo*	
525	**Madagascar** *www.herrickstamp.com*	
320	**Maldives** *www.stamperija.eu*	
320	**Mozambique** *www.stamperija.eu*	
525	**Netherlands** *www.herrickstamp.com*	
417	**Nevis** *www.igpc.com*	
101	**India Post** *www.indiapost.gov.in*	
320	**Niger** *www.stamperija.eu*	
328	**Norway Post** *www.posten.no/frimerker*	
417	**Palau** *www.igpc.com*	
417	**Papua New Guinea** *www.igpc.com*	
116	**Phila Post/La Poste—France** *www.laposte.fr*	
525	**Portugal** *www.herrickstamp.com*	
111	**Pos Indonesia** *www.posindonesia.co.id*	
328	**POST Greenland** *www.stamps.gl*	
107	**Post Philately Luxembourg** *www.postphilately.lu*	
328	**Posta—Faroe Islands** *www.stamps.fo*	
328	**Posti Group Finland**	

Countries (continued)

417	Qatar *www.igpc.com*	417	St. Kitts *www.igpc.com*	320	Togo *www.stamperija.eu*
103	Romfilatelia—Romania *www.romfilatelia.ro*	525	St. Maarten *www.herrickstamp.com*	417	Turks & Caicos *www.igpc.com*
525	Royal Mail—Great Britain *www.herrickstamp.com*	417	St. Vincent and the Grenadines *www.igpc.com*	417	Tuvalu *www.igpc.com*
320	São Tome & Principe *www.stamperija.eu*	102	Tahiti—French Polynesia *www.opt.pf*	329	United Nations Postal Administration *www.unstamps.org*
320	Sierra Leone *www.stamperija.eu*	110, 112, 114	Chunghwa Post (Taiwan) *www.post.gov.tw*	331	United States Postal Service *www.usps.com/stamps*
320	Solomon Islands *www.stamperija.eu*				

Agencies representing more than one country:

525	Herrick Stamp Co. *www.herrickstamp.com*	328	Nordica
417	IGPC *www.igpc.com*	320	Stamperija Philatelic Agencies *www.stamperija.eu*

Stamp printers:

311	Ashton Potter *www.ashtonpotter.com*
313	Stamps to Go *uspsstampstogo.com*

Special Exhibit:

117   The Mauritius "Post Office" Issue Printing Plate
www.davidfeldman.com/the-mauritius-post-office-plate/

Societies

CLUBS AND ORGANIZATIONS PARTICIPATING AT World Stamp Show–NY 2016.

875/ 877	Allied Military Government Collectors' Club *amgcc.boards.net/*	881	British North America Philatelic Society—BNAPS *www.bnaps.org*
777	American Air Mail Society—AAMS *www.americanairmailsociety.org*	1378	British West Indies Study Circle *www.bwisc.org*
832/ 835	American Association of Philatelic Exhibitors—AAPE *www.aape.org*		Burma (Myanmar) Philatelic Study Circle *burmamyanmarphilately.wordpress.com/ burma-myanmar-philatelic-study-circle/*
1476	American First Day Cover Society—AFDCS *www.afdcs.org*	879	Canal Zone Study Group—CZSG *www.canalzonestudygroup.com*
	American Helvetia Philatelic Society—AHS *www.swiss-stamps.org/*	683	Carriers and Locals Society—CLS *www.pennypost.org*
677	American Philatelic Congress—APC *www.americanphilateliccongress.org*	1656	CartoPhilatelic Society—CPS *www.mapsonstamps.org*
	American Philatelic Research Library—APRL *www.stamplibrary.org*	1276/ 1278	Cats on Stamps Study Unit of the American Topical Association—COSSU *catstamps.info*
721	American Philatelic Society—APS *www.stamps.org*		Chess on Stamps Study Unit—COSSU *www.chessonstamps.org*
1652	American Revenue Association—ARA *www.revenuer.org/*		China Stamp Society—CSS *www.chinastampsociety.org*
1280	American Society of Polar Philatelists—ASPP *www.polarphilatelists.org*	1276/ 1278	Christmas Philatelic Club *www.christmasphilatelicclub.org*
721	American Stamp Dealers Association—ASDA *www.americanstampdealer.com*	1660	Christmas Seal and Charity Stamp Society—CSCSS *www.seal-society.org/*
1276/ 1278	American Topical Association—ATA *www.americantopicalassn.org*		Cinderella Stamp Club of Great Britain—CSC *www.cinderellastampclub.org.uk*
1276/ 1278	Armenian Philatelic Association *www.armenianphilatelic.org/*	639	Collectors Club—CC *www.collectorsclub.org*
	Art Cover Exchange *artcoverexchange.org*	879	Colombia-Panama Philatelic Study Group—COPAPHIL *www.copaphil.org*
	Association International des Experts Philateliques		
	Auxiliary Markings Club *www.postal-markings.org*	1380	Confederate Stamp Alliance—CSA *www.csalliance.org*
1381	Bechuanalands and Botswana Society—BBS *www.bechuanalandphilately.com*	675	Cuban Philatelic Society of America—CPSA *www.cubapsa.com*
1378	Bermuda Collectors Society—BCS *www.bermudacollectorssociety.com*	1276/ 1278	Earth's Physical Features Study Unit *www.webring.org/l/rd?ring=thematicstamps;id= 13;url=http%3A%2F%2Fwww%2Eepfsu%2Ejeffhayward%2Ecom%2F*
1276/ 1278	Biology Unit		
	Boston 2026 World Stamp Show *www.boston2026.org*		
1378	British Caribbean Philatelic Study Group—BCPSG *www.bcpsg.com*		

318

782	Ebony Society of Philatelic Events & Reflections—ESPER *www.esperstamps.org*	679	Machine Cancel Society—MCS *www.machinecancel.org*
	Egypt Study Circle—ESC *www.egyptstudycircle.org.uk*		Masonic Stamp Club of New York *www.mscnewyork.net*
681	Ephemera Society of America—ESA *www.ephemerasociety.org*	679	Meter Stamp Society—MSS *www.meterstampsociety.com*
1283	Falkland Islands Philatelic Study Group—FIPSG *www.fipsg.org.uk*	777	Metropolitan Air Post Society—MAPS *www.mapsnewyork.org*
	Federación Interamericana de Filatelia (FIAF)	1282	Mexico-Elmhurst Philatelic Society International—MEPSI *www.mepsi.org*
	Fédération Internationale de Philatélie—FIP *www.f-i-p.ch*	1280	Military Postal History Society—MPHS *www.militaryphs.org*
1375	Fellowship of Samoa Specialists—FSS *www.samoaexpress.org*	781	National Duck Stamp Collectors Society—NDSCS *www.ndscs.org*
774	France and Colonies Philatelic Society—FCPS *www.franceandcolps.org*	1376	Nepal and Tibet Philatelic Study Circle—NTPSC *www.fuchs-online.com/ntpsc/*
1381	G. B. Overprints Society—GBOS *www.gbos.org.uk*		Nicaragua Study Group—NSG *www.facebook.com/pages/Nicaragua-Study-Group-postage-stamps-and-revenue-stamps-of-Nicaragua/200224964632*
1474	Germany Philatelic Society—GPS *www.germanyphilatelicsocietyusa.org*		
1276/ 1278	Graphics Philately Association *graphics-stamps.org*	1276/ 1278	Old World Archaeology Study Group *www.owasu.org*
	Guyana Philatelic Society *www.guyanastamps.com*	883	Ottoman and Near East Philatelic Society—ONEPS *www.oneps.net*
875/ 877	Haiti Philatelic Society—HPS *haitiphilately.org*	1375	Pacific Islands Study Circle—PISC *www.pisc.org.uk*
	Hong Kong Study Circle—HKSC *www.hongkongstudycircle.com*	1375	Papua Philatelic Society—PPS *www.communigate.co.uk/york/pps*
1376	India Study Circle—ISC *www.indiastudycircle.org*		Peru Philatelic Study Circle—PPSC *www.peru-philatelic-study-circle.com*
	Indonesian Philatelic Interest Group	637	Philatelic Foundation—PF *www.philatelicfoundation.org*
778	International Association of Olympic Collectors—AICO *aicolympic.org*	1379	Philatelic Society for Greater Southern Africa—PSGSA *www.psgsa.org/*
875/ 877	International Cuban Philatelic Society—ICPS *www.cubafil.org*		Philatelic Specialists Society of Canada *www.philatelicspecialistssociety.com*
875/ 877	International Philippine Philatelic Society—IPPS *www.theipps.info*	1281	Pitcairn Islands Study Group—PISG *www.pisg.net*
	International Postal History Fellowship—IPHF	876	Plate Number Coil Collectors Club—PNC3 *www.pnc3.org*
882	International Society for Japanese Philately—ISJP *www.isjp.org*	1478	Polonus Philatelic Society—PPS *www.polonus.org*
	International Society of Guatemala Collectors *www.guatemalastamps.com*	883	Post Mark Collectors Club—PMCC *www.postmarks.org*
1374	International Society of Worldwide Stamp Collectors—ISWSC *www.iswsc.org*	1382	Postal History Foundation—PHF *www.postalhistoryfoundation.org*
776	Iran Philatelic Study Circle—IPSC *www.iranphilately.org*	677	Postal History Society—PHS *postalhistorysociety.org*
	Le Club Philatelique Saint-Pierre et Miquelon *www.clubphilatelique.com*	881	Postal History Society of Canada—PHSC *www.postalhistorycanada.net*

681	Postal Label Study Group—PLSG *www.postal-label-study-group.info/plsg/index.html*		Spanish Philatelic Society—SPS *www.spsforum.net*
1275/ 1277	Postal Order Society—POS *www.postalordersociety.blogspot.com*	677	Spellman Museum of Stamps & Postal History—SM *www.spellmanmuseum.org*
681	Poster Stamp Collectors Club—PSCC *www.posterstampcc.org*	778	Sports Philatelists International—SPI *sportstamps.org*
878	Precancel Stamp Society—PSS *www.precancels.com*	1281	St. Helena, Ascension and Tristan da Cunha Philatelic Society—SHATPS *www.shatps.org*
675	Puerto Rico Philatelic Society *www.philapr.com*		St. Pierre & Miquelon Philatelic Society *stamps.org/SPM*
1377	Rhodesian Study Circle—RSC *www.rhodesianstudycircle.org.uk*	1652	State Revenue Society—SRS
1279	Rocky Mountain Philatelic Library—RMPL *www.rmpldenver.org*	880	The Perfins Club—PC *www.perfins.org*
780	Rossica Society of Russian Philately—ROSSICA *www.rossica.org*	1276/ 1278	The Petroleum Philatelic Society International
775/ 874	Royal Philatelic Society London—RPSL *www.rpsl.org.uk*	1658	The Postal Museum *www.postalmuseum.org*
881	Royal Philatelic Society of Canada—RPSC *https://www.rpsc.org*	738	U.S. Philatelic Classics Society—USPCS *www.uspcs.org*
	Sarawak Specialists Society	875/ 877	U.S. Possessions Philatelic Society—USPPS *www.uspps.net*
1482	Scandinavian Collectors Club—SCC *www.scc-online.org*	1480	Ukrainian Philatelic and Numismatic Society—UPNS *www.upns.org*
783	Scouts on Stamps Society International—SOSSI *www.sossi.org*	1276/ 1278	United Nations Philatelists, Inc *www.unpi.com*
1276/ 1278	Ships on Stamps Unit *www.shipsonstamps.org*	1275/ 1277	United Postal Stationery Society—UPSS *www.upss.org*
	Smithsonian National Postal Museum *postalmuseum.si.edu/*	736	United States Stamp Society—USSS *www.usstamps.org*
1650	Society for Czechoslovak Philately—SCP *www.csphilately.net/*	1280	Universal Ship Cancellation Society—USCS *www.uscs.org*
779	Society for Hungarian Philately—SHP *www.hungarianphilately.org*		Vincent Graves Greene Philatelic Research Foundation *www.greenefoundation.ca*
774	Society for Thai Philately—STP *www.thaiphilately.org*	1379	West Africa Study Circle *www.wasc.org.uk*
1375	Society of Australasian Specialists/Oceania—SASO *www.sasoceania.org*		Westfield Stamp Club—WSC *www.westfieldstampclub.org*
774	Society of Indo-China Philatelists—SICP *www.sicp-online.org*		Women Exhibitors
1274	Society of Israel Philatelists—SIP *www.israelstamps.com*		World Stamp Show-NY 2016 Social Media Followers *www.facebook.com/ny2016*
	Society of Postal Historians—SPH *s429868656.websitehome.co.uk*	777	Wreck & Crash Mail Society—WCMS *www.mapsnewyork.com/home.html*
1383	South African Collectors Society, UK *www.southafricacollector.com/*		Zeppelin Study Group *www.ezep.de/zsg/zsg.html*
	Space Unit of the American Topical Association—SU *www.space-unit.com*		

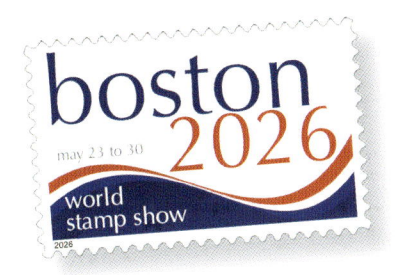

Mark your calendars.

AMERICA CELEBRATES its 250th anniversary in 2026, and Boston will be the center of attention. Planning is already underway to ensure that stamp collecting is a big part of the fun. To find out more about the next great, once-a-decade U.S. postage stamp event, visit boston2026.org

To meet the organizing committee and learn more before you leave NY2016, please join us for a public information session on Saturday, June 4, at 1pm in 1E07. And don't forget: it's all happening in Boston, May 23-30, 2026.

Boston 2026 World Stamp Show, Inc. Registered as a 501(c)(3) public charity.

SPINK

350TH YEAR
LONDON 1666

THE OLDEST AND BOLDEST COLLECTABLES AUCTION HOUSE

With an outstanding reputation since 1666, Spink is proud to command the largest expert philatelic network around the world. All Spink sales are promoted on the Spink App, Spink website and Spink Live, Spink Insider Magazine and the largest press coverage in the Philatelic world. Join Spink in making its 350th year a year to remember!

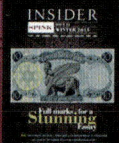

REPUTATION ACHIEVES RESULTS
CONSIGN YOUR PHILATELIC MATERIAL FOR SALE BY AUCTION OR PRIVATE TREATY

WORLD RECORD
U.S. The J. E. Safra
24c. INVERTED JENNY
Realised: $575,100

WORLD RECORD FOR AN ITEM SOLD IN SINGAPORE
Straits Settlements, $500
Realised: S$264,000

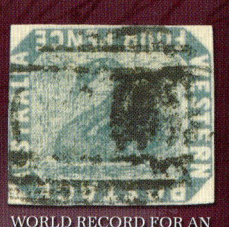

WORLD RECORD FOR AN ITEM OF WESTERN AUSTRALIA
4d blue showing variety FRAME INVERTED
Realised: £122,400

WORLD RECORD FOR AN ITEM OF ITALIAN ERITREA
1878, "Bay of Assab"
Realised: €40,800

WORLD RECORD FOR A DIE PROOF OF ANY COUNTRY
Realised: HK$2,040,000

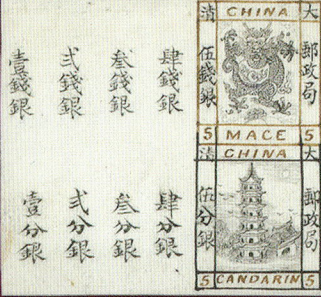

WORLD RECORD FOR A STAMP ESSAY OF ANY COUNTRY
Realised: HK$4,800,000

WORLD RECORD FOR CHINA'S MOST ICONIC STAMP
Realised: HK$6,240,000

YOUR TRULY GLOBAL PARTNER

SPINK LONDON
69 Southampton Row
London
WC1B 4ET
Tel: +44 (0)20 7563 4000
Email: concierge@spink.com

SPINK NEW YORK
145 W. 57th St.
New York
NY, 10019
Tel: +1 212 262 8400
Email: usa@spink.com

SPINK CHINA
4/F Hua Fu Cmerl Bldg.
111 Queen's Road West
Hong Kong
Tel: +852 3952 3000
Email: china@spink.com

SPINK SINGAPORE
360 Orchard Rd.
#06-03A Intl' Bldg.
Singapore 238869
Tel: +65 6339 8801
Email: singapore@spink.com

SPINK SWITZERLAND
Via Balestra 7
6900 Lugano
Switzerland
Tel: +41 91 911 62 00
Email: switzerland@spink.com

#SPINK_AUCTIONS   WWW.SPINK.COM